Advanced Praise f

"We are all lucky that Tyler Tichelaar loves history. This book is a monumental accomplishment. Tyler has already proven himself a master of historical fiction and fact. By writing about Kawbawgam, he took on the most extreme challenge, researching local Native American history. In doing so, he became a myth buster, trying to reveal the real stories, names, and dates. I collect Native American photographs, and I now look at them with a whole new understanding."

— Jack Deo, Owner, Superior View Photography

"Tyler Tichelaar's careful and thoughtful research put forth this important book documenting the life of a loved community member, Charlie Kawbawgam. You'll find answers and understanding in its pages."

— Cris Osier, Executive Director, Marquette Regional History Center

"Tichelaar's book is an invaluable compilation of research in local and regional history, but more importantly, it begins to integrate Native history into the dominant Anglo-American narrative by focusing on Charles Kawbawgam. Arguably there would not be a viable Native community in Marquette today (and maybe even no Marquette) if not for this extraordinary individual, skilled cultural mediator, and leader who guided his people during a difficult time of transition for Native peoples. As the author acknowledges, the history of this area remains incomplete without these stories and voices, so there is much work to do, and Tichelaar's book provides an excellent introductory guide."

— Rebecca J. Mead, History Professor, Northern Michigan University

"Tyler Tichelaar's meticulous research is helping to clarify and correct the record regarding Native American history in the Upper Peninsula."

— Beth Gruber, Research Librarian, John M. Longyear Research Library, Marquette Regional History Center

"Tichelaar's extensive and well documented research fills the gaps between the legend and the man, a must read for any local history buff."

— Larry Buege, Author of the Chogan Native American series

"This Kawbawgam biography is a noteworthy work that has been thoroughly researched. Through this historical biography, the author presents us with one of the few Ojibwa histories of the Upper Peninsula and ultimately connects regional history with that of the United States. For a Yooper or outsider this is a valuable piece of history to be read and included in your library."

— Russell M. Magnaghi, History Professor Emeritus,
Northern Michigan University

"Meticulously researched and highly readable, *Kawbawgam* is a serious biography of one of the most famous but least understood figures in Marquette County's past. This book enriches our knowledge of local Native American history and will be an invaluable resource for future scholars."

— Adam Berger, PhD, Marquette Regional History Center

"Tyler Tichelaar sorts fact from fiction concerning Kawbawgam and Marquette's early history. This book is thoroughly researched and long overdue."

— Jo Wittler, Curator, Marquette Regional History Center

"Kawbawgam is a thorough and well-researched portrait of someone whose name is familiar to everyone in central Upper Michigan, yet few have bothered to delve into the depths of his story. Tyler Tichelaar separates fact from fiction as he tells a tale full of adventure and pathos, politics and war, kindness, coercion, and compromise. You won't soon forget this book."

— Sonny Longtine, Author of
U.P. People and *Murder in Michigan's Upper Peninsula*

A Microcosm of the 19th Century
Ojibwa Experience in Upper Michigan

KAWBAWGAM

The Chief, The Legend, The Man

Tyler R. Tichelaar

Author of *My Marquette*, *Haunted Marquette*,
When Teddy Came to Town, and The Marquette Trilogy

Never forget the past.
Tyler R. Tichelaar

Kawbawgam: The Chief, The Legend, The Man

Marquette Fiction

1202 Pine Street

Marquette, MI 49855

www.MarquetteFiction.com

All efforts have been made to source properly all quotations.

ISBN-13: 978-0-9962400-7-9

Library of Congress Control Number: 2020902828

Printed in the United States of America

Cover Design and Interior Layout: Larry Alexander

Publication managed by Superior Book Productions

www.SuperiorBookProductions.com

"We all recognized our indebtedness to Charlie
and I for one shall never forget it."

— A prominent Marquette citizen
The Mining Journal, January 8, 1887

Contents

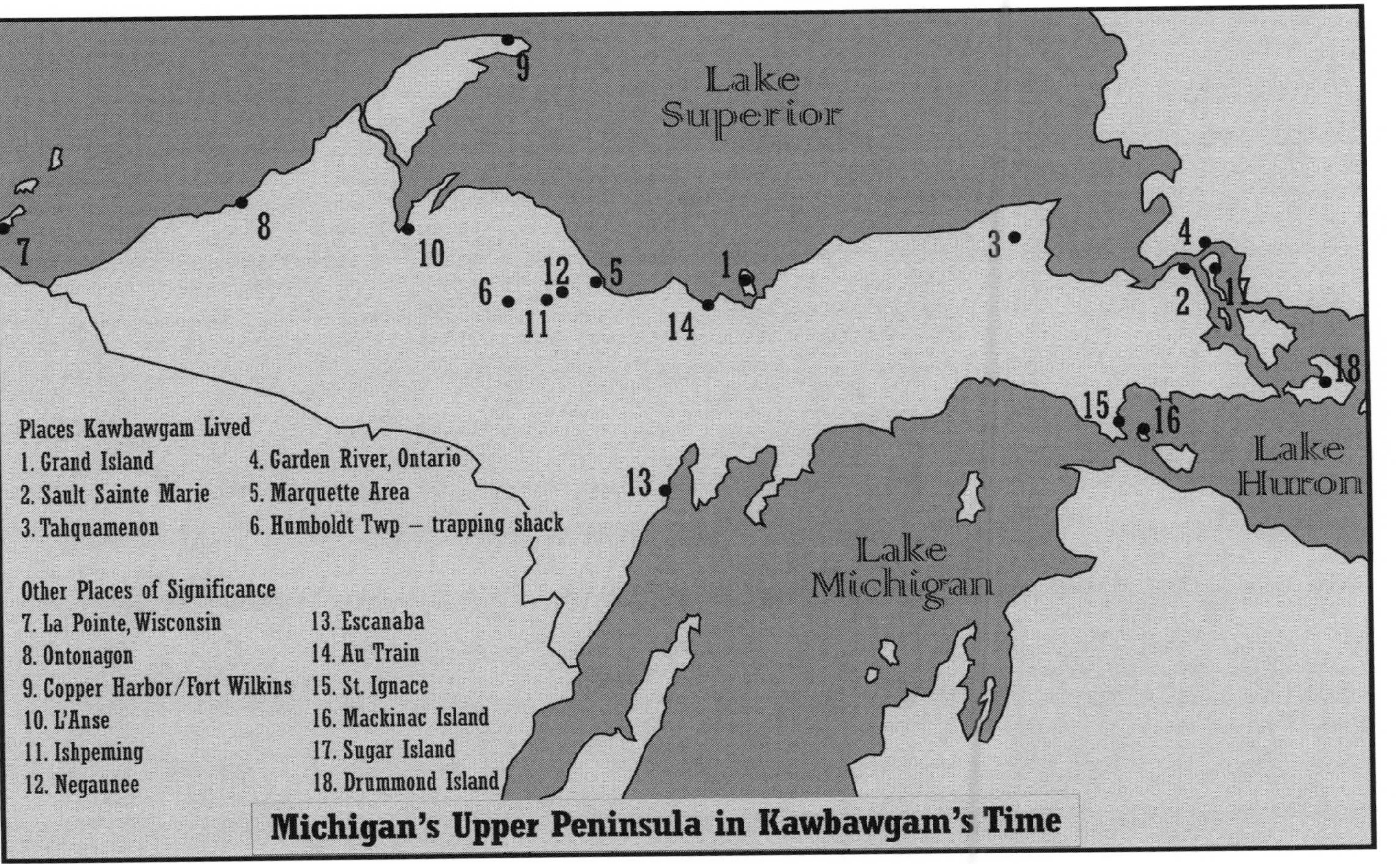
Lake Superior
Lake Michigan
Lake Huron
1
2
3
4
5
6
7
8
9
10
11
12
13
14
15
16
17
18
Places Kawbawgam Lived
1. Grand Island
2. Sault Sainte Marie
3. Tahquamenon
4. Garden River, Ontario
5. Marquette Area
6. Humboldt Twp — trapping shack
Other Places of Significance
7. La Pointe, Wisconsin
8. Ontonagon
9. Copper Harbor/Fort Wilkins
10. L'Anse
11. Ishpeming
12. Negaunee
13. Escanaba
14. Au Train
15. St. Ignace
16. Mackinac Island
17. Sugar Island
18. Drummond Island

Michigan's Upper Peninsula in Kawbawgam's Time

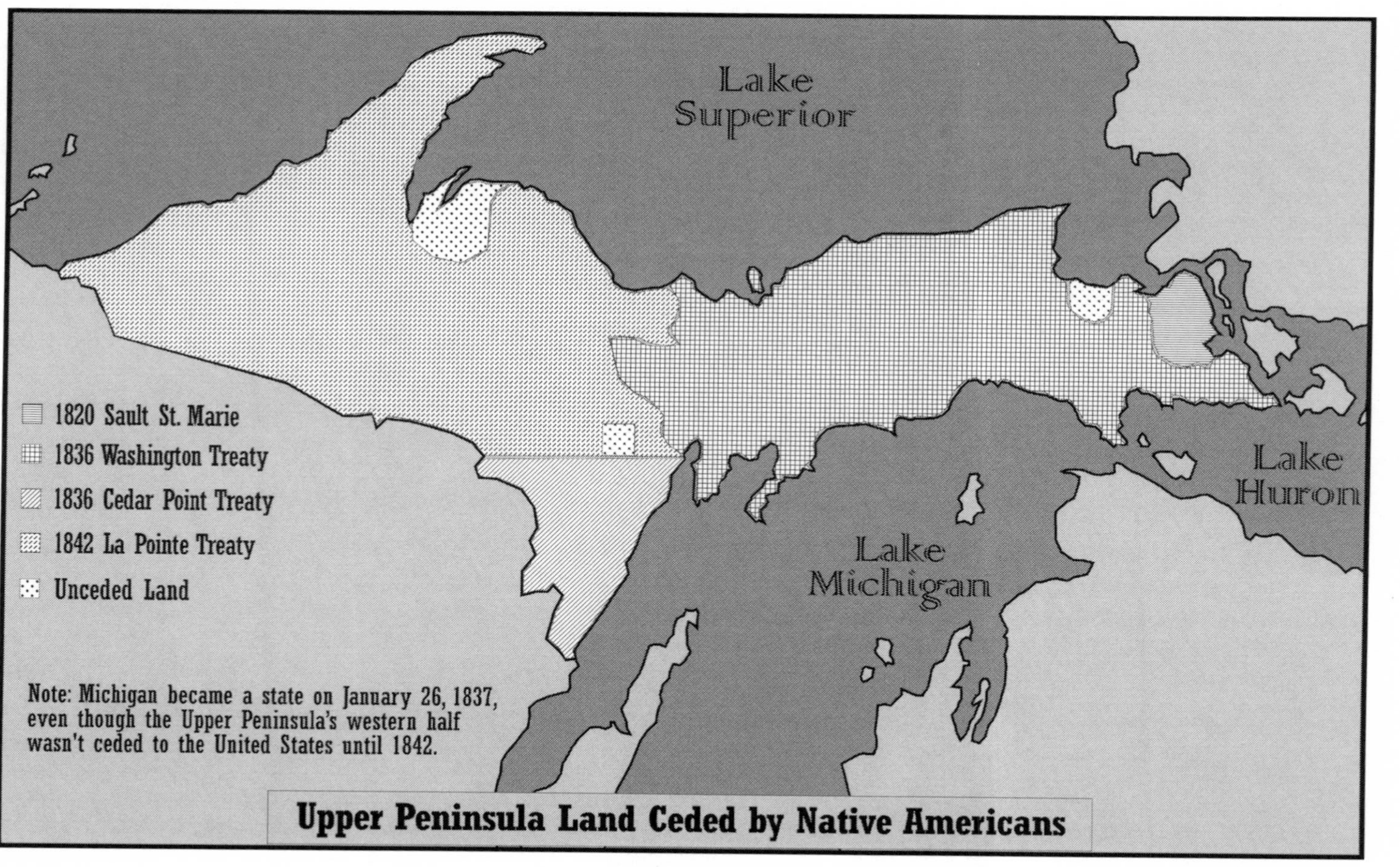
Lake Superior
Lake Michigan
Lake Huron
1820 Sault St. Marie
1836 Washington Treaty
1836 Cedar Point Treaty
1842 La Pointe Treaty
Unceded Land
Note: Michigan became a state on January 26, 1837, even though the Upper Peninsula's western half wasn't ceded to the United States until 1842.
Upper Peninsula Land Ceded by Native Americans

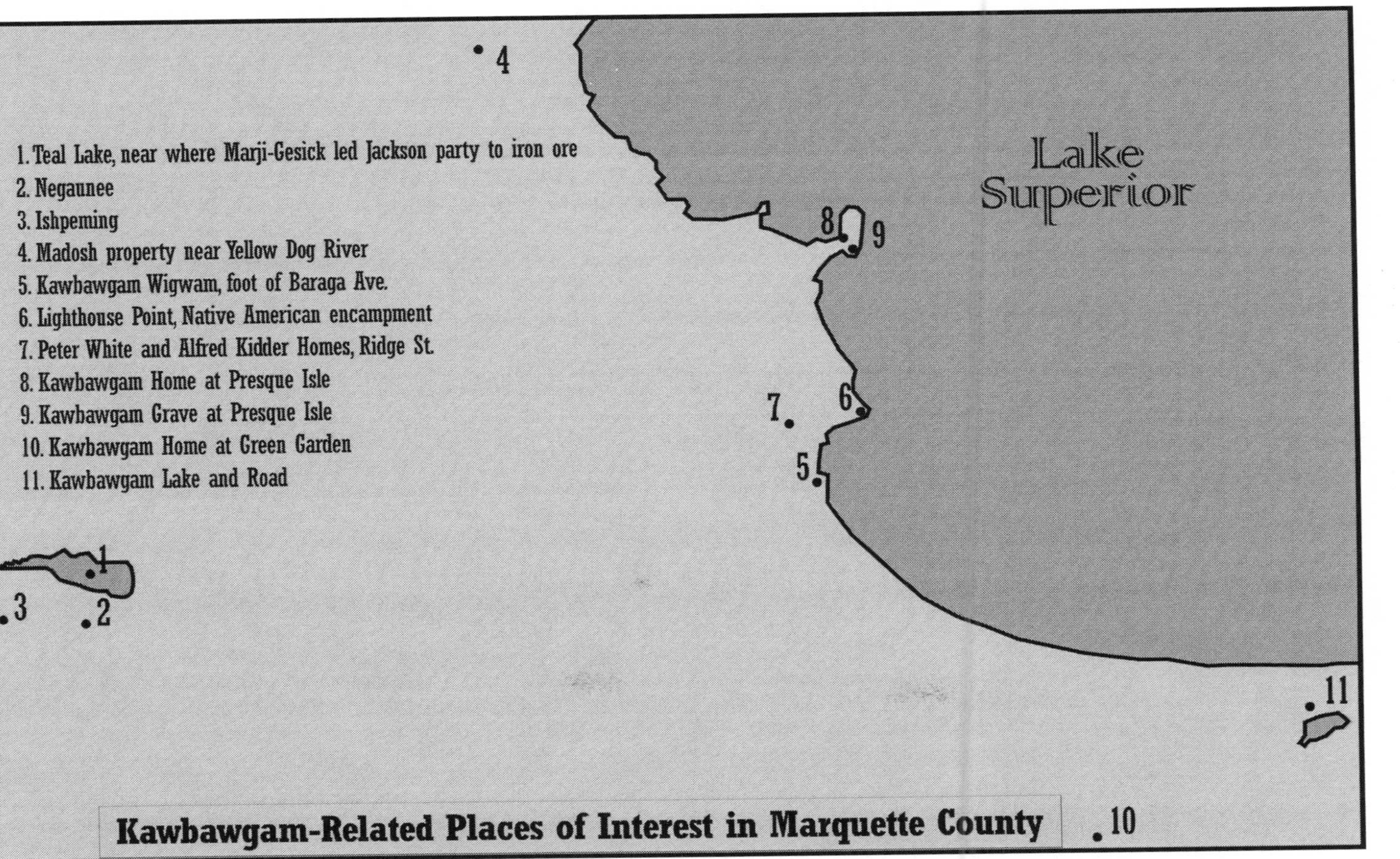

Kawbawgam-Related Places of Interest in Marquette County

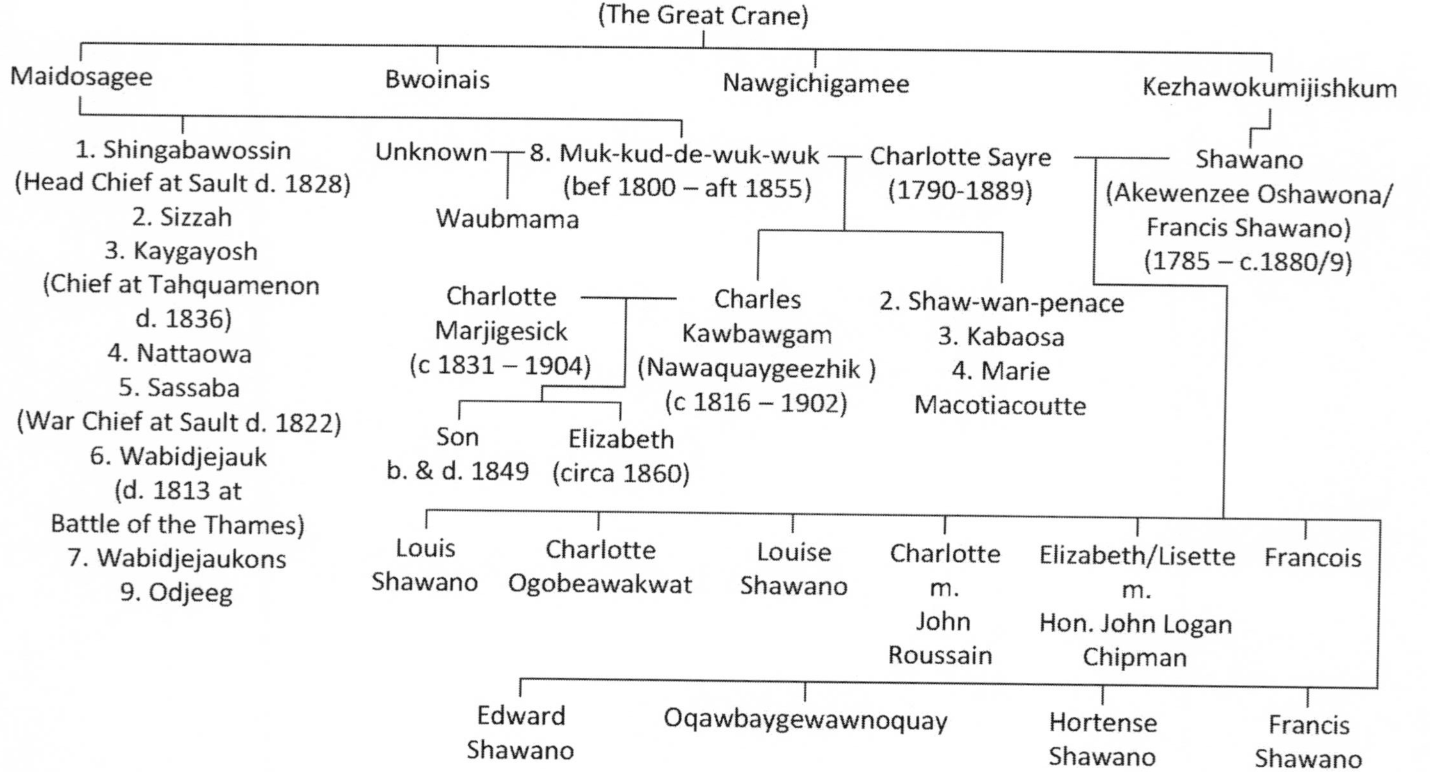

Kawbawgam's Family - The Crane Clan
Gitchejeedebun
(The Great Crane)
Maidosagee
Bwoinais
Nawgichigamee
Kezhawokumijishkum
1. Shingabawossin
(Head Chief at Sault d. 1828)
2. Sizzah
3. Kaygayosh
(Chief at Tahquamenon
d. 1836)
4. Nattaowa
5. Sassaba
(War Chief at Sault d. 1822)
6. Wabidjejauk
(d. 1813 at
Battle of the Thames)
7. Wabidjejaukons
9. Odjeeg
Unknown
8. Muk-kud-de-wuk-wuk
(bef 1800 – aft 1855)
Waubmama
Charlotte Sayre
(1790-1889)
Shawano
(Akewenzee Oshawona/
Francis Shawano)
(1785 – c.1880/9)
Charlotte
Marjigesick
(c 1831 – 1904)
Charles
Kawbawgam
(Nawaquaygeezhik)
(c 1816 – 1902)
2. Shaw-wan-penace
3. Kabaosa
4. Marie
Macotiacoutte
Son
b. & d. 1849
Elizabeth
(circa 1860)
Louis
Shawano
Charlotte
Ogobeawakwat
Louise
Shawano
Charlotte
m.
John
Roussain
Elizabeth/Lisette
m.
Hon. John Logan
Chipman
Francois
Edward
Shawano
Oqawbaygewawnoquay
Hortense
Shawano
Francis
Shawano

Marji-Gesick Descendants

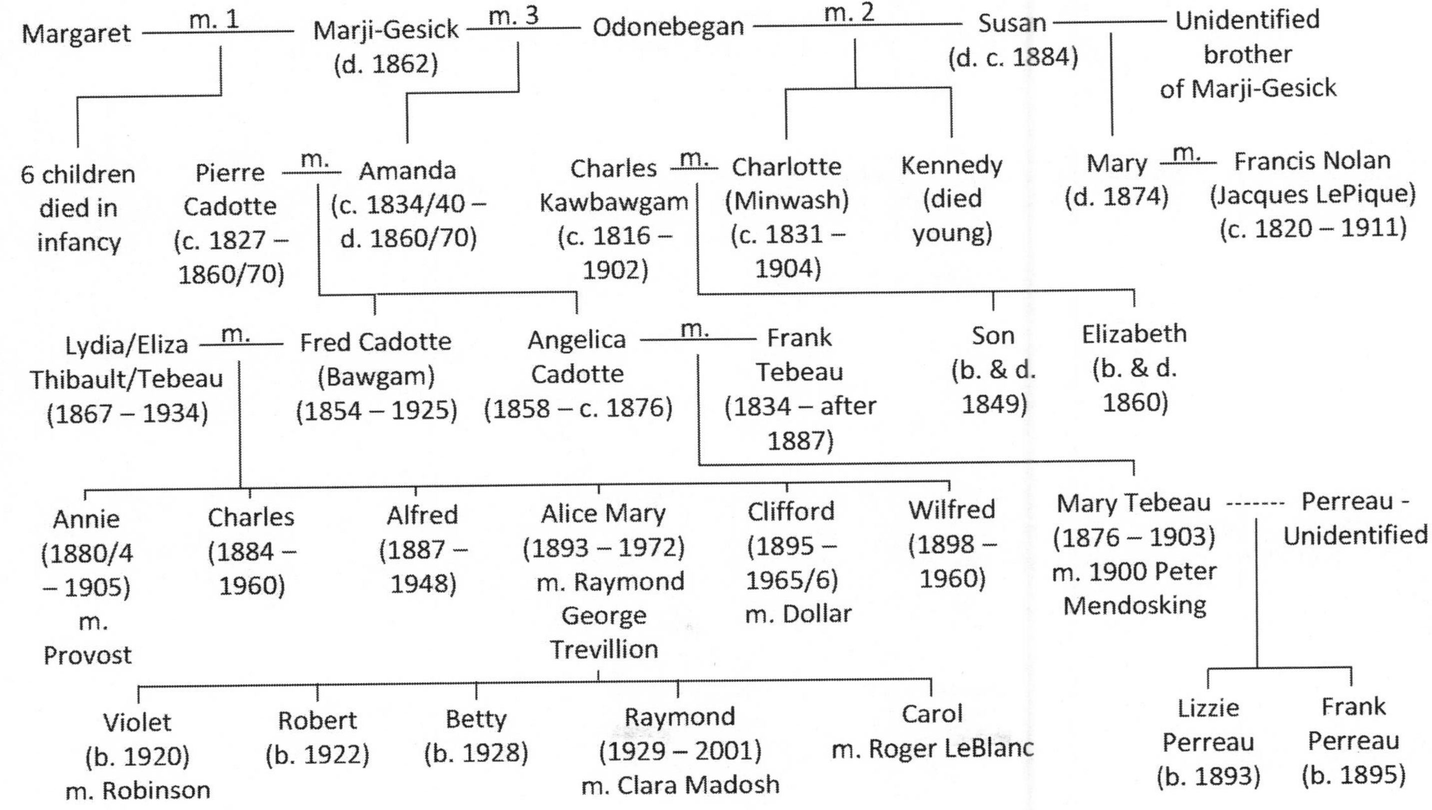

Madosh Family

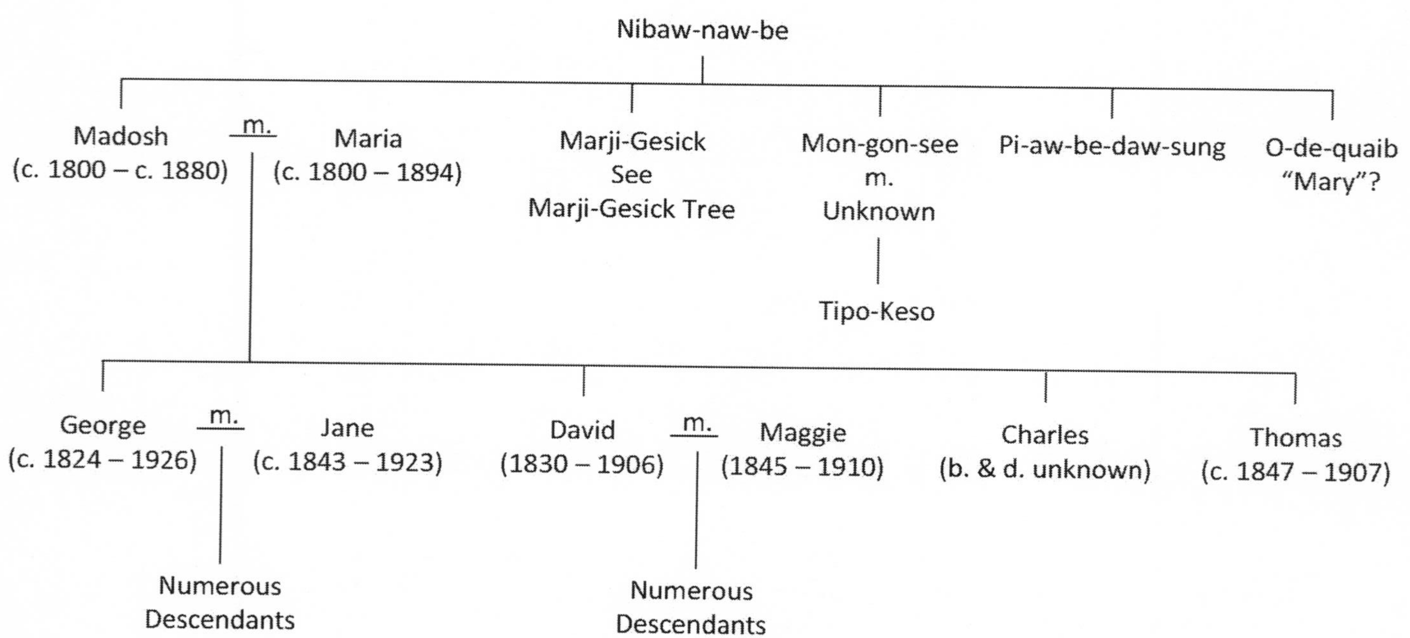

Graveraet Family

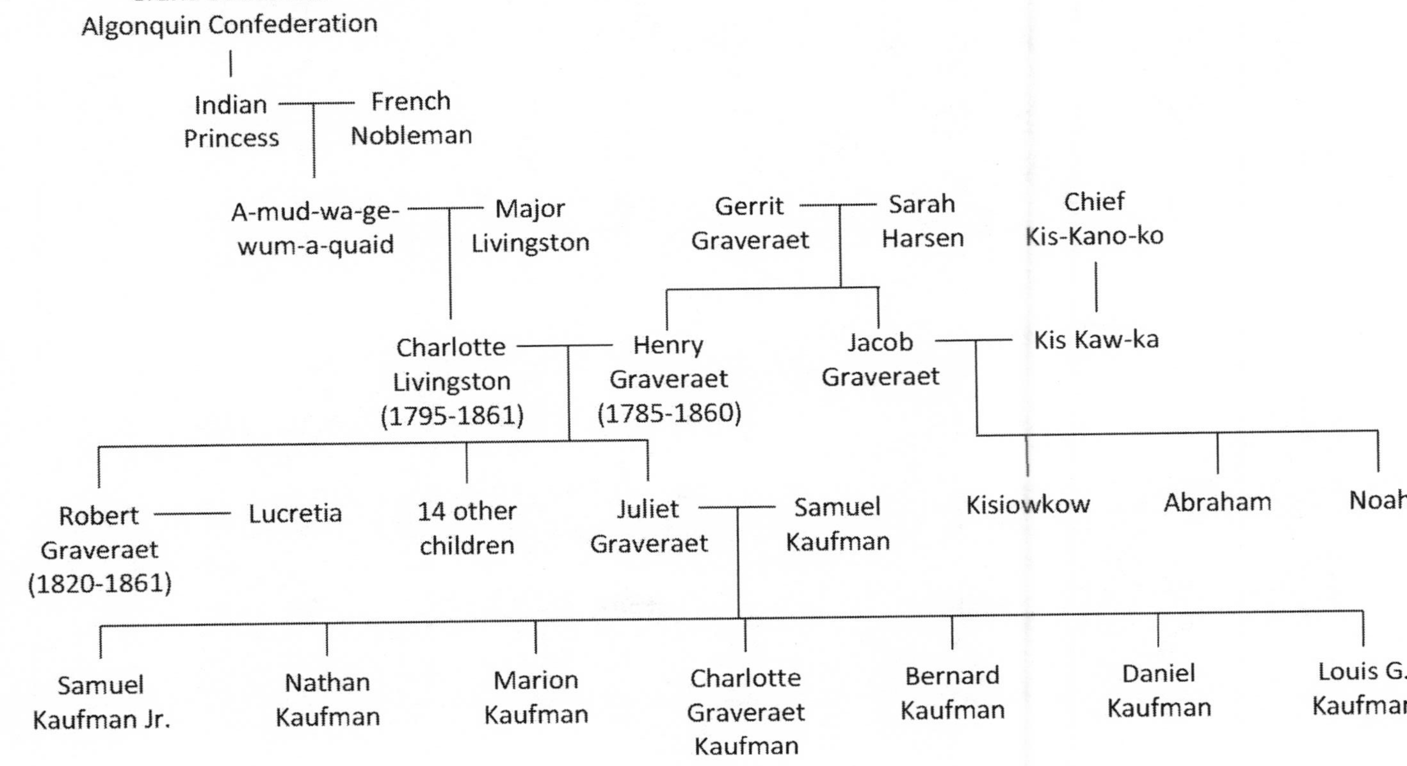

Chief Charles Kawbawgam

Introduction

IN 1888, A TALL, SLIM, Ojibwa man went fishing at the Dead River, which marked the border between Presque Isle, the little peninsula that jutted out into Lake Superior and had recently become a city park, and the city of Marquette in Michigan's Upper Peninsula. The man, known to most as Chief Kawbawgam, was likely in his early seventies, although he did not know for certain his own age. What he did know was that his people had been in this land for centuries before the white man came. In his lifetime, he had seen the change from a handful of French and British traders to a population explosion of Americans across Michigan's Upper Peninsula. He had lived throughout the eastern and central Upper Peninsula and even in Ontario. Often, he had been forced to move because of the encroachment of white Americans. However, he had also befriended many whites.

But at the moment, all those events were far from his mind. Today, he was intent on catching a meal for himself, his wife Charlotte, their great-niece Mary, who lived with them, and the extended family members who lived around them. There were always many mouths to feed. Fortunately, the earth always provided for them. The Ojibwa had long been fishermen, and having grown up at Sault Sainte Marie, Charles Kawbawgam had learned to fish at the St. Mary's Rapids, which had once teemed with whitefish. Now he fished along the shores of Presque Isle Park, where he lived at the grace of his benefactor, Peter White, one of Marquette's leading businessmen. White had befriended him in 1849 when White was just a boy of eighteen, shortly after arriving in Iron Bay as a member of the party that had founded Marquette.

More recently, White had secured Presque Isle from the US Government to preserve as a park for Marquette. Kawbawgam and his wife Charlotte had moved from Presque Isle when they heard it would become a park, but White and some other friendly white men had built the Kawbawgams a home there and assured them they could remain at Presque Isle for the remainder of their lives. Their home was a wooden frame house, a far cry from the wigwams Kawbawgam had lived in most of his life, but he and Charlotte had adapted to it, just as they had adapted to the many other changes they had seen throughout the nineteenth century.

Today, Kawbawgam had made his way to the Dead River. At his age, it was becoming harder to move quickly, and his eyesight was not what it had been; he dreaded the day when he would no longer be able to fish or hunt. He knew his eyesight would have made it difficult to tie a fly or hook a worm, but he had never liked the white man's fishing pole anyway. Carrying a sucker net, he waded into the river. The water was chilling to his old bones, but he had gotten far enough into the river where he might have had some luck had he not heard someone shouting behind him.

Turning around, Kawbawgam saw a white man emerging from the forest. The old Ojibwa took one look at the man and knew there would be trouble. He couldn't see the man's face very well because he was so far away, but something in the man's tone told Kawbawgam this one was no friend to Indians.

"What do you have there?" the man shouted to him, approaching the riverbank.

Kawbawgam did not answer. He understood English, but his own English was not the best, so he rarely spoke it. He simply continued walking toward the shore, not sure how he would deal with this man.

"You've got a net there, don't you?" said the man. "You know it's not the season for fishing with a sucker net."

By now, Kawbawgam had nearly walked back to the bank. He did not respond to the man, instead enjoying the return of warm air on his bare feet. He looked over to where he had set his shoes a few feet farther up the bank.

"Do you hear me?" the man asked.

"Indians fish all seasons," Kawbawgam finally said, looking straight at him.

"No," said the man. He was several inches shorter than the tall Indian chief, but Kawbawgam knew smaller men were often the most aggressive. Still, he felt he was within his rights.

"Yes," said Kawbawgam. "Treaty say so."

"What treaty?" asked the man. "I don't know about any treaty. I'm an officer of the State of Michigan, and it's not the season to fish with nets. I'm going to have to write you a citation."

Kawbawgam wasn't sure what a citation was. He only knew this man was giving him a hard time, even though his people had been fishing here for generations before this man was even born.

Kawbawgam stood there and stared at the man while he took out a small tablet of paper and began scribbling on it.

"You Indians think you can get away with breaking the law just 'cause you're Indian," the man said.

"Not breaking law," said Kawbawgam.

"You are. Anyway, it's up to the judge what he does with you. He oughta lock you up to make an example of you," said the man. He handed the piece of paper to Kawbawgam.

"What it say?" asked Kawbawgam.

"What's it say?" repeated the man in amazement. "It says you broke the law. It says you were caught fishing illegally with a sucker net out of season. It says you'll have to pay a fine."

"Fine?"

"Yes. You know—a penalty. You'll have to pay money for committing the misdemeanor of fishing with a net out of season."

"Who pay?" asked Kawbawgam, realizing it was a stupid question, but irritated enough to want to argue.

"You pay. You take that to the judge down at the Marquette County Courthouse and he'll decide how much the fine will be."

Kawbawgam took the paper from the man and stared at it for a minute. He could barely speak English. He certainly couldn't read it. He'd have to get someone to explain it to him, perhaps Peter White.

Kawbawgam stuffed the piece of paper in his pocket.

"Hey, don't wreck that citation," said the man. "If you don't go to the court, I'll have you arrested."

Kawbawgam stared at the man.

"And I need to confiscate this," said the man, grabbing the net from Kawbawgam's hand before the old man knew what was happening.

The man took the net and broke it over his knee.

Kawbawgam remembered a time when he could have broken this man over his own knee.

Not replying, he walked over to his shoes.

"That's right. You put your shoes on now and get out of here," the game warden barked. "And you can bet I'll check with the judge to make sure you paid that citation. Otherwise, I'll find you and have you arrested."

Kawbawgam bent down to pick up his shoes. Then he carried them home. He wasn't going to sit down on the ground and put his shoes on in front of this man.

He acts like he owns the land and the fish, Kawbawgam thought as he walked home. *Charlotte won't be happy that there won't be any fish for supper. But despite how the white men don't act like Christians toward the Indians, Gitche Manitou looks after us.*

*

Chief Charles Kawbawgam is not well known by most people. He is not a figure of national renown, but only local renown among the Ojibwa, the residents of Upper Michigan, and especially, the people of Marquette, Michigan. Although Kawbawgam is a household name in Marquette, if not for his and his wife's prominent gravestone at Presque Isle Park, it is questionable whether most residents would even know his name today.

Personally, as a lifelong and seventh-generation resident of Marquette, I can't remember when I didn't know about Chief Kawbawgam. As a boy, my grandfather Lester White told me his father had been friends with the chief. Over time, as a lover and author of local history, I came to know the general details of Kawbawgam's life that most locals know. According to the sign beside his grave, "Charley" Kawbawgam was born in 1799 and died in 1902, having lived 103 years. His wife, Charlotte, is buried beside him. She was the daughter of Chief Marji-Gesick. The sign also tells us that Presque Isle was their home and will be into eternity. Books about Marquette's history frequently mention how when the first settlers came to Marquette in 1849, Chief Kawbawgam was already there, and he let several of the settlers live in his cedar bark wigwam until they could build homes of their own.

The only other incident of note usually recorded about Kawbawgam is that he was a "good Indian"[1] who never got into trouble with the law except once when an overzealous game warden gave him a citation for fishing out of season with a sucker net, as we have just seen, although the details of this incident are not fully known—I have fictionalized the scene for dramatic purposes.

From such facts, a very meager biography of Kawbawgam can be created. But such a biography leaves out many of the most interesting facts of Kawbawgam's life and also the experiences of the Ojibwa during his lifetime as the white races "conquered" the land and spread across Michigan's Upper Peninsula.

Kawbawgam's story is not as dramatic as that of Pocahontas, Geronimo, or Tecumseh, yet it is one worth telling. Few Americans today are ignorant of the terrible crimes eighteenth and nineteenth century white Americans committed against the Native Americans throughout the United States as they stole their land through dishonest and misleading treaties, and murdered them, sometimes overtly, sometimes subtly through policies that forced their removal under horrible conditions.

And yet, in Upper Michigan, no extreme violence occurred between Native Americans and whites, at least not after the War of 1812. As a result, I grew up believing the settlement of the Upper Peninsula by whites had been peaceful, and even that the Native Americans had welcomed the white settlers, all because I had heard how Kawbawgam himself had welcomed the white settlers and helped them during Marquette's early years.

The truth is far more complex and far more fascinating.

It is time that Charles Kawbawgam's full story be told. It is time to remove many of the misconceptions about him and the status of his people, the Ojibwa, during his lifetime. This story deserves to be told because it is part of the history of all the people who call Upper Michigan home, and indeed, part of the history of the United States, especially when we consider that the whites took the Upper Peninsula from the Ojibwa because of its mineral resources—resources that ultimately helped the Union win the Civil War, helped the United States win two World Wars, and continue to power the iron industry today. No person in the United States has not benefited from the iron industry, and so here in Kawbawgam's life story is also the tale of how that industry began—an industry that provides us today with everything from automobiles to nails and guns. And as that iron industry was birthed, the traditional Ojibwa world began to pass away.

Kawbawgam's story is the tale of a vanishing world. He was born into an Upper Peninsula with few whites in it. He grew up at Sault Sainte Marie, in a time and place where the few Europeans in the area—primarily of French and British descent—often intermarried with the Native population, creating a métis (mixed race) world. He spent a childhood in an atmosphere largely filled with tolerance and understanding of the Native Americans, and then he saw it quickly change into one marked by racism and intolerance as the Americans spread westward, hungry for the Upper Peninsula's mineral riches, as well as its other natural resources, including fish and lumber. Kawbawgam saw settlements of largely nomadic Native Americans with the occasional wooden house built by a white man be replaced with cities of thousands of whites who encroached on Native American camping, fishing, and even burial grounds. Kawbawgam was among the Native Americans left to fend for themselves in small communities on the outskirts of white men's cities. But he also learned how to befriend the whites, thereby ensuring the survival of himself and his people without forced assimilation or removal.

This is Kawbawgam's story, but it is also the story of every American—it is our shared history that too often we forget or deny. It is the story of a simple, noble man who tried to carve out a place for his people in the margins of an industrial revolution. It is the story of how he earned respect from white Americans during his lifetime. And it is the story of how his memory has been respected, but also how his name and image have been appropriated by white Americans for their own purposes in the more than a century since his death.

I hope you come away from this book respecting the fine line Kawbawgam often had to walk. I hope you come away with a better understanding of a past too often romanticized, and whose realities are more fascinating than any fictional account. I hope, ultimately, you agree with me that Upper Michigan's history needs to be revised so none of its citizens are left out.

Tyler R. Tichelaar
Marquette, Michigan
November 1, 2020

A Note on Spelling, Word Choice, and Sources

THE OJIBWA LANGUAGE IS DIFFICULT to translate and even to spell in English. Furthermore, over the centuries, various spellings have been used for the different Native American tribes and the names of many of the Native people mentioned in this book. I have tried to give alternate spellings and even explanations for them where possible, but for the sake of easy recognition by readers, I have overall opted to use the most commonly known spellings, even though they may not always be the most accurate to the Ojibwa tradition and language. For example, the name of Kawbawgam's father-in-law, Chief Marji-Gesick, is probably not spelled in a manner that reflects how it was pronounced, especially considering there is no "r" sound in Ojibwa; however, it is so well-known a spelling that for the sake of the lay reader who is not familiar with Ojibwa, I have retained the spelling that has most frequently appeared in histories.

I have also made specific choices about the names of various Native American tribes, for example opting for Ojibwa over Ojibway, Ojibwe, Chippewa, Anishinaabe, or Anishinabek. That said, I am aware that Ojibway is probably the closest to the correct pronunciation. I have also opted for Sioux over Dakota or Dakota Sioux.

These choices were not easy to make, and they may not be the best or most optimal choices. My choices certainly do not reflect any disrespect to Native Americans, some of whom may disagree with them. They have simply been made for the ease of the reader.

I have also striven to leave out the niceties of such pronunciations and spellings from the main text and instead include them in footnotes. I hope lay readers will read the footnotes, which I have placed at the bottom of pages for easy reference. I have also included endnotes for the sake of citing my sources. The endnotes are solely citations and do not include any additional information about the topic so there is no need to consult them unless one is interested in pursuing a source further. For this reason, the endnotes are at the back of the book.

I have tried to be as meticulous as possible about my sources. However, in many cases I have not been able to pinpoint sources of research. For example, the Marquette Regional History Center has many folders full of newspaper clippings from *The Mining Journal*. Unfortunately, while a newspaper article might refer to Kawbawgam or another subject, the original collectors of these items sometimes failed to notate the pages or dates when the newspaper articles appeared and I have not always been able to locate this information. There were also many handwritten documents I found that do not have dates or even their authors' names on them. However, my endnotes and bibliography pages should provide enough information for people to verify sources or conduct their own search to pinpoint details I have been unable to verify myself. I would also like to note that over the course of its history, Marquette's *The Mining Journal* has also been known as *The Daily Mining Journal* and *The Weekly Mining Journal*. To remove confusion and simplify, I have just referred to it as *The Mining Journal* in all instances. If a source cannot be found in *The Daily Mining Journal*, it is likely in *The Weekly Mining Journal*. I have also alphabetized *The Mining Journal* sources under "T" in the bibliography to avoid confusion.

Finally, I do not by any means consider this book the final say on Kawbawgam. No doubt there are many articles and other sources in existence that I did not find, but that future historians may be able to locate to expand on the work I have begun. Regardless, I hope this book will provide a greater understanding of Kawbawgam and the Ojibwa experience in Upper Michigan in the nineteenth century.

Chapter 1
Kawbawgam's Birth and Family Background

MOST BIOGRAPHIES BEGIN WITH A sentence stating that their subject was born on such and such a date at such and such a place. Such a statement is impossible to make with any accuracy for Charles Kawbawgam because the Ojibwa of his day did not keep written records. Several historians, pseudo-historians, and people who knew Kawbawgam have given various approximate dates for his birth, ranging from 1799-1832. Kawbawgam's own statement about his age should, one would think, be the most reliable source of information, but because Kawbawgam did not write English and only spoke it minimally, everything of importance he said about himself has been filtered down to us by his interpreters, so even the reliability of these statements is questionable. Therefore, several statements regarding his age need to be considered to determine the most likely date for his birth.

Birthdate

First, let us tackle the general belief that Kawbawgam lived to be 103 years old, having been born in 1799 and died in 1902. These are the dates on the sign beside his grave, which serve as a source of wonder to those who visit his final resting place at Presque Isle Park in Marquette, Michigan. Furthermore, Marquette County's death records list his age as 103.[1]

The idea that Kawbawgam was born in 1799 stems from a statement he made regarding his age in 1849, the year Marquette was founded. At that date, Peter White, later Kawbawgam's great friend, arrived to help found the city, along with Robert Graveraet. This event and White and Kawbawgam's first meeting will be discussed in more detail in Chapter 4. For now, it is significant to note that Peter White, eighteen at the time, had already learned to speak Ojibwa so he could converse with Kawbawgam when he first arrived in Marquette. Forty years later, in 1889, White recalled that he had asked Kawbawgam soon after they met how old he was. Kawbawgam had replied, "I am fifty. I spent twenty years at the Soo; twenty years on Tonquoemenon bay [sic Tahquamenon Bay], and ten years on the Canadian side."[2] This statement would place Kawbawgam's birth in 1799. However, as we will see, Kawbawgam likely came to Marquette a year or two before it was officially founded, which is not accounted for in his math, and he likely rounded up his sense of years to the nearest decade, so this statement is not necessarily reliable. Furthermore, we are getting this information through Peter White, who seems to have taken great pride in later life over his friend Kawbawgam's advanced age. White had a reputation as a teller of stories, so he may have exaggerated Kawbawgam's age or not recalled in 1889 what Kawbawgam had actually told him forty years earlier, although in 1905, he stated that he had recorded what Kawbawgam told him in his diary at the time.[3a] We cannot know, therefore, whether White exaggerated or misremembered or whether Kawbawgam simply stated what he believed was true at the time.

On other occasions, Kawbawgam made statements concerning his age that make it seem more likely he was born several years after 1799. During the lawsuit his wife Charlotte conducted against the Jackson Iron Company in 1882, which will be discussed in Chapter 8, Kawbawgam was called upon as one of the witnesses. At that time, he told the court he was either seventy-six or seventy-seven, which would place his birth year as 1810 or 1811.[4] In 1888, when the lawsuit was again before the courts, *The Mining Journal* reported that Kawbawgam was seventy-five,[5] which would put his birth at 1813, although it is unlikely *The Mining Journal* reporter knew the chief's true age.

Our best source for determining Kawbawgam's age comes from a statement he made to Homer Kidder. Between 1893 and 1895, Kidder would record many of Kawbawgam's Ojibwa stories and the events of his life. Kawbawgam told Kidder that his earliest recollection was seeing

---

a. This diary no longer seems to exist. It is not in the collections of any of the three major places where White's papers are located: the Marquette Regional History Center, the Bentley Historical Library at the University of Michigan, or the Burton Historical Collection at the Detroit Public Library.

his uncle walking up a hill in Sault Sainte Marie in a British officer's red coat. The Ojibwa had been allies of the British during the War of 1812, so Kawbawgam apparently thought this incident happened during that war (1812-1815), which would make his birth closer to 1810 if we assume he was two to five at the time when one is likely to have their first memory. However, this incident actually happened in 1820 when Lewis Cass, then Michigan Territorial Governor, visited the Sault to convince the Ojibwa to cede land there to the United States so a fort could be built. The Ojibwa opposed this idea, and we know from other sources that at least one of them, the war chief Sassaba, wore a British uniform to the meeting with Cass as a sign of protest and to show that the Ojibwa remained loyal to the British.[6] Sassaba was the brother of Kawbawgam's father, and because of the tension that Sassaba's behavior caused at the Sault,[7] as will be discussed in Chapter 2, it is not surprising that this uniform would be part of Kawbawgam's first memory. If Kawbawgam's first memory is then from 1820, his birthdate is more likely between 1815 and 1818. Another *The Mining Journal* article that appeared soon after Kawbawgam's death says he was probably born about 1819,[8] but this date seems too late for him to have had his first memory in 1820. Surprisingly, his marriage record from 1847 says he was twenty-five at the time,[9] putting his birth as late as about 1822, but again, this date is unlikely.

Finally, one of Marquette's first residents, Mrs. Samuel (Eliza Anna) Barney, stated that when she arrived in Marquette in 1850, Kawbawgam was "only about eighteen."[10] That would suggest he was born about 1832, but such a date is far too late. For one, it would make him the same age or younger than his wife Charlotte, and Ojibwa men usually took younger brides. Furthermore, it does not align with his brother-in-law Jacques LePique's memories of living near Kawbawgam's family in the Sault in the 1830s, so we can dismiss Mrs. Barney's statement. She made this statement when she was eighty years old, some sixty-five years after she first met Kawbawgam, so her memory may have failed her. She also, as we will see, had reason to dislike Kawbawgam and belittle the praise he received for living to be more than one hundred. That said, given that he appeared to be twenty-five in 1847 and eighteen in 1850, Kawbawgam may have looked young for his age in his youth, but then how are we to take Peter White's belief that he was fifty in 1849?

In any case, Kawbawgam was probably in his mid to late eighties at the time of his death, rather than the famous age of 103 usually cited for him. Notably, several other Native Americans in the Upper Peninsula claimed to have lived for more than a century at this time, whether through a vain desire to appear older than they were or from simply being ignorant of their true ages. White Americans also liked to promote this idea of Native Americans living to advanced ages, Peter White being just one example.

Real Name

Just as confusion exists over Kawbawgam's birth date, so there is confusion over his name. Johann Georg Kohl (1808-1878), a German travel writer and historian who lived among the Ojibwa in 1855 at La Pointe, Wisconsin, and at L'Anse and Sault Sainte Marie, Michigan, noted that the Ojibwa he met tried to conceal their real names when asked for them. To learn an Ojibwa's name, you usually had to ask others who knew the person. Wives also often evaded questions about their names by giving their husbands' names. They appeared to feel that giving their names was beneath their dignity.[11] Possibly, they also believed that if an enemy knew your true name, it allowed the enemy to have power over you.[12] Kawbawgam's true Ojibwa name was Nawaquay-geezhik (Noon Day), which was listed in the Treaty of 1855 (spelled there as Naw-o-ge-zhick).[13] However, he rarely used it, preferring "Kawbawgam," a pet name given to him as a boy by his mother. Its meaning has never been properly explained, and when Homer Kidder interviewed Kawbawgam in the 1890s, he did not receive a satisfactory answer to his inquiries about it.[14] The only source that has offered an interpretation of it is a 1965 article in Marquette's *The Mining Journal*, which claims it means "undulating,"[15] a suggestion perhaps that the boy Kawbawgam moved about quickly with a wave-like motion. The reliability of this translation, however, is questionable, and the article does not give its source for such an interpretation. Furthermore, the Ojibwa often gave new or altered names to each other when they married, and rather than referring to their in-laws by given names, they would refer to them in a roundabout manner such as "the man who is son-in-law."[16] Consequently, Kawbawgam may have been reluctant to share his nickname's meaning. He and his mother seem to have taken it to their graves with them. However, if it did mean "undulating," it suited him because he spent his life undulating between his traditional Ojibwa lifestyle and the Americans' efforts to bend the Ojibwa to their will through assimilation or removal efforts.

Ancestry

More confusion exists over Kawbawgam's parentage. Kawbawgam had at least one stepfather who has often mistakenly been cited as his father. His mother had at least two and possibly three husbands.

Kawbawgam's father was Muk-kud-de-wuk-wuk (Black Cloud).[17b] Muk-kud-de-wuk-wuk lived either on Grand Island or on the mainland across from Grand Island where the city of Munising, Michigan, is today. Muk-kud-de-wuk-wuk's name appears in the 1820 treaty with the Chippewa at the Sault where it is spelled as Macadaywacwet.[18] Other sources say he also signed the 1836 Treaty with the Chippewa as a chief of the second class,[19] and the 1842 Treaty of La Pointe, but I have not found his name listed in either place. Two Native Americans with similar names are listed in the 1842 treaty—from the Lac de Flambeau band, May tock cus e quay, and from the Lac Vieux Desert band, Medge waw gwaw wot—but neither appear to be Kawbawgam's father given the locations associated with them.[20] However, Muk-kud-de-wuk-wuk did sign the 1854 Treaty with the Chippewa at La Pointe, where he is listed under the La Pointe band as "Mac-caw-day-wa-quot, or the Black Cloud 2[d] chief."[21] We do not know how long Muk-kud-de-wuk-wuk lived, but Kawbawgam stated that he was present at the 1855 council of the four Algonquian nations, which Kawbawgam himself attended.[22] On Kawbawgam's death certificate, his father's full name is given as Charles Makadoaque, a sign that Kawbawgam was, in a sense, named after his father.[23] It is unknown where "Charles" came from as a family name, but it obviously resulted from a British or French influence, the French having been in the Great Lakes region since the early seventeenth century and the British being the dominant European power in the area from the time they had won the French-Indian War (1756-1763) until the War of 1812.

Through his father, Kawbawgam could claim an illustrious ancestry. His great-grandfather was Gitcheojeedebun, known as the Great Crane because he was the head chief of the Ojibwa's Crane clan. Gitcheojeedebun would have four children, the mother of whom is unknown. The oldest child was Naidosagee/Maidosagee who would be Kawbawgam's grandfather and also the head chief.[24] Besides Muk-kud-de-wuk-wuk, Naidosagee would have eight other sons, all Kawbawgam's uncles. The three most significant were Shingabawossin (d. 1828), head chief at the Sault like his grandfather had been; Sassaba (1790-1822) a warrior chief at the Sault; and Kaygayosh (d. 1836), chief at Tahquamenon and later head chief at the Sault after Shingabawossin died. As previously mentioned, Sassaba is believed to be

b. Kawbawgam's father's name has had several variations due to various translations of the name into English, including Muk-kud-d-wuk-kwuk; Makadoaque (the name that appears on Kawbawgam's death certificate) (Nertoli p. 6), and Mukcawday mawquot (a spelling Homer Kidder recorded during his interviews with Kawbawgam) (Bourgeois p. 14-15).

the uncle who wore the British uniform and provided Kawbawgam's first memory.[25] Consequently, Kawbawgam, besides being a chief himself, was at birth the son, nephew, grandson, and great-grandson of chiefs. In time, he would also be the stepson, brother, half-brother, and son-in-law of chiefs.

Before marrying Kawbawgam's mother, Muk-kud-de-wuk-wuk had previously married a woman whose name is unknown. With her he had two children, Joseph Thompson (also known as Waubmama, White Woodpecker, or White Pigeon), and John Kabaosa (b. 1805 and also known as Jones).[26] It is not known what became of Muk-kud-de-wuk-wuk's first wife. Some chiefs had more than one wife, so she may have still been married to Muk-kud-de-wuk-wuk when he married Kawbawgam's mother, but given that Kawbawgam was the oldest child of that marriage and likely born about 1816, many years after the birth of his youngest paternal half-brother, it is more likely Muk-kud-de-wuk-wuk's first wife died not long after the birth of her second child.

Kawbawgam's mother was Charlotte Sare or Sayre. Her Ojibwa name was Bechanokwetokwe (One Cloud Woman). Charlotte's parents' names are not known. Some researchers have speculated she was Charlotte Sayer Pemousse, daughter of Chief Pemousse.[27] There was a large Sayer family at the Sault at this time, which is likely the same as the Sayre family, but how Kawbawgam's mother was related to them has not been determined. In any case, Charlotte was born about 1790-1800 in Wisconsin or Canada, and died on February 15, 1889 at the Sault.[28] Perhaps Kawbawgam inherited his longevity from her. Charlotte was of mixed race, being both Ojibwa and Scottish, although what percentage of Scottish blood she had is not known.[29] Her surname suggests her father, not her mother, was of Scottish descent. Scottish traders, as well as English and French traders, often married Native American women. Regardless, her Scottish blood reflects that Kawbawgam was born into a métis world, and that even he himself was métis, despite many newspaper reporters toward the end of his life repeatedly stating Kawbawgam was "pure Indian."

Kawbawgam's parents are believed to have had four children:

1. Charles Kawbawgam
2. Shaw-wan-penace (aka Oshawwunnebenace/South Bird, Shawonong (from the South) who would also be a chief (This child, however, may be confused with Kawbawgam's half-brother Edward Shawano, since Shawano is also translated as "from the South.")

3. Kabaosa, born after 1816.[c]
4. Marie Macotiacoutte (probably a form of her father's name), who was baptized on December 25, 1821 in Green Bay, Brown County, Wisconsin,[30] but probably born before 1818 by which time Charlotte Sayre and Muk-kud-de-wuk-wuk had parted.

Kawbawgam's parents were not together for much longer than seven years. The marriage was dissolved when another chief from the Sault, Shawano (South Wind)[31d] was on a hunting trip to the Grand Island area and became so taken with Charlotte that he took her and her children to the Sault with him.[32e] Despite being separated from his father, Kawbawgam appears to have maintained a relationship with him until the end of his father's life.

The marital situation of Kawbawgam's parents was not unusual among the Ojibwa, although it was often grossly misunderstood and frowned upon by European and Christian contemporaries who equated such behavior with polygamy rather than divorce. Bishop Frederic Baraga, the most famous missionary to Upper Michigan's Native Americans, worked tirelessly to convert the Natives from his arrival in Upper Michigan in 1843 until his death in 1868. Baraga's biographer, P. Chrysostumus Verwyst, in his *Life of Bishop Baraga*, remarks, "Polygamy was one of the great impediments to his [the Native American's] conversion. This great evil had gradually almost entirely disappeared prior to Baraga's arrival in the Indian country."[33] However, this statement misunderstands the Ojibwa concept of marriage at the time. Polygamy had existed in earlier centuries and continued, but it seems to have been rare by the nineteenth century. German author Johann Georg Kohl stated that another well-known writer on the Ojibwa, whom he doesn't identify, said the Ojibwa didn't think it respectable to have multiple

---

c. This child may be confused with Muk-kud-de-wuk-wuk's son John Kabaosa, believed to be born in 1806. They may be one and the same. It is unlikely this child was named for a deceased older brother since we know John Kabaosa was alive around 1836 when he moved to Ontario with his father and brother Waubmama, as we will see later.

d. Shawano's name is also often written as Sha-wa-no or Sheweno Kwwainzegor Ka-ga-qua-dung and even Francis O'Shawwano and Francis Chavinane or Chavineau.

e. Notably, Shawano was a cousin to Kawbawgam's father, also being a grandson of the Great Crane. Maynard (p. 7) claims Shawano outranked Muk-kud-de-wuk-wuk and exercised his right as a major chieftain to take Charlotte from her husband, but this does not reflect Ojibwa custom. More likely, Charlotte fell in love with Shawano.

wives, and Kohl himself testified that the Ojibwa he met considered it simply horrible to be in a position to support multiples wives.[34] By Kawbawgam's time, polygamy was not as common as divorce. It was not unusual for men or women among the Ojibwa to put aside a spouse and choose another. Toward the nineteenth century's end, Jacques LePique, Kawbawgam's brother-in-law, would state that divorce was practiced by the Ojibwa earlier in the century, remarking, "When they didn't like one another, they didn't tie them up like you do; they had a better way of marrying in them days."[35] Kawbawgam's father-in-law, Chief Marji-Gesick, had multiple wives, although he lived with them at various times rather than all at once. The Ojibwa saw no sin in this; however, whites did, which resulted in Chief Marji-Gesick's marital relations becoming an item of contention when years later his daughter Charlotte tried to claim her father's rights when she took the Jackson Iron Company to court, as we will see in Chapter 8.

The confusion over Kawbawgam's parentage was best clarified upon his death by Detroit lawyer William B. Cady. Cady sent a letter dated January 8, 1903 to Marquette's *The Mining Journal* after Kawbawgam's obituary had been printed with some misinformation about Kawbawgam's parentage. Cady had been hired several years earlier to handle some land claims concerning the heirs of Kawbawgam's stepfather Shawano. At that time, Cady had spoken through an interpreter to Kawbawgam and his half-brother Edward, who succeeded Shawano as chief at the Sault, and assembled the following facts.[36] Kawbawgam and another child were born to a lesser chief who lived on or near Grand Island. Another chief, Shawano, from the Sault then came and took away the lesser chief's wife along with her children to the Sault. Later, Kawbawgam's mother and Shawano had four children of their own: Louis, Edward, Charlotte (Mrs. Roussain), and Lisette (Mrs. Chipman).[37]

Shawano was born at Drummond Island in 1791, so he would have been about twenty-six when he married Kawbawgam's mother, while she was likely in her late teens by that time. (Shawano was apparently also previously married, having a son named Edward who would have been Kawbawgam's stepbrother.)[38]

Charlotte and Shawano had the following children:[39]

1. Louis B. Shawano born circa 1818/1823. Died March 26, 1910.
2. Charlotte Ogobeawakwat, born circa 1822. Died March 6, 1922 in Garden River, Ontario, Canada. Married John Cornelius Katawkequonabee Wahlen on May 18, 1848.

3. Louise Shawano, born circa 1826. Died October 3, 1906 in Sault Sainte Marie, Michigan.
4. Charlotte Shawano, born circa 1828. Died July 8, 1912 in Sault Sainte Marie, Michigan. Married John Roussain.
5. Elizabeth/Lisette Shawano, born June 5, 1835 at Sugar Island near the Sault. Died July 2, 1864 in Detroit. Married John Logan Chipman.
6. François, baptized July 21, 1836 in Sault Sainte Marie, Michigan.
7. Edward Shawano, born circa 1838. Died September 20, 1899 in Sault Sainte Marie, Michigan.
8. Ogawbaygewawnoquay, born circa 1840.
9. Hortense Shawano, born circa 1841. Died after 1845.
10. Francis Shawano, born June 6, 1842 in Manitowaning, Ontario, Canada.

Altogether then, Kawbawgam's mother had fourteen children. To trace the history of all of them and their descendants is beyond the scope of this book, but we know at least a few of them remained significant in Kawbawgam's life into adulthood.

Kawbawgam's half-sister Charlotte married John (Jean) Roussain in Sault Sainte Marie on June 24, 1846.[40] She would have been about eighteen at the time and he about twenty. We know almost nothing about Charlotte, but John Roussain's obituary from the January 5, 1890 *Democrat* (Sault Sainte Marie newspaper) states:

> Death of John Roussain, of Sugar Island
>
> Ex-Supervisor John Roussain died at his home on Sugar Island, last Saturday night at 11 o'clock, aged 64 years. Mr. Roussain was one of Chippewa county's oldest settlers and for eight years represented Sugar Island township in the board of supervisors. He was a member of the G. A. R. post, of this city, under the auspices of which the burial took place Tuesday. Two sons, James and Robert, survive him. In many respects Mr. Roussain was a character. For a long time he controlled the political situation on Sugar Island and came to be known as the "boss" of the Island. Many will be found to remark "Old John had a big heart and always meant well."[41]

The Roussains had five children, including a daughter Harriet, and two sons, John Jr. and Benjamin, who apparently preceded their father in death.[42] One of the other sons has to be named Robert because he appears in the

1880 census as living with his grandparents, Chief Shawano and Charlotte (Sayre) Shawano.[43] I have been unable to unravel the Roussain family tree, but a Eustace Roussain (who may have been John Roussain's father or an uncle—he is referenced in a letter from John as we'll see in Chapter 4), had children by three Ojibwa sisters, Shauwunnanbanoqua, Wanwausumoqua, and Payahaubuoqua.[44] John Roussain's brother also married an Ojibwa woman. Two Roussain brothers, who may be John and his brother, were said to have created strong trading relationships with their Ojibwa relatives.[45] If John Roussain was not métis, his children would be, and marriages between French-Canadians and Natives were common at this time.

More surprising was the marriage of Kawbawgam's younger half-sister, Lisette (Elizabeth), to John Logan Chipman, an American, in 1852. This marriage drew quite a bit of attention, partially after the fact because Chipman became a prominent Michigan politician. More about Lisette and Chipman will be presented in its proper chronological place in Chapter 5.

Kawbawgam's half-brother Edward was selected by Chief Shawano to become chief of the tribe at the Sault upon his death.[46] It is important to note that chieftainship was not hereditary, although often members of the same family were chosen to be chiefs. We will look later at how Kawbawgam achieved chieftainship himself. Because Edward was chosen to be his father's successor, in agreement with the 1855 treaty, he was educated at government expense and sent to school at Albion College, Lansing, and Oberlin before returning to the Sault.[47] By 1846, Albion had established an "Indian Department" to educate "Those Indians who are expected to become Preachers, Interpreters or Teachers of Schools among their Aboriginal Brethren of the West" according to its 1846 catalog. It included the sons and daughters of tribal leaders as well as common Native American children. While many of these Native Americans adopted white names, Edward Shawano was one of the few who retained his Native name. While at Albion, Edward was elected to the Clever Fellows Society, the only mention of his attendance.[48] This education was for the government's benefit as much as Edward's since the government likely wanted him to assimilate and lead his people to become model Indians who lived like whites. Unfortunately, Edward's education would be largely for naught as we will later see in Chapter 7.

Since Kawbawgam's mother lived until 1889, Kawbawgam likely stayed in touch with her and his family throughout most of his life, although few details have been recorded about his relationships with his relatives during his adult years.

Catholicism

Kawbawgams' parents appear to have been Catholic, and while a baptism record does not exist for Kawbawgam himself, some do exist for his siblings. As noted above, his full sister Marie Macotiacoutte, was baptized on December 25, 1821 in Green Bay, Brown County, Wisconsin.[49] Since this baptism took place after we know Charlotte Sayre was with Shawano, it may show that Kawbawgam's father was not Catholic but his mother and stepfather were. We also have a baptismal record for Kawbawgam's half-brother François from July 2, 1836. The record lists him as François M. Chawenon/Shawenon. He was baptized by Jean-Baptiste Proulx and the sponsors were Louis and Marie Nolin. (The Nolin family will play a significant role in Kawbawgam's story.)

Based on his siblings' baptism records, we can assume Kawbawgam was Catholic from childhood. While it is unlikely he was baptized at Grand Island, he probably was baptized as a child at the Sault. No Catholic church existed at the Sault when Kawbawgam was a child, but in 1818, Father Provencher, while en route to Fort William, baptized forty-one children at the Sault. A mission was established there soon after, and other priests sporadically visited the area until Bishop Frederick Resé established regular Catholic services at the Sault in 1834. The following year, the first St. Mary's church was built and a parochial school begun.[50] Therefore, we can assume Kawbawgam was baptized by the time he was in his late teens if not in his childhood, although he probably did not attend the Catholic school since by all accounts, even as an adult, he could not read or speak English well. Protestant schools at the Sault were also established in the 1820s, but it is doubtful he would have attended these. He was definitely Catholic by the time he married in 1847 since the ceremony was performed by the Jesuit priest, Father Jean-Baptiste Menet. However, we do not know whether Kawbawgam regularly attended Mass. It is also noteworthy, as we will see, that Kawbawgam held onto the stories of his ancestors, which shows this was a time when religious beliefs were in flux among the Ojibwa between Christianity and their traditional religion. Baptism records for members of the Roussain family at the Sault, into which Kawbawgam's half-sister would marry, reflect this transitional period; for example, the baptism record of Josephte Roussin [Roussain] on August 17, 1835 lists her parents as Jean-Baptiste Roussain and Brunetta, an "Indian" and a "pagan."[51]

Clan

The Ojibwa were divided into numerous clans. Originally, five clans existed, but by the nineteenth century, they had further divided into twenty-one, according to mid-nineteenth century Ojibwa historian William Whipple Warren in *History of the Ojibwa People*,[52] although Warren's contemporary Henry Schoolcraft only listed fifteen.[53] A person belonged to their father's tribe. Everyone was required to marry outside their clan so they would not marry their close relatives.[54] To marry someone of your clan was considered one of the great sins and punishable by death.[55] This taboo shows the Ojibwa were knowledgeable about the problems caused by incestuous relationships and had their own moral codes prior to their interaction with Europeans, something most white writers of the time ignored or dismissed. Certain clans were also linked together as phratries, providing special hospitality and mutual assistance to one other.[56] Each clan was then broken down into bands of fifty to two hundred people.[57]

William Whipple Warren

Each clan had a totem, which was a bird or animal. According to legend, these totems came from six strangers who arrived from the bottom of a great salt water lake in human form. The strangers originally gave the Ojibwa five totems, although Warren lists six: crane, catfish, bear, martin, wolf, and loon. These five or six clans made up approximately 80 percent of the Ojibwa population during the nineteenth century, and the remaining totems were offshoots of them.[58] The Crane clan held predominance over the others and provided the region's hereditary chiefs.[59] Kawbawgam was born into the Bosinasse or Echo-Maker Crane totemic clan that resided at the Sault, and which claimed prominence over all other clans by hereditary rights.[60]

That the Crane clan resided primarily at the Sault is not surprising since the Ojibwa were, according to legend, led there by a crane. This event dates back several hundred years to when the Ojibwa separated from the other Algonquin peoples. The Ojibwa were one of the principal branches of Algonquins, the others being the Ottawa (Odawa), Potawatomi, Delaware, and Menominee.[61] The Potawatomi and Ottawa were most closely related to the Ojibwa, and according to Ojibwa legend, the three nations first resided along the shores of a great salt sea to the East (the Atlantic Ocean). Eventually, they moved west along rivers until they reached the Straits of Mackinac. There the three nations decided to go their separate ways. The Ojibwa chose to go north and west, ultimately settling in Michigan's Upper Peninsula, Wisconsin, and the north shore of Lake Superior in what is Canada today. The Ottawa settled primarily in Ontario and Lower Michigan while the Potawatomi settled in southwestern Michigan, around Lake Michigan's southern shore, and up into Wisconsin.

Legend states that upon separating from the Potawatomi and Ottawa, the Ojibwa were led to the Upper Peninsula by a crane that circled overhead. Its voice begged them to follow it, and eventually, it led them to the rapids of the St. Mary's River, where today Sault Sainte Marie stands. For this reason, the Ojibwa at the Sault came to call themselves "Boweting inini," meaning "People of the Falls."[62] Another story regarding the crane and the falls tells of the founding of Sault Sainte Marie. Today, a statue of a crane and two children stands in front of the Chippewa County Courthouse in Sault Sainte Marie. The statue includes a plaque with the following explanation:

> The statue depicts the Chippewa Legend of two young brothers who fled their wicked mother, who was pursuing them with the intent to kill them. When they reached the north shore of the St. Mary's Rapids they were met by a crane, who after hearing their story carried them to the south shore of the rapids. The crane then met the mother on the north shore and agreed to transport her to the other side. Instead, the crane dropped the mother in the rapids. When she hit the stones below, the mother's skull cracked open and her brains became the whitefish that inhabit the rapids to this day. The crane adopted the boys and one of them remained in the area, married the daughter of the crane, and founded Bahweting.

Regardless of how the Ojibwa arrived at the Sault, they remained because the rapids at the St. Mary's had a heavy concentration of fish, which became a primary source of food for them. The Ojibwa's oral traditions suggest they arrived about the year 1400.[63] The Ojibwa even had a story about the origin of the St. Mary's rapids, saying the rapids were created when the trickster spirit Nanabozho stepped on a beaver dam.[64] The Ojibwa called the area Bahweting, but later the Jesuits would rename it Sault Sainte Marie—French for St. Mary's Falls—to honor the Virgin Mary. The French would consequently call the Ojibwa at the St. Mary's River "Saulteurs."[65]

The Crane Statue in front of the Chippewa County Courthouse, Sault Sainte Marie, Michigan

Ojibwa fishing on the St. Mary's River at the Sault circa 1890. The International Railroad Bridge, built in 1887, is in the background. Note that the fishermen are using nets. George Shiras III said that at the time the near-shore waters of Lake Superior were so teeming with whitefish that the Natives never thought to resort to the white man's habit of using a fishing pole.[66]

In time, the Ojibwa split into the northern and southern Ojibwa, the southern staying in the Upper Peninsula and Wisconsin along Lake Superior's south shore, the northern moving into Canada along Lake Superior's north shore. This division happened about 1640, contemporary to when the first Europeans arrived in the area.[67]

Despite these divisions, the Ojibwa, Ottawa, and Potawatomi remained closely allied. They frequently met at Michilimackinac just south of the Straits of Mackinac for military and political reasons. Their meeting was known as the Council of the Three Fires.[68] The three nations would go to war together against the Iroquois Confederacy, the Sioux, and later against the British when the nations sided with the French in the French-Indian Wars (1754-1763), and then against the Americans when the nations sided with the British in the Northwestern Indian Wars (1785-1795) and the War of 1812 (1812-1815).

While many members of the Crane clan resided at the Sault, the clan had spread throughout the area, claiming it was also the first clan to pitch its wigwams and light fire near La Pointe, Wisconsin.[69] The clan's Echo-Maker designation refers to the loud, far-reaching cry of the crane; the Crane clan's members were said to have equally loud, ringing voices.[70]

The Loon totem also claimed to be the head chiefs of the Ojibwa, citing that loons have rings around their necks like the chief wampum (a beaded necklace worn by the chiefs), but all the other clans disagreed on this point and acknowledged the Crane clan as the chief clan.[71]

During Kawbawgam's youth, his paternal uncle Shingabawossin[f] was recognized by the Ojibwa as the head chief from the Crane clan at the Sault. Significantly, Shingabawossin was acknowledged by Governor Cass of Michigan as the head of the entire Ojibwa tribe in the 1825 treaty made at the Sault.[72] Shingabawossin stood 6'3" and, according to Henry Rowe Schoolcraft, then Indian agent at the Sault, he was "well proportioned, erect in his carriage, and of a commanding and dignified aspect. Of a turn of mind deliberate and thoughtful, he is at once respectful and respected." Shingabawossin once traveled from the Sault 400 miles to La Pointe to fight with Waubojeeg (White Fisher or White Crane), the chief there, against the Sioux at the battle of Falls of the St. Croix River.[73] Both Shingabawossin and Waubojeeg's daughter, Susan Johnston, would be significant people in Kawbawgam's early world, as was Kawbawgam's other uncle Sassaba, who wore a British officer's uniform when Governor Cass came to the Sault in 1820.

Kawbawgam's uncle, Chief Shingabawossin, head of the Crane Clan at Sault Sainte Marie in the 1820s

At this time, the Americans began to manipulate the position of chief among the Ojibwa. While Shingabawossin was already acknowledged as a chief by his people, Cass and Schoolcraft decided to recognize him as head chief.[74] The Ojibwa did not acknowledge anyone as a head chief, but the British and Americans enforced their own ideas of hierarchy and monarchy upon Native Americans, so they saw a head chief as equivalent to a high king over several minor kings. Cass likely chose to designate Shingabawossin as the head chief because he was the most amiable chief at the Sault in 1820, as we will see in Chapter 2. Such designations, usually conferred upon various chiefs with medals, caused confusion and resentment among the Ojibwa because it disrupted their traditions. In most cases, the chiefs chosen by the whites were not acknowledged as such by the Ojibwa.[75] Often, they were men agreeable to or easily coerced by whites into agreeing to deals beneficial to the whites. Shingabawossin seems to have been an exception since he was already a chief and well-respected by his people prior to Cass' arrival.

f. The name is often hyphenated as Shin-ga-ba-wos-sin.

The Ojibwa actually had two levels of chiefs. Civil chiefs were of the first rank while war chiefs were of the second.[76] However, no chief really had authority over the others. The Ojibwa had a long history of government, but no organizational hierarchy. Leadership was maintained through oratory.[77] Chiefs would get together to discuss issues and come to agreements. To become a chief, one had to show leadership abilities as a great warrior, show great wisdom in times of crisis, or be born into it. Chieftainship was not by primogeniture or necessarily hereditary, but it usually passed from one family member to another.[78]

Kawbawgam achieved his own status as a chief through his family relationships, although the details of this process are not clear. He may have had a right to chieftainship through his biological father, or perhaps through his stepfather, although when his stepfather Shawano died in 1884, his chieftainship passed to his biological son Edward, Kawbawgam's half-brother. By this time, Kawbawgam was not living at the Sault, so it stands to reason Edward, who did reside there, would become the chief in the area. Kawbawgam would move to Marquette in the 1840s shortly after marrying Charlotte, daughter of Chief Marji-Gesick, who was part of the Madosh family in Marquette County. Kawbawgam likely became acknowledged as a chief by virtue of his being Marji-Gesick's son-in-law and probably succeeded him as chief upon his death, although this is conjecture. Arthur Bourgeois, in his introduction to *Ojibwa Narratives*, says Kawbawgam became a chief after the death of Chief Madosh (Kawgayosh) a head chief recognized by the US Government, who was Chief Marji-Gesick's brother.[79] However, as I'll discuss in Chapter 7, this seems unlikely.

Childhood and Native Beliefs

We know very little about Kawbawgam's childhood. Because his family was Catholic, we can only speculate to what degree he grew up experiencing the typical Ojibwa lifestyle prior to the nineteenth century. This topic is important because Kawbawgam was obviously a leader in his community as an adult, but it is hard to know to what degree he adopted white ways, especially when it came to religious beliefs.

Traditionally, Ojibwa boys and girls would make prepuberty fasts, abstaining from food and fixing their minds on the spirit world. The fasts' purpose was so the child would hopefully acquire a guardian spirit, which was often visualized as a person or animal. This spirit would give them sound advice, knowledge, and possibly even power to influence the course of future events.[80]

German writer Kohl wrote about such experiences in 1855 after interviewing Ojibwa at L'Anse, Michigan. This fact suggests such practices were still common among the Ojibwa, despite the influences of Christianity, well into the nineteenth century. Kohl describes the children who made these fasts as:

> ...able, at the tenderest age, to fast for days on behalf of a higher motive, retire to the most remote forests, defy all the claims of nature, and fix their minds so exclusively on celestial matters, that they fell into convulsions, and attained an increased power of perception, which they did not possess in ordinary life.[81]

The children would make their "dream-beds" in the trees, about ten to twelve feet off the ground. According to the Ojibwa, the good spirits and dream genii reside high in the air while the Matchi-Manitou wanders about on the ground and annoys people, so the dreamer needs to be above where the Matchi-Manitou's snakes, toads, and other animals would disturb him. The children were also warned that if they had bad dreams, they were to return home and try later, over and over, until the right dream came.[82]

In particular, Kohl interviewed Agabe-gijik (The Cloud), an older Ojibwa who recounted his dream from his youth to Kohl. This Ojibwa was likely a generation older than Kawbawgam. He describes a spirit coming to him who ordered him to follow him, and he did so through the air. He felt like he and the spirit were ascending a mountain until they came to a summit where he found a wigwam and four men sitting around a large white stone. From there the four men told him to ascend and he did so, rising higher and higher in the air and seeing an abundance of birds and game below him, which meant he was to be a famous hunter.[83]

If Kawbawgam had such a dream experience, one has to wonder what the spirits showed him. Did he realize he had a destiny to become a chief among a small band of his people at Marquette, or that he would be involved in founding a city at the heart of the great iron industry the Americans would develop?

As a Catholic, did Kawbawgam also hold on to old beliefs that an Ojibwa leader should develop an intimate, long-term relationship of reciprocity with spirit persons? The spirit persons would then provide him with material help and create a balance among the various powers in the Ojibwa universe to allow him and his people to survive and be secure. Similarly, as the Ojibwa converted to Christianity, they came to believe the "blessings" of white technology and skills would result from respectful behavior toward the white man's god.[84]

We can only guess what Kawbawgam's religious beliefs may have been. How did he reconcile a belief in Christianity with the traditional Ojibwa religious beliefs and myths and legends he grew up hearing? That these legends were important to him is reflected in the fact that in the 1890s he would remember so many of them and recount them to Homer Kidder to ensure they would be preserved.

Conclusion

Chief Kawbawgam's origins and family background remain cloaked in obscurity. Similarly, his early years are largely lost to us from a lack of historical record. In Chapter 3, we will delve into the parts of his life that are fairly well-documented, beginning with his marriage to Charlotte in 1847. First, however, in Chapter 2, we will set aside Kawbawgam himself and look at an overview of the state of the Ojibwa and their relations with the Americans who arrived at the Sault when Kawbawgam was hardly more than a toddler. The coming of the Americans would be the most significant force of change to the Ojibwa way of life, and it would affect Kawbawgam's own behavior and relationships with white Americans as an adult.

Chapter 2
Ojibwa and American Relations at Sault Sainte Marie: 1820-1845

At the time of Kawbawgam's birth, Sault Sainte Marie consisted of just a handful of permanent buildings owned by whites or métis. However, numerous Native Americans also resided in the area in less permanent structures. The St. Mary's Falls had long made the Sault a gathering place, especially for its fishing and fur trade. For nearly two centuries, the French had come to the area to trade with the Native Americans, and the British for nearly a century. While other tribes were frequently at the Sault, the dominant tribe there was the Ojibwa.

The Ojibwa Before 1820

Although Kawbawgam would be known as the "Chief of the Chippewa" by his contemporaries, he was rightfully a member of the Anishinaabe, a word that has been variously translated as "The People," "The Original People," or "Spontaneous People."[1] This name implies the Anishinaabe were the first people made by the Creator, or according to some of their creation stories, they just simply appeared. The name Anishinaabe was corrupted by the French as "Ojibwa" or "Ojibway" and then further corrupted by the British into "Chippewa." One possible meaning of Ojibwa is "gathering," a reference to how its members gathered or stitched together their moccasins, which were designed differently from those of other Native American tribes.[2] The name may also refer to the "puckering" of the moccasins; they were roasted until they puckered to make them waterproof.[3]

Prior to 1820, the Ojibwa of Upper Michigan lived a nomadic lifestyle, largely free from rules and strictures. In winter, they would disperse as individual families to hunt deer and small animals. In March, they would gather together to tap maple trees and process maple syrup to use as seasoning, make candy from, and mix with water to create refreshing drinks.[4] In summer, they would come together to gather wild plants and fish at the Straits of Mackinac and the St. Mary's Falls and to socialize with their fellow tribal members. In the autumn, they would hunt game and gather wild plants, berries, and nuts. Then they would move into their winter quarters where families "owned" land for trapping and subsisted on food they had stored up during the rest of the year. The Ojibwa had no real concept of land ownership; instead, they saw themselves as stewards of the land. Fish was their primary food, composing about 75 percent of their diet. They also derived high nutritional value and antioxidants from maple syrup. They were not farmers, so they did not grow corn or maize; instead, wild rice was their grain substitute.[5]

No strong or central government existed among the Ojibwa.[6] They believed no one individual should have authority over another. Even their greatest chiefs had no more power than did a child, but the chiefs were revered for their wisdom. Because the Ojibwa had no true hierarchy, each community member had to cooperate with everyone else if the tribe or family units and clans were to survive. Everyone was considered equal so everyone had to do his or her share of the work and everyone shared what they had. Because they did not believe in property, no need or desire existed to accumulate belongings; consequently, greed and theft were unknown.[7] Although the Ojibwa had no central government, they were divided into clans, as we saw in Chapter 1, and each clan was governed by its own group of chiefs.

As stewards of the land, the Ojibwa were reverent toward everything. They did not swear or curse because it would have been disrespectful. They were not prone to drunkenness until the Europeans arrived and introduced them to alcohol, which would result in many problems for them.[8]

Approximately 25,000 Ojibwa resided in the Lake Superior Basin in independent bands in the seventeenth century when Europeans first began to explore the western Great Lakes.[9] One Ojibwa legend states that when the first white men, the French, arrived at Great Turtle Island (Mackinac Island), a crane and bear were on shore to welcome them—a metaphor for the two clans that greeted the French. It was said that, as a result, the Crane and Bear clans were the favorites of the French explorers.[10] When German writer

Johann Georg Kohl visited the Lake Superior region in 1855, he asked Peter Jones, an Ojibwa, about the coming of the white men, and specifically, who had first brought the news of white people to the Ojibwa. Jones replied that no one had brought the news. Rather a great jossakid (a seer) had experienced a vision in which he saw the French and their large canoes and described them to his fellow Ojibwa, who then decided to travel east to see the white men and report about them to the rest of the tribe. When the Ojibwa met up with the French, they were kindly received, and the French sent them home with presents of colored cloth.[11]

The history of French and Ojibwa relations is beyond the scope of this book, but it is worth noting that the French were largely tolerant of the Ojibwa, and the Ojibwa later claimed they were the favorite Native American tribe of the French. Besides trading with them, the French notably brought Christianity to the Ojibwa through the Jesuit missionaries. In fact, the Sault is Michigan's oldest city, dating back to 1668 when Father Marquette established a mission there. For the most part, the Ojibwa were open to Father Marquette and his fellow priests' message; many converted to Christianity, although how much the Ojibwa understood Christianity is questionable; they often blended it with their own traditions and beliefs, as will be discussed in Chapter 11 when we look at some of the Ojibwa legends Kawbawgam shared with Homer Kidder.

In the next century, the British made inroads into the Upper Great Lakes, resulting in the French-Indian War of 1756-1763. The Ojibwa and other Native tribes were not happy about the British winning the war, resulting in a massacre of British soldiers at Fort Michilimackinac at the Straits of Mackinac in 1763. In time, however, the Ojibwa became loyal to the British.

The good years of Ojibwa and British relations would only last for a few decades. Following the American Revolution (1775-1783), the Treaty of Paris fixed the St. Mary's River as the border between Canada and the United States, meaning that the Sault, Mackinac Island, La Pointe, and other key Ojibwa areas of settlement were now under American control. The British, however, remained in the area until 1794 when the Jay Treaty was signed.[12] At that point, the Americans took over the fort at Mackinac Island, which had replaced the earlier mainland Fort Michilimackinac.

The American incursion into the Upper Peninsula would make little difference to the Ojibwa during this period, but in the early nineteenth century that would quickly change.

The Ojibwa and Anti-American Feelings

The Jay Treaty of 1794 had allowed for the Ojibwa to move back and forth over the United States/Canadian border without trouble since they had relatives on both sides of the St. Mary's River.[13] This freedom, however, was little consolation to the Ojibwa when they began to hear horror stories about American encroachment upon other Native American tribes' lands. Kawbawgam's ancestors had lived in a métis world where Native Americans, Europeans, and children of both races had mutual respect for one another. But by the time Kawbawgam was born, this métis world was quickly vanishing. In 1809, the Northwest Company would forbid its agents to marry Native Americans. Soon the Native Americans and those of mixed race would find themselves second-class citizens in a white American world. What had been a world of tolerance would become increasingly racist as the nineteenth century progressed.[14]

The Treaty of Greenville (1795) and the Treaty of Detroit (1807) also caused the Ojibwa and métis at the Sault to view Americans negatively because the treaties dismantled Native American independence and power. The Treaty of Greenville was basically a forced secession of most of Ohio and other parts of the Northwest Territory to the United States, and the Treaty of Detroit ceded southeast Michigan and the northernmost part of Ohio to the United States.

In 1797, General James Wilkinson of the US Army, stationed at Detroit, traveled to Mackinac Island and the Sault to discuss the benefits of being American with the Ojibwa and to distribute American flags and presents to them, hoping to strengthen US relations with the tribe. The Ojibwa were not impressed by these actions and remained loyal to the British.[15] Earlier in 1795, Congress had created a factory system—a chain of well-stocked trading posts staffed by government agents—intended to attract Native American loyalty to the United States through trade. As part of this system, in 1809, Joseph Varnum, Jr. was appointed to open a factory on Mackinac Island. Varnum offered fair prices to the Native Americans for their furs and other goods to try to draw them away from the British, but the Native Americans continued to trade with the British because British goods were superior. In addition, fear began to spread that American farmers planned to invade the Upper Peninsula to take Native American lands.[16]

At this point, Americans had no real interest in settling the Upper Peninsula, but rumors of its mineral riches—specifically its copper—were already spreading. Because Isle Royale in Lake Superior was known to have had prehistoric copper mines, in 1800 US President John Adams directed Congress to employ an agent to collect information relative to copper, as well as to determine the land ownership of the Upper Peninsula and persuade the Native Americans to cede it to the United States. However, the following year, President Thomas Jefferson decided to halt a planned copper expedition so the secession of land was also postponed.[17] It would be another forty years before serious copper exploration would begin in Upper Michigan's Keweenaw Peninsula, today known as the "Copper Country."

Native dislike of Americans at this time also resulted from President Jefferson closing all the American ports in 1807. This situation meant that when Joseph Varnum arrived at Mackinac, he had to tell the Ojibwa they could no longer trade with their friends and neighbors in Canada.[18]

All these factors contributed to a strong anti-American feeling among the Native Americans of the Great Lakes region. The situation reached its climax when several Native Americans tried to stir up anti-American feelings and call for a return to traditional Native American culture and values.

In 1807, Le Maigouis (the Trout), an Ottawa who was brother to a principal chief at L'Arbre Croche in Lower Michigan, began to preach to his people that they should avoid all contact with the whites and quit practicing white ways, including drinking liquor, keeping domestic animals, and wearing white clothes. Le Maigouis insisted that any Native American women who were coupled with white men must demand legal marriages. He also preached against Native Americans trading liquor between themselves. Le Maigouis traveled north to Lake Superior to encourage this return to traditional Native values. He told his fellow Native Americans that the Americans "are not my children, but the children of the evil spirit. They grew from the scum of the great water, when it was troubled by the evil spirit, and the froth was driven into the woods by a strong east wind. They are numerous, but I hate them."[19] This talk excited the Native Americans enough that they started passing wampum belts (belts made of beads) from tribe to tribe to spread the word to prepare for war. At Fort Mackinac, Captain J. Dunham was concerned enough about this agitation to make plans to arrest Le Maigouis, but Le Maigouis not only eluded him but managed to speak to the Ojibwa in the shadow of the fort's walls.[20] He then went to Indiana to meet with Tecumseh, a Shawnee warrior and chief, and Tecumseh's brother Tensquatawa, known as the Shawnee Prophet, who were also working to resist American advancement.

Captain Dunham also called for a council of Ottawa and Ojibwa at Detroit, but the Native American leaders refused to meet with him, believing the council just another effort to persuade them to cede more land to the United States. The Ojibwa and Ottawa said of the other Native Americans of the Lower Peninsula, "If they are fools enough to throw away their hunting ground, let them do it. However in this quarter we will do no such thing. And, we hope, My Father, you will not think of taking our lands beneath for we have so little to spare."[21] By the fall of 1807, the Ottawa at L'Arbre Croche had begun to adhere strictly to the Shawnee Prophet and Le Maigouis' preaching. They quit wearing hats and refused to consume liquor, which ruined the business of the traders at Mackinac Island.[22] At the Sault, the Ojibwa wife of fur trader Michael Cadotte became interested enough in Le Maigouis' message to infuriate her husband, who consequently beat her. Directly after this event, his storehouse was pillaged, presumably by the Ojibwa as punishment for how he had mistreated his wife.[23]

Tensquatawa, the Shawnee Prophet, brother of Tecumseh

Meanwhile, the Shawnee Prophet and Tecumseh were encouraging Native Americans in Indiana and its vicinity to rise up against the American advance upon the frontier. Like Le Maigouis, the Shawnee Prophet preached that Natives must give up white ways so the Great Spirit would no longer be angry with them.[24] Tecumseh would initiate Tecumseh's War, but be unsuccessful in getting the US government to rescind the 1809 Treaty of Fort Wayne and other land-cession treaties. He most famously initiated the Battle of Tippecanoe in 1811 in Indiana, although the American forces, led by future US President William Henry Harrison, caused the Native forces to retreat.

Americans blamed the British for this anti-American feeling among the Native Americans. As a result, several Congressmen pushed for war with Britain, which was declared on June 18, 1812.[25]

The Cass Expedition of 1820

In the War of 1812, the Ojibwa sided with the British. Consequently, they were deeply saddened when the Americans won the war and the British retreated from Fort Mackinac and other outposts in the area. The British moved their headquarters to Drummond Island, where their presence still caused considerable trouble to the American government as it tried to establish itself in the area. For many years, loyal Native Americans would travel to Drummond Island to collect gifts from the British, infuriating the American government. Not until 1822 would Drummond Island become part of the United States, and the British would not evacuate it until 1828.[26]

American encroachment finally reached the Sault in 1820 when US Secretary of War John C. Calhoun commissioned an expedition to explore the Great Lakes for evidence of its legendary mineral riches and to establish relationships with the tribes that had fought with the British in the war. This expedition would result in Kawbawgam's first memory of seeing his uncle, the warrior chief Sassaba, walking down the street in a British uniform to show his hostility toward the expedition.

The expedition, led by Michigan Territory Governor Lewis Cass, also included Henry Rowe Schoolcraft, the expedition's mineralogist who would later be the Indian agent at the Sault, and James Doty, a journalist, who would later write about the expedition to gain publicity for it.[27] At Mackinac Island, the party would be joined by Lieutenant John Pierce, who was in charge of twenty-two soldiers at Fort Mackinac. Pierce was brother to future US President Franklin Pierce.[28]

Lewis Cass, Governor of the Michigan Territory

The Cass party arrived at the Sault by batteaux. According to Doty's journal, forty-two men were in the company, including ten Native Americans, who were of the Shawnee, Ottawa, and Ojibwa tribes.[29] Approximately sixty men were on the expedition, some of whom planned to begin a trading post at the Sault. Schoolcraft described the Sault as consisting of fifteen to twenty buildings with five or six French and English families residing there, besides the Native Americans who were believed to number about two hundred and had about forty lodges erected in the area.[30] Cass and his men would be entertained by Mrs. Johnston, the Ojibwa wife of John Johnston.[a] Johnston, the most prominent citizen at the Sault and a wealthy fur trader, was away on a business trip to his native Ireland.[31]

Cass came to the Sault with the intention to persuade the Ojibwa to cede land to the United States so a fort could be built there, but this mission did not start out on a good footing. Cass met with the local Ojibwa leaders, including George Johnston, the métis son of John Johnston. The Ojibwa were immediately suspicious of Cass and his men and still felt loyalty to the British. When they expressed their feelings to Cass, he told them, through an interpreter, that the United States already held their land as a result of the 1795 Treaty of Greenville. This statement infuriated the chiefs, who said they knew nothing of this treaty.[32] Cass explained that despite the treaty, the United States was willing to repurchase the land from them. Kawbawgam's uncle, Chief Shingabawossin, agreed that the Ojibwa would cede the land on the condition that there would be no fort or garrison built upon it, which Cass promised.[33]

---

a. The Johnstons were the most prominent family at the Sault so Kawbawgam likely knew them in his youth. Mrs. Johnston's Ojibwa name was O-shaw-gus-co-day-way-qua, which has been translated as Daughter of the Green Mountain, Green Meadow Woman, or Woman of the Glade. Later, she would be baptized and be known by the name Susan. Mrs. Johnston was the daughter of Waubojeeg, the chief at La Pointe. Johnston met the family when he provided aid to Waubojeeg's father, Mamongazida, who had been taken financial advantage of by some traders and left with nothing to survive the winter. Johnston immediately fell in love with his future wife, but Waubojeeg told Johnston to return for the winter to Montreal, and if in the spring, Johnston still loved her and had not yet found a white woman, he would consent to the marriage. Johnston returned in the spring and the two were married, although O-shaw-gus-co-day-way-qua was apparently forced into the marriage and afterwards ran away from Johnston. Her father then beat her and brought her back to Johnston. After that, the two seem to have lived happily together and had a large family. Mrs. Johnston became famous at the Sault for her hospitality, and many travelers left written records of visiting the family. Although Mrs. Johnston could understand English, she always spoke Ojibwa and retained her Native dress. For more about the Johnston family, I recommend reading *The Invasion* by Janet Lewis (a fictional account) and *The John Johnston Family of Sault Ste. Marie* by Elizabeth Hambleton and Elizabeth Warren Stoutamire.

John and Susan Johnston

Despite this promise, Chief Shingwaukonse, from Grand Island, opposed the ceding of land,[34] which included a Native burial ground. When Cass then threatened to occupy the riverbank whether the Ojibwa renewed the lease or not, the young war chief Sassaba, brother of Shingabawossin, became angry. Clad in his British uniform, complete with epaulettes and a silver gorget that indicated rank as a brigadier general in the British army, Sassaba, also known as "the Count," haughtily told Cass that he and his brother Waubejechauk had fought with the British against the victorious Americans at the Battle of the Thames, where his brother had been killed.[b] Because of his brother's death, Sassaba felt hatred for the Americans, so he would not cede them any land.[35] Sassaba then kicked aside the present of tobacco Cass had thrown at his feet, and after violently thrusting his lance into the ground, he stormed out.[36]

The council then broke up, with the other chiefs embarrassed by Sassaba's behavior.[37] Meanwhile, Sassaba went to his wigwam where he ran up a British flag. When Cass saw the flag, he was infuriated and immediately tore it down.

---

b. For whatever reason, perhaps out of respect for his father, in 1819 the British had recognized Waubejechauk's eight-year-old son, Negenagoching, Kawbawgam's first cousin, as head chief, despite Shingabawossin being regarded as head chief by the Ojibwa. Negenagoching would grow up to be known as Joseph Sayer when older; he would live a typically métis lifestyle near his métis relatives (Chute 30).

The Johnston House as it appears today

He then entered Sassaba's wigwam and lectured him that if the British flag was ever flown again, he was prepared to "set a strong foot upon their [the Ojibwa's] necks and crush them to the earth."[38c]

Soon both sides were arming for battle. Sassaba was busy convincing his warriors he was in the right, while the Americans were preparing to hold their ground. Meanwhile, the Ojibwa women and children jumped into canoes and paddled up the river to safety.[39] Very possibly, Kawbawgam and his siblings were among those children.

By this point, Mrs. Johnston decided to take matters into her own hands. She sent her son George to bring the chiefs to her house to discuss the situation. Since she was a chief's daughter and highly respected among the Ojibwa at the Sault, the chiefs agreed to come. Upon their arrival, Mrs.

---

c. Despite this dramatic behavior, Cass was often kind toward Native Americans. In his captivity narrative, John Tanner recounts how Cass gave gifts to an Indian family after one of their members was murdered. Cass also showed kindness to Tanner himself when Tanner was trying to reunite with his Kentucky family, from which he had been kidnapped by Native Americans while still a child (Tanner, Chapter 13).

Johnston told the chiefs she had magic power given to her through a vision-trance to stop calamities. She convinced the chiefs of the uselessness of plotting against the Americans. George also warned the chiefs that even if they only fired one gun upon the Americans, it would ruin their entire tribe.[40] Ultimately, the Johnstons convinced the chiefs not to fight, and then the chiefs sent Shingwaukonse to Sassaba to stop him and the warriors he was amassing. When he confronted Sassaba, Shingwaukonse told him he had been authorized by the chiefs and elders to stop him, to which Sassaba replied, "You was [sic] a war leader when my brother fell in battle; he was killed by the Americans, and how dare you come to put a stop to my proceedings?" He then raised his war club and struck at Shingwaukonse, grazing his shoulder. Undeterred, Shingwaukonse convinced the party to desist from violence and Shingabawossin further pacified Sassaba. Afterwards, Shingwaukonse was honored by the Ojibwa for stopping a volatile situation.[41]

The treaty was signed on July 16, 1820 in George Johnston's office. Per the terms of the treaty, the Ojibwa ceded sixteen square miles of land at the Sault to the United States in exchange for a "quantity of goods" and perpetual fishing rights.[42] The treaty would be signed by fifteen chiefs, the first among them being Shingabawossin. Shingwaukonse signed last, requesting his name be fixed as Augustin Bart. As previously stated, Kawbawgam's biological father also signed the treaty as Macadaywacwet. Sassaba refused to sign the document.[43] Witnesses of the treaty included Schoolcraft and Doty.[44]

After signing the treaty, General Cass gratefully realized the debt the United States Government owed to Mrs. Johnston for her actions and also that he probably owed her his life.[45] Later, in gratitude for Mrs. Johnston's actions, the United States Government would give Mr. Johnston a land grant near the Sault.[46] However, Mrs. Johnston was not jubilant over stopping the bloodshed. She knew she had saved her people from a violent destruction by the Americans but that the treaty also likely marked the beginning of the end for her people.[47]

That Kawbawgam's first memory is of his uncle Sassaba wearing a British uniform to this meeting is significant since it marked the moment when the Sault officially became American. Kawbawgam was there at the moment his people lost their role as stewards over their ancestral lands; he would be among the first generation of Ojibwa to grow up in the United States of America.

Left: *Statue of Mrs. Johnston in the Johnston House's garden*
Right: *This ancient burial ground along Water Street in Sault Sainte Marie is likely the burial ground the Ojibwa were concerned about having disturbed when Cass arrived. In 2005, it was enclosed. Shingabawossin referred to the place as "Our Ancient Burial Ground." On this hill also resided the Adjimag or Sacred Mountain Ash Tree. On a calm, cloudless day it would give forth a sound of distant rolling drums, causing the Ojibwa to believe a manitou (spirit) resided there. Offerings of twigs and prayers were made at the tree's base.* [48] *The obelisk in the center of the burial ground was erected in 1905 to commemorate the fiftieth anniversary of the Sault Locks and lists among the principal commissioners of the celebration Marshall Charles Harvey and Peter White, Kawbawgam's good friend, who went to Washington, DC to get the government to fund the celebrations.*

Henry Schoolcraft as Indian Agent

In the years following the expedition, Cass continually tried to keep the Native Americans from trading with the British. In 1821, calling the Native Americans "my children," he asked them not to travel to Drummond Island to receive gifts from the British.[49] Despite these pleas, the Native American tribes would continue to deal with the British for decades. Nor can they be blamed since Cass reneged on his promise that the Americans would not build a fort at the Sault.

In July 1822, Colonel Hugh Brady arrived at the Sault to establish Fort Brady. With him came Henry Schoolcraft, who would be installed as the Indian agent. During the installation, Schoolcraft had his first opportunity to address the Native Americans in his new capacity. Colonel Brady also addressed them, promising that their burial grounds and encampment area would not be encroached upon by the government.[50] The speeches were well received by Chief Shingabawossin, but Chief Sassaba remained unhappy. He made a brief, violent speech, and then when George Johnston rebuked him, he left the council.[51] Despite this disturbance, Schoolcraft wrote in his journal that the event went well and that he promised to study the Ojibwa's customs and language so he could deal justly and amicably with them. He also hired Yarns, an Irishman married to an Ojibwa, to be a translator and help him learn Ojibwa and other Native languages.[52] Governor Cass had written how the best way to know the Native Americans was to study them in their homes,[53] and that is what Schoolcraft now proposed to do.

George Johnston

Brady was truthful in his promise that the fort would not encroach upon Native lands, but encroachment by other whites soon resulted as the natural consequence of the population explosion at the Sault. Two-hundred-fifty soldiers had arrived at the fort, plus the families of the married officers, meaning the whites now equaled or outnumbered the Native Americans.[54]

Although peace was maintained at the Sault in the years that followed, plenty of tension remained. Because American forts frequently changed their commanders, it hurt the establishment of good relations between the locals, including the Natives, with the military. At Mackinac Island, the military didn't hire local workers to help build the fort, which also caused unhappiness. In addition, the Natives were subject to Indian agents who sometimes used

Fort Brady, Sault Ste. Marie

their power to keep the Native Americans out of the trade loop as a way to punish or discriminate against them.[55]

The American Fur Company contracted with the Native Americans for fish as well as fur; the fishing industry was second only to the fur industry and fish was a major source of food and income for the Native Americans. However, as more Americans moved into the area, they began to see the Native Americans as intruders upon their businesses.[56] Within fifteen years, the Americans had disenfranchised the old French, British, and métis traders.

This situation may partly explain why John Johnston would in time consent to his daughter Jane marrying Henry Schoolcraft; the marriage was one way for Johnston to stay in the Indian agent's good graces, for his children's sake, if not his own, since he was not an American citizen and couldn't trade. While Johnston and his family had been very prominent at the Sault and would remain so as long as Schoolcraft was the Indian agent there, after Johnston's death, white Americans saw Johnston's children as métis, and therefore, of a lower class. When, in 1825, the Erie Canal was completed, it made passage to the Sault easier, bringing more white Americans to the area, and ultimately leading to the destruction of the Sault's cosmopolitan French-Native world. Discrimination against Native Americans and métis increased during this period, resulting in many French, métis, and Native Americans moving across the river to live in the more tolerant Canadian Sault.[57]

With an American fort and an Indian agent established at Sault Sainte Marie, no pretense could remain that the Sault was British or French rather than American. Because the Americans were completely ignorant of Ojibwa beliefs and what was sacred to the Ojibwa, Schoolcraft found himself in an uneasy position of constantly trying to keep peace in the community. Soon after the fort was built, a problem arose when a sacred manitou tree was desecrated because an officer had removed one of the poles placed there to appease the manitou (spirit) who might be the cause of someone's sickness.[58]

In April 1823, Chief Shingabawossin made a speech to his people about how the Great Father, the American President, was good to the Indians.[59] He was one of the first chiefs to espouse the cause of peace with the Americans, although his brother Sassaba opposed it. Doubtless, Shingabawossin realized it was futile to resist the Americans.[d]

Schoolcraft's marriage to Jane Johnston, who was half-Ojibwa and half-Irish, likely softened him toward the Native Americans. For example, in 1824, when the Natives complained that white settlers were encroaching upon their fishing encampment in direct violation of the 1820 treaty, Schoolcraft advocated that in the future the Natives draw the maps for the treaties so they would be clear about what lands were involved, rather than relying on an interpreter's pointing finger or waving hand.[60]

---

d. Sassaba would not have a happy ending. Following the signing of the 1820 treaty, his behavior became quite abnormal. He was often seen wandering about at the Sault clad in nothing but a wolfskin (his name means wolf) with the animal's tail trailing after him (Chute 34-5). On September 25, 1822, he had a drinking bout with some friends at Pointe aux Pins, just north of the Sault. Returning to the Sault by canoe with his wife and child, and apparently still intoxicated, his canoe was swept into the rapids and he and his family drowned. However, it has been suggested such behavior was a sign that he was trying to appeal to spirits for assistance. (See Chute p. 35 for additional interpretations of his behavior.) Bayliss and Bayliss make a good point in *River of Destiny* that "Properly viewed, he [Sassaba] was a sincere patriot who, regardless of personal consequences, refused to recognize the conquest of his country" (315). Kawbawgam, who was said never to drink alcohol, may have had vivid memories of how his uncle Sassaba's death affected his family, since he would have been about five or six at the time. He certainly would have grown up hearing stories about his uncle Sassaba. His uncle's death may have made a great imprint on Kawbawgam, affecting how he treated white people and perhaps influencing his moderate and temperate behavior.

Henry Schoolcraft

Schoolcraft definitely became more interested in the Native Americans than his position required. He ultimately interviewed hundreds of Native Americans about themselves and their history. This process may be considered the first oral history program in America.[61] The Natives also seemed, for the most part, to trust him and asked him to help them settle matters of importance. For example, he was asked to determine the succession of title of chief from the Crane totem at the Sault. To arrive at an answer, he interviewed various family members and traced the family back three generations to Gitcheeojeedebun, the Great Crane leader of the mid-eighteenth century (Kawbawgam's great-grandfather).[62]

Despite his interest in Native American history and lore and even his marriage into a métis family, Schoolcraft was well aware of his precarious position. He was a white man seeking to look after Native American concerns, but primarily to benefit the US Government by keeping the Natives peaceful and convincing them to sell their lands, including mineral rights. He was also surrounded by a growing white population at the Sault that had little sympathy for the Natives, while the old guard—the métis, French, and British—had become second-class citizens or moved to Canada. Consequently, Schoolcraft must have felt divided in his loyalties and struggled to maintain balance in the community and in his own heart.[63]

Jane Johnston Schoolcraft

Elmwood, Schoolcraft's home and also the Indian agency, was the largest home in the Sault when it was built. Here it is in 2019.

Henry Schoolcraft and Racism

Schoolcraft obviously had a great reverence for the Native Americans he dealt with, but that did not stop him from holding beliefs of white superiority. He wanted to be a friend to the Natives, but that friendship hinged on helping them assimilate into American society or removing them from being in the way of whites and the United States' westward expansion.[64] Consequently, Schoolcraft was in many ways a man of contradictions.

Schoolcraft's marriage to Jane Johnston makes his racism even more interesting. Many biographers and contemporaries have speculated that he found Jane's mixed blood exotic; this overlooks that being métis was common at the Sault, although it was not back in Schoolcraft's native New York.[65] That he promoted his wife as a Pocahontas (an Indian princess by right of Jane's grandfather having been Chief Waubojeeg) and an educated marvel (she was mostly educated by her father, although a brief stay in England and Ireland as a child when her father went on a business trip there was exaggerated into her having received an extensive and polished European education) also reflects his own discomfort in having married a half-Native woman and his efforts to whitewash her ethnicity. Schoolcraft even tried to whitewash his children, although that might be interpreted as an attempt to protect them by assimilating them. While he was opposed to Native children being sent to boarding schools to be indoctrinated into American ways, he had no problem with sending his own métis (one-quarter Ojibwa) children to such schools.[66]

The Johnston family certainly educated Schoolcraft on the Ojibwa's strengths. Soon after arriving at the Sault, Schoolcraft's contacts with the local

Natives caused him to write in his diary in 1824, "It was amazing to find him [the Native American] a man capable of feelings and affections, with a heart open to the wants and responsive to the ties of social life. But the surprise reached its acme when I found him whiling away a part of the tedium of his long winter evenings in relating tales and legends for the amusement of the lodge circle."[67] Schoolcraft became enamored with Native lore and recorded much of it, but he also appropriated it for his own purposes. The Johnstons told him many Native American stories, several of which he published in his literary magazine, the *Literary Voyager*, which was passed about the Sault in manuscript form in the 1820s. In 1839, Schoolcraft published *Algic Researches* about his research into Native American lore, but even the book's title is suspect. He invented the word "Algic" as a shortened form of Algonquin. When he gave a copy to his sister-in-law, Eliza Johnston, she appreciated the gift but felt he had written condescendingly about Jane's Ojibwa ancestry. However, Schoolcraft was always aware that he was writing for an American audience so he felt the need to whitewash the Native American stories.[68] Native Americans themselves also may have whitewashed their stories for the white audiences they told them to, making them sound more Christian or leaving out sexual anecdotes. As a result, today we often have filtered versions of Native tales, but these modified works served as a bridge between cultures, replacing American fear and distaste with more understanding and respect for Native Americans and their culture.

Henry Wadsworth Longfellow at the time he wrote The Song of Hiawatha

One of the biggest bridges between white and Native cultures would be Henry Wadsworth Longfellow's epic poem *The Song of Hiawatha*, published in 1855. Longfellow borrowed from Schoolcraft's writings, but also appropriated Native lore for his own purposes. While he retained the Upper Peninsula setting of the stories, he named his hero Hiawatha after a legendary New York Iroquois. Regardless, he did bring the Ojibwa to the attention of a wider audience.

Schoolcraft's interest in the Ojibwa language is also worth noting. He compiled an Indian grammar and dictionary years before Bishop Frederic Baraga, who generally receives the most attention for his dictionary. Schoolcraft knew Ojibwa better than almost any white man of the time, although he always had an Ojibwa interpreter to help him, and he sometimes despaired of ever learning the language accurately.[69] And even in his efforts to learn the Ojibwa language, his white arrogance is apparent. He wanted a monosyllabic Ojibwa language, so in creating his dictionary, he reduced polysyllabic words to monosyllabic ones.[70]

In other ways, Schoolcraft supported giving credit to Native American culture. For example, he advocated for the use of Native American names for new townships and counties, especially as a member of the Legislative Council of the Territory of Michigan.[71]

Schoolcraft's efforts on behalf of the Native Americans make him a man ahead of his time, while still a product of his racist society. For example, he once wrote that "vague symbolisms and mental idiosyncrasies" had left the Native American without a government or God,[72] and "A mythology appears indispensable to a rude and ignorant race like the Indians."[73]

Schoolcraft was largely in favor of Native American assimilation, although on July 13, 1837, he wrote that "almost everything which has been attempted to better the condition of the Native Americans has failed."[74] One wonders whether the Ojibwa of his day felt the same way or whether they even wanted to be "bettered"—and by whose definition of "better"? Regardless, assimilation was strongly promoted by many whites in the early nineteenth century. Reverend Verwyst, in his life of Bishop Baraga, wrote at the end of the nineteenth century that "two or three successive intermarriages with the whites are sufficient to transform the Indian into a white."[75] If that were true, Schoolcraft's children, or at least his grandchildren, could be considered white. In the nineteenth century, Pocahontas' descendants included the prominent Virginian Randolph family who were viewed as proof that assimilation worked.[76] However, assimilation did not mean any true merger of civilizations. In *Pocahontas*, Robert S. Tilton explores how Pocahontas was used as an argument for assimilation in the nineteenth century. He argues, "The Enlightenment fantasy of absorption would actually be nothing less than a quiet genocide of the native population, which would ultimately be more effective than a military campaign."[77] Whites were not willing to share their land with Native Americans; they simply thought that by marrying Native Americans, they would more easily gain their land and whitewash the Natives into white citizens.

Not everyone favored assimilation. The preferred solution was removal of the Native Americans as the American republic spread west, turning territories into states. On a visit to Washington, DC, Schoolcraft was thrilled to meet President Andrew Jackson, who had been the strongest proponent of Indian removal. Schoolcraft even presented the president with maple syrup that his wife Jane had prepared. Robert Dale Parker, Jane's twenty-first-century biographer and the editor of her collected poems, notes that this small token is an example of how Jane was integrated/assimilated into the system exploiting her and her people.[78] Twenty-first century Ottawa historian Eric Hemenway says, "Schoolcraft's annual reports and letters show his racism and bigotry, which was common for the times, but he was a standout.... He was always advocating that we [Ottawa] be removed because of our insurmountable barbaric state."[79] This statement suggests Schoolcraft only favored assimilation for those Native Americans whom he viewed as more advanced, including his family members. Through assimilation, he was able to keep his in-laws at the Sault. He also practiced nepotism, hiring his brother-in-laws for government jobs until people complained and he ultimately lost his post.

After losing his position as Indian agent, Schoolcraft moved his family to New York, and soon after, in 1842, Jane died. Her death would cause the American author and supporter of women's rights, Margaret Fuller, to write, "By the premature death of Mrs. Schoolcraft was lost a mine of poesy."[80e]

As for Schoolcraft, he remarried in 1847 to Mary Howard of South Carolina. Both of his children by Jane—John Johnston Schoolcraft and Janee Schoolcraft—were unhappy about the marriage because of how quickly it happened. Mary's neurotic behavior, Southern manners, and pro-slavery beliefs—she would be the author of the pro-slavery novel *The Black Gauntlet* (1860)—did not help matters, even though Janee Schoolcraft married Mary Howard's half-brother Benjamin Howard.[81] As métis, the Schoolcraft children may have seen the plight of their Native American relatives as not much better than that of the African-American slaves Mary wanted to keep in chains.

---

e. Jane Johnston Schoolcraft is the first known Native American literary writer and poet, and she may be the first to write poems in her native language. Her achievement equals that of the first African-American poet Phyllis Wheatley (1753-1784), and the first American poet Anne Bradstreet (1612-1672), all three notably female. Jane's poetry has been collected in a scholarly edition *The Sound the Stars Make Rushing Through the Sky: The Writings of Jane Johnston Schoolcraft* (the book's title reflects the meaning of her Ojibwa name) edited by Robert Parker and published by the University of Pennsylvania. Today, her poetry is often anthologized in collections of Upper Michigan, Native American, and women's literature.

Henry would die penniless on December 10, 1864 in Washington, DC. His wife would live until 1878. John Johnston Schoolcraft died soon after his father in April 1865 at the age of thirty-five. Janee would survive until 1892, but she would lose all her children in infancy, thus ending the Schoolcraft line. However, Henry Schoolcraft's legacy lives on. The work he did at the Sault would directly affect Kawbawgam and all the Upper Michigan Ojibwa.

Treaties

While Schoolcraft served as a buffer between the United States Government and the Ojibwa, he could not stop the government's desire to acquire Native American lands; he could only try to get good terms for the Native Americans—or at least for his relatives, depending on how skeptical of a view we want to hold of Schoolcraft.

Although Kawbawgam was too young to be involved in the first several treaties signed between the Ojibwa and the US Government, his stepfather, uncles, and the other chiefs at the Sault did help negotiate and sign them, and Kawbawgam would definitely be affected by them.

The 1820 treaty was the first of several that would cause the Ojibwa to cede more and more of their land to the encroaching Americans. As we have seen, the Ojibwa were coerced into signing this treaty by Governor Cass. By it, they ceded sixteen square miles of land on the bank of the St. Mary's River in exchange for a "quantity of goods" and perpetual fishing rights at the falls, plus the right to encamp and fish on the ceded land.[82]

More treaties followed, signed at Prairie des Chiens on the Mississippi River in 1825, Fond du Lac in Wisconsin in 1826, and Butte de Mort, near Green Bay in Wisconsin, in 1827. Each of these treaties was signed by Shingabawossin, listed as first chief of the Ojibwa nation, and also by Waishkey, Mrs. Johnston's brother. Waishkey now resided at the Sault with his sister.[83] The 1826 treaty provided a $2,000 annuity to be paid in Sault Sainte Marie, which Schoolcraft would distribute. It also granted $1,000 a year to maintain an Indian School at the Sault.[84] Although we know nothing of Kawbawgam's formal education, if he received any, it is possible he could have attended such a school, though unlikely since he did not learn to speak much English until his later years and did not read or write it to the best of our knowledge.

In 1836, the Treaty of Washington was signed. This treaty also occurred through coercion of the Native Americans, this time by the local fur traders. By this point, the fur trade was in decline from the near-extermination of most fur-bearing animals in the area. In an effort to make the Native Americans work harder to get furs, the traders continually enticed Native Americans with alcohol, which caused further problems.[85] Sadly, the traders took advantage of the Native Americans, causing them to fall into heavy debt for the goods they received. This debt forced the Natives into once again feeling they had to sell their land. Consequently, an Ottawa delegation went to Washington, DC to try to sell Drummond and Manitou islands and part of the Upper Peninsula to the US government. Lewis Cass, by now US Secretary of War, was thrilled to acquire more land for Michigan and the United States, but to make things appear legal, he ordered Schoolcraft to collect a more complete delegation of Native Americans. This time Mrs. Johnston's brothers, Waishkey and Keewyzi, went as representatives from the Sault, along with Maidosagee, a headman representing Kawbawgam's uncle, Chief Kaygayosh from Tahquamenon. However, the traditional Crane chiefs at the Sault had not agreed to this deal and were angered as a result, including Shingabawossin and Kawbawgam's stepfather, Shawano.[86f] Waishkey and Keewyzi were originally from La Pointe, not the Sault, and of the Caribou clan rather than the Crane clan, which usually had predominance in these matters. Schoolcraft probably only invited the Ojibwa he knew would agree to the treaty so he could stay in Cass' good graces. Furthermore, Waishkey and Keewyzi were his wife's uncles, so he was clearly practicing nepotism. The Johnstons and their relatives did receive substantial money from the treaty.[87]

Ultimately, the Ottawa and Ojibwa ceded ten million acres of land to the United States in exchange for $600,000 to be paid over twenty years. Money was also provided for education, missions, agricultural implements, and medicine. An additional $300,000 was set aside to pay the debts to the traders. Another $150,000 was set aside to go to métis relatives, and $30,000 went to the chiefs. Finally, the Natives had the right to remain on the land to earn a living by fishing, hunting, and gathering.[88] This right included immunity from state law, which means Kawbawgam would have been within his rights to fish with a sucker net out of season when he was cited in 1888, as we saw in the introduction.[89] By the time the 1836 treaty was made, Kawbawgam was about twenty years old, so he was likely well aware of what the treaties said, receiving information from his elders. The land ceded included most

---

f. Among the signers of the treaty was Nawbungeezhig, whose name has been translated as Noon Day (Cleland, *Rites of Conquest*, p. 227), but I do not think this can be Kawbawgam since he would have only been about twenty at this time.

of the northern Lower Peninsula, and the entire eastern half of the Upper Peninsula, the dividing line running from just east of where Marquette is today along the Chocolay River to where the city of Escanaba lies.[90]

The treaty had to be approved by Congress, and when it went to the US Senate, some modifications were wanted. While the treaty originally was to provide for certain reservation lands being permanently set aside for the Natives, the Senate wanted this land to be set aside only for five years. Schoolcraft called the Native American chiefs to Mackinac Island (he had moved the Indian agency there from the Sault in 1833) to convince them to agree to this stipulation. They eventually did agree after he told them if they did not ratify the changes, no payment of goods, services, or money would be made to them. The government hoped by this ploy to bring about the removal of the Native Americans westward, but Schoolcraft assured the Ojibwa this was not likely to happen in the foreseeable future.[91] Regardless, frequent threats of removal of the Ojibwa would follow for decades.

According to Andrew Blackbird, the Ottawa author of *History of the Ottawa and Chippewa Indians of Michigan* (1887), the goods the Native Americans were to receive from this treaty were also not distributed properly and the whites stole some of the goods from them, but when the Natives complained to Schoolcraft, he said he could do nothing about it.[92] Certainly, the treaties were not mutually beneficial.

Native American Immigration to Canada

Because the Americans were not keeping their promises, about 1835, Chief Shingwaukonse proposed that the Ojibwa should move across the St. Mary's River to the Canadian side of the Sault. For his services in the War of 1812, Shingwaukonse had been granted land by the British on the Canadian side. Regardless, Shingwaukonse had remained on the American side. During this time, he had become close to his mentor Kaygayosh, one of Kawbawgam's uncles. Kaygayosh had been a chief at Tahquamenon, which may explain why Kawbawgam resided there for twenty years, as he would later tell Peter White. When Shingabawossin died in December 1828, Kaygayosh, as the next oldest living brother of the Crane clan, assumed the duties of head chief at the Sault. He would hold that position until his death in 1836.

At this time, Shingwaukonse was considering how aligning himself with various Christian denominations might help him have more clout with the American government so that the government would keep its promises. Along with Kaygayosh and Reverend McMurray, Shingwaukonse basically created a lobby group. With about twenty-five to thirty followers, he went to Francis Audrain, the sub Indian agent at the Sault (the main office had been moved to Mackinac Island by Schoolcraft by this point) to complain about the American failure to keep its promises and to make clear that if their demands were not met, many of the Ojibwa would move to Canada.[g]

Eventually, Shingwaukonse did move to the other side of the St. Mary's River and established the Garden River community opposite Sugar Island. Soon after, Kaygayosh decided to join Shingwaukonse, partly because he felt Schoolcraft was corrupt for giving Waubojeeg of the Caribou clan, Schoolcraft's wife's uncle, preference over him and other members of the Crane clan. As stated earlier, Schoolcraft had intentionally assembled a group of chiefs to go to Washington to negotiate the 1836 treaty, but he felt the Crane clan, which leaned toward British interests, should be left out of the negotiations. Although eventually Schoolcraft included Kaygayosh, it was more of a concession to him than an acknowledgment that the Crane clan still had political power among the Ojibwa.

When Kaygayosh joined Shingwaukonse's group, his younger brother, Kawbawgam's father Muk-kud-day-wuk-kwud, along with two of Muk-kud-day-wuk-kwud's sons, John Kabaosa and Waubmama, went with him.[93] Kawbawgam may well have joined them since he also told Peter White that he spent ten years living on the Canadian side of the Sault. Because Kawbawgam listed Canada as the last place he lived when he recounted his life history to Peter White, it may indicate he moved to Canada in the 1830s or early 1840s and that was the last place he resided before returning to the Michigan side of the Sault, where he met Graveraet and agreed to come to Marquette. Since Kawbawgam's statement that he lived at Tahquamenon also suggests he was close to his uncle Kaygayosh, it is not unlikely he followed his uncle, father, and brothers to Canada. It also shows he probably retained a relationship with his father despite his mother's marriage to Shawano. Furthermore, Kawbawgam's brother John Kabaosa was his full brother, who also would have gone with him and his mother to the Sault in childhood, which shows

g. Shingwaukonse was an Ojibwa leader of great foresight who was adept at dealing with the Americans and later the Canadians to get what was best for his people, often allying himself with ministers from various denominations whom he thought best able to help serve his political ends for his people. His political astuteness may well have influenced Kawbawgam's own ability to maintain peace between the Ojibwa and white Americans when he later resided in Marquette. Shingwaukonse's full story is told in Janet Chute's *The Legacy of Shingwaukonse.*

family ties with Muk-kud-day-wuk-kwud were likely not estranged despite his parents' separation.

This branch of Kawbawgam's family apparently remained with Shingwaukonse's group in Garden River. We do not know when Muk-kud-day-wuk-kwud died, but he may well have died in Canada. Further information on John Kabaosa has not been found, but Waubmama definitely stayed at Garden River and had a family there. In the early 1890s, Kawbawgam mentioned to Homer Kidder that Waubmama resided at the Sault (he may have meant just at the St. Mary's Rapids and he probably meant the Canadian side of the Sault) and was chief by the English treaty.[94] In 1884, Waubmama would attend the Grand Council at Cape Croker in Canada and support Chief Ogista, son of Shingwaukonse, when Canadian government officials tried to remove him. Waubmama's name meant "White Woodpecker" or "White Pigeon," but he would also adopt the more English name Joseph Thompson. Since we know Waubmama had grandchildren, his descendants likely still reside in Canada today.[95]

Meanwhile, when Kaygayosh died in 1836, a council of Ojibwa at the Sault chose Kawbawgam's stepfather, Shawano, to become head chief there.

Statehood and Mineral Exploration

In Michigan, the Ojibwa remained on their reservations and their traditional way of life continued with some modifications. When, in 1837, Michigan became a state, a dispute arose between Michigan and Ohio over who owned the City of Toledo on their shared border. Famously dubbed the Toledo War, with only one shot being fired, this dispute was settled when Ohio was given Toledo, and Michigan was compensated by receiving the Upper Peninsula. Notably, the United States did not even have the right to the western half of the Upper Peninsula at the time. Not until the 1842 Treaty of La Pointe was signed was the western half of the Upper Peninsula and northern Wisconsin ceded by the Ojibwa to the United States. By all reports, most Michiganders felt they had lost the Toledo War since Upper Michigan was considered little more than a wilderness and a frozen wasteland, but that belief was soon to change.

It had long been rumored that the Upper Peninsula had vast mineral resources, including rich veins of copper throughout the peninsula, although later it would be established that the copper was only in the western Upper Peninsula, primarily the Keweenaw Peninsula. In 1844, Douglass Houghton led a party to the Upper Peninsula to explore for minerals. At that time, copper had become a desirable commodity because telegraph lines were made from copper wire. The first Morse code telegraphic message had been sent on May 24, 1844, and the telegraph was quickly spreading throughout the United States and the world as a means for long-distance communication.[96]

Douglass Houghton

Houghton's expedition led to extensive reports of mineral riches available in the Upper Peninsula, causing an influx of would-be miners to the Sault. This population explosion resulted in the establishment of two hotels there. Previously, the schooner *Detroit* had made one trip a week to the Sault, but now, two other vessels also started making the trip. Soon, so many people were arriving in the Sault with copper fever that the hotels could not house them all and many would-be miners had to camp out near the rapids, where "amusement could be had in watching the Indians and half breeds in their birch bark canoes catching the delicious white fish."[97]

One wonders how amused the Natives were by this situation, although some reputably created an income for themselves by giving rides in their canoes to whites who wanted to shoot the rapids. Peter White was a teenager at this time, having been born in 1830, and having already left home to work on the Great Lakes, so he witnessed this growth at the Sault with his own eyes. He did not meet Kawbawgam at this time, but events were under way to bring about their meeting in the near future.

Among those who came to the Sault with copper fever was Philo Everett, a young businessman from Jackson, Michigan. Everett's journey, as we will see in the next chapter, would bring him into contact with Kawbawgam's family—and in the process, change the future of the Upper Peninsula and of Kawbawgam himself.

Chapter 3
Marriage and Mining

On July 12, 1847, Charles Kawbawgam married Charlotte, the daughter of Chief Marji-Gesick. Years later, Charlotte would testify that she and Kawbawgam were married at the Sault by a Catholic priest.[1] The actual marriage record is at the Chippewa County Courthouse and states:

> A Catholic Priest under written certify that July the 12th a Thousand Eight Hundred and Forty Seven, I have married Charles Makatakwat twenty five years old of Saut[a] Ste Marie son of Makatakwat and Charlotte, with Charlotte Madjikijiki of Saut Ste Marie twenty one old daughter of Madijkejiki and Bahamikirkoh in presence of Bawdry and John Sause, both of Saut Ste Marie the 12th July 1847
>
> G. B. Menet
>
> S.J.S.[2b]

This document is significant because it tells us Marquette was founded after the date of this marriage since Kawbawgam was considered Marquette's first resident and he later said he came to Marquette after he was married. The marriage by a priest is not surprising since Kawbawgam was probably already Catholic since we know his siblings had been baptized. Charlotte may have converted to Christianity to marry Kawbawgam since there were

---

a. Saut was a common spelling at the time for Sault.

b. The handwriting is difficult to read so the spelling of some of the names may be a bit off in my transcription. However, Marji-Gesick's name does appear to have two different spellings.

no white settlers yet in the central Upper Peninsula where her father Marji-Gesick lived, nor do we have any evidence that Marji-Gesick ever became a Christian. The ages on the record are wrong; Kawbawgam was probably closer to thirty or thirty-one while Charlotte, as we will see, was probably about sixteen.

Traditionally, Ojibwa men married in their late twenties. Marriage usually occurred only after the man had a sense of his purpose based on his dreams,[3] an aspect of Ojibwa spirituality we can't know whether Kawbawgam subscribed to since he was Catholic. However, perhaps he felt a sense of purpose in helping to found Marquette not long after he married.

Before following Charles and Charlotte Kawbawgam's married life, it is important to understand Charlotte's family background and the invaluable role her father would play in the iron industry as a result of his meeting Philo Everett. The iron industry would drastically change the Upper Peninsula by encouraging white settlement, and ultimately, cause Kawbawgam and his new bride to move to the future site of Marquette.

Chief Marji-Gesick

Marji-Gesick[c] was the son of Nibaw-naw-be (Nibawnawbé), a name that means "merman."[4] Marji-Gesick's own name probably means "moving day," or possibly "moving sun," "morning sun," or "first light of day."[5d] Other sources suggest it means "bad day" or "hard day," referencing the Ojibwa's nomadic lifestyle. Because moving from one place to another can be difficult,

---

c. As with all Ojibwa names, there are various spellings of Marji-Gesick. Rebecca Mead, in an article about the Jackson lawsuit, chose to spell Marji-Gesick's name as "Matji-gigig," a spelling Kenn Pitawanakwat at the Northern Michigan University Center for Native American Studies believed most accurate (Mead p. 1). I have opted to retain the spelling most frequently used so Marji-Gesick will be easily identified by my readers, although with the understanding that this spelling is not phonetically accurate. Notably, there is no "r" in the Ojibwa language (Berger, "Mah-je-ge-zhik Was Remarkable Man").

d. The "morning sun" translation I have only seen in the article "The Guardian of Presque Isle" in *The Mining Journal* on January 8, 1887. An alleged photo of Marji-Gesick in the Marquette Regional History Center's collection has written on the back of it that his name was "translated by joking pioneers" as Moving Day, and that a more correct translation would be Stormy Sky or Thunder Cloud. I find this explanation unlikely since Gesick clearly seems to mean "day" in Ojibwa, given that Kawbawgam's real name, Nawaquay-gee-zhik, meant Noon Day. The photo is in the folder "Indians—Marji-Gesick, Marji-Gesick Family," and labeled as catalog no. 1951.1.31(1).

a moving day could be a bad day.[6] Although chieftainship was not necessarily hereditary, Marji-Gesick's wife Susan, Charlotte's mother, would state in court that Marji-Gesick "was recognized as chief at Marquette from his birth."[7] Marji-Gesick had three brothers and four sisters all by the same mother and father.[8] Two of his brothers, Madosh and Man-gon-see, would also become chiefs. Man-gon-see is often recorded in history as "Mongoose," although his name actually means "Little Loon." Man-gon-see would live near Goose Lake in Marquette County at least as late as 1857.[9] Madosh would reside closer to Lake Superior, just west of Presque Isle, in the area of Little Presque Isle and Wetmore Landing. It has been said that Kawbawgam became chief of the local Ojibwa who resided along the lakeshore after Madosh's death, although the truth of this statement is unknown. Marji-Gesick's other brother, Pi-Aw-Be-Daw-Sung, and his sister O-De-Quaib are no more than names to us today, although we know Pi-Aw-Be-Daw-Sung signed the 1855 Treaty of Detroit.[10] Marji-Gesick may have also had a sister named Mary who would operate a type of hotel in Marquette in 1849, as we will see.[11e] His other two sisters' names have been lost to history.

Marji-Gesick's birthdate is not known, though it was likely in the 1790s. Little is known about his life before 1831 when Charlotte was born. In the 1830s and 1840s, he had a small band of warriors over whom he was chief. An estimated eighty-one Ojibwa were living at the Chocolay River's mouth in 1830, and less than one thousand were believed to be scattered between the Chocolay River and the Sault,[12] with both Grand Island and Tahquamenon being other significant Ojibwa settlements. Marji-Gesick's band primarily lived along the Chocolay, Carp, Dead, and Pine Rivers.

Henry Rowe Schoolcraft spent the summer of 1831 studying the local Ojibwa along Lake Superior, especially between Munising and L'Anse. At that point, Marji-Gesick was just a young chief. His summer camp was at Pine River, and his daughter Charlotte would have been born there that summer. Schoolcraft may have met Marji-Gesick at this point since he knew most of the Ojibwa chiefs.[13]

Prior to Charlotte's birth, Marji-Gesick had been married to Margaret, by whom he had six children, all of whom died young. His second wife, Susan, Charlotte's mother, would state that he had three children already

---

e. Boyer is the only source for the possibility that Marji-Gesick had a sister named Mary. However, it is highly likely since his wife Susan testified that he had four sisters (State of Michigan Supreme Court. Jeremy Compo vs. The Jackson Iron Company, p. 21).

when she married him,[14] which might suggest Susan and Margaret were his co-wives for a time and Margaret's other three children were born while he was with Susan, or more likely that three of Margaret's six children had died by the time Susan and Marji-Gesick were married. Marji-Gesick and Susan would themselves have two children, Charlotte and a son, Kennedy, who died young.[15] Later, Marji-Gesick married a third wife, Odonebegan or O-Do-No-Be-Qua,[16] by whom he had four children, but the only one whose name we know is Amanda.[f] The other children likely died young. Notably, the influence of whites was already clear in these name choices for Marji-Gesick's children. Among his children were also two sons named William and Joseph who were alive in 1845, but must have died soon after.[17] The mother(s) of these boys is unknown.

A lot of misinformation about Marji-Gesick's family has been reported, including that he also had sons named Cadotte and Mongoose, but Pierre Cadotte was actually his son-in-law who married his daughter Amanda, and Mongoose was Marji-Gesick's brother.

Marji-Gesick's wife Margaret was living as late as 1849 when Marquette was founded; she was among the Ojibwa who greeted the first white settlers to Iron Bay. Nothing is known about Odonebegan. Susan, Charlotte's mother, would live well into the late nineteenth century and testify during Charlotte's lawsuit against the Jackson mine. Charlotte's marriage record is the only place where Susan is listed by an Ojibwa name, Bahamikirkoh. Everywhere else she is called by her white name Susan.

Susan's testimony provided most of what we know about her and Marji-Gesick's early lives. She stated that during "the fall and winter season we [the Ojibwa] would all scatter around hunting.... We all came out in the spring of the year from the hunting ground on the lake shore and we would make one camp." The summer Susan was sixteen, about a month after they had all come to the lake, she married Marji-Gesick. He was older than she was, but she had known him a long time. She stated, "Marji Gesick came to me and inquired if I would marry with him—stay with him. I accepted the

---

f. Genealogist John P. DuLong states that Margaret and Odonebegan are the same woman and that Amanda is her daughter (Dulong p. 55). During the Jeremy Compo vs. The Jackson Iron Company trial, Charlotte would state that Fred Cadotte, Amanda's son, was Marji-Gesick's grandson, and that "the first wife had a daughter that was the mother of this boy," meaning Amanda was Margaret's child (State of Michigan Supreme Court. Jeremy Compo vs. The Jackson Iron Company, p. 34).

offer and during that day or evening he came in and we became as man and wife and stayed together after that.... That was the general custom." Susan stated that Marji-Gesick already had another wife, by whom he would have six kids, and three of them had already been born when she married him. She also stated she was his second wife (no mention of Odonebegan, who may have been his third wife). Susan also stated that Charlotte was about five at the time of the first treaty of Mackinac (the 1836 treaty), which tells us Charlotte was born about 1831. Susan goes on to say she and Marji-Gesick had married about 1830, at which time there were no whites or even Ojibwa at the mouth of the Carp River except her family and that of Marji-Gesick. They lived together for six years and had two children. After they married, they lived different places along Lake Superior, including at Grand Island and L'Anse. When they had resided at the mouth of the Carp, Susan's family had lived on the east side of the river, and Marji-Gesick's parents also lived there with their four sons and four daughters, all of whom had families. Both Marji-Gesick and Susan's families lived in one wigwam along with an old man named Gog-Wa-Gon. She also stated that her and Marji-Gesick's son (Kennedy) had died at Presque Isle and his death had caused distance between them, so they lived together only intermittently after that.[18] Notably, Susan stated that after she and Marji-Gesick grew distant, she had a daughter by another man. This child, Mary, would marry Francis Nolin, better known as Jacques LePique. LePique would testify during the trial that Mary's father had been one of Marji-Gesick's brothers, although he did not specify which brother.[19] LePique would be a key figure in the Kawbawgams' life, as we will later see.

Little is known about Charlotte's siblings, but we do know Charlotte's Ojibwa name was Minwash, meaning "Sailing with the Wind."[20] It did not mean Laughing Whitefish as is often stated. That name was the invention of John Voelker for his novel *Laughing Whitefish* as will be discussed in Chapter 13.[21] Some sources have said that Charlotte married when she was about eighteen or nineteen, and her marriage record says she was twenty-one, but she was probably about sixteen.

We know little else about Marji-Gesick and his family until 1845 when he helped to make history. At that time, he resided at the mouth of the Carp River and had thirty warriors under him. Other Ojibwa were living in the vicinity of what would become Marquette where they were cultivating potato patches, which when left unattended, were discovered and dug up by the newly arrived whites.[22]

It is unlikely Marji-Gesick ever became a Christian because he always had an Ojibwa praying house near his home. He would construct new ones whenever he moved. This praying house was a wigwam with its only opening in the roof; Marji-Gesick would climb over the open top to enter it. Inside, he would pray for the young men of his tribe to be brave, honest, and industrious. Sometimes he would remain in the praying house for three or four days.[23] His brother Mongoose (Little Loon) also had a praying house on a pine plain some distance south of his lodge near Goose Lake. The praying house was about the size and shape of a common stack of hay and had a small hole on one side just large enough to crawl through.[24] Marji-Gesick's Native religion also made him superstitious, as we will see.

The Discovery of Iron Ore

William Austin Burt

In 1845, white men were flocking into the Sault, intent on discovering copper. Philo Everett, a merchant from Jackson, Michigan, was one of these men.

Everett had heard of the discovery of copper in the Upper Peninsula, but he had no knowledge of the discovery of iron ore that had happened the year before, despite many sources mistakenly saying he did. William Burt had accidentally discovered the iron ore in 1844 near Teal Lake in Marquette County. Burt had been surveying the land when his compass went haywire because of the mineral deposits there. Some sources say Everett had a copy of Burt's survey map in hand and was looking for iron. However, the truth is Everett knew nothing about the iron at the time and was only looking for copper. It wasn't until he met Louis Nolin[g] at the Sault that Everett heard about the

g. The Nolin family will play a significant role in Kawbawgam's life so it is worth noting here that some records spell the name as Nolan, but I have opted to use Nolin as the more frequent spelling. Jacques LePique (Francis Nolin), Charlotte Kawbawgam's brother-in-law, was the son of Louis Nolin.

other shiny rocks that were a different color than copper and decided to try to find them.

Burt had been surveying the previous year to create six-mile wide townships in the Upper Peninsula, moving east from the Sault. While surveying, he was also collecting some mineral samples for Professor Charles Jackson. Notably, Burt's party included two Ojibwa, who went by the names of John Taylor and Michael Doner, and likely served as guides.[25h] On September 19, 1844, six miles south from Teal Lake, Burt noted a strong magnetic disturbance in the area, which made it clear iron was in the vicinity. However, nothing more was done regarding the iron ore at this time.

In 1845, Professor Jackson published an article on copper samples that he said were "undoubtedly valuable" for "profitable mining." This article was responsible for causing the copper fever in Upper Michigan.[26] According to Swineford, Dr. Jackson also got ore from his friend Peter Barbeau at the Sault, who in turn got it from an Indian Chief—this may have been Marji-Gesick, although Swineford does not specify.[27] Swineford summarizes from Dr. Jackson's 1849 report, stating that:

> in the summer of 1844, during his first visit to the Lake, he obtained from Peter B. Barbeau, then a trader at Sault Ste Marie, a fine specimen of specular iron ore which had been given to Mr B. by an Indian chief. He also learned at the same time that this chief knew of a mountain mass of ore, somewhere between the head of Keweenaw bay and the headwaters of the Menommee [sic] river. The next summer he informed Mr. Lyman Pray, of Charlestown, Mass, what he had heard, and suggested to him the propriety of looking up the mountain in question. Mr. Pray immediately proceeded to the Sault, where he employed the son of the Ojibway chief as a guide, and went with him to L'Anse, from thence, guided by the Indian, he traversed the then unbroken forest and found the mountain. On his return he informed Dr. Jackson that he had traveled four miles around the mountain and found only the same kind of ore, *and no rocks.* To Mr. Pray, therefore, he ascribes the honor of the first practical discovery of iron ore in the upper Peninsula of Michigan,

h. We know nothing else about these Ojibwa, but Alfred Swineford says they were both dead by 1876, the year he published *History and Review of Copper, Iron, Silver, Slate and Other Material Interests of the South Shore of Lake Superior.*

saying that "no linear surveys had then been made, and it is probable no white man had ever before explored that locality."

Swineford goes on to say perhaps it is the Republic "mountain" that Pray explored.[28] Notably, Jackson makes no comments about Burt's discoveries even though he published his report in the same volume of *Public Documents* that was filled with three pages of Mr. Burt's discoveries.[29] Unfortunately, who the son of the chief was who accompanied Pray is not known. The chief could not have been Marji-Gesick since he had no sons old enough for such a task, so more likely it was a chief who resided at the Sault.

Swineford also states that according to Peter Barbeau:

> Achille Cadotte, a French and Indian half-breed, was, in 1845, informed by an old Indian chief, then living at the mouth of Carp River, (now within the corporate limits of the city of Marquette,) that he knew where there was a mountain of iron ore, and went with the chief to see it. The name of this chief was "Man-je-ki-jik," (Moving Day.) Cadotte then communicated his discovery to Mr. John Westren, who went with him to the mountain, and under his direction about a ton of the ore was carried down from what is now the Jackson mine to the mouth of the Carp, taken from there to the Sault in canoes, and thence to Detroit. That Mr. Barbeau is mistaken in at least one particular, is proved by the well substantiated fact that Mr. Westren did not visit Lake Superior until 1846.[30]

While the timing of this event is unclear, as Swineford notes, in 1845 Marji-Gesick definitely knew the location of the iron ore and led the Everett party to it. However, this tale of Achille Cadotte is worth mentioning because it shows Swineford knew who Marji-Gesick was and, therefore, he likely would have named him earlier in referring to an Indian chief if the chief were Marji-Gesick; therefore, one or two other chiefs, likely residing at the Sault, must have also known the location of the iron ore. One of these chiefs may have been Marji-Gesick's brother Madosh. Also of interest here is that Achille Cadotte's brother, Pierre Cadotte, would sometime in the near future marry Marji-Gesick's daughter, Amanda, with rather disastrous consequences, as we shall see.

Everett was among those who had read Professor Jackson's reports on copper, and he was determined to try to make his fortune by prospecting. To raise capital, he convinced eleven neighbors to share in the expedition's expenses. This group formed the Jackson Mining Company.[31] Everett applied for a permit from the Secretary of War, which he received on June 19, 1845, and the next day, he left for Lake Superior with three of his fellow investors, S. T. Carr, Edward Rockwell, and William Monroe. They took a steamship to Mackinac Island, then bought a coasting boat they put on a steamer to take them to the Soo, planning to portage the boat over the St. Mary's River and into Lake Superior so they could ship supplies to Copper Harbor, at the tip of the Keweenaw Peninsula where the copper deposits were located.[32]

Philo M. Everett

However, Everett's plans changed when he arrived at the Sault. There he met Louis Nolin, who agreed to bring him to the copper deposits.[33] However, an Ojibwa woman, Tipo-keso, who happened to be the daughter of Marji-Gesick's brother Man-gon-see, also met Everett at the Sault. When Everett told Tipo-keso what he was looking for, she told him her uncle Marji-Gesick could show him where the copper deposits were near Teal Lake, saying she had just returned to the Sault from Teal Lake and a mountain of rock and mineral was there that was too heavy for the Ojibwa to use. Tipo-keso gave Everett directions and sold him a boat for his journey.[34] Notably, the Ojibwa did not really understand the significance of copper or iron ore to the white men at this time, nor did they recognize the difference between the two minerals. They simply knew they were "shiny rocks." Nolin told Everett he knew where the rocks Marji-Gesick's niece spoke of were, not realizing they weren't copper, although he saw samples Everett showed him and told him they did not look like the ore he'd seen. This information was enough for Everett to agree to go to what is now Marquette County to investigate whatever minerals might be there.

Everett hired Nolin to "pilot, pack, and cook" as guide for the trip, and Nolin was extraordinary at the task. He was a métis of mixed French and Ojibwa blood. More importantly, he was thick of chest, over six feet tall, and could shoulder a ninety-pound pack with ease. In addition, Everett later wrote that Nolin had "an intelligent countenance and pleasant address, and [was] very polite."[35]

Nolin brought Everett and his party to Teal Lake in present Marquette County, but once there, they could not locate the ore deposits. At this point, Everett was ready to give up and travel on to the Keweenaw Peninsula to look for copper. Fortunately, before leaving, he met Marji-Gesick, who agreed to lead him to the ore deposits.[36]

What happened next has often been mistold. From Everett we have the most accurate version of the events based on his testimony when Charlotte Kawbawgam sued the Jackson mine. Marji-Gesick agreed to show Everett's party where the iron ore deposits were. Everett himself did not go with Marji-Gesick into the forest to find the deposits, only Carr and Rockwell went. Marji-Gesick took them into the forest a ways, but he was too superstitious to bring them all the way, so Carr approached the ore deposits alone.[37]

One false story claims that Burt's party, while surveying the previous year, had discovered iron ore under a fallen pine tree and that Marji-Gesick had learned of this discovery and then brought the Everett party there. However, Everett later refuted this story. The Burt party did not locate the iron ore, despite Burt's compass going haywire because of the ore's nearby presence. Marji-Gesick clearly already knew where the iron ore was. Nor was it a small deposit under a fallen pine tree. In fact, Everett's testimony instead refers to a two-foot tall little pine tree by a ledge that was marked as the center of the property where the discovery was made.[38] This tree was later cut down and made into a desk.[39]

The ore was far more than what could have been hidden under a pine tree. In a November 18, 1845 letter to Captain G. D. Johnson, Everett described the ore as "a mountain of solid ore, 150 feet high. The ore looks as bright as a bar of metal just broken."[40] In his 1887 "Recollections," Everett states:

> On arriving at Teal Lake, we found the ore.... There lay the boulders of the trail, made smooth by the atmosphere, bright and shining, but dark colored, and a perpendicular bluff fifty feet in heights, of pure solid ore, looking like rock, but not rock, and on climbing a steep elevation of about seventy feet, the ore cropping out in different places all the way, we came, at the top, to a precipice many feet deep. Hundreds of tons of ore that had been thrown down by the frost lay at the bottom. It was solid ore, but much leaner than that on the other side. From all that could be seen, it seemed that the whole elevation for half a mile or more was one solid mass of iron ore. No rock could be seen, and all that visited it came to the same conclusion, until the mine was fairly opened.[41]

This was the famous "iron mountain" that was often described in early Marquette County sources. Unfortunately, the pine tree myth has been repeated numerous times, and even the monument that was placed in 1904 where the ore was found mistakenly states that it was found under a pine tree.[42]

According to Everett's biographer, his great-grandson Frank B. Stone, it is believed the fallen pine tree story was fabricated in the later nineteenth century for publicity appeal.[43] How late in the century is questionable, however, because Swineford mentions it in 1876, stating:

> The precise spot where this discovery was made, was until a year or two ago, and maybe yet, distinguished by the remains of a huge pine stump, the upturned roots of which revealed to Carr and Rockwell the first knowledge of an iron range from which nearly ten million tons of ore have since been mined. The trunk of this tree, which at the time of their visit had been freshly uprooted, was afterwards sawn into lumber and carefully preserved to be afterwards manufactured into mementoes.[44]

It is strange that the pine tree story is not true since one would think an iron mountain would have a far greater appeal from a storytelling perspective.

The pine stump at the Jackson Mine,
which may have become more famous than it deserved

Indeed, the iron mountain became a sort of tourist attraction in Marquette's early years. The best-selling nineteenth century American novelist Constance Fenimore Woolson, sister-in-law to Samuel Mather who would found the Cleveland Iron Company, wrote the first short story set in Marquette, which appeared in *Appleton's Journal* on February 15, 1873. Titled, "On the Iron Mountain," it tells the story of a young woman, Helen Fay, who journeys with a small party of visitors from the East to Marquette. Once there, they decide to see the Iron Mountain. Woolson describes the setting as:

> Marquette, on Lake Superior, is now a busy town, soon to be a city; it has railroads on shore and fleets of steamers and vessels on the water, people to do business and business to do, all coming from the Iron Mountain behind it. But, in 1853, it was a lonely settlement in the woods, with one little stamping-mill stamping on the ore with wooden legs; a few houses of those hopeful pioneers, who so often sow the seed in the West and so seldom reap the harvest; and a swampy, rocky, sandy, corduroy road, inland to the mine. The Iron Mountain stood there, great and wonderful, waiting for capital. Capital has come, and dug and blasted into its sides for years; but it remains great and wonderful still.[45]

The iron mountain has long since vanished from the landscape, but we can still imagine how stunning and wonderful it seemed to Everett and his companions.

Convinced a fortune was to be made from the iron ore deposits, Everett now went to Copper Harbor to file his claim.[46] Along the way, he looked for copper without success and stopped in L'Anse where he met the Ojibwa there and attended services held by Father Frederic Baraga at the mission church.

Ojibwa Superstitions About Minerals

As for Chief Marji-Gesick, he immediately regretted showing the white men where the iron was because he was superstitious. Nor was he the only Native American superstitious about the mineral deposits in Upper Michigan. Decades before, the white men had heard stories of the famous Ontonagon Boulder on the western end of the Upper Peninsula. In fact, the 1820 Cass Expedition made a point of traveling down the Ontonagon River to see the boulder. The boulder, which weighs 3,708 pounds and is pure copper, was much respected by the Native Americans who made offerings to the boulder's manitou (spirit or life force) and asked it for health and wellbeing.[47] Already word of the boulder's fame had spread, so the American government wanted to remove it and bring it East. Cass hired an Ojibwa named Waub-ishkee-penaysee (White Bird) to show him where the boulder was located. Waub-ishkee-penaysee led the Cass party to the boulder, but he later regretted it. He believed the boulder's manitou was angry at him for betraying it. When Cass gave him a silver medal for his assistance, Waub-ishkee-penaysee was embarrassed and saw the medal as a sign of disgrace. His tribesmen also reprimanded him for showing the boulder to the whites, and he had a series of misfortunes that followed after the event.[48] In 1826, the whites returned to try to remove the boulder, but they only succeeded in hacking off parts of it.[49]

German traveler Johann Georg Kohl also recounts the story of the Ontonagon Boulder as he heard it from a Native American fur trader who took it. Kohl states that in 1827, Chief Keatanang showed the boulder to white men. The chief said the boulder was important to his father and grandfather, and it had the power to defeat foes, give long life to the Ojibwa, and help them catch beaver and kill bear. He traded the boulder for many goods, and then prayed that the Great Spirit was not angry with him. He gave five pounds of tobacco as a sacrifice to appease the boulder's spirit. Keatanang always regretted selling the boulder and claimed many misfortunes befell him, but later, he became a Christian, found peace, and stayed friends with the trader to whom he sold it.[50]

Eventually, the boulder would be removed in 1843 by Julius Eldred after he paid the local Ojibwa $150 for it, only to learn a group of Wisconsin miners already owned it, so he had to repurchase it from them for $1,365. (The miners obviously knew its worth better than the Ojibwa.) At this point, the War Department laid claim to the boulder, but Eldred was able to get the boulder to Detroit and make money by displaying it until the government took him to court and successfully obtained possession of it. In 1860, the boulder was placed in the Smithsonian Institution where it remains to this day.[51]

Efforts have since been made to return the Ontonagon Boulder to Upper Michigan, the most significant efforts being by the Ojibwa of the Keweenaw Bay Indian Community. In 1991, an assessment was initiated after the tribe requested the boulder be returned to them as a sacred object. A preliminary investigation decided insufficient evidence existed to establish that the boulder had been a sacred object, according to the Native American Graves Protection and Repatriation Act's definition of a sacred object. After consultations with the tribe in 1998 and 1999 and a visit to the boulder's

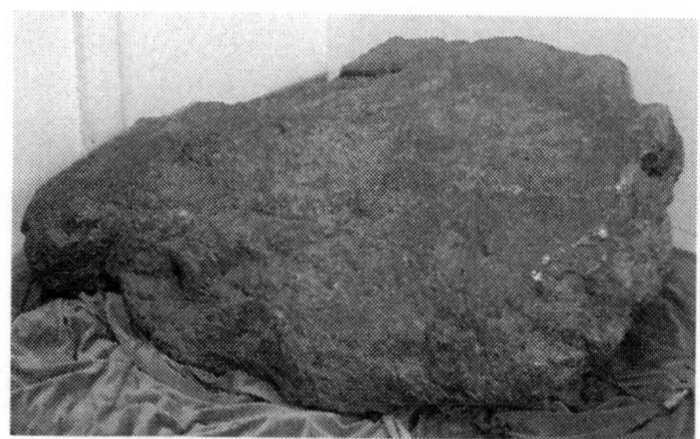

The Ontonagon Boulder, on display today at the Smithsonian

original location, in 2000, the Repatriation Office decided the right to possess the boulder belonged to the Smithsonian Institution.[52] To compensate, the Ontonagon Historical Museum has a replica on display.

The Ojibwa also held superstitions regarding silver and copper. Kohl records that the Ojibwa had great reverence for copper itself and ascribed power to the pieces of it they would find scattered about the land. They would carry such pieces in their medicine bags, often wrapping them in paper, and they would be handed down from father to son.[53]

As for silver, Swineford, writing in 1876, states:

> Some forty or fifty years ago, when John Jacob Astor and the American Fur Company had a station or trading post, at the mouth of Iron River, the Indians were known to have constantly in their possession silver in its native state in considerable quantities, and the men are now living who have seen them with large chunks as "big as a man's fist," but no one ever succeeded in inducing them to tell or show where the hidden treasure lay. A superstitious fear always clung to them, and does even to this day, that if they showed to any white man a deposit of mineral, the great Manitou would punish them with death. Two instances of this kind, proving the superstitious fears of the Indians in this regard, are of comparatively recent date. Several years since, a half-bred Indian brought to Ontonagon some very fine samples of vein rock, carrying considerable quanties [sic] of native silver. His report was that his wife had found it on the south range where they were trapping, and to test his story he was sent back for more. In a few days he returned, bringing with him quite a chunk, from which was obtained eleven and one-half ounces of native silver. He returned home, went among the Flambeaux Indians and was killed. His wife, to this day, refuses to listen to any proposals from friend or foe to show the location of the vein, clinging with religious tenacity to the superstitions of her tribe.

> The present Nonesuch copper vein was discovered by an Iron River half-breed, and shown to some white men. The poor fellow soon sickened and died. His relatives and friends shook their heads and said they knew it would be so. These instances are mentioned to show the superstition of the red man on the discovery of mineral veins, and to account in some measure for the long delay and failure in tracing up the rich deposits of minerals which have so long been known to exist in the Iron River district.
>
> In 1846 or '47 quite a distinguished party then on the lake exploring, surveying, and examining the wonderful mineral discoveries of Lake Superior, were induced by an Indian to go up Iron River to see a big rock of native silver. They started eager to find the great riches before them. The Indian led them a fearful and useless hunt of several days, but at last the party became tired and disgusted and told the Indian before starting (from their camp in the morning) that if he did not bring them to the silver rock before night they would shoot him. After traveling till noon the Indian brought them to the bank of a small stream and told them to sit down and he would find it. In a short time he returned and told them that the great Manitou had become displeased with him and had turned the great silver rock into a rock of stone. This he showed them and the whole party returned disgusted, weary and ragged, but the Indian was seen no more.[54]

What are we to make of this last story? Swineford calls the men "quite a distinguished party"—distinguished how? First, they threatened the Native American, and then, we are told he was "seen no more." The details of what became of him have been lost to history, but we can imagine. Superstition or not, showing the white men where the minerals were would be detrimental to the Ojibwa's way of life.

Marji-Gesick's Share in the Jackson Mine

Despite his superstition, Marji-Gesick could not turn back the tide once Everett's party saw the iron ore deposits. Marji-Gesick was also aware that the United States owned all the mineral rights to the land as agreed to from its treaties made with the Ojibwa.

Everett and his party, with their claim now established, returned downstate, but the next year, investors Berry and Kirtland returned from Jackson. At this point, they gave Marji-Gesick a certificate that stated:

River du Mort, May 30, 1846

This may certify that in consideration of the services rendered by Madjigijig, a Chippewa Indian, in hunting ores of location No 593 of the Jackson Mining Co., that he is entitled to twelve, undivided one-hundredths part of the interest of said mining company in said location No.

A.V. Berry Superintendent
F.W. Kirtland, Secretary

Berry and Kirtland did not have the authority to give this certificate, so when they reported it to their partners, some objections were made. The problem was that the stock had already all been issued, but the partners finally agreed unanimously to find a solution to honor it, although as late as 1848, no solution had been found.[55] That year, the company became incorporated as the Jackson Mining Company for a thirty-year period. At one of the early meetings of the new corporation, inquiry was made concerning the reservation of eighteen shares of unassessable stock for the Native Americans, at which time the meeting was informed of the certificate given to Marji-Gesick for twelve shares, and apparently other Natives not named received documentation for the other six shares (although no later claim on those shares ever came forward). Some company accounts stated these six shares belonged to Marji-Gesick's two sons, three for each son, though both had died by the time claims were made upon the shares by Charlotte.[56] We know Marji-Gesick had a son, Kennedy, by Susan, but in the deposition that F. W. Kirtland provided during Charlotte Kawbawgam's lawsuit against the Jackson Iron Company, he referred to "Joseph Marji Geesick and William" each receiving three shares.[57] Philo Everett, in his deposition at this time, did not name the boys, but did refer to one, of whom he stated, "but the boy got drowned, I believe."[58] We know Kennedy drowned so perhaps he was also known as Joseph or William. Otherwise, it's not known who was the mother of these two sons who obviously died young.

By February 1848, the Jackson Mining Company was beginning to process iron.[59] Meanwhile, the certificate became Marji-Gesick's most prized possession. He kept it in a little birchbark box in his wigwam and brought it with him wherever he went. Even when he went fishing, he would bring the box and place it in the bottom of his canoe.[60] In the years that followed, it is not clear whether he made any effort to receive compensation from the Jackson Mine. We are told the only compensation he received was a suit of clothes and some trifling articles.[61] Berry and Kirtland either gave him these

Rev. John Pitezel

with the certificate, or he got them later as an appeasement when he asked for something in return for his shares.

Little is known about Marji-Gesick's life between when he received the certificate and his death, which was probably about 1862, but a few incidents have been related concerning him. In January 1846, when the Methodist missionary John H. Pitezel, who was stationed at L'Anse, traveled to Grand Island, he stopped on the way at Marji-Gesick's wigwam and spent the night there. In his book *Lights and Shades of Missionary Life*, Pitezel described the hospitality Marji-Gesick offered him and his two Indian guides, stating:

> On the evening of the fourth day we reached Carp river, near the now flourishing town of Marquette. Here was then one solitary wigwam, occupied by an Indian family. I had worn my moccasins through; my feet were both badly blistered, and my limbs so wearied that I could scarcely drag my snow-shoes along. The sight of a human habitation, though but an Indian lodge, gave me such joy that I was involuntarily moved to tears. Here we were warmly received. One of the men had just taken a deer. Mah-je-ge-zhik's wife made us a warm cake, cooked venison and some potatoes, and made us a dish of tea—all neatly and well served, and which had a relish not common at sumptuous feasts. Our hostess then dried and mended my moccasins, and seemed to take pleasure in doing all she could to minister to our wants.[62]

Later in the same book, Pitezel recalls the incident, stating:

> I stated, also, that, in January, 1846, I passed on snow-shoes over the ground where we now worshiped, to visit a band of Indians at Grand Island, and that then there was no trace of civilization at Carp river. Remarked that I could never forget the day of my arrival at this place. I was excessively fatigued. My feet were badly blistered, and when I had reached the wigwam of Mah-je-ge-zhik, I was so rejoiced that tears involuntarily crowded to my eyes. That I was much refreshed on a repast of small potatoes and fresh venison.[63]

In the next chapter, we will catch a couple of more glimpses of Marji-Gesick during Marquette's early years.

In 1847, Marji-Gesick's daughter Charlotte would marry Kawbawgam at the Sault. They may have lived there for a short time; however, Marji-Gesick's action of showing the Jackson party where the iron ore was located would eventually cause the Kawbawgams to relocate to the Carp River.

Chapter 4
Marquette's Founding and Early Years

EARLY IN THE MORNING OF May 18, 1849, a longboat appeared on Lake Superior's horizon. Charles Kawbawgam stood on the shore of what would soon be known as Iron Bay, not far from his wigwam, and watched the boat approach. Could he know at that moment he was taking part in one of the most significant events in the history of Michigan's Upper Peninsula? It may not even be too much of a stretch to say it was one of the most significant events in American history because the iron ore that would be shipped out of Iron Bay would fuel American industrialization and be integral to the United States' ability to win the Civil War and two World Wars.

The events set in motion four years earlier by Kawbawgam's then future father-in-law Marji-Gesick in showing the Jackson party the location of the iron ore had directly resulted in Kawbawgam moving to Iron Bay, where on this day the city of Marquette would be officially founded. A lot had happened in the four years between. They had been filled with efforts by numerous men to start an iron industry, and those men had often come into conflict with one another.

In 1846, the same year members of the Jackson party returned to Upper Michigan and gave Marji-Gesick his certificate for shares in the mine, another group of prospectors started a silver and lead mine at the cove at Presque Isle, just a few miles north of Iron Bay. Calling themselves the New York and Lake Superior Mining Company, they erected a fort-like structure by the cove for protection from the Ojibwa.[a] Fifteen men and two women made up the Presque Isle mining community. They dug three pits at Presque Isle, two of which became continually swamped with water. The venture was unsuccessful and quickly folded the next year.[1] In 1847, Everett returned to the Carp River and hired some of the men from the now defunct silver mine at Presque Isle to cut a road from the lakeshore to the site of the Jackson mine. At the mine, Everett and his colleague Ariel N. Barney built the first settlement of any size in what would become Marquette County as they prepared to start mining.[2]

By this point, others were also interested in mining iron ore. Dr. Edward Clarke of Worcester, Massachusetts, decided he would go to the Keweenaw Peninsula (the Copper Country) to look for iron. When he stopped at Mackinac Island, he met Robert Graveraet and told him of his plans. Clarke then went on to the Copper Country but found no iron. When Clarke returned to Mackinac Island, Graveraet told him where iron could be found near Teal Lake.[3] Clarke soon set about preparing to begin an iron company near the Jackson Mine with the help of Graveraet and a few others.

As a result, Robert Graveraet would become a major player in the history of iron mining in Upper Michigan. Because Graveraet would recruit Kawbawgam to come to Marquette, it is worth providing some background information on him.

Robert Graveraet

Like most of the older families at the Sault and on Mackinac Island, the Graveraets were a métis family. According to family legend, their roots in North America went back at least a century to the days when the French were still the dominant European power in the Great Lakes. In 1755, a council had been held at Montreal of all the local Native American tribes. To this council, the Grand Sachem of the Algonquin Confederation brought his daughter, an "Indian princess." A young French nobleman at the council fell in love with the princess and married her. They lived at Montreal, where they had a daughter of their own. In 1774, a Scottish officer, Major Livingston, part of a British delegation to Montreal, met the nobleman's métis daughter and married her. They then had multiple children, including a daughter named

a. An official fort, Fort Wilkins, had also been constructed at Copper Harbor at the tip of the Keweenaw Peninsula to protect the copper mining interests from the Native Americans as well as to maintain peace among the unruly miners. No issues, however, erupted between the miners and Native Americans at Fort Wilkins or Presque Isle.

Charlotte. Charlotte would marry Henry Graveraet, and they would become the parents of Robert and his many siblings.[4]

Henry Graveraet, of Dutch ancestry, was born in Pennsylvania in 1785. He came to Mackinac Island in the early 1800s where he met Charlotte.[5] Among Henry's siblings was a brother, Jacob, who also had no qualms marrying into a Native American family. While Henry married the granddaughter of an "Indian princess," a term basically used for any chief's daughter since the time of Pocahontas, Jacob did better by marrying a true Indian princess, Kis Kaw-ka, the daughter of Chief Kis-Kano-ko. He and his bride settled in Lower Michigan along the Saginaw River. Jacob and his wife would have a daughter, Kisiowkow, and two sons, Abraham and Noah—a strange mix of Native American and biblical names.[6]

Meanwhile, Henry and Charlotte Graveraet settled at the Straits of Mackinac. At one point, Charlotte taught school in St. Ignace, possibly before her marriage.[7] In total, the couple would have sixteen children, the most notable being their fourth child, Robert (b. 1820), and their fifteenth child, Juliet (b. 1842). Juliet would marry Samuel Kaufman in Marquette in 1862 and be mother to several prominent and wealthy sons who would play significant roles in Marquette and even on a national stage in finance in the late nineteenth and early twentieth centuries.[8]

By 1824, Henry Graveraet was working under the Indian subagent, George Boyd, at the subagency on Mackinac Island. However, that year Boyd wrote to Governor Cass saying he'd had to discharge Henry Graveraet for drunkenness. He had reinstated him because Henry had to provide for his family, but now Boyd wanted to discharge him again.[9] Alcoholism may have been a family trait, and Robert Graveraet would later also develop a reputation, although perhaps undeserved, for being a drunkard.

Robert and his siblings attended the Indian mission school founded at Mackinac Island in 1823. It is not known how long Robert attended school, but it was not uncommon at the time for boys to leave school at age fourteen or younger. When Robert was fourteen, in 1834, he was hired as an Indian interpreter by Henry Schoolcraft.[10]

The Graveraets, unashamed of their Native blood, used it to their advantage. They knew the Schoolcraft family well, especially after the Indian Agency was moved to Mackinac Island. At one point, Robert's mother Charlotte wrote to Jane Schoolcraft to make sure the Graveraet family was included when the US Government made its payments to the Native Americans. As part of the 1836 treaty, the Graveraet children were listed with the other children of mixed blood who were to have money awarded to them.[11] The same treaty, under the 7th article, notes that Robert Graveraet was paid for his work as an interpreter for the Indian Department at Michilimackinac, on March 28, 1836, and both Graveraet and Schoolcraft's signatures testify to this. There were also two vouchers for a salary as interpreter for $75.[12]

Despite their relationship with the Schoolcrafts, both Robert and Henry Graveraet testified against Henry Schoolcraft over the distribution of goods at Mackinac in 1836.[13b] Schoolcraft still hired Robert in 1839 to accompany him on a journey to Elk Rapids, along with a Native American interpreter and a Native American blacksmith named Isaac George.[14]

Robert Graveraet's other activities are not known until the late 1840s after he met Clarke. He then became one of the four men credited with the founding of Marquette because of the partnership he formed with Clarke and the other Marquette Iron Company founders. About this time, Graveraet also met Kawbawgam at the Sault and enlisted him to help establish the Marquette Iron Company's claim and found the town of Worcester, originally named for Worcester, Massachusetts, but later renamed Marquette. Who can claim to be the individual "founder" of Marquette is open to question. Philo Everett and the Jackson party had erected the first permanent buildings, but it was the Marquette Iron Company that truly made progress happen. Clarke returned to Massachusetts where he received the assistance of Waterman A. Fisher and Amos Harlow, both also from Worcester. Fisher would be a silent partner, solely putting up money for the venture. Harlow and Clarke would both return to Marquette, though Harlow is usually credited with being the founder of Marquette since he was the company manager. However, Graveraet seems to have done the bulk of the physical preparation, including engaging in some unscrupulous behavior, as we will see.

When Kawbawgam arrived in Marquette with Graveraet is not clear since Kawbawgam could not always be relied upon to give accurate statements about the timing of events in his life. He did say it was after his marriage, which took place in July 1847. The events of that summer until May 1849 when Graveraet and Peter White arrived in Marquette are important for understanding how the iron industry developed, so a brief outline will be presented before resuming focus on Kawbawgam's role in Marquette's founding.

---

b. This statement comes from a November 6, 1925 letter by Olive Pendill. Pendill, the first historian of the Marquette County Historical Society, was descended from the Barbeau family at the Sault, so she may have learned this information from older family members.

The Jackson, Cleveland, and Marquette Iron Companies

Not much happened with the Jackson Mine until the summer of 1847 when a crew arrived to run a forge. That summer, two bloomeries were built and an earthen dam was constructed to operate them. Twenty-four men and two women lived in one large cabin through the following winter. On February 10, 1848, the first bloom was made and the first iron bar struck from it.[15] A road was also built from the lake to bring in cargo for the forge. Among the earliest workers of the forge was Ariel N. Barney.

Meanwhile, the Cleveland Iron Company had been formed by men from Cleveland, including Samuel Mather, whose sons Samuel Mather, Jr. and William Gwinn Mather would become giants of the iron industry. The Cleveland Iron Company built a location near the Jackson mine, but it did not interfere with the Jackson.

Then, in the summer of 1848, men representing the Marquette Iron Company tried to jump the Cleveland Iron Company's claim. Robert Graveraet, Captain Samuel Moody, and John H. Mann arrived, went up to the mines, and in the absence of the man in charge of the Cleveland location, burned down the Cleveland company's building, built one of their own, and stated they would shoot anyone who attempted to take back possession.[16]

The following winter of 1848-49, Robert Graveraet told Edward Clarke he thought the controlling stock of the Jackson Mining Company could easily be bought out. Waterman Fisher of Worcester was convinced to furnish money to buy out the Jackson, and Amos Harlow agreed to invest his small machine shop in Worcester, Massachusetts, in the venture and go to Upper Michigan to manage the mine. Before they were even certain they could obtain shares of the Jackson, Clarke and Harlow went to Detroit to purchase supplies, but they did not purchase teams or tools because they assumed they would get those when they took possession of the Jackson. In July 1849, Graveraet and Harlow arrived in Marquette and

Ariel Barney

Jackson Mine South Pit 5 from 1857

took possession of the Jackson's dwelling on the lakeshore. This resulted in Everett having to sleep in the Native Americans' quarters when he went down to the lakeshore.

By the time Clarke arrived in Marquette, he realized he could not get his hands on the Jackson's stock. Therefore, the Marquette Iron Company would not be able to use the Jackson's tools, teams, or laborers. They were now basically trespassers. The men of the Marquette Iron Company then decided to build a forge of their own. They removed a log dwelling near the Dead River, brought it to Iron Bay, and then vacated the Jackson building. Clarke then went to Milwaukee to hire forty French and German immigrants to work in Marquette. Next, he went to the Sault where he became ill with cholera and died within a few days.[17] The cholera would soon spread to Marquette.

Meanwhile, the Cleveland Iron Company went to the land office commissioner at Washington, DC, and explained how Graveraet, Moody, and Mann had unscrupulously taken possession of their mine. The commissioner awarded the mine to the Cleveland Iron Company, thus ending the dispute.[18]

Later, John Burt—son of William Austin Burt, whose compass had first sensed the iron ore—arrived at the land office in the Sault to make a claim for his own location nearby, but Graveraet intensely opposed the matter until Burt made peace with him by giving him half of the mining right.[19]

From this short history, we can see Marquette was founded by rival iron companies all trying to operate side-by-side or eliminate their competition. Furthermore, the iron industry's growth would soon change the role of the Ojibwa in the area.

Kawbawgam and Founder's Day

In recent years, May 18, 1849 has been celebrated in Marquette as "Founder's Day," although the date the city was actually founded has been disputed. Furthermore, while the Marquette Iron Company and Amos Harlow are viewed as the city's founders, a good argument can be made that Philo Everett was the true founder since he arrived first and began the Jackson mine. May 18 is actually the date Robert Graveraet returned to Marquette with Peter White and a handful of other men to establish a permanent settlement. Harlow and his family would follow them within a couple of months. By this point, Kawbawgam was already settled at the mouth of the Carp River and awaiting their arrival. Consequently, in many later newspaper articles, Kawbawgam would be referred to as Marquette's "first resident."

How Graveraet met Kawbawgam and convinced him to move to Iron Bay is unknown. Perhaps life at the Sault was no longer palatable to Kawbawgam, who had already moved around a few times, both to Tahquamenon and Ontario. In 1845, the Ojibwa at the Sault were again complaining that the whites were threatening to crowd them out of their reservation lands at the St. Mary's River.[20] In 1847, there was also talk of moving the Lake Superior Ojibwa to Minnesota.[21] Perhaps Kawbawgam thought he had a better chance of survival if he moved to a new area; perhaps he needed income, and Graveraet likely paid him something; perhaps Charlotte wished to move closer to where her father lived. In any case, the decision was made.

Years later, during Charlotte's lawsuit against the Jackson Iron Company, Kawbawgam testified:

> I lived at Presque Isle since a year after Marji-Ge-Shik had told the Jackson Company about the mine location. I came from the Sault and am part of the Chippewa Tribe. I knew Mary before I came up here from the "Soo." I knew Mary about eight years down at the "Soo," and I knew her mother Susan, at the "Soo." I came to Marquette after

> I had married Charlotte. I was married to Charlotte seven years before I came to Marquette. I knew Charlotte when about fifteen and married her about that time.[22]

This statement gives some clarification to the timeframe of Kawbawgam's move, but it is also problematic. If Kawbawgam came the spring after Marji-Gesick showed the Jackson Company the iron ore's location, it would have been in 1846, at which time Charlotte was about fifteen, as Kawbawgam says. However, Kawbawgam also says Charlotte and he had already been married for seven years when they came to Marquette. Since we know they were married in July 1847, more likely they were married less than a year before they came. Possibly they did not arrive until the spring of 1849, just before Graveraet returned with Peter White, although more likely, they came in the summer or fall of 1847, or sometime in 1848. The "Mary" referred to is Charlotte's half-sister (Susan's daughter) who would marry Francis Nolin (Jacques LePique). Nolin was the son of Louis Nolin, who had accompanied Everett in trying to find the iron ore.

During the Jackson Iron Company trial, Charlotte's mother Susan also testified, stating that her daughter came with Graveraet to Marquette.[23] Some authors have written that Kawbawgam married Charlotte after he came to Marquette, but this information is obviously incorrect given Kawbawgam, Charlotte, and Susan's testimonies, and the Kawbawgams' marriage record showing they were married in the Sault. Charlotte herself testified that "the paper [the Jackson mine certificate] was given about a year before we came here from the Soo."[24] That would mean they arrived in 1846, which is at least a year too early. Kawbawgam would state he came "the year after the Company took up this location—the Jackson Company—the spring after."[25] This could mean 1847 after the Jackson had a claim, or 1848, the year the company began to build, both possible dates. It should also be noted that both Charlotte and Kawbawgam's words were translated and the translator may have misunderstood them, plus they were recalling events that had happened decades earlier so their memories may have been faulty. Because Kawbawgam also stated that Mr. Harlow (who arrived in 1849) came after,[26] we can definitely say the Kawbawgams arrived in Marquette between July 12, 1847, the date of their marriage, and May 18, 1849, the date Graveraet and Peter White arrived.

In the above statement, Kawbawgam also stated that he lived at Presque Isle since a year after Marji-Gesick told the Jackson Company where the iron ore was. However, Presque Isle is a few miles north of Iron Bay where Kawbawgam was living when Graveraet and White arrived. Since Kawbawgam was living at Presque Isle when he gave the trial testimony, he could have been just simplifying the statement for the court, or perhaps he thought of Presque Isle and Marquette as one place and did not distinguish between them. It is possible Kawbawgam settled at Presque Isle when he first came to Marquette but moved at some point prior to May 18, 1849 to just north of the Carp River's mouth, which flows into Iron Bay south of the current city of Marquette. There Kawbawgam built a large cedar bark wigwam which the early settlers would know as the "Bawgam House" or "Boggam House" and which may have been at the bottom of what is today's Baraga Avenue.[27] However, Peter White would later state of Marji-Gesick that "the old chief's palace used to be only four or five hundred feet from the present [1886-1902] humble home of the Kawbawgams at Presque Isle"[28] so it is likely the Kawbawgams did first live at Presque Isle near Charlotte's father and then later moved to where downtown Marquette is today once the white settlers began to arrive. In fact, Peter White also stated, "The place where we came ashore was called Jackson's landing at that time, which indicates, of course, that we were not the first white men who had landed there. There were two small log houses on the point, five or six birch-bark wigwams, and the whole outfit inhabited by Indians."[29] This statement suggests the Ojibwa may have been scattered along the lakeshore for a couple of miles from Presque Isle to what would become Marquette's lower harbor.

Graveraet and Peter White arrived in Marquette in a longboat. Various numbers have been given for how many men were in it, but Peter White, who is our primary source for what happened that day, stated there were "three men and seven hearty healthy boys,"[30] himself included as one of the boys. Years later, White would state:

> We succeeded in crowding our large Mackinac barge up the rapids or falls, at Sault Sainte Marie, and embarking ourselves and provisions, set sail on Lake Superior for the Carp River iron region. After eight days of rowing, towing, poling and sailing, we landed on the spot immediately in front of where Mr. George Craig's dwelling house stands (on the south shore of Gaines' Rock). That was called Indian Town and was the landing place of the Jackson Company.[31]

In 1889, White also reminisced about these events to the Marquette YMCA in a forty-five page speech he titled "My Recollections of Early Marquette."

When Kawbawgam died, White shared the speech with *The Mining Journal*, which quoted from it as follows:

> On the 18th day of May next will occur the fortieth anniversary of as lovely a morning, as charming a day as the month of May ever produced in any country.
>
> On that morning, as early as 6 o'clock, when not a ripple disturbed the glass-like surface of Lake Superior, a large Mackinaw boat might have been seen rapidly approaching what is now known as "South Marquette."
>
> The craft had ten occupants. It would have been fair to describe them as three men and seven hearty healthy boys.
>
> The seven were the oarsman and they were pulling with a will—long, strong, deep, regular strokes, that the boat show what the sailors call a "bone in her teeth" for these boys had been told that morning when breaking camp at 4 o'clock at Shot Point, that their destination was in sight, and if they did as well as they sometimes did that a landing would be made inside of two hours, that the long trip—nine days of coasting would be ended, and the new Eldora [sic Eldorado] would be reached—and it was accomplished.
>
> The time which your patience will allow me to read this paper will not, I fear, permit me to name, or particularize this party, and I will briefly say that, I believe they are all, save one, dead.
>
> As the boat struck the beach a tall, powerful, swarthy individual with an aboriginal face and form, who seemed to be about forty-five or fifty years old, greeted the party with a cheer and a hearty welcome and seized the boat painter, assisted the crew to land the boat high and dry in about one minute of time.
>
> Then he was introduced as "Charley Kaw-baw-gam."
>
> He conducted the party to his hugh [sic] cedar bark wigwam.
>
> It was built like a one-story house with gable ends only with no ceiling or upper floor.
>
> There was a large opening (perhaps a large square) in the center of the ridge for the purpose of a chimney or rather smoke escape, which also furnished light, in lieu of windows.
>
> The entire structure was covered, roof and sides, with cedar bark.
>
> The door was hung from the top with a piece of duck that had

served its time with a boat sail. The newly arrived party took their first breakfast in that house—boiled and fried whitefish, unequalled potatoes, fried venison and good coffee and bread.

In those primitive days butter was unknown.

Charley's wife, Charlotte, was a bright intelligent looking woman, who made everything neat and clean in and about her house.

Charlotte, was a born princess. Her father was the king of his tribe. His place was four or five hundred feet from her present home.

He was the great Chief "Madje Geeshick" Moving Day. Charlie, too was a prince. His father was a Chief of the Sault Ste. Marie band of Chippewas. His name was "Shau-wa-no" sometimes called "Shau-Wo-no-Nodin" South Wind. So you see that this party was at once royally entertained.

Let us digress from the thread of my story here to tell you that John Logan Chipman, a lawyer of distinction, son of a very learned judge of the Supreme Court of Michigan, himself for many years and many times re-elected judge of the Supreme Court of Detroit, and now a re-elected member of Congress from the First District of Michigan; wooed, and married Lizette, a daughter of Chief Sha-wa-no and sister of Charles Kaw-baw-gam.[c]

The landing place where the party landed near Kaw-baw-gam's dwelling was called "The Jackson Landing."

There were two small log houses there, and perhaps nine or ten birch bark wigwams, all occupied by "Lo the Poor Indian."

There was a small clearing, not to exceed five acres and beyond that a dense almost impenetrable thicket or forest was found on every side.

The whole lake front from Light House Point nearly to the mouth of the Carp river, was one mass of foliage that overhung the water and in some places immersed itself in the water.

It was as a whole, the most beautiful day I ever beheld. There is no other place on the South Shore of Lake Superior as handsome as was Marquette Bay at that time.[32]

---

c. The original of White's speech is among his papers in the Burton Historical Collection at the Detroit Public Library. In the original manuscript, White digressed here to discuss Kawbawgam's present state and complain about American cruelty to the Indians, which *The Mining Journal* saw fit to omit. I quote this section later in Chapter 12: A Local Celebrity.

White's description suggests that Kawbawgam was expecting the party, although how Graveraet communicated that they were coming we cannot know.

In the first reminiscence quoted above, White goes on to state:

> We put up that night at the cedar house of Charlie Bawgam. It is true his rooms were not many, but he gave us plenty to eat, clean and well cooked. I remember that he had fresh venison, wild ducks and geese, fresh fish, good bread and butter, coffee and tea, and splendid potatoes.[33]

(Note that White contradicts himself about the butter.) In this same first reminiscence, White went on to describe how Graveraet and party traveled inland the day after their arrival and spent a few minutes visiting with both the Everett party at the Jackson Forge and then at the Cleveland Mine, known as Moody's Location, where Captain Moody and John H. Mann had spent the previous summer and winter. Then until July 10, they lived inland, taking possession of the iron mountain until Harlow arrived when they returned to live along the lakeshore.[34]

In the two months before Harlow arrived, a 16' x 18' log house was built near the lakeshore. It would be occupied by Graveraet. Sixty feet behind it was another log house known as the St. Mary's Hotel, run by two "squaws," Margaret and Mary. Margaret was most likely Marji-Gesick's first wife. The Mary referred to appears to have been his sister, rather than Charlotte's half-sister. Most of the party, however, lodged in Kawbawgam's "Boggam House."[35] According to Kenyon Boyer, who broadcast a series of Historical Highlights about Marquette on radio in the 1950s, Marji-Gesick and his sister Mary supplied the settlers with fish and meat.[36] The efforts of Marji-Gesick and his band, of which Kawbawgam was now a member, have even been credited with helping to prevent the whites from starving during the long bitter winters that followed by providing them with food and teaching them how to find game.[37] Approximately five or six Ojibwa families were settled along the lakeshore with the white settlers at this time.[38]

What the Boggam House and perhaps even the St. Mary's Hotel looked like can be gathered from a description Bourgeois provides in his introduction to *Ojibwa Narratives* of typical Ojibwa homes of the period:

> [The Ojibwa's] more stationary dwelling consisted of an elliptical dome-shaped structure made of a pole frame covered with rolls of birchbark and cattail matting. The largest examples could house

> several families. The interior sheltered woven cedarbark mats, woven bags, a variety of birchbark containers, carved wooden bowls, ladles, bow and arrows, snowshoes, cradleboard, fish lures, nets, and line, and perhaps lacrosse racquets, flute, drum, and (rarely) sculptured imagery in human and animal form. Tanned hide clothing, medicine bag, and knife sheath occasionally featured dyed porcupine quillwork, or later, glass bead decoration arranged in floral designs, while patterns in silk applique were sparingly applied toward the end of the eighteenth century.[39]

Peter White was likely one of those who lived in the Boggam House that summer. He could already speak Ojibwa, so he had a better chance than most of the other settlers, excepting Graveraet, to get to know the local Ojibwa, and he was able to converse with Kawbawgam.[40] White and Kawbawgam's meeting on May 18 would be the start of a friendship that would last fifty-three-and-a-half years until Kawbawgam's death. Because he met Kawbawgam in his youth and Kawbawgam did not speak English, White would become one of the major sources of information about Kawbawgam.

Peter White

Peter White would become one of Kawbawgam's best friends and later in life be described as his "benefactor" and "protector," and he would also become one of Marquette's wealthiest and most prominent citizens, so it is worth pausing here for a brief summary of his life prior to his first meeting with Kawbawgam so we have a better understanding of him.

Peter Quintard White was born in Rome, New York, on October 31, 1830. His parents were Dr. Stephen White, an Episcopalian clergyman, and Harriet Tubbs White. White's paternal grandparents were Captain Stephen White, who had commanded Fort Stanwix in 1777 during the American Revolution, and Mary Quintard White.

White's mother died while he was a child. When he was nine, his family moved to Green Bay, Wisconsin, where he attended school and his father remarried. Several historians have written that Peter White ran away from home at thirteen. Mrs. Samuel Barney, who knew White well in Marquette's early days, clarifies why he left the family. Peter White's brother had told her mother-in-law, Mrs. Barney, that after his mother died, his father could not do anything with Peter and the family was even afraid he might kill someone:

> ...so his father bonded him out to an old half breed who kept a little store on Mackinac Island and that is where Peter learned to talk French and Indian. He was bonded out until he was twenty one and he was not fourteen years old at that time.... He was such a good boy that the old half breed would not keep him.[41]

According to a 1905 article in the *Detroit Free Press*, White also spent time attending a "half-breed Indian School on Mackinaw Island, under Capt. Gage."[42] There he would have had time to learn Ojibwa. Captain Gage may have been Morgan L. Gage, who was a captain with the Michigan 1st volunteers and stationed at Fort Mackinac in 1847.[43] Any other details of White's time on Mackinac Island have been lost to time. However, he would always remain well versed in Ojibwa. Late in his life, White would meet the former Governor of New York, William D. Hoard, whose dad had been a missionary to the Oneida Indians in the area of New York where Peter White's family had originated and who had also become an Indian interpreter. During their meeting, Hoard poured the Oneida language into Peter White's ear and White responded by pouring out Ojibwa, which led to the bystanders beginning an involuntary Native American dance.[44]

Peter White

In time, White left Mackinac Island and went to Sault Sainte Marie. He was hired to work on a schooner that sailed back and forth from Detroit to the Sault. At one point, White fell while boarding the ship and broke his arm. The Detroit doctors thought the arm would need to be amputated, but Dr. Zina Pitcher recommended waiting. When the swelling subsided, Pitcher reset the arm. White was forever grateful to him.[d]

While waiting for his arm to heal, White worked as a clerk in a store in Detroit, then worked at the Waugoshance Lighthouse. He then spent two

---

d. Interestingly, Pitcher had also been Henry and Jane Schoolcraft's doctor when their son, William Henry, died, as detailed in Schoolcraft's *Ojibwa Lodge Stories*, which includes copies of the *Literary Voyager* and even a poem Pitcher wrote in William Henry's memory. Pitcher would serve as Mayor of Detroit twice in the 1840s. After Pitcher's death, Peter White arranged to have flowers planted on his grave every year (Williams 32).

Ackerman Lith 379 Broadway N.Y.
VIEW NEAR CARP RIVER, LAKE SUPERIOR.
Marquette Regional History Center

Marquette circa 1850

years on Mackinac Island, finishing his schooling and working as a school clerk.[45]

Graveraet, of course, was at Mackinac Island, so it wasn't long before he met White and enlisted him to help establish the town of Marquette. Always up for an adventure, White accepted, little imagining that this would be the last of his wanderings about the Great Lakes. While he would make many more trips during his lifetime, including to Washington, DC and even Italy, White would call Marquette home for the remainder of his life—fifty-nine years.

Mrs. Barney's Memories of Kawbawgam

Anna Eliza Barney, who was previously mentioned as giving the youngest date for Kawbawgam's likely birth and knowing details about Peter White's running away, arrived in Marquette in July 1850 after marrying her husband Samuel Barney, son of Ariel N. Barney. In 1847, Samuel had come to Marquette and the Jackson mine with his parents. In 1915, Mrs. Barney provided her reminiscences of Marquette's early years, including her first encounter with Chief Kawbawgam, which did not make her his fan. She states:

> The papers said that Charlie Kaw-baw-gam was over one hundred years old. That is a mistake. When I was here he was only about eighteen and Pa (Mr. Barney) [her husband] was twenty-one! The

> first thing I seen him [Kawbawgam] I scolded him. There used to be piles of little winter birds and when I would throw out crumbs from the table, the birds would come and feed. Didn't this fellow come with a shot gun and shoot right in amongst them and was picking up what he had killed and the little ones with broken wings and was putting them into a sack, and he said it was "wolf bait." He was going to a wolf trap. There was wolves around Marquette then, many of them.[46]

Mrs. Barney can't be blamed for being upset that the birds she loved were killed. Nor is it surprising that Kawbawgam would trap wolves. We will see later that he trapped when he lived at Presque Isle.

Native American Contributions to Early Marquette

While Marquette's history has been told in other places, the role Native Americans played in its earliest years and throughout the nineteenth century is usually glossed over. Other than Kawbawgam, little mention is made of the other Native Americans in Marquette in its early days or of their contributions. This omission needs to be rectified. The Native American settlement at Marquette was never as large as at other places like Sault Sainte Marie and L'Anse, but it was still at this time an integral part of the community. The 1850 census only lists eight Native Americans in Chocolay Township—two males, two females, and four children, and none were listed in Marquette Township. The 1860 census lists twenty-seven in Marquette. (The Kawbawgams are not included on the 1850 census, but they are on all the later censuses.) Since censuses were taken in the summer, they probably did not include Native Americans who were traveling or living in the forest at the time. There must have been far more Ojibwa around Marquette than the censuses record since in 1839 Schoolcraft counted 961 Native Americans in the Upper Peninsula with eighty-one at the Chocolate (Chocolay River).[47] Regardless of these small numbers, Native American contributions were significant for the white settlers from the time Marji-Gesick led the Everett party to the iron ore.

Because a road was needed to haul the ore from the mines to the lakeshore, in the late 1840s, Kawbawgam and three or four other Ojibwa were engaged to help build this road; in fact, Kawbawgam is said to have cut the first tree that would open the wilderness to the mine.[48] Everett's party had already built a road in the fall of 1846 or 1847,[49] so it is not clear whether Kawbawgam was involved in creating that road or a later one.

Olive and Amos Harlow

Kawbawgam not only provided shelter to the settlers, but he operated the Boggam House as a hotel, though he never charged anyone to stay there. It was located at the foot of where Baraga Avenue is today.[50]

As previously mentioned, Margaret and Mary, Marji-Gesick's wife and sister, also ran a hotel for the whites. We do not know to what extent this meant the Ojibwa tried to make money off the whites' presence. However, they must have realized the whites weren't leaving, so they tried to get what compensation they could out of them, and they stayed busy as more settlers arrived.

Among Marquette's most significant early settlers were Amos Harlow and his wife. Harlow arrived in Marquette on July 6, 1849, and the next day, accompanied by an unnamed Native American, he went to inspect land he had purchased near the mouth of the Dead River. Seeing the land was unsuitable for a town site, he returned to the Sault where he purchased another parcel of land.[51] Harlow's wife Olive and her mother, Martha Bacon, had traveled to the Sault with Harlow. Now, because he had business to see to there, the women traveled by schooner to Marquette without him and he followed a few weeks later. When Olive and her mother arrived in Marquette, they spent the first night in a small hut. Olive later described how she slept on a bed made of birch poles and pine boughs over a dirt floor. She amused herself by "looking at the stars through cracks in the roof."[52] Upon emerging the next morning, she saw a wigwam for the first time, and her curiosity overcame her. She recounted: "Anxious to see all the novelties of my new country, I looked inside the blanket door and saw two squaws. We exchanged giggles and I retreated."[53] Obviously, Olive did not think she needed to knock, which she doubtless would have done before entering a white person's home. Since she refers to two female Indians, it may have been the St. Mary's Hotel that she intruded upon.

While the Ojibwa were willing to help and perhaps profit from the whites, when the cholera spread that summer from the Sault to Marquette, they quickly fled. Peter White recalled, "We were all frightened, but the Indians who lived here then—to the number of 100—had embarked in their boats and canoes within sixty minutes, and started over the water to escape a disease to them more fearful than the small-pox."[54] The cholera continued for several weeks. Peter White joined Dr. Rogers in helping to care for many of the settlers who came down with the disease, especially after the doctor himself became ill.[55] Fortunately, no one seems to have died from the disease, and once the epidemic was over, the Ojibwa returned to Indian Town. Whether Kawbawgam and his family fled is not recorded, although it seems unlikely since they were operating Marquette's first hotels.

Both Graveraet and Peter White were instrumental in working with the Ojibwa in Marquette's early days. That first summer, Graveraet needed to send someone south on an errand to Bay de Noquet, where the city of Escanaba is today. He chose Peter White, who then chose some Ojibwa to accompany him. White's biographer, Ralph Williams, writing in 1905, provides a white man's view of Graveraet and White's relations with the Ojibwa and this specific mission.

> This extraordinary man [Graveraet] was attracted to Peter White for they had a common facility of language. Graveraet spoke English, French, German and several Indian dialects. He was highly educated. Peter White spoke several languages also, a gift wholly native, for his mind was practically undisciplined. He seemed to have the faculty of absorbing language by association. Throw him in contact with an Indian and Peter White would acquire his tongue within a month. Graveraet was therefore attracted to a boy whom the Chippewas followed after as though they were his personal retinue. The Chippewas liked Peter because he could tell them stories in their own language. It was even said that he had a greater hold upon the Indians

> than Graveraet, who had lived among them for years. Therefore when Graveraet wanted anything done he summoned Peter. One day he sent him upon a mission of some delicacy to Escanaba. This meant a trip overland across the peninsula—a mere nothing nowadays, but a considerable undertaking through a continuous forest for a boy of eighteen. Two Chippewas, Mongoose [Marji-Gesick's brother] and Jimmeca, volunteered to accompany Peter. This is one of the chief recollections of the man's life, which is not surprising since it was the first trip he ever undertook through the wilderness on foot. They carried their provisions on their backs. The Indians were of incalculable aid to Peter in following the trail. When one tree is blazed the Indian seems to know by instinct where to look for the next blaze and so the trail was followed with reasonable accuracy. There is nothing more monotonous, however, than following a trail, either on horseback or on foot. On the fourth day Peter began to despair. The woods seemed endless.[56]

The passage goes on to say that Peter told himself he would never go in the woods again, but, of course, he would do so many more times in the years to come.

Decades later, at an unknown date, Peter White would give an address at the opening of the Escanaba high school which says he and his Ojibwa companions did not travel all the way by foot on that journey south.

> My first visit here [Escanaba] was in November 1849. I started from Marquette on the 27th of the month with two Indians, Mongoos and Jimmeca. We went to the main river several miles above the West Branch and there we made a raft and came down the river. We were seven days coming, where now we leave Marquette at 6 and get here before bedtime.[57]

White had probably returned to Marquette by the second week of December. He would have found the community greatly worried that it would not survive through the winter. A supply ship was expected before the winter shipping season closed, which was usually in December. Day after day passed and no ship came. Eventually, the German settlers decided they would walk to Milwaukee to spend the winter, realizing the settlers would never survive with so many mouths to feed.

However, an Ojibwa from L'Anse arrived in Marquette with word that the supply ship was stranded in L'Anse Bay. Someone was sent after the Germans to tell them to return. Meanwhile, Captain Moody and James Broadbent walked on snowshoes to L'Anse. Arriving there, they found the supply ship, the *Swallow*, trapped in the ice. Captain Moody then decided the *Siscowit* would have to bring the supplies to Marquette. Captain Bendry of the *Siscowit* tried to protest his ship could not go to Marquette either, but Captain Moody told him the people there were starving, and then he had all the supplies from the *Swallow* moved onto the *Siscowit*. A large number of Ojibwa from L'Anse were enlisted to cut a passage about two or three miles long out into the ice so the *Siscowit* could reach open water and make it to Marquette. If not for the bravery of those Ojibwa on dangerous ice, the people in Marquette might have perished that first winter. Despite the sails being frozen stiff and immovable and a coating of ice a foot thick on the *Siscowit*'s deck by the time it arrived in Marquette, it did sail into Iron Bay on Christmas Day—a true Christmas miracle for the desperate settlers.[58]

Even with the ship's arrival, the winter remained difficult. In 1887, *The Mining Journal* ran an article about Kawbawgam in which it quoted "a prominent citizen," who was probably Peter White. The citizen stated:

> During the winter of '49-'50 and of '50-'51 provisions ran scarce. It was impossible to obtain more, and the two hundred men in the settlement would have had a hard time of it if it had not been for Charlie Baw-Gam and his father.[e] They came to the rescue and day after day brought in venison, ducks, rabbits, and wild geese, while they set nets and supplied all of us with whitefish and trout from the bay. They kept the settlement supplied with game for months until navigation opened again and supplies were received. We all recognized our indebtedness to Charlie and I for one shall never forget it; they kept us from starvation."[59]

Native American Mail Carriers

During the winter of 1849-1850, Marquette only received mail three or four times because no ships could travel on the frozen lake so mail had to be carried overland. The mail was delivered through Wisconsin to the Upper Peninsula. Amos Harlow, who had taken on the role of deputy postmaster, employed Jimmeca to go to L'Anse to fetch the mail for $10 a

---

e. This "father" reference most likely refers to Marji-Gesick, Kawbawgam's father-in-law, though it could also refer to Shawano, his stepfather, who visited Marquette that first year, according to James Kelley's article that will be quoted shortly.

trip[60] (about $333 in 2020). Jimmeca likely made the seventy-mile journey by snowshoe.

The following winter, the government had still made no provision to deliver mail to Marquette so Peter White volunteered to go regularly to L'Anse to fetch it. Harlow was skeptical that White was strong enough for the job, but White was insistent. White's biographer, Ralph Williams, describes how White enlisted the Ojibwa to aid him:

> He got two Indians to go with him. His influence with the Indians was great and they would have gone with him to the pole. Hundreds of letters were written by the men when they learned that Peter was going to carry the mail. The whole town saw him off. The mail was very heavy, and what with the provisions, which also had to be carried, made a staggering load for his back. The mail was taken to L'Anse where other carriers were met. Peter established a station where he might meet the carriers in the woods. It was as primitive as it well could be, Peter hanging the mail bag to the limb of a tree where the relay might get it. On the second trip he secured a dog sled and a team of dogs to ease his burden. The sled was flat, like a toboggan and the dogs were mongrels, stout curs, capable of making between four and five miles an hour. They had to be fed at short intervals to keep their temper and spirits at normal pitch. They became wildly excited at the scent of wolves and were almost unmanageable on such occasions. The mail was securely strapped to the sled, Peter traveling alongside of it on snowshoes, controlling the leading dog by a string rein and using a staff to stop the sleigh by pushing it into the snow. He made nine of these trips during the winter and they furnished the base for many of the legends of the upper peninsula. The lore of the French Canadian, in particular, is full of stories of Peter and his Indians and his dog sleds.
>
> For these nine trips Peter received the aggregate sum of three dollars.[61]

Williams goes on to say that pledges had been made to pay Peter White more, amounting to $1,200, but they never materialized.

White tells a slightly different story in his own words:

> We had been able to send mail our [sic] by L'Anse until the troops were taken away from Copper Harbor, but that had stopped. I was still supposed to be the only white man who knew the way to Lake

> Michigan, or Bay de Noques. An Indian would not do, because he could not be admittd [sic] as a proper person to take an oath. So I carried the mail out five times during the winter, for which I was to have two hundred dollars a round trip. It was a glittery prospect. But I never got the money. However, I am like a good many other people up in this country,—I had the experience.[62]

Clearly, White was intelligent enough to develop a better mail delivery system, but one wonders just how smart he was when Jimmeca made less than half as many trips for more than three times the amount ($10 per trip compared to Peter's $3). However, while White's is a household name in Marquette today, Jimmeca's name is all but forgotten.

Mail delivery continued by dogsled for many years with Peter White and the Ojibwa regularly involved in it. In January 1854, White and six Ojibwa took three dogsleds to Green Bay, Wisconsin, a distance of about 175 miles, to fetch the mail for Marquette.[63]

The US Postal Service also hired Ojibwa men to deliver mail from the Sault to Marquette and Mackinac.[64] Certainly, these mail carriers not only provided communication for the whites in the community, but they probably brought word to Kawbawgam and other Ojibwa in Marquette of their relatives at the Sault.

D. P. Maynard, who in 1972 wrote the most extensive biography of Kawbawgam (twenty pages) until the publication of this book (unless one counts Homer Kidder's *Ojibwa Narratives*, which has biographical information sprinkled throughout it), stated that besides Peter White and Jimmeca, Kawbawgam himself helped to deliver mail by dogsled for the settlers.[65] I have been unable to locate Maynard's source for this statement so I cannot say whether it is true. Given that Maynard was a member of a pioneer Marquette family, it's possible he heard oral traditions that Kawbawgam delivered mail.

By 1855, mail delivery was improving in the Upper Peninsula. In February of that year, Mrs. Everett wrote to a friend hailing a new road being built to Bay de Noquet where the city of Escanaba would soon be founded. Escanaba itself is an Ojibwa name that means either "land of the red buck" or "flat rock," and an Ojibwa village had long been there before it became a place of interest for the white settlers from which to ship iron ore.[66] In her description of the new road, Mrs. Everett remarks upon Native Americans and the mail:

> The long talked-of road from here to Bay de Noquette is now opened, and the first team arrived here yeaterday [sic] with sixty bushels of grain, the first load of anything ever brought by the overland route to Lake Superior. Hitherto dog-trains have been employed to transport the mails; and one enterprising citizen succeeded last winter in transporting a few barrels of pork by the same means.
>
> Those were the days of small things, not to be despised, for without the inventions of the untutored Indian, we should now be scolding about the postmaster general not sending our mail, which we had very good reason to do in the early part of the winter.
>
> There have been up to this time over sixty bushels of mail matter drawn by dogs brought to this place; for the future there will be sleighs for the convenience of travelers and the mail *once in ten days.*
>
> You will perceive that to Marquette belongs the praise of having persevered and overcome every obstacle in her way, and the honor (if there is any) of having outdone every other town on the lake, being the only one in communication with the little world outside this desirable region.
>
> Detroit people had better be looking out, or Chicago will usurp the trade of this whole upper country. With a railroad from this place to Lake Michigan we can laugh at Deroit [sic]; and hie for Boston or New York without so much as saying, 'By your leave.'[67]

What inventions exactly the Native Americans made for the mail to be delivered more smoothly is not known—perhaps Mrs. Everett refers to the snowshoe—but despite their ingenuity, Native American assistance would soon become unnecessary with the coming of technology. That same year, the *Sebastopol*, Marquette's first locomotive, arrived to haul ore from the mines to the lake. Prior to that, a plank road had been built and men had used mules to pull cars of ore. Already the pioneer days were passing away.

However, mail delivery by sled dog would continue for decades with Native Americans being an integral part of the process. A photograph taken at the Sault shows several Native American or métis mail carriers who regularly traveled to Marquette and Saginaw to deliver mail. These men would have been relatives or friends of the Kawbawgams as their names attest. Besides mail, they likely carried verbal news between the Ojibwa at the Sault and those at Marquette. The photograph has been dated to 1871 or possibly as late as the winter of 1886-7, the last year mail carriers may have operated since the railroad reached the Sault the next year.[68] These men reflect how close the Kawbawgams must have remained to their relatives in the Sault.

According to the Bayliss Public Library, identifications are (left to right) Geo. Bernier, Louis Cadotte, Eli Gurnoe, William Miron, Unknown, Antoinne Picquette.

Taken in front of State Lock Administration Building, corner of Portage & Gurnoe Alley (Douglass – Later Osborn Blvd.), Sault Sainte Marie.

The "Unknown" has written above it "John Boucher."

However, an interpretive panel on Water Street that features the photograph identifies the "Unknown" man as Gob Shawano.

Louis Cadotte was a cousin to Charlotte's brother-in-law Pierre Cadotte. Later, a John Gurnoe from the Sault would come to testify for Charlotte when she sued the Jackson Iron Company, so Eli Gurnoe must be his relative. I have been unable to identify Gob Shawano, but he was surely a relative of Kawbawgam's stepfather, if not a relative of Kawbawgam himself.

A German Visitor's Perspective

On August 3, 1850, Friedrich Karl Ludwig Koch (1799-1852) visited Marquette. He had been sent by the Duke of Bruanschweig (Brunswick) to develop a guide for Germans who would be attracted to immigrating to the United States to work in the mines or woods. Koch was a German mathematician and an assistant forge master. Koch's report, which was not translated into English until recent years, describes early Marquette as "uncommonly livable." Koch visited the Carp and Dead Rivers and traveled inland to the Jackson forge. He was not impressed with the destruction to the landscape around the forge, but overall, he felt the area beautiful and rich in iron deposits.

During his one-week visit, Koch also observed the Native American community in south Marquette. He wrote, "Indians and their women were camped in tents and log houses and present every evening and morning at their fires, a Gypsy-like appearance. By the way they are somewhat civilized—although fishing and hunting are still their main pursuits and they do not appear ragged."[69]

Native American New Year's Celebrations

In the fall of 1850, Mr. Everett's family moved to Marquette, staying in the Barneys' hotel until they could build a home of their own. By the early 1850s, several people had opened hotels or boarding houses in Marquette. It is not known how long the St. Mary's Hotel or Boggam House operated, but they probably only lasted a year or two. The white settlers would have wanted something more typical of the style of hotel they were accustomed to.

According to the Everetts' daughter, Mrs. Daniel (Emma) Ball, when the Everetts arrived in Marquette, there were only twenty buildings, including a store and the company barn.[70] The family soon moved into a simple house on Front Street, which they would share with the Burt family, resulting in an occupancy of fourteen people.

In 1879, Mrs. Philo (Mehitable) Everett wrote a memoir of those early days in Marquette. She recalls fondly the New Year's Day surprise she received from Chief Marji-Gesick, which Kawbawgam no doubt joined in:

> January 1st, 1851 opened mild and pleasant, but not anticipating New Year's calls I had not spread my table with tempting luxuries, but had sat down to think over the happy days spent far away, and of the many friends who perhaps would miss my hospitalities and greetings, when the door of my parlor-dining room—and kitchen (all in one) opened, and there before me was a group of laughing Indians of all ages, from the brave old chief May-je-ki-jik and his squaw, to all the little niches, and all the members of the tribe he could muster. As the outer door opened, all the other members of my family fled through an inner door and looked through a crack to see how I would receive my callers, but I had no time to arrange a program, for the old chief rushed up and greeted me with a kiss, and all the rest followed his example. One young brave had painted his

face to indicate he was in love instead of having an engagement ring to proclaim the fact. I cannot tell exactly how the red paint was put on, but it was in lines pointing to his heart. His long black hair was braided and hung down the sides of his face, and braided in it were small brass thimbles strung on a soiled pink ribbon, and when he moved his head they produced a tinkling sound. The old chief appeared in his accustomed blanket and embroidered leggings and moccasins, and his wife had on a rather scant broadcloth skirt, elaborately embroidered with porcupine quills and beads. Fortunately I had plenty of good substantial food to set before them, and they went away satisfied. Of course I felt honored, as I should that such distinguished guests had put on their best attire to call on me. Every New Year after that for a number of years I spread table for them, and they never failed to come and "eat salt" with me, and I have always had their friendship and good will.

Mehitable Everett

Later in the day Mr. Jed Emmons, of Detroit, and Mr. R. J. Graveraet and Captain S. Moody called. I had rather suspected that these two gentlemen had induced my first callers to pay me their respects but they disclaimed all knowledge of it. Mr. Graveraet informed that the Indians always made it a point at Mackinac and the Sault to call upon the white people, and probably the fashion had reached here.[71]

It's nice to see from this passage that no apparent animosity existed between the Everetts and Graveraet and Moody, despite the initial issues between them over mining claims. However, that Mrs. Everett thought Graveraet and Moody may have put the Ojibwa up to the visit suggests some skepticism about their friendship.

Mrs. Everett goes on to say of Marji-Gesick, "The brave old chief sleeps with his fathers in an unknown grave, and of him much praise could be said, but I must leave him for some future time, to come down to the present, January 1st, 1879."[72] Unfortunately, Mrs. Everett never found a future time to tell us more about Marji-Gesick.

Graveraet was accurate in the information he gave Mrs. Everett about the Ojibwa custom of paying calls to whites on New Year's Day. The Ojibwa had adopted this tradition from the French.[73] Similar calls of Native Americans upon white villagers are known to have happened at the Sault in 1830 and 1844. The Natives apparently sought cakes, kisses, and whiskey from the whites, which suggests their purpose in the visits was rather self-serving.[74]

Rev. Verwyst, writing in 1900, describes such New Year's celebrations and other holidays as he observed them celebrated by the Ojibwa, doubtless several decades earlier in his life and at places such as L'Anse, about seventy miles west of Marquette, where the Catholic Church had a heavy influence upon the Ojibwa and Bishop Baraga had worked diligently to found a mission. Verwyst tells us:

> Our Catholic Indians beautifully decorate their churches for Christmas and Corpus Christi. They will cheerfully devote whole days to this laudable work and spare neither time nor expense to decorate the church nicely. Christmas is preëminently an Indian holyday, on which all, even the most lukewarm, attend the midnight mass. On New Year's day they go from house to house wishing each other a "Happy New Year." It is the day of universal good will and reconciliation. They all go to the priest and shake hands with him, wishing him, too, a Happy New Year, and kneel down to receive his blessing. In going from house to house, they receive everywhere little presents and occasionally a little "fire water," too. On the eve of All Souls' days, that is, in the evening of the first of November, they go to the church and each time they pray for a deceased parent, child or dear relative, they ring the bell, and this goes on sometimes until midnight or till the priest, tired of the endless dingling, locks the church. This ceremony they call "Niba-madwessing," night ringing, whilst people are sleeping.[75]

Similarly, Andrew Blackbird, in his *History of the Ottawa and Chippewa Indians of Michigan*, says of the Ojibwa and Ottawa:

> They used to observe many holidays, particularly Christmas, New Year, and Corpus Christi. At New Year's eve every one of the Indians used to go around visiting the principal men of the tribe, shooting their guns close to their doors, after screaming three times, "Happy New Year!" then bang, bang, altogether, blowing their tin horns, beating their drums, etc. Early on New Year's morning they would go around among their neighbors expressly to shake hands

> with one another, with the word of salutation, "Bozhoo," children and all. This practice was kept up for a long time, or until the white people came and intermingled with the tribes.[76]

Interestingly, Blackbird blames the whites for the end of the New Year's celebrations, although the tradition was initially adopted from them.

Although Mrs. Everett left us no further record of her interactions with Marji-Gesick, Frank B. Stone, great-grandson of the Everetts, notes that the Everetts' friendship with Marji-Gesick was continued after his death by Charles and Charlotte Kawbawgam. In fact, photographs exist of Kawbawgam that were taken near the end of his life by the Everetts' grandson, J. Everett Ball, as we will see in Chapter 12.[77]

In 1921, the Everetts' daughter, Emma Everett Ball, further recalled the role of the Ojibwa in early Marquette:

> The Indians had a camp just where the old south shore freight depot is. There were several birch bark camps there. Father and Mr. (?) Charles Johnson got their meals there, and if they had to stay over night, that was the first place. Mary Campbell took me to see Old Mary and Margaret.... There was no camp of Indians east of the places I said. It was an unbroken wilderness there."[78]

Within a few years, however, that wilderness would change into a substantial city.

Catholicism Comes to Marquette

Whether or not the Kawbawgams were actively Catholic, they had had no opportunity to practice their faith since they had moved to Marquette. Then in 1853, Father Jean-Baptiste Menet established a mission there. The Kawbawgams probably were among those who welcomed him since he had married them.

Father Menet was a Jesuit who had arrived at Sault Sainte Marie in 1846. While itinerant priests had visited the Sault prior to that, Menet was the first resident pastor there.[79] He was described by nineteenth century Marquette diocese historian Antoine Rezek as:

> of medium stature, inclined to be stout, with a dark, smooth shaven complexion, dark hair and eyes. He was a man of rare personal charm and was gifted with extraordinary talents. He wore an expression of determination but possessed a loving disposition, being sober, tolerant and congenial. He spoke several languages

> including Russian, and was conversant on all topics. From the pulpit, he ranked high and was inclined to be a dramatic orator.[80]

During these years, Menet traveled a great deal and in 1852 established the first Catholic Church on the Canadian side of the Sault, and later in 1864, at Garden River, where Chief Shingwaukonse had gone. In 1853, he established a mission in Marquette, saying Mass in a log house on Spring Street. The Kawbawgams may have attended the Mass or at least had interaction with him at this time.

Then in 1855, the first Catholic church was built in Marquette, later to be replaced in 1864 by the first St. Peter's Cathedral. The first priest would be Father Duroc.

Father Menet remained at the Sault during this time and his name appears on the records of several of Kawbawgam's other relatives there, including the baptism record of Louis Shawano's daughter Catherine in 1855.[81] In 1857, the Upper Peninsula became its own diocese and Bishop Baraga established his see at the Sault, moving in with Father Menet. The two would work together for many years, but eventually had a disagreement and Father Menet left Upper Michigan, dying in Quebec in 1868.[82] Meanwhile, in 1864, Bishop Baraga reestablished the see of the diocese at Marquette and had St. Peter's Cathedral built.

How much the Kawbawgams participated in the Catholic religion throughout their lifetimes is unknown. However, the family obviously remained Catholic since in 1875, Charlotte's niece Angelica Cadotte would be married to Frank Tebeau by Bishop Ignatius Mrak, successor to Bishop Baraga. That the bishop himself performed the ceremony may reflect some friendship between the Kawbawgams and the bishop or at least recognition that the Kawbawgams were of high status among the Ojibwa community.

In 1872, St. John the Baptist Catholic Church was established in Marquette. It was the church the French Catholics frequented. Charlotte's nephew, Fred Cadotte, would be married in St. John's in 1880 and his funeral would be held there in 1926. In 1894, Charles and Charlotte Kawbawgam would participate in a parade hosted by the Society St. Jean Baptiste. The society, founded in 1875, had among its purposes to keep the French language alive among its members and see that the French language was taught to their children.[83] Given that the Cadottes were of French ancestry, as were many of the other métis families the Kawbawgams associated with and their relatives intermarried with—including the Thibeault/Tebeau and Perreau families, as we will see—it is possible they attended St. John's after it was established. That

Kawbawgam's funeral would be held at St. Peter's Cathedral in 1902, may be due to his role as a chief and because Peter White, who handled the funeral arrangements, felt the cathedral a more appropriate place for his funeral.

Unfortunately, we do not know if the Kawbawgams regularly attended Mass, but from the time Father Menet established his mission in 1853, they would have had access to Catholic priests so they could practice their religion in a more official way. Since the Kawbawgams did not understand much English, and would have understood even less Latin—the language the Mass was held in—it is possible they did not attend Mass at all. Perhaps instead they were visited by the local priests who spoke Ojibwa and may have conducted separate religious services for the Ojibwa community. Many of the priests at this time, having been missionaries before Marquette was founded, spoke Ojibwa, including Bishop Baraga and Bishop Mrak. More research into Ojibwa religious practices in Marquette at this time certainly needs to be done.[f] That said, the Kawbawgams retained some belief in their Ojibwa religion and traditions, as will be explored in Chapter 11.

Angelique—The Harlow's Native American Cook

Another Native American woman[g] of some prominence in early Marquette because of her interaction with the whites was Angelique. About 1857 or 1858, she came to live with the Harlow family as their cook. Little is known about Angelique's time in Marquette, her interaction with the Harlow family, or even how long she remained with them. However, she is famous for having had a remarkable experience on Isle Royale a few years prior to Marquette's founding when she and her French-Canadian husband, Charlie Mott, were stranded there in the winter of 1845-46 by a man who had promised to bring them provisions and take them away before winter but never did. Hers was a terrifying tale of survival, including her husband coming down with a fever and threatening to kill her with a knife, thinking she was a sheep, because of his hunger. Eventually, her husband died and Angelique had to remain on the island with his corpse until she was finally rescued in the spring. She even managed to catch and snare rabbits using her hair to create the snares. Her story is a reminder of how close the settlement in Marquette also came to starvation that first winter, if not for the ingenuity and help of the Ojibwa.

---

f. I have been unable to learn whether the Kawbawgams regularly attended Mass or were members of St. Peter's or St. John's. A search of the Diocese of Marquette's archives yielded no records for the Kawbawgams.

g. Swineford says Angelique was a "half-breed" (Swineford 63).

Another tale about Angelique is that she once made a wager with a Frenchman that she could carry a barrel of pork to the top of an adjoining hill and back. She won it with ease, and upon her return, she volunteered to carry the barrel up again with the Frenchman on top of it.

Angelique died at the Sault in 1874.[84]

Ojibwa Place Names

By 1857, not only was Marquette growing, but the settlement that had grown up about the Jackson mine was large enough to be given a name. The Ojibwa were consulted and the name "Negaunee" was decided upon, meaning "the first, or pioneer" in their language. In 1858, it was decided that the town growing up around the Cleveland Mine also needed a name. When asked to help name it, Peter White said because the mine was located on the highest ground between Lake Superior and Lake Michigan, it should be named to reflect its altitude, so he chose the Ojibwa word "Ishpeming," which means "high place" and also "heaven" in an abstract sense.[85] Also, on April 17, 1856, Worcester's name was officially changed to Marquette,[86] a name the ship captains had already been using for the area. The city was named for Father Jacques Marquette (1637-1675), the Jesuit missionary, because legend says he once held a Mass on Iron Bay, during which time he converted numerous Ojibwa.

More Glimpses of Marji-Gesick

A few more glimpses of Chief Marji-Gesick come to us from this period that show what a jovial man he was.

The first is from an article by Captain James Kelley that was published in the *Marine Review* in 1909. In it, Kelley describes how he arrived in Marquette on July 6, 1849. He contracted with Graveraet and Harlow for one year to put up the buildings and machinery for the Marquette Iron Company.[87] Kelley was eighty-two when he wrote the article, which means he would have been only twenty-two when he arrived in Marquette. In the article, he describes how he helped clear land for the building of the town and also the mines. He had particularly fond memories of the Native Americans, and provides us with a look at Marji-Gesick, Kawbawgam, and their relatives at this time.

> I shall never forget the day we started the mill. The Indians both male and female were there astonished and delighted. They went to the engine and looked at Gates, then to the mill to see Harding and Sawyer, then came to me and seemed to wonder how I could do such a mighty thing. They were my good friends always.

Soon after we arrived, Bawgam's little child died. Peter White came to me and asked if I could make a coffin for it. Said they would be very grateful if I would. I made it of boards from packing boxes and stained it with some red chalk. They were very grateful and said "Meguech, Meguech" (many thanks).

At that time the Indian lodges consisted of Charley Bawgam, his wife Charlotte, his sister Lisette and his little boy, Madjigigig and his wife Margaret. My first visit to Kawbawgam's lodge was the evening after we arrived. Peter White and his half breed companions (Jim, Harry and Wayne) invited me to visit them. I was introduced in due form. After a while I proposed to have a smoke and with a handful of cigars intending to pass them around, and as Charley, a chief's son, I offered to him first, thinking he would take one. To my surprise he took them all and said "Meguech." I was about to explain but Peter told me not to do so. The joke was on me, and the boys enjoyed it. In the winter they had their feast and I was invited and went. I was at the seat of honor at the side of the Chief Shawano, Charley's father, who came up from the "Soo" to preside at the feast. We had stewed venison, partridge, muskrat and beaver tail and roast dog. I ate of all but the muskrat and dog.

Shawano (from the south) was a fine noble-looking man, the most powerful athletic man I ever saw. He was nearly six feet tall, but his immense breadth of shoulder and powerful limbs made him appear about medium height. His expression was dignified but friendly and intelligent. He gave Peter White his Indian name "Shob-wa-wa" and myself he called "Shob-was-e-gay." The Indians do not use the white man's name when speaking of or to him, but use the Chippewa name. It is said of Shawano that he would take the entire contents of a barrel of pork, 200 lbs., in his pack and carry it when packing for the United States surveyors. The Indians were always my friends and honorable men. They would not lie, steal, drink whisky or swear; in fact did not know how to swear. (These vices belong to the white man.)[88]

Kelley goes on to describe the arrival of the Harlows, his first encounter with wolves, and how, with the help of Peter White, Harding, and a Hollander (probably a German or Dutch man), he built the forge shop 150 feet long, 50 feet wide, and 14 feet high, which would hold ten forges.[89] He concludes his article by saying that in the summer of 1850, Mr. Long arrived as general manager. Since his own agreement with the company had ended, he decided to return to Boston. On the way home, Kelley's ship stopped in the Soo "where I met some of our natives from the location who said that they came to bid me good-bye. Among them were old Margaret and Lisette."[90]

Kelley had other memories he did not include in this article but had written a few years earlier in a 1906 letter to Peter White. Perhaps he felt them not proper to print in an article. However, the letter gives us a good look at Marji-Gesick's personality.

> Charlie Bawgam was a good fellow and Lisette was a nice modest girl. She did not like Gates, I suppose he made unsettling propositions to her, he was inclined that way. When I arrived at the "Soo" on my way home, (after making the trip to Ontonagon) she and Margaret met me at the landing and Lisette gave me a ring and many kind wishes. She knew I had a picture of a young lady in my pocket.
>
> I shall always remember Achille Cadotte he was a fine specimen.[h] So was Charlie's father the old Chief—I have a Chipaway Hym [sic] Book that formerly belonged to James Hillyard. Madigigegeg was quite a joker for a Indian. I was getting back to camp from hunting one day and as I passed on the trail from the indian lodges everything quiet, not a sound, then something touched my ear, I turned around and there was Madgigigig stark naked marching almost in lock step with me, and he roared and laughed and laughed as I never heared [sic] an Indian before or since.[91]

Kelley's reminiscences are fascinating since little is known about Kawbawgam's sister, Lisette, and it gives us a date for one of Kawbawgam's children who died young. We also have insight into Shawano and Marji-Gesick from these stories, and it shows just how much the Ojibwa moved about the peninsula, thinking nothing of a trip from the Sault to Marquette to celebrate a festival in the fall, despite a distance of 165 or so miles.

Another early pioneer befriended by Marji-Gesick was Sidney Adams. Adams arrived in Marquette in June 1850 when he was only nineteen. Adams had come to Marquette after his mother died of tuberculosis. Knowing himself to be of a frail constitution, he had taken his doctor's advice to come

---

h. Besides being a fine specimen, Achille was apparently far more enterprising than his brother Pierre. In fact, before there were locks at the Sault, he had been ingenious enough in 1839 to haul the fifty-ton schooner *Algonquin* out of the river near old Fort Brady and take her on rollers down Water Street and Portage Avenue, launching her into Lake Superior at the portage in Ashmun's Bay into Lake Superior (Bayliss et al. p. 283).

to the Lake Superior region where it was believed the environment would be conducive to his health. Upon arriving in Marquette, Adams went to the general store and bought an axe for fifty cents from Peter White, who was the clerk there. Then he commenced business by cutting cord wood and selling it. This led to Adams meeting Marji-Gesick. *The Mining Journal* later summarized a talk about Adams given by his son-in-law, Dr. James H. Dawson, in 1938. According to *The Mining Journal*:

> When Mr. Adams first started his wood chopping operations in south Marquette he looked up from his work one day and was surprised to see a huge Indian closely looking down at him.
>
> After deliberate inspection, he slowly announced, laying a forefinger on the boy's chest: "You sick. You sick here. Bimeby you come die. Eat balsam."
>
> He took the boy and showed him the balsam, took some pellets of gum from the tree and ate them; made a wad of balsam boughs, lay on his back on the ground and placed the wad between his shoulders, removed it; put it under his head, shook his head and replaced the wad of balsam boughs between his shoulders; arose and forcibly conveyed the idea to the boy to sleep in the open.

Sidney Adams

> **Was Valuable Advice.**
>
> This advice the boy followed for years. He waxed strong. The Indian was Maja Gesic, chief of the Chippewas, father [sic] of Charlie Kawbawgam.
>
> Disregarding all the great scientific advances that have been made in the field of preventive medicine, since 1850 to our present 1938, no specialist in pulmonary diseases could give more valuable advice to a subject of Mr. Adams' heredity than did this sage of the forest on this occasion.
>
> With this early introduction to the red man there grew up beteen [sic] the Indians and himself, an intimacy that was one of his most

> cherished contacts during the years. This friendship was extended by them to his little child, Bertha, her father's constant companion from the age of three years. She was often parked in the forest with the horse and buggy while her father strolled deep in the woods inspecting timber; returning to the buggy, he found the child gone.
>
> Some Indian had wandered along, put the child on his shoulder and carried her to see an unusual bird's nest, a hornet nest, an unusual mound of active ants, thus cultivating a love of nature, which children and woman she possessed in a most remarkable degree and which was a supreme pleasure to her through life. She also loved the Indians.[92]

Dr. Dawson was married to Bertha. That he remembered the story his father-in-law had told him about Marji-Gesick is not surprising given his own interest in medicine.

One last memory of Marji-Gesick is questionable. It comes from Carroll Watson Rankin, best known as Marquette author of the children's novel *Dandelion Cottage* (1904). In 1935, Rankin published a three-part series of reminiscences about what life was like in Marquette's early days. In it she states, "Marjigeegies, the famous Indian, who in 1845 led Mr. P.M. Everett to the site of the Jackson mine and the discovery of iron ore, once brought me a fawn, tied up in his red bandana handkerchief."[93] Fred Rydholm slightly altered this story when he recounted it in his book *Superior Heartland* by stating that Rankin was good friends with Chief Marji-Gesick when she was a little girl. Marji-Gesick lived near the mouth of the Carp River while her family lived below the bluff on Lake Street. He would tap on her window at night and once brought her a fawn. He also used to pull her pigtails when he would come to visit.[94] Possibly these slight additions Rydholm heard from Rankin herself, whom he knew when he was a child. Sadly, this charming story is impossible since Marji-Gesick died no later than 1862 and Rankin was not born until 1864. Perhaps Rankin confused Marji-Gesick with Kawbawgam or another Ojibwa.

Carroll Watson Rankin

Helen Longyear Paul

A similar version of the story comes from Mr. Lynn R. Swadley, who along with Negaunee historian Robert Dobson was trying to determine Marji-Gesick's final resting place. According to Swadley, Rydholm told him that his Sunday school teacher, Helen Longyear Paul, had known Marji-Gesick as a girl and she had been given the gift of a fawn by him. One day Mrs. Paul took her Sunday school class for a drive to Negaunee and showed them where there were some spirit houses marking Ojibwa graves. There she pointed out Marji-Gesick's grave. Rydholm remembered this and later showed the site to Swadley in the mid-1990s. The location is not far from the Carp River and County Road 492.[95] It is odd that Rydholm, in the mid-1990s, would say this story is from Mrs. Paul since he had already published the story about Mrs. Rankin receiving a fawn from Marji-Gesick in his book *Superior Heartland* in 1989. I believe Rydholm confused Mrs. Paul and Mrs. Rankin, unless Marji-Gesick was prone to bringing fawns as gifts to numerous little girls. However, like Mrs. Rankin, Mrs. Paul was not born until after Marji-Gesick's death, in fact 1884. Therefore, I'm afraid we must dismiss both stories as apocryphal.

No more is known of Marji-Gesick, other than the events surrounding his death, which will play an important role in the Kawbawgams' story and be discussed in future chapters.

A Native American Sault Migration

Little has been written about other Native Americans who came to Marquette from the Sault about this time, but others did come, perhaps partially attracted by Kawbawgam's presence there. They include the Bass, Pine, and Madosh families. While I have been unable to learn more about the Bass family, the Pine family may have come to Marquette to work in the mines. They were descendants of Chief Shingwaukonse (Little Pine). Historian Janet Chute notes that at the Sault, members of the Sayer (possibly relatives of Kawbawgam's mother Charlotte Sayre), Nolin, and Pine families transferred their skills as mineral explorers to the working of small iron, copper, and silver ore operations in Ontario on the ceded townships of Laird and Duncan or on the Bathchewana tract.[96] Some of those who came to Marquette may have done the same. Paul Pine would later play a pivotal role in the Kawbawgams' lives by being an interpreter during Charlotte's lawsuit against the Jackson Iron Company. The Madosh family was also at the Sault, where several of Chief Madosh's children had been born. Chief Madosh moved to the Marquette area soon after the city's founding. That his brother Marji-Gesick was in the area, coupled with the mining boom, would have been reason for such a move.

Two of Kawbawgam's close relatives also came to the area. Four letters to Peter Barbeau (1800-1882) in the Judge Joseph H. Steere collection at Bayliss Library in the Sault reveal that the Native American population was quite mobile at this time.

Peter Barbeau

Barbeau was a French-Canadian who settled in the Sault in 1822. He worked for the American Fur Company and had a trading post on the Baraboo River. (The river was named for him, based on Native American pronunciation of his name.) In 1842, Barbeau left the American Fur Company and began his own store and trading post. A large collection of business letters to him exist from numerous people, including Peter White, Robert Graveraet, and Frederic Baraga. Most of the letters are from people writing to obtain items Barbeau sold.

Among the letters are two by John (Jean) Roussain, who had married Kawbawgam's half-sister Charlotte, and two by Chief Shawano, Kawbawgam's stepfather and Roussain's father-in-law. What is surprising is that three of the letters were written from "Carp River"—the name for the post office at Marquette at the time—and one from Au Train, which suggests both Roussain and Shawano were at least temporarily living in the Marquette area in the 1850s. The letters show how dependent at this point the Native Americans were upon the payment of monies from the US Government as determined by the treaties. The handwriting on all four letters looks different, which suggests they were dictated to people who could write. Roussain's two letters could be by the same hand, but Shawano's two letters definitely are not. Roussain may have been literate given that he would later be township supervisor at Sugar Island; however, we know Joseph Perrault, the moderator (accountant) for the Baie de Wasai School at Sugar Island for twenty-seven years in the late nineteenth century couldn't read or write,[97] so there's no reason why the township supervisor necessarily had to. We can be fairly certain Shawano did not write and maybe did not speak English, considering that Kawbawgam did not speak much English until his later years. It was not uncommon in the early twentieth century at Sugar Island for the Native Americans to ask the postmistress, Delia Laramie, to write letters for them and read the letters that came back in response,[98] and that was probably also the case in Marquette and other areas of the Upper Peninsula. In fact, records show that half the residents at the Sault were illiterate in 1850.[99] Below, the letters are quoted in full because it is rare to find Native American letters from this time, and for what they reveal about these two relatives of Kawbawgam.

Saut Ste Marie Feby 5, 1851

Mr P B Barbeu

Please pay, when the money is Received on Indian Claims to Spalding & Bacon, the amount coming to me, on my a/c [account] of Seventy Six & 98/100 Dollars the same being included in your claim

John Roussain

Barbeau in response wrote as a note to himself on this letter:

P. S. I will pay the amount that may be due John deducting his Share of Collection, if ever Paid whatever that money may be.
P. B. Barbeau

Carp River
July 15, 1854

P B Barbeau Esq

Sir,

I received your letter by L Ermatinger, wanting me to send and get a bale of goods to the amount of my childrens mony, I am very much oblge to you for your kind offer and would be glad to accept of it were I in want of anything in that line, But if the Indian payment should take place soon I wish you would get the money from the old man, to be subject to my order and I wile pay you for your trouble I wrote to Eustache[i] Some time ago to get you to buy me a fishing Boat about 18 or 20 feet Bottom he wrote Back to me Saying that there was none to

i. Eustace Roussain, as stated in Chapter 2, is likely John's father and "the old man" referred to in this letter.

be got. Now I wish you would try and get me a good one and send it up and I will pay the Cash for it on the delivery here So you can get your mony an return Boat or you Can take your pay out of the money above spoken of either way its no difference to me I do not want one to Cost me forty or fifty dollars, you tell the old man to let you have the mony at the payment, if you cannot buy about let me know as soon as you can

Your Truly

J Roussain

Carp River

Oct 18th 1852

Sir

I enclose thirty dollars here with twenty of it you will apply on my acct the other ten you will please send me that much worth of Brandy. And another thing if you will do it you will me a great favor. That is to find me a half Bbls [? Maybe 13 lbs] of Lard. I shall never forget my indebtness to you having been sick and not being able to do anything all last winter was that made me behind hand this spring but now I am well and will be able to do something if you send me up anything you will please direct them to J Roussain for I am not in the place half of the time, I received your tobacco & Brandy which was drank by all the Indians that we could get to come

Your truly

Kewainze Shawwanon

Send me some of that Martin medicine that I was talking to you about last fall

Au Train Feb 18th 1856

My dear Sir

I hasten to answer the receipt of your kind letter, which came to hand by the mail carriers; Pray accept my hearty thanks for the trouble, & interest you take in my affairs, during my absence, from the Saut, as well as for the kidness which you have always shewn me, hoping that an opportunity may offer, in which I may be able to prove to you my gratitude therefor. Permit me to grant you full authority, to act for me, during my present absence as you may think fit.

With regard to the five dollars which I attended [attached?] in my former letter, it was as follows. [illegible] Badon's husband borrowed four [?] dollars from me, to pay his way up the Lake, & he was to return me five, by the return of the Steamer Superior, directed to the Post Master himself with a request for him to keep it for me, until it was called for, as, I did not expect to be at the Saut myself.

My reason for not having mentioned the name of the person, from whom I expected the money, was only on account of showing a little courtesy to my son in law [perhaps John Roussain], but I think that it is no longer necessary [sic], to be so fastidious, especially when a person is only expecting his own returned.

I remain dear Sir
Yours
Most sincerely
Akiwioe [?] Shawino

Robert Graveraet, Peter White, Racism, and Marginalization

By the early 1860s, Marquette's pioneer years were over, and with their passing came not only the passing of Marji-Gesick about 1862, but also that of Robert Graveraet in 1861.

Because Graveraet and White were the two white men Kawbawgam was most involved with in Marquette's earliest years, it is worth saying a bit more about them and the reputation Graveraet acquired following his death, which may be due to racism toward his Native American blood, as well as a misunderstanding over something Peter White said.

Graveraet and White appear to have remained close until Graveraet's death. An untitled manuscript contends that at one point, Graveraet found Peter White on the street in Marquette and he took him in and cared for him. (Whether White was drunk, destitute, or ill is not clear.) Graveraet, according to this document, also gave Peter White some land. The implication is that White took advantage of Graveraet, who ended up dying penniless.[100]

Ernest Rankin, a local historian who was at one point President of the Marquette County Historical Society, took an interest in Graveraet and the rumors that he had a bad end. Rankin traced these rumors to a vague remark Peter White made toward the end of his life, referring to Graveraet as "the lamented Robert J. Graveraet" and adding, "He had many virtues but his end was sad indeed."[101] Because White did not elaborate on the details of that

Ernest Rankin

death, his words were misinterpreted to mean Graveraet met an unseemly death. As a result, rumors spread that Graveraet had either committed suicide by gunshot, died in a duel with an angry husband whose wife he'd committed adultery with, or died on the street as a drunk. None of these stories are true. Rankin solved the mystery of Graveraet's death by finding his obituary and realizing that he simply died unexpectedly on June 4, 1861 at age forty-one of a stomach hemorrhage.[102]

By all accounts, Graveraet, despite his early claim-jumping attempt against the Cleveland Mine, was a respectable citizen as his June 15, 1861 obituary in the *Detroit Free Press* testifies:

> Robert J. Graveraet, widely known as the representative of Lake Superior and its iron region, died at 40 years and eight months. He was an Indian Agent at Mackinaw but being of an adventurous disposition, turned his attention to exploring, and with a few others, discovered what is now known as Bruce Mines in Canada on Georgian Bay. Disposing of his interest in that mine, he came to Marquette in 1846—a complete wilderness, and might justly be called the 'Father of Marquette.' He has done much toward developing the iron resources of this county and inaugurating the manufacture of iron from our native ore. His desire to represent the county in a more public capacity, and on a wider field of usefulness than a local agent of an iron company, caused him to lose the agency of the Collins Iron Works, on his being elected Senator from the U.P., in the State Legislature, in the fall of '56, but his prominence as a politician, and his character as a man, were the means of his being appointed Receiver of the U.S. Land Office, by President Buchanan. He was also Superintendent of the Marquette and Ontonagon Railroad, and had the line surveyed under his personal supervision. We are informed it was at considerable pecuniary sacrifice to himself. After the survey was completed, Mr. Graveraet was not actively engaged in business, but continued to show up, at every opportunity, the vast resources of the country, besides taking a prominent part in all political movements. He was a firm and devoted Democrat and we are an

> ardent admirer of the illustrious statesman whose death, alas, we are now called to mourn and announce.[103]

It is interesting to note that the newspaper calls Graveraet the "Father of Marquette" rather than Everett or Harlow.

Mrs. Samuel Barney, in her 1915 reminiscences, stated, "I often think R. Graviat [sic] didn't get much praise, but you know him and Peter White was awful bad friends for a while."[104] Barney seems to be suggesting that White, who outlived Graveraet as well as the Harlows, did not see that Graveraet got enough credit for his role in Marquette's history.

The full extent of relations between White and Graveraet is not known, but from 1851-1854, White managed Graveraet's properties for him; White did not get full payment for doing so until 1855. In 1857, Graveraet borrowed money from White, ultimately owing him $2,144.20 ($56,615.13 in 2020). In 1858, White instituted foreclosure proceedings on Graveraet's land. Graveraet accused White and his partner of hindering the just payment of his debts by holding his property without sufficient claims.[105] Consequently, it is not surprising that bad feelings arose between the former friends, especially since Graveraet had originally been White's boss and now their financial situations were reversed. While White may not have always sung Graveraet's praises in his later years when recalling Marquette's past, it is notable that he never badmouthed Graveraet. His

Samuel and Juliet Graveraet Kaufman

statement that Graveraet came to a bad end, therefore, has been blown out of proportion.

One can't help wondering what role racism played in the decline of Graveraet's reputation after his death, and whatever Peter White's faults, no one can say he was racist toward Native Americans. It was well-known that Graveraet had Native American blood. In fact, the US Government had given lands to the heads of métis households (probably as a result of the 1855 treaty, which will be discussed in the next chapter), so Graveraet received some land in Marquette. This property would be inherited by his sister Juliet and her husband Samuel Kaufman, who also resided in Marquette. In time, they would sell the property.[106] While Graveraet did not have any children, Samuel and Juliet Kaufman would have several who would become wealthy and prominent bankers and marry into high society families. People, doubtless jealous, derided the Kaufmans as social climbers and even dishonest. In addition, rumors spread that the Kaufmans had Jewish blood (debate still ensues over whether this was true) and their Native American blood was also not forgotten. One or both of these ethnic heritages has often been given as the reason the Kaufmans never gained admittance into the exclusive Huron Mountain Club, founded in 1889 by John M. Longyear, Peter White, and other prominent Marquette and Detroit residents and located about forty miles northeast of Marquette. It has been long believed in Marquette that Samuel and Juliet's most prominent son, Louis Graveraet Kaufman, would build his fabulous log cabin mansion, Granot Loma, on Lake Superior, as a response to his not being admitted into the Huron Mountain Club.

Racism and rumor were also used to disparage Graveraet's wife, Lucretia. Lucretia may have been the daughter of Ariel N. Barney, one of the original settlers who came to work in the Jackson mine. Lucretia's parentage is not clear but the 1850 Marquette census lists a Lucretia Marney, age twenty-five. The surname may be a typo for Barney. This Lucretia is believed to have become Graveraet's wife.[107] Ariel Barney became a prominent Marquette resident who would serve as both Marquette's first justice of the peace and seven times as a probate judge. Mrs. Barney was the first white woman to arrive in Marquette County. If the Barneys were Lucretia's parents, she came from a well-respected family. However, Ernest Rankin notes that stories circulated of Lucretia being described as an "Indian squaw," going about town wrapped in a blanket and smoking a black pipe.[108] Obviously, this was not reputable behavior for a Victorian woman. If Lucretia was the Barney's daughter, this behavior seems highly unlikely. The Barneys did not have Ojibwa blood, so such a lie only adds further malice to the rumors about Robert Graveraet. Lucretia died in 1855, at which time Graveraet wrote a letter to his friend Peter Barbeau at the Sault describing his heartache over the loss of his wife.[109]

No evidence suggests that Peter White intended to disparage Robert Graveraet's reputation. In fact, in Ralph Williams' biography of Peter White, which White no doubt oversaw and approved since it was published during his lifetime, there is nothing but glowing praise for Graveraet:

> Graveraet was not an ordinary man. He would be singled out as a natural leader among thousands. He was ambitious; he had a will of iron; he had the faculty of winning men; he was generous, gentle, but firm; he had great intelligence and energy; and his mother had given him a constitution that did not know the meaning of fatigue. For grace of bearing and beauty of proportion Graveraet challanged [sic] instant admiration; and moreover his muscles were of steel.[110]

Fred Rydholm

One cannot give higher praise. It puts to rest Mrs. Samuel Barney's claim that Robert Graveraet did not get enough credit.[j] It is a shame no photograph of Graveraet exists to verify what this incredible man looked like.

If White did have negative feelings toward the Graveraet family, it may have been more likely due to the behavior of two of Graveraet's sisters toward him. In *Superior Heartland*, Fred Rydholm, writing in 1989, records a rumor that was passed along orally in Marquette for more than a century, although no circumstantial evidence exists for it. It is of interest to us here because it reflects white beliefs about Native Americans and that whites could be as superstitious as the Ojibwa.

---

j. Notably, Mrs. Samuel Barney never referred to Robert or Lucretia as her in-laws so it is questionable whether Lucretia was a Barney. One also wonders why Lucretia, though twenty-five, wasn't living with her family according to the 1850 census if she were unmarried.

Rydholm states:

> The legend, one of many told about town, is that Peter White had sold Sam Kaufman some land years earlier [before 1878] and had given him a bad deed. Now it seems that if anyone should have known how to make out a deed, it would have been Peter White, so it appeared that the act was deliberate.
>
> One of Mrs. Kaufman's sisters, a Graveraet, put an Indian curse on Peter because of it. We must remember that these were different times, and an Indian curse was much dreaded and much believed. When his children came down with diphtheria, Mr. White was said to have begged on bended knee to her to lift the curse, but to no avail. All the male children of the family died in the epidemic, and there was no one left to carry on the proud White name.[111]

The 1878 diphtheria epidemic actually resulted in the death of three of White's children (eldest son Morgan, son Mark Howard, and daughter Sarah). White's niece by marriage, Ellen Mather, also died. However, no evidence exists that a bad deed was sold or a curse placed. Nor is it known which of Graveraet's sisters placed the curse. If a curse was placed, one wonders why White did not enlist his friend Kawbawgam's aid to get it lifted, especially considering Kawbawgam was a chief, although Graveraet's sister may not have bowed to his authority.

Even if the story of the curse is true, it did not affect Peter White's behavior toward the Ojibwa. In the years that followed, he would be one of the few whites who would maintain fair relations with them, and he often criticized Americans for their negative attitudes and policies toward Native Americans as we will see in Chapter 12.[112] White's relationship with Kawbawgam probably helped his positive perception of Native Americans, but even prior to knowing Kawbawgam, he must have had a deep respect for the Ojibwa to have learned their language by the time he was eighteen. In upcoming chapters, we will see how White and Kawbawgam's friendship strengthened throughout their lives.

The Ojibwa would need their few white friends as the nineteenth century continued. With the coming of the railroads, the Ojibwa's homelands were usurped. Despite their friendliness toward the early settlers and their assistance in establishing Marquette, their lifestyle did not mesh with that of the more industrious and profit-driven whites, and consequently, they were pushed to the community's margins, although perhaps partly by their own choice so they could maintain their traditional lifestyle.

By the 1860s, Kawbawgam and the other Native Americans had moved from the foot of what is today Baraga Avenue to Lighthouse Point and other outskirts of Marquette. Although the Ojibwa had always been nomadic by choice, the United States now sought to get them to settle on reservations and become farmers, and/or assimilate into white communities. Kawbawgam and Charlotte did become fairly sedentary, staying in the Marquette area the remainder of their lives. However, as we will see, they would relocate their home several times in the next few decades before permanently making their home at Presque Isle.

Chapter 5
Back at the Sault, 1846-1856

Iron mining spurred Marquette's rapid growth during the 1850s. As the riches from the mines became more important to US industry, a need arose to increase the speed and amount of ore shipped, so a canal was proposed at Sault Sainte Marie. This canal would not be possible without further encroachment upon Native American land; therefore, the 1855 Treaty of Detroit was signed, the last treaty to be made between the Ojibwa of Upper Michigan and the United States Government. Because the Sault was Kawbawgam's childhood home and where most of his family remained, and because the canal was vital to the iron industry, we will now return to the Sault to catch up on the events there that affected the Ojibwa during Marquette's infancy.

Changes at the Sault

Not long after Kawbawgam left the Sault, the Ojibwa's presence there became less dominant. By the late 1840s, many of the Ojibwa had left the Sault to live at Naomikong Point at the foot of Whitefish Bay so they could take advantage of working for the fishery that had been built there.[1] Because the Ojibwa had moved to the point, the Methodist mission also moved there, led by the Rev. Peter Marksman (Ma-dwa-gwun-a-yaush), an Ojibwa chief who had converted to Methodism.[2] This move resulted in a division among the Ojibwa who professed Christianity. The Protestant Ojibwa were now at Naomikong Point, while the Catholic Ojibwa, under Kawbawgam's stepfather, Chief Shawano, remained at the Sault.[3]

With the coming of the mining boom, the Sault changed dramatically. The copper and iron mines' need for ships and freight to expand their operations meant that freight had to pass through the Sault. The August 22, 1846 *Lake Superior Journal* printed the following description from the *Cleveland Herald* of how the Sault had changed in recent years, including for the Ojibwa:

> The contrast at the "Soo" now and several years ago is striking. Then, the ancient little village presented an almost antediluvian appearance, and the romantic scenery of the Sault had not been marred by the hand of enterprise and improvement. The Indian trader and Indian fisherman lived on as their fathers lived before them, and the bark huts and bark lodges were huddled together without much regard to streets or town regulations. Now the Indian lodges have mostly been driven out to the immediate vicinity of the foaming rapids—streets have been opened—docks built and large warehouses erected—comfortable dwellings, stores and commodious hotels have arisen—and the former Indian path across the portage has become a well-traveled road, on which new dwellings are springing up. Several buildings have been erected at the head of the portage, and a dock and warehouse are soon to be built. In addition to the new buildings now occupied at the "Soo", some twenty are now being constructed, and marked improvements have been made along the river below the town. Settlements have begun on Sugar Island, at the 'Sailor's Encampment', and a few other points before reaching the DeTour, and the primitive wildness of scenery has been broken by pioneer industry.[4]

Kawbawgam's Sister Lisette

In Marquette, Kawbawgam was doubtless aware of these changes from messages he would have received from relatives or by their visits. One wonders how often he also traveled back to the Sault. Did he make the journey in winter to witness the marriage of his sister Lisette (Elizabeth) to a white man? Lisette married John Logan Chipman on February 6, 1852 in Sault Sainte Marie.[5] At the time of the marriage, Chipman was twenty-one and Elizabeth sixteen. Chipman would later become a major Michigan politician, so it is worth looking briefly into his and Lisette's histories and marriage.

John Logan Chipman was born on June 5, 1830 in Detroit. His father, Henry C. Chipman, was a lawyer who served on the Supreme Court for the

Michigan Territory, and his grandfather, Nathaniel Chipman, had served as a senator from Vermont and was on the Vermont Supreme Court.[6] After attending public schools and the University of Michigan, at the young age of sixteen, Chipman was hired as an explorer for the Montreal Mining Company in the Lake Superior region. After five years in this role, he met Lisette at the Sault about 1851, and in 1852, they would be married. The details of their romance will be described below.

John Logan Chipman in his youth

In 1853, Chipman became an assistant clerk in the Michigan House of Representatives. However, he apparently remained in the Upper Peninsula because he then studied law and was admitted to the bar in 1854 while a resident of the Upper Peninsula. Not only did he practice law in the Lake Superior region (presumably at the Sault), but he became a candidate for public office while residing there and received practically all the votes in the Upper Peninsula, although votes cast elsewhere led to his defeat.[7]

Chipman also aided the US Government in making the Treaty of Detroit with the Native Americans at the Sault and in paying them their annuities. On the 1855 treaty, he is listed as "secretary."[8] In a collection of speeches given in Congress to honor Chipman following his death in 1893, and later published in 1895 as a monograph in the Congressional Series, his fellow Michigan congressman, Mr. Weadock, said of Chipman, "His experience and familiarity with the Indians gave Judge CHIPMAN a warm appreciation of the race, which he has always held and which he handsomely expressed in one of his finest speeches in Congress."[9]

In another memorial speech, Mr. McMillan of Michigan describes Chipman's early acquaintance with the Native Americans and then quotes a former speech Chipman had made:

> While yet a boy he left his studies to become an explorer in the wilds of the upper peninsula of Michigan; and from the free air of the pine forests and the invigorating breezes of the Great Lakes he drew those forces which so often controlled his life. For his forbears

he had perhaps a silent regard. For the wild life of the explorer and for such quiet as the camp fire brings, he had a fondness which made the memories of the darting canoe and the tangled forest the happiest of his life.

It was his intimate acquaintance with Indian life and history and his sympathy with the Indian in his present condition that made Judge CHIPMAN an effective and eloquent advocate in his behalf. In one of his speeches he thus forcibly stated the duty of the nation to its wards:

> I have known the Indians from my earliest youth. I have slept in their lodges; I have mixed with them as a friend. I have seen them fresh from the war dance, with the scalp still reeking with the blood undried upon its surface. I know them all. I know that of all the people on this continent they are more like the whites than any other. They are fond of this country; they are unplacable; they are haughty; they have a pride by birth; they have all the characteristics, and I must add that they have all the vices which grow out of, and are a part of, the nature of the white people. And, Mr. Chairman, it is because they are so like us that we have found it so extremely difficult to manage them and so difficult to subdue them.
>
> In my state, by the treaty of 1854,[a] in which I had the honor to take a part—a very humble part—we provided for dissolving the tribal relations and for the allotment of lands in severalty. That was the beginning of that plan of settling the Indian question with us; it has worked well. The Indian all over the northern country is a citizen. He is a voter, and in Michigan, Wisconsin, and Minnesota, the tribes who were parties to that treaty are, almost all of them, feeling all the good effects of it. I can say to the gentleman that they are increasing in number and are living a civilized life. They live the lives of agriculturists, lumbermen, and fishermen, and follow the pursuits which are followed by people of like opportunity and like pecuniary circumstances in the same country. They are a living example that the Indian condition

a. McMillan is likely referring to the 1855 Treaty of Detroit, which will be discussed shortly. Interestingly, Chipman's brother-in-law, Kawbawgam, was among the chiefs who signed this treaty.

> may be changed, for I have seen the fathers of these very people, wearing war paint on their faces and scalp locks on their heads, indulging in all the horrid orgies of striking the post, and singing their songs of triumph over enemies they had just killed or tortured. The children of these very people have made their progress, and to say that the humane influence of education and religion persistently pursued will not better the conditions of a people is simply to ignore the providence of God and to deny the progress which has been made on this continent.[10]

It is worth noting that Chipman's statement that the Native Americans are more like the whites than any other race on the continent is a veiled reference to African-Americans and perhaps the few Asians on the continent at the time whom Chipman obviously thought inferior to both the whites and the Native Americans. One also has to wonder just where he saw Native Americans engaging in warfare since no such battles are known to have occurred in Michigan in the 1850s or later—perhaps he was exaggerating by playing upon Native American stereotypes to bolster his argument of how much the Native Americas had progressed in such a short time. It is also noteworthy that in his speech, while he talks about how intimately he has known the Native Americans, he does not mention that he married one.[b] Nor do any of the memorial speeches mention his marriage. All that said, Chipman was obviously a great friend to the people he mixed his blood with, and he sought their best interests, even if they were countered by his white man thinking. The date of this speech is unknown, but it would have been made during his time in Congress from 1887 to 1893, by which time Native Americans had largely assimilated—a time period roughly forty years after Chipman had himself lived at the Sault.

We know next to nothing about Lisette's married life with Chipman other than the births of her children. In 1856, she gave birth to a son Henry, who would have been named for his paternal grandfather. Like his father, Henry would grow up to be an attorney in Detroit. In fact, soon after his birth, in 1857, the family left the Upper Peninsula for Detroit where Chipman became city attorney from 1857 to 1860. Next came a daughter Elizabeth, named for her mother and known in the family as "Lizzie." She was born circa 1858 and would marry Henry C. Buhl of Detroit. Another son,

b. I have not read all of Chipman's speeches or been able to locate them, but he seems to have been walking a fine line not to reveal his own personal interest in the matter.

Edmund, arrived about 1863. He also would grow up to be a lawyer. Finally, on April 21, 1864, Lisette gave birth to Charlotte, who was likely named for her grandmother, Charlotte Sayre (Kawbawgam's mother), although Lisette also had an older sister, Charlotte (b. circa 1828)[11] and, of course, the baby had an aunt Charlotte in Charlotte Kawbawgam, so Charlotte was obviously a popular family name. Unfortunately, Lisette died soon after on July 2, 1864 in Detroit,[12] when her last child was just a little more than two months old. Another source says the Chipmans had a daughter born in the early 1850s, a son Henry born in 1856, and a daughter born in 1858.[13] Still yet another source claims they had five children: Harry, b. 1855, Henry b. 1856, Lizzie b. 1862, Edmund b. 1863, and Charlotte b. 1864.[14] This information all comes from genealogy websites, none of which contain further information about the children. I have been unable to determine the accuracy of these statements or any additional details about the children.

After Lisette's death, Chipman married again, this time to a white woman,[c] while also staying busy raising his children and continuing his political career. In 1865 and 1866, he was a member of the Michigan House of Representatives for the First District of Wayne County. In 1866, he lost an election as Democratic Candidate for the US House of Representatives for Michigan's 1st congressional district. He then served as attorney of the Detroit police board from 1867 to 1879. Next, he was elected judge of the superior court of Detroit on May 1, 1879. He was reelected in 1885 and resigned in 1887 following his election to the Fiftieth Congress as a member of the United States House of Representatives for Michigan, a position he would be reelected to three times and serve in until his death of pneumonia in Detroit on August 17, 1893.[15]

John Logan Chipman while a Congressman

While Chipman's speeches in Congress may not have blatantly mentioned his Native American marriage, his obituary in the Sault Sainte Marie *Democrat* did not shy away from the issue. On August 19, 1893, it ran the following:

---

c. I have been unable to determine the second wife's identity, which suggests Chipman did not have children with her and she may have also predeceased him.

A SOO ROMANCE

Death of J. Logan Chipman Revives His Career Here

MARRIED AN INDIAN PRINCESS

Then He Civilized and Educated Her and was Happy

The late Detroit Congressman Dedicated the Chippewa County Court House and was a Factor Here in the Early Days

Congressman J. Logan Chipman of Detroit, a brother-in-law of Edward and Louis Shawano, of this city, and John Roussain, of Sugar Island, died in Detroit at 7 o'clock Thursday morning, of hypostatic pneumonia. While Judge Chipman had been ailing for some time his death was not expected....

In 1851 he became engaged to a charming young lady in the Soo, a member of one of the first and best-to-do-families. They fell out in some way and the young lady bestowed her smiles on an officer at Fort Brady. This enraged Chipman and he almost at once sought the hand of Lizzie Shawano, the full blooded Indian daughter of the head chief of the Chippewa. The wooing was swift and they were wed. Lizzie is spoken of as a beautiful Indian girl. She left here with her gay young husband to go to Detroit attired in her Indian garb, with her hair hanging in a glossy plait down her back and her head covered with a government blanket. At first Chipman's refined mother and sisters were greatly shocked, but they sensibly made the best of the occasion and at once proceeded to civilize and educate the young princess, ala Pocahontas. When she came to the Soo in later years the Indian wife is spoken of as having been as fine a lady as the land afforded. Four children were born to this union and the marriage was a happy one. Then the Chippewa princess died. Of her children who still live Harry Chipman, the Detroit Lawyer, is the "John Randolph, of Roanoke."[d] Another child, and the only daughter, married into the family of Buhl, the wealthy Detroit furrier. J. Logan Chipman mourned his wife for a time and then married again—a white woman....

---

d. This is a reference to the prominent Randolph family of Virginia being descended from Pocahontas. (President Thomas Jefferson's mother was a Randolph.) The article implies Lisette was a northern Pocahontas and the ancestor of an equally illustrious Michigan family.

> John Logan Chipman was born at Detroit, June 5, 1830, and was educated in the schools of that city and in the University of Michigan. He comes from a celebrated family, being the son of Judge Henry Chipman, a well-known and honoured name in Detroit history and a grandson of United States Judge and Senator Nathaniel Chipman, of Vermont. His mother was a South Carolinian, from whom he takes his middle name.[16]

The *Democrat* may have made a mistake in saying Elizabeth (Mrs. Buhl) was the only daughter since it mentions four children and Charlotte was believed to be the youngest; the article only names Elizabeth and Harry, but not Edmund or Charlotte.

Chipman and Lisette's courtship was common knowledge at the time. Mrs. Juliette Starr Dana, who made a tour of the Great Lakes in 1852, met Chipman at Eagle River, by whom she and her traveling companions were "very polited [sic] treated." She described him as "a Mr. Chipman, a young lawyer of Detroit, who in a fit of despair on being refused by the parents of a lady to whom he was very much attached married a full blooded squaw."[17]

An article recalling the Sault's past mentions that Chipman visited Lizzie one Saturday evening and convinced her to be his wife, then went to find a parson to perform the ceremony at once. He found the Methodist minister, whom the article's author believed was the Rev. Pitezel. The minister tried to convince him that such a marriage would lead to lifelong regret. Chipman replied, "I asked you to marry me, not to advise me, and if you will not, someone else will." Seeing that reasoning with Chipman was useless, the parson then performed the ceremony. Mr. and Mrs. Chipman then lived for a while with Chief Shawano on his island. Chipman made a stir the next day when he attended the Baptist mission and a general of the army passed around a slip of paper among the choir members that said, "Chip has married the chief's daughter." Apparently others showed regret for his hasty action, but he stood by his wife. He also seemed to be helpful to his in-laws, including helping his brother-in-law, Edward Oshawano, with educational opportunities.[18]

That Kawbawgam's brother-in-law became a US congressman seems very significant. We do not know how well-known it was, once Chipman became a politician, that his wife was an Ojibwa, but the marriage certainly influenced him in his support of Native Americans. It is possible that his wife's early death helped him politically by whitewashing his past a bit. Little is known about his children. Did they try to pass as white? They may have, given that his sons became lawyers.

It is also not known what, if any, contact the Kawbawgams had with the Chipmans once they moved to Detroit. It seems unlikely the families stayed in touch, especially after Lisette's death and since the Kawbawgams did not write or speak English. However, as we will see, Chipman stayed in touch with his brother-in-law Edward Oshawano.

The Sault Canal

Sault Sainte Marie had been the gateway to Lake Superior since prehistoric times, but only after Upper Michigan's mineral riches came into high demand did being able to travel swiftly and easily from Lake Superior to the lower Great Lakes become a priority. Because of the St. Mary's River's falls that connected Lake Superior to Lake Huron, ships could not travel safely from one lake to the other. In the past, French voyageurs had portaged their vessels to avoid the rapids. Then in 1796-1798, the Hudson's Bay Company constructed a sluiceway for the passage of loaded batteaux around the falls of St. Mary's with a gradual incline to a lift lock. This lock would be destroyed in 1814 during the War of 1812. Plans by the Americans to build a new canal and lock at the Sault were continually delayed in the decades that followed. It didn't help that in August 1838, the Native Americans protested a proposed canal.[19] Fort Brady closed at the Sault following the end of the Mexican War in 1848, but a threat of Native American hostilities at the Sault caused it to reopen in 1849. That threat may have been due to removal threats and the proposed building of the canal.[20] Once mining began in Upper Michigan in the 1840s, it became clear the canal would be vital for business, so the Natives' objections were ignored. In 1848, when a survey for the canal was made, Chief Shawano led a delegation to Washington, DC to ensure his people's title to the local rapids fishery be recognized under the 1820 and 1836 treaties.[21] It is possible, but probably unlikely, that Kawbawgam joined this delegation since he was probably in Marquette by then.

For years, those in favor of the canal had tried to rally support for it in Washington, DC. Their efforts paid off on August 26, 1852 when a bill was signed into law granting Michigan 750,000 acres of federal land to help finance the canal's construction and the use of government land for the canal. In January 1853, the Michigan Legislature approved a canal bill for two tandem locks, each 70 x 350-feet long, with nine-foot lifts. The law required that the canal be completed within two years.[22]

Charles Harvey, the general manager for the canal project, now set about moving the Ojibwa from the land needed for the canal. He went to each log cabin and paid its occupants ten to fifteen dollars per cabin. He told the occupants they must leave the area in twenty-four hours. Chief Shegud protested this action as a violation of the treaties since the land wanted for the canal had previously been set aside as reservation land. He also eloquently pled for the observance of the 1820 and 1836 treaties so that the Native American cemetery would not be disturbed.[23] Regardless, when the first shaft for the locks was dug in July 1853, the Indian graves were desecrated. The dead were dug up and their bones flung into muddy pits.[24] An article written in 1899 by Mrs. Thomas D. Gilbert recalled this event, saying:

> The first shaft of the first canal, was sunk right down through their bones, to the great distress of the surviving Indians, to whom the spot had been reserved forver [sic] by treaty with the government. Another chief, Shegud, a man of noble presence of unusually intelligent mind, of great oratorical power, eloquent, impassioned in speech, on that sorrowful day when he saw the first shaft sunk went to the missionary, who was also his pastor, and in never to be forgotten words expressing his deep feeling, asked if Mr. Bingham

The Soo Locks, circa 1865. Native American houses and fishing sheds can be seen filling the space between the locks. The insert photo is of Charles Harvey, head of the canal project.

would go with him to the "great father at Washington" to remonstrate against the desecration, and claim fulfillment of government promise. The matter was thoroughly discussed, and unjust as it seemed, it was decided protest was useless. The car of progress, like the car of Juggernaut, does not pause or turn aside in its relentless march, lest dead men's bones be crushed, or living hearts be broken. The saddest face I ever saw, was the dark face of that native nobleman as he yielded to the inevitable.[25]

Despite these actions, many Native Americans remained in the area, living beside the locks. It wouldn't be until the fall of 1884 that the last Native American homes were moved from the site.[26]

The two-year deadline for the canal was met, and on June 18, 1855, the first steamer sailed through the locks.[27] Shipment of iron ore from Marquette to the lower Great Lakes would now be much faster.

Threat of Removal

While the Ojibwa were watching their former lands, and even their sacred graveyard, being decimated by the canal's construction, they were also facing threats of removal to Minnesota or farther west. After the 1842 treaty was signed, which ceded the western half of Upper Michigan and northern Wisconsin to the United States, the American Fur Company tried to encourage the Native Americans to move to Minnesota. The government also continued its threats of removal. In its May 22, 1850 issue, the *Lake Superior Journal* argued that the agitation for removal of Native Americans was clearly led by the American Fur Company in its efforts to dominate the Indian trade.

Frederic Baraga, first Bishop of the Marquette Diocese, known as "The Snowshoe Priest." People remarked that he grew to resemble the Native Americans he served.

Both Methodist minister John Pitezel and Catholic priest Frederic Baraga protested removal as did many other whites. In L'Anse, the Ojibwa had Father Baraga purchase land for them so they could remain in the area. Whites in the L'Anse area also supported allowing the Native Americans to remain because they needed workers to help with the large potato crops. Some Native Americans hired lawyers to take their case to Washington, DC. Despite these efforts, US President Zachary Taylor signed a removal order on July 7, 1850, just two days before his death. Fortunately, Taylor's death led to a temporary suspension of the removal order. His successor President Millard Filmore did not reinstate the order, and by 1853, President Franklin Pierce had veered away from removal.[28]

In 1853, the Michigan legislature passed a joint resolution of Congress in favor of allowing the Native Americans to remain.[29] By this point, arguments were being made that the Ojibwa at L'Anse, who numbered about 600 within two villages and who had houses, a church, and a school, had assimilated to white men's ways. The Ojibwa there had learned to farm and they understood the value of money and property. Many had abandoned their traditional costumes for American clothing, and they were even learning to read and write in both English and Ojibwa.[30] Throughout the Upper Peninsula, the threat of removal caused not only the Ojibwa to protest, but many whites, including missionaries and newspaper editors.[31] The German visitor Johann Georg Kohl noted during his 1855 visit to Upper Michigan that when earlier reports had circulated that the Ojibwa would be removed, many on the south shore of Lake Superior had packed up their belongings and moved to the Canadian shore rather than leave the Great Lake.[32]

To settle the removal question, in 1854, two US commissioners met with the Lake Superior Ojibwa at La Pointe and signed a treaty in which the Ojibwa ceded their land claims in Minnesota in exchange for lands in Michigan. The Ojibwa from L'Anse, Lac Vieux Desert, and Ontonagon were involved in this treaty. The government also promised to pay annuities, provide equipment for agricultural improvements and clothing, and send the Ojibwa a blacksmith and an assistant to help them.[33]

1855 Treaty of Detroit

In 1855, to settle any outstanding claims of Michigan's Native Americans against the United States Government, Indian Commissioner George W. Manypenny and Indian Agent Henry C. Gilbert met with Native American leaders in Detroit. John McDougall Johnston, brother of Jane Johnston Schoolcraft, was the meeting's official interpreter.[34] While the result of this meeting is usually referred to as the Treaty of Detroit, in fact three treaties were signed at Detroit in July and August of that year. The first was signed by the Ojibwa and Ottawa, the second by the Ojibwa at the Sault, and the third by the Ojibwa who resided at Saginaw in Lower Michigan.

The first treaty was quite lengthy and contained specific listings of land allotments to various groups of Native Americans in Michigan, including at the Sault. It also canceled out all the former treaties made with the Ojibwa and Ottawa.[35] Below are a few paragraphs from the first treaty specific to the Native Americans at the Sault, which follow the treaty's land allotment discussion:

> Should either of the bands residing near Sault Ste.; Marie determine to locate near the lands owned by the missionary society of the Methodist Episcopal Church at Iroquois Point, in addition to those who now reside there, it is agreed that the United States will purchase as much of said lands for the use of the Indians as the society may be willing to sell at the usual Government price.
>
> The United States will give to each Ottawa and Chippewa Indian being the head of a family, 80 acres of land, and to each single person over twenty-one years of age, 40 acres of land, and to each family of orphan children under twenty-one years of age containing two or more persons, 80 acres of land, and to each single orphan child under twenty-one years of age, 40 acres of land to be selected and located within the several tracts of land herein before described, under the following rules and regulations:
>
> Each Indian entitled to land under this article may make his own selection of any land within the tract reserved herein for the band to which he may belong—Provided, That in case of two or more Indians claiming the same lot or tract of land, the matter shall be referred to the Indian agent, who shall examine the case and decide between the parties.
>
> For the purpose of determining who may be entitled to land under the provisions of this article, lists shall be prepared by the Indian agent, which lists shall contain the names of all those persons entitled, designating them in four classes. Class 1st, shall contain the names of heads of families; class 2d, the names of single persons over twenty-one years of age; class 3d, the names of orphan children under twenty-one years of age, comprising families of two or more persons, and class 4th, the names of single orphan children under twenty-one years of age, and no person shall be entered in more than one class. Such lists shall be made and closed by the first day of July, 1856, and thereafter no applications for the benefits of this article will be allowed.

> At any time within five years after the completion of the lists, selections of lands may be made by the persons entitled thereto, and a notice thereof, with a description of the land selected, filed in the office of the Indian agent in Detroit, to be by him transmitted to the Office of Indian Affairs at Washington City.[36]

The second treaty, because it concerned Kawbawgam's relatives specifically, is given in its entirety below:

At the City of Detroit
in the State of Michigan
Treaty with the Chippewa of Sault Ste. Marie

Articles of agreement made and concluded at the city of Detroit, in the State of Michigan, the second day of August, 1855, between George W. Manypenny and Henry C. Gilbert, commissioners on the part of the United States, and the Chippewa Indians of Sault Ste. Marie.

> ARTICLE 1. The said Chippewa Indians surrender to the United States the right of fishing at the falls of the St. Mary's and of encampment, convenient to the fishing-ground, secured to them by the treaty of June 16, 1820.
>
> ARTICLE 2. The United States will appoint a commissioner who shall, within six months after the ratification of this treaty, personally visit and examine the said fishery and place of encampment, and determine the value of the interest of the Indians therein as the same originally existed. His award shall be reported to the President, and shall be final and conclusive, and the amount awarded shall be paid to said Indians, as annuities are paid, and shall be received by them in full satisfaction for the right hereby surrendered: *Provided*, That one third of said award shall, if the Indians desire it, be paid to such of their half-breed relations as they may indicate.
>
> ARTICLE 3. The United States also give to the chief, O-shaw-waw-no, for his own use, in fee-simple, a small island in the river St. Mary's, adjacent to the camping-ground hereby surrendered, being the same island[e] on which he is now encamped, and said to contain less than half an acre: *Provided*, That the same has not been heretofore otherwise appropriated or disposed of; and in such case, this grant is to be void, and no compensation is to be claimed by said chief or any of the Indians, parties hereto, in lieu thereof.

e. This was "island No. 5," later known as Oshawano Island (Hearings p. 576).

ARTICLE 4. This agreement shall be obligatory and binding on the contracting parties as soon as the same shall be ratified by the President and Senate of the United States. In testimony whereof, the said George W. Manypenny and the said Henry C. Gilbert, commissioners as aforesaid, and the undersigned chiefs and headmen of the Chippewa Indians of Sault Ste. Marie, have hereto set their hands and seals at the city of Detroit the day and year first above written.[37]

Most noteworthy is that this treaty overturned the 1820 treaty and left the Ojibwa with no fishing rights in the St. Mary's River, which had provided them with livelihood and sustenance for centuries. It is not surprising, however, since the Ojibwa had already been thrown out of their lands to build the canal. In the third article, the chief referred to is Shawano, Kawbawgam's stepfather. The small island he received was across from the Ojibwa's former encampment on the mainland. One wonders whether Shawano tried illegally to fish from his island. He would be the last permanent chief to make his home at the rapids.[38] Some sources add that it was stipulated in the treaty (though it wasn't but may have been by some other private agreement) that Shawano would be succeeded by his son Edward (Kawbawgam's half-brother); consequently, Edward, who was seventeen at the time of the treaty, was to be educated at government expense.[39] Mrs. Thomas D. Gilbert, who remembered Edward from his youth stated that he attended the boarding school of the Baptist mission of the Sault with his brother (which one is unknown) and that she remembered him as "a bright and promising youth, capable, ambitious, and proud, feeling his own capacity and his position as 'crown prince;' but the circumstances of life were against him."[40] What happened with Edward's education will be discussed in Chapter 7.

An article written years later describes a visit paid by some white Americans to Shawano near the end of his life on his island. One of the party had once been a young girl whose parents he had known. Shawano had attended religious services at her father's mission, so on this visit, she sung an old hymn in his language for him. The article asks when these visitors departed, "What were his thoughts? Were these his guests, his friends or his foes? Was he glad that he stood there in the sunset of his life and of his race? And was there a crown for that noble head waiting in the 'happy hunting grounds' beyond the glowing sunset?" Interestingly, the article also describes him as a "grand old man" with a "Websterian head and iron grey hair, hat in hand, kingly in manner."[41] Later, we will see his stepson, Kawbawgam, also described as an Ojibwa version of Daniel Webster.

The land granted to Shawano may have partly been compensation for how the canal had made refugees of Shawano's band of Ojibwa at the Sault when their homes had been bought up by Harvey. However, the treaty also made it clear that the Ojibwa were no longer welcome along the canal or to fish in the rapids—in other words, they were not wanted in town or as part of the white civilization. The Ojibwa were given land allotments because the United States wanted them in one place, and for their migrant bands to be disbanded.[42] However, Indian Commissioner Manypenny's allotment scheme was ill-advised and poorly executed. It ran counter to Ojibwa tradition since the Ojibwa didn't see land as property one could own. Nor could they, as the government desired, become self-sufficient farmers when the land they were given had poor soil and Upper Michigan's short growing season did not make farming practical.[43]

The allotment turned out to be a bureaucratic disaster. The selection lists were made and canceled at least four times. Certificates were not issued when scheduled, and the first patents were not sent to the individual Native Americans until 1873—eighteen years after the treaty! The good land at the Hay Lake Reserve was discovered to have been taken by land speculators just days before the treaty was signed. The rest of the land was swampland or open water, which meant there was not enough land to accommodate all six Ojibwa bands at the Sault. Chiefs Shawan and Shawano then collected annuity payments from individual members of their bands so they could purchase land for them; however, the government soon condemned the land purchased for non-payment of taxes, leaving the two bands homeless. Meanwhile, the other four bands acquired land allotments at Iroquois Point; they would eventually become the Bay Mills reservation. In 1871, Chief Shawan asked the chiefs of the four bands to allow his band to settle with them, which they agreed to; consequently, five of the six bands would become part of what is today the Bay Mills Indian Community. Shawano's band, however, remained homeless.[44]

A party from the Sault traveled to Detroit to sign the treaties, including Chief Shawano and Kawbawgam (still apparently involved in Sault and clan politics despite his move to Marquette; the trip would be the longest recorded one of his life). Shawano is listed first as O-shaw-waw-no-ke-wain-ze, a chief, and Kawbawgam is listed by his real name, Naw-o-ge-zhick, as a headman.

The full list of signers from the Sault follows. The L. S. after their names likely designates them as being from the Lake Superior region.

> O-shaw-waw-no-ke-wain-ze, chief, his x mark. [L. S.]
> Waw-bo-jieg, chief, his x mark. [L. S.]
> Kay-bay-no-din, chief, his x mark. [L. S.]
> O-maw-no-maw-ne, chief, his x mark. [L. S.]
> Shaw-wan, chief, his x mark. [L. S.]
> Pi-aw-be-daw-sung, chief, his x mark. [L. S.] (Marji-Gesick's brother)
> Waw-we-gun, headman, his x mark. [L. S.]
> Pa-ne-gwon, headman, his x mark. [L. S.]
> Bwan, headman, his x mark. [L. S.]
> Taw-meece, headman, his x mark. [L. S.]
> Naw-o-ge-zhick, headman, his x mark. [L. S.]
> Saw-gaw-giew, headman, his x mark. [L. S.]

Kawbawgam's brother-in-law John Logan Chipman is listed as secretary on the treaty and John M. Johnston and George Johnston are listed among the interpreters.[45] The treaty was signed on July 31, 1855.

Life definitely changed for the Ojibwa after the canal and the treaty. In 1856, Manypenny, still commissioner of American Indian Affairs, wanted to encourage Native Americans to build houses. He believed in developing "civilized" habits in the Native Americans so he gave them all a house and "a good cook stove with cooking utensils, a table, bureau, chairs, bedstead, looking glass, and many smaller articles."[46] Manypenny may have had good intentions, but assimilation was only good from the white Americans' perspective. Native Americans no longer had any choice but to assimilate.

Nor did the government keep its promises to the Native Americans. Just before the twentieth century began, the Ottawa and Ojibwa descendants sued the federal government for money still owed them from the 1855 treaties. The US Court of Claims sided with the Native Americans, but in order to distribute the money owed, a census was required to determine who should benefit. As a result, in 1908, the Durant Roll of Native American descendants was made—an important genealogical document today and evidence that the US government could not follow through on its promises in a timely manner. During this time, Native Americans were basically wards of the government. They remained so until 1924 when the Indian Citizenship Act went into effect. Then the impoverished Native Americans were declared citizens,

Johann Georg Kohl

which basically meant since they were no longer wards, they had to fend for themselves.[47]

As previously noted, German writer Johann Georg Kohl lived among the Lake Superior Ojibwa for six months in the time leading up to the signing of the 1855 Treaty of Detroit. In his book *Kitchi-Gami: Life Among the Lake Superior Ojibway*, he captured the sentiments of several of the Ojibwa about the changes they had experienced in recent years. While Kohl was visiting the Ojibwa at La Pointe, American agents arrived there to begin political discussions with them. Everything the Ojibwa said was translated by government interpreters. Following is how one Ojibwa man responded to the agents at this meeting.

> "When the white men first came into this country and discovered us, we received them hospitably, and if they were hungry, we fed them, and went hunting for them. At first the white men only asked for furs and skins. I have heard from our old men that they never asked for anything else. These we gave them gladly, and received from them their iron goods, guns, and powder.
>
> "But for some years they have been asking land from us. For ten years they have asked from us nothing but land, and ever more land. We give unwillingly the land in which the graves of our fathers rest. But for all that we have given land in our generosity. We knew not that we were giving so much for so little. We did not know that such great treasures of copper were hidden in our land.
>
> "The white men have grown rich by the bargain. When I look round me in this assembly, I notice rich golden watch-chains and golden rings on the clothes and fingers of many men; and when I look in the faces of the people who are so richly adorned, I always see that their colour is white, and not red. Among the red men I never see anything of the sort! They are all so poorly clad! They are miserably poor! How poor they are, I must request you to judge by personal inspection. I have brought some of our poor sufferers here, that you may see them. There they come! There they are! How wretched do they look!"
>
> (At this passage of the speech a number of old wrinkled squaws and children clothed in rags pressed forward to heighten the effect.

They certainly looked wretched enough; but, although we could all see this, the speaker described their scanty clothing, their thin and bowed forms copiously, and then proceeded:)

"And through whom have they fallen into this lamentable condition? You have become rich through us, and these have grown poor through you. Your golden chains, your dollars, and all you brag of, have been taken from them and from us. We promised thee"—the speaker here turned to the chief American official—"that we would open our ears to what thou wouldst say to us, and keep it in our heads; but now thou shouldst hear what we say to thee, and keep it in thy head!

"We are not only poor, but we have also debts. At least, people say that we have debts. On the former treaty and payment we also paid debts. I fancied then we paid them all. But now the old question is addressed to us. A number of old things are brought against us from an old bag. Where these debts come from, I know not. Perhaps from the water!" (I must here remind the reader that the Ojibbeways transfer the evil principle to the depths of the lake.)

"But you say we have debts. It may be that we have them. We must pay these debts. The just and recognised debts we will pay. But the question is, how? On other treaties and payments the whole of our debts were taken in a lump from the moneys coming to us, and the rest divided among us. This is not good. I say, it is better and more just that each man should receive his full payment, and settle for himself with his creditors. Each knows best for himself what he owes. I know exactly what I owe, and will pay it. But I do not wish that the innocent, and these our poor, should suffer by the deduction of these debts from the total sums belonging to the tribe. That is my opinion. And I speak not only for myself, but also for the majority of the chiefs and for the young men, and for these poor widows, orphans, and sick!

"Our debts we will pay. But our land we will keep. As we have already given away so much, we will, at least, keep that land you have left us, and which is reserved for us. Answer us, if thou canst, this question. Assure us, if thou canst, that this piece of land, reserved for us, will really always be left to us. Tell me if you and we shall live in friendship near each other, and that you will never ask this land from us. Canst thou promise this? That is what I wished

> to ask of thee. That is all I have to say. But no! I have still one thing. The chiefs, my brothers, have commisioned [sic] me to mention one point more, and lay another question before thee. It would be unjust of me not to speak it out openly. If I kept it to myself, it would be a heavy burden upon me. It would weigh on my breast. It would terrify me in my dreams. Father, thou knowest we are glad to see thee here. We salute thee with joy. Thou hast said that thou camest to us in friendship and kindness. We received thee here in the same way. We wish, therefore, to place confidence in thee, and not to speak to thee with a forked tongue. We will speak to thee with a simple tongue. We wish to lay before thee not only our thanks but our grievances.
>
> "Father, the point is this. In our former treaties—yes, in all former treaties—it was settled that a certain sum should be deducted from our tribute for blacksmiths' shops, schools, and other establishments among us. We have *heard* of those moneys. But we have *seen* nothing of these works. They have not come to us. We know not where those moneys are gone, or where they went off in smoke. We beg thee, examine into this closely. This we beg thee much. I could say much more on this point. But I will now sit down. For I am not accustomed to wear these new Europeans trousers which have been given me, or to stand long in them. They annoy me. Hence I will cease to speak and seat myself."[48]

Kohl goes on to say that with this comical turn the speaker sat down and was applauded. Today, rather than applaud, we are more likely to weep over these words.

Toward the end of Kohl's visit to Lake Superior, he traveled to Sault Sainte Marie. There he spoke to an elderly Ojibwa woman known as Old Aurora, who summarized Ojibwa history for him. She begins her history by stating:

> "Ah!" old Aurora, La Rose's mother, said to me, with a sigh, this morning, when I called once again to listen to her stories—"ah!" she said, "my head has grown quite weak lately. I have lost my memory. The Ojibbeways have all lost their memory. The Americans have made them weak. Our people do not talk so much about their own affairs now as they used to do. They no longer feel the same pleasure in telling the old stories, and they are being forgotten, and the traditions and fables rooted out. You often ask after them, but you seldom find any one who can give you the right answer. Our nation

is fallen; and this came quite suddenly, since the Kitchimokomans, or 'Long-knives,' entered our country."[49]

The Long-knives was an Ojibwa name for the Americans. Kohl goes on to discuss how he has heard the Ojibwa were largely free and independent under the French and British, but not under the Americans. Then he shares how Old Aurora told him more of the old times in broken Canadian-French, ending with the time when the Americans gained power as a result of the War of 1812 and how times have changed in the four decades since then.

> "When the English were at war with the Americans (1812-1814), the savages were almost as kindly disposed to the former, their old friends, as before to the French, and they helped the English, and stood up for them, and sent their braves to help them against the Long-knives. When the English made a peace with them, and gave up to them the whole southern half of Lake Superior, the savages[f] would not hear of it, and still lived for a long time in good friendship with the English, and were, from ten to twenty years, as independent on the lake almost as they had been before.
>
> "Now, however, since the copper mines have been discovered, and the great steamers have appeared on the lake, and since the canal has been dug, which brings their ships easily from Huron Lake into our waters, and that all the men have come to seek copper, and look at our lake, it has all been over with the Ojibbeways. Their strength is broken, and they have lost their memory. Their tribes have melted away, their chiefs have no voice in the council. Their wise men and priests have no longer good dreams, and the old squaws forget their good stories and fables."[50]

Kohl concludes his book by describing how he said his goodbyes as he left Lake Superior:

> I bade adieu to many worthy men—perhaps for ever.... Rapidly disappearing nations remained behind me, whom I shall never see

f. It seems unlikely Aurora would refer to her people as "savages." However, as Kohl notes, she spoke in Canadian-French. Kohl wrote his book in German and it was later translated into English. He may have known French well enough to follow what Aurora told him, although with most of the Ojibwa he spoke to, he had an interpreter who translated Ojibwa into English for him. Kohl then wrote his experiences in German, and eventually his German book was translated into English, so it is hard to know what has been lost in the multiple translations concerning specific word choices and meanings.

again, and who yet appeared to me so deserving of a thorough study, when I had myself scarce laid my fingers' ends on them. Hundreds of questions crossed my brain, which—had not the last grain of sand fallen in my hour-glass—I should have wished to propose to the willing echo of the lake, and reap copious replies. I felt like the poet when he described Hiawatha's departure:

And I said : Farewell for ever!
Said : Farewell, O Hiawatha!
And the forests dark and lonely,
Moved through all their depths of darkness,
Sighed : Farewell, O Hiawatha![51]

Longfellow's *The Song of Hiawatha* would not be published until November 10, 1855, a few months after Kohl left, so these thoughts actually came to him after his departure and he is just adding emotion to the scene. However, the poem's success would cause the Ojibwa and the Upper Peninsula to be seen through Longfellow's eyes by many visitors in the years to come. And even Kohl, who no doubt mourns the disappearing Ojibwa way of life, in the end chooses to romanticize the Ojibwa and see only what he wants by doing so.

The year 1855 marks three significant events that one might say closed the curtain upon the Ojibwa's traditional way of life: the opening of the Sault Canal, the Treaty of Detroit in which they ceded the last of their lands in Upper Michigan, and the publication of *The Song of Hiawatha*, for now that the Ojibwa were no longer a threat to the United States' growth, it was safe for Americans to romanticize them. Their old way of life was now over. From 1855 on, the Ojibwa would reside on reservations or on the fringes of Upper Peninsula communities. They would be viewed as curiosities by tourists and often seen as pests and undesirable by the white Americans they lived among. Their leaders, including Chief Kawbawgam, as we shall see, would have to master the art of diplomacy to maintain good relations with the whites; the Ojibwa did this by fitting into the white stereotype of the "good Indian"—one who assimilated to white ways, did not break the law or get drunk, and altogether, did not cause any trouble for whites. It was the only way they could ensure their people's survival in a now dominant white American world.

Chapter 6
Jacques LePique

So far, Jacques LePique has only been briefly mentioned in these pages. However, he played a significant role in the Kawbawgams' lives for multiple reasons. He knew the Kawbawgams from their childhoods, he married Charlotte's half-sister Mary, and he and the Kawbawgams would later have their Ojibwa stories written down by Homer Kidder. Therefore, a biography of LePique, including his interactions with the Kawbawgams, will give us better insight into Kawbawgam's story and world. In many respects, LePique's life was more fascinating than Kawbawgam's, although LePique is not as well remembered since he has no visible monument like the Kawbawgams have at Presque Isle Park.

Jacques LePique

LePique was born in Manitoba in Cree Country about 1820, which makes him just a few years younger than Kawbawgam, and about eleven years older than Charlotte. His real name was Francis Nolin. His father, Louis Nolin, as previously related, was the man Philo Everett hired at the Sault to show him where the iron ore was in Marquette County. LePique's grandfather, Louis Nolin, Sr., had been an

Irish boy left as an orphan in France. He was adopted by a French couple who later left him their money. At that point, Louis Nolin emigrated to the Sault. Kawbawgam told Homer Kidder of Louis Nolin, Sr. that "the Ojibwas married him to a girl named Kitchi Agenayquay" (LePique's grandmother, Big Angeline). Kawbawgam goes on to say, "So he had brothers-in-law and they used [to] make up stories about him, as the Indians often do about their brothers-in-law."[1] This detail is important because Kawbawgam told a story to Homer Kidder in the 1890s about Louis Nolin, Sr., to whom the Ojibwa gave the name Kitchi-Nonan, meaning "the Great or Wise Nolin."[2] But with this statement, Kawbawgam was also poking fun at his own brother-in-law relationship with LePique, who was present when this remark was made. We will look more closely at the stories about Kitchi-Nonan and the other stories the Kawbawgams and LePique told to Kidder in Chapter 11. Characteristic stories about Louis Nolin, Sr. were also recorded by Henry Schoolcraft in his book *The Indian in His Wigwam or Characteristics of the Red Race in America.*[3] Schoolcraft would have personally known Louis Nolin, Sr. at the Sault.

Louis Nolin, Sr. and Big Angeline were the parents of Louis Nolin, Jr. who married Mary Adolph. Mary, like her husband, was half Native American and half European.[4] Louis Nolin, Jr. met his wife at the Sault, and then they immigrated to the Red River country, among the Crees, and later to the Black Hills of Dakota where LePique (Francis) was born at Blackstone Falls, a place LePique believed was in Montana.[5] One source says that besides being LePique's parents, the Nolins were also the parents of Louis, Louisa, Angeline, Joseph, and Moses;[6] another source says he had two sisters, one of whom was named Sophie.[7a] Like most Ojibwa, LePique had a nickname: Buk kaw kaw duz or Bakakadoose ("Skinny man" or "thin fellow").[8] Alfred Kidder, Sr. would later give him his French nickname Jacques LePique ("Jack of Spades" or "the Joker"). English speakers would corrupt it into Jack LaPete.

LePique's father was a trader during his youth, which explains the family's many moves. His father's trading would lead to the great adventure of LePique's life when he was twelve. He and his father journeyed to the Arctic to hunt for furs and walrus tusks to trade with the Hudson's Bay Company.[9]

---

a. If LePique had a sister named Sophie, she is not to be confused with the Sophie Nolin who married William Cameron, the lighthouse keeper at Grand Island, who was his cousin. Sophie Nolin Cameron told Lewis Henry Morgan that LePique was her "father's brother's son and she called him her brother." (Lewis Henry Morgan Journals, Vol. 2, p. 346).

When violent fighting broke out between the Cree and the Sioux, the Nolin family moved back to Red River and then lived at Pembanon until Jacques was thirteen. More fighting among the Native Americans caused them to move to Fond du Lac (modern-day Duluth, Minnesota). When Jacques was fourteen, they traveled east along Lake Superior to return to the Sault. They would migrate various places along Lake Superior's south shore in the years that followed.[10]

These migrations when Jacques was about fourteen resulted in his befriending Marji-Gesick and his daughter Charlotte and later Charles Kawbawgam. When the Nolin family were still in Fond du Lac, Louis Nolin, Jr. bought a large canoe, and the entire family paddled along the coastline to the Sault. Speaking of himself in third person, LePique recalled of this journey:

> One day as they passed Presque Isle, they saw a wigwam at the mouth of the Dead River, and going ashore, they found Matji-gijig [Marji-Gesick] sitting on a log on the beach, smoking his long pipe and painted up as if for some ceremony.
>
> "Well," said Jacques' father, "what are you doing today?"
>
> "Oh," replied Matji-gijig, "I am doing nothing today, for it is Sunday."
>
> "How do you know it is Sunday?"
>
> "Why, look around," said Matji-gijig. "See how clear and bright it is. There's not a cloud in the sky. So it must be Sunday."[11]

This brief anecdote is yet another example of Marji-Gesick's sense of humor. In the years that followed, LePique would get to know the chief well and eventually become his son-in-law. This was not his first meeting with Marji-Gesick, however, since he would later testify that he saw Charlotte as a papoose at Grand Island or the Sault (LePique gave two contradictory accounts of when he first saw Charlotte),[12] which would have been likely a couple of years before this incident, about 1831 or 1832.

During their first winter back at the Sault, the Nolins lived on the Canadian side with Michael Adolph, LePique's uncle. The next winter, they stayed on the American side. During that time, LePique first met Kawbawgam.[13] LePique stated: "That was when we lived at the Sault. Our house stood about half way along the canal and Kawbawgam's people lived on the point opposite a little island in the rapids."[14]

LePique later told Homer Kidder about a medicine man's visit during this time to Kawbawgam's mother when she was ill.

> That morning Kawbawgam and I were out in a canoe in the rapids, fishing for whitefish with a scoop net; and when we started ashore at noon, we saw that some Chippewas had camped near by. One of them was a young fellow about fifteen who had a red plume of hair fastened on his head. He went towards the point with a pole on his shoulder, and when we came along, he was fishing from the rocks. Another man in the party was an old Indian called by the French Shalot Toulouse. He was just going in to see Ka-ga-qua-dung (Kawbawgam's stepfather) [Shawano] and after talking a while he looked round and saw Kawbawgam's mother lying in the corner.
>
> He said: "Who is that? Who's that lying over there?"
>
> The Chief said: "That's my wife."
>
> "And what's the matter with her?"
>
> The chief said: "I'm afraid it's consumption. I don't know whether there's a remedy for that disease."
>
> "Well, I don't know," said Shalot. "I wish you'd go and give a pipe to that boy fishing on the point. That boy's a devil of a fellow." "Maybe," says he, "that boy can help her. Maybe he can do something for your wife."
>
> Well, Ka-ga-qua-dung took a pipe—the pipe of peace, we call it—filled it with Kinnikinnick and gave it to us to take it to the boy. So we went down on the rocks and offered it to him.
>
> He looked at us and said: "I don't know if I can accept that pipe, my friends, my time is not yet up," says he. "It's the Great Spirit himself that came to me in my dreams when I was fasting. Well, I'll take the pipe but I have no medicine rattle."
>
> I said, "We can make one in a few minutes." I was used to making them.
>
> So I went home and asked my father for a tin powder flask. He wanted to know what I was going to do with it and I told him that a medicine man was going to doctor the chief's wife. My father said he would come to see the performance.
>
> I went back and said to the boy, "What shall I put into the [cavity], shot or what?" "Oh no, nothing," said the boy. "You put a cork in the flask and raise it on a pole, and the Great Spirit above will put rattlers

> in it. Light a pipe when you get it up on a pole. If the rattlers come into the flask while I am smoking the pipe, we can cure the chief's woman. But I don't know, because my time was not to begin till I'm married and have one child." "But," says he, "we'll try anyway."
>
> The boy began to smoke and we no sooner raised the flask on the pole than we heard rattlers jingling in it. That was a miracle.
>
> "I will come this evening," said the boy. "You must get a white cloth for the place where the spirit lives is very clean. And I want two candles and a piece of blue ribbon about that long" (Jacques held his hands about a foot apart) "because the place where he lives is sky-blue, I want seven crackers and a little wine (about a pint) in a dish and also whiskey (less than a pint) in another dish."
>
> He said that when he came in the evening he would put into the whiskey-dish seven bones which he would bring himself.
>
> In the evening he came to operate. He began to tell about his (fasting?).[15]

Unfortunately, Kidder lost the pages of his manuscript that completed the story, but he remarked when editing the manuscript that "My recollection is that in the operation, the boy put in his mouth the little hollow bones which he had previously placed in the whiskey dish, and by applying them to the woman's body, sucked out the disease and cured her."[16] Kawbawgam's mother did survive. In fact, she would live until 1889.

The Nolin family next moved to Grand Island because the American Fur Company offered Louis Nolin, Jr. employment to run the trading post there. That next spring, LePique said the family went to the Sault with furs. During that visit, as he later told Kidder, he first saw Charlotte Kawbawgam as a baby on a cradle board.[17] This chronology, however, seems odd since this would be the spring of 1835 or 1836, by which time Charlotte would have been about five. LePique probably did not remember all these details accurately when he reported them to Homer Kidder, or he may have been born a few years earlier than 1820 or have been younger than thirteen when the family moved to the Sault. He also made another statement during Charlotte's court case against the Jackson Iron Company that makes it more likely that he first saw Charlotte at Grand Island and not on that particular visit to the Sault:

> I know [sic] Charlotte Ko-Bo-Gum. When she was tied to a board—a papoose, down at Grand Island, at Bay Furnace. Her mother Susan had a little camp built alongside of the hill. Margi was

a sort of sub-chief. Susan and Margi lived in the same camp together. Margi died in my boat, the next point above Presque Isle.

I was living with the tribe at Bay Furnace when Charlotte was a papoose. We had an American trading post there.[18]

The fur trading cabin of Abraham Williams, the first Euro-American settler at Grand Island, circa 1840s, now at the Alger County Historical Society. Louis Nolin, Jr., LePique's father, may have worked from a very similar cabin.

A métis named Dube, who was from Saginaw and president of another fur company, now convinced Louis Nolin, Jr. to leave the American Fur Company and keep his own trading post at Grand Island, which he did, resulting in the family remaining there for another couple of years. Then they returned to the Sault. After that, they moved from place to place for several years. In 1837, LePique's mother died, a date Jacques knew because it happened about the time he heard Queen Victoria had been crowned.[19b]

By this point, LePique was in his late teens and ready to set off on his own. He would work on several different schooners on the Great Lakes. In 1844, he decided to go with some other young men to Lake Huron around Alpena and Thunder Bay to hunt and trap for the winter. Then in the spring of 1845, they traveled to Detroit to sell their furs. There, LePique happened

b. Queen Victoria's coronation was June 28, 1838, a little over a year after William IV died and she became queen. Kidder says "crowned" but may mean simply that LePique heard Victoria had become queen in 1837.

to meet his father. His father introduced him to several men from the Jackson Iron Company's party who had been with him the year prior when he had helped Everett find the iron ore.[20]

LePique briefly returned to Thunder Bay, then went to the Sault where he again met men from the Jackson party. At this point, he joined the party and traveled on the *Independence* to the Dead River's mouth just north of where Marquette would be founded. They then canoed along the shore near Lighthouse Point where Prior's boathouse later stood (believed to be the foot of Marquette's Hewitt Avenue today).[21] Interestingly, Kawbawgam, according to LePique, was already camping at this spot, which means it was later than 1845 and probably 1847 or 1848. LePique stated, as previously noted, that Kawbawgam and three or four other Ojibwas were engaged by the Jackson Iron Company to cut a road to the mine and that Kawbawgam cut down the first tree.[22] While this is all very plausible, it is confusing since this would be a few years before Graveraet would have been involved with the Marquette Iron Company, yet Kawbawgam stated that he came to Marquette first with Graveraet, so LePique's recollection of when events happened may be off by a few years.

LePique was hired at this time to be a packer to carry pork over from the Dead River. He remained in the area for two or three months and then returned to the Sault in a bark canoe with John Roussau, a métis.[c]

By this point, LePique's father had died. LePique, now about twenty-five, was left to care for his orphaned siblings. He also wanted to go to Red River to look up some relatives. On the way there, he saw the *Michigan* in the harbor at La Pointe. On board was a métis lawyer, John Martel, who told him an Ojibwa delegation was headed to Washington, DC, to try to recover lands

Jacques LePique

c. Kidder says Roussau was a brother of Kawbawgam's sister (Kidder, *Ojibwa*, p. 146). However, Roussau was probably Kawbawgam's brother-in-law, John Roussain, and Kidder misunderstood LePique's explanation of the relationship. Kidder also got the spelling wrong based on LePique's correct pronunciation of the name since in French consonants at the end of words are usually not pronounced (Boyer, "Kawbawgam," p. 2).

about Lac de Flambeau that they wanted as a reservation. Martel persuaded LePique to join the delegation as an interpreter. After some traveling about, the delegation recruited fourteen members. Money, however, was not available for the journey, so when they arrived in St. Louis, Missouri, they rented a hall and performed Native American dances to raise money. They continued to give performances as they made their way down the Mississippi to New Orleans, then back up the river, and along the Ohio River to Cincinnati. From there, they took the stagecoach and boats to get to Pittsburgh, Philadelphia, Baltimore, and eventually, Washington, DC.[23]

Martel arranged an interview with US President James K. Polk and the Commissioner of Indian Affairs. First they went to the commissioner, who did not understand their requests and said he couldn't give them money to travel home, but he'd put in a good word for them with the president. Eventually, they were driven to the White House where they saw President Polk. LePique described the president as a little man in a stovepipe hat; however, he had expected to see a man with a crown and scepter.[24] After listening to them, President Polk told them they would need a petition to raise money to get back home. A petition was then drawn up and presented to Congress. Some members of the House of Representatives wanted to hear a talk about Indian affairs and how they were being treated so a Native American named Nigawnub gave a talk and LePique interpreted it before Congress. The next day, Congress voted that the delegation be given $5,000 to pay their travel expenses.[25]

James K. Polk, 11th President of the United States, 1845-1849

The delegation remained in Washington for some time. A week later, President Polk hosted a supper for them. He and the First Lady were the only people at the party not in Native American costume. The plates and glasses were upside down, and beneath the glasses were papers that gave orders to a military store to render each bearer a suit of clothes. Under the plates was forty dollars in gold ($1,301 in 2020) and a gold ring for each. President Polk, calling the members of the delegation "my red children," explained that the gifts were from him and his wife. After supper, the delegation performed a war dance.[26]

The delegation now left Washington, and its members returned to their respective homes. Despite the kindnesses shown to them, the Native Americans never succeeded in getting their reservation; the matter never even went before Congress.[27] Although LePique returned to the Sault, he would travel to Washington every year for the next four years (circa 1849-1852) as a hired interpreter.

After that, LePique returned to Marquette where he married Charlotte Kawbawgam's younger half-sister, Mary, who was about thirteen at the time. LePique would have been well into his thirties by then. LePique and his bride moved to L'Anse, but when they lost their house and belongings in a fire, they snowshoed the seventy or so miles to Marquette where the Kawbawgams had a little house on the hill above the Marquette Rolling Mill on Lake Street. The next year, LePique built a house at Presque Isle. Unfortunately, that house also burnt. Then he built a second house at Presque Isle and remained living in it for ten years, until about 1866, give or take a couple of years.[28]

In 1850, Peter White introduced LePique to George Shiras I, who came to the area to go fishing. This would be the beginning of LePique's longtime friendship with the White and Shiras families. In 1871, LePique would accompany twelve-year-old George Shiras III on a trip to a hidden lake about twenty miles east of Marquette, which he had first visited a year or two before as a mail carrier on a railroad survey.[29] This would only be the first of many expeditions LePique and George Shiras III would engage in as will be shared later.

Shiras, who would become a world famous wildlife photographer, was eager to go bear-hunting when he first met LePique. He recalled, however, that LePique convinced him otherwise:

> Jack grimly rolled up a shirt sleeve, exposing a deeply scarred and shriveled arm. The injury, he said, was the result of a fierce encounter with a bear 10 years before.... Jack's misadventure had been due to his falling on top of a big bear asleep between two logs. In its endeavor to escape, the animal had seized him by the arm, under the natural impression that anyone taking such liberties should be repelled by force.[30]

The remainder of LePique's story will be told through his interactions with the Kawbawgams in the ensuing chapters. We will now return to the Kawbawgams and the general situation of the Native Americans in Marquette and throughout the Upper Peninsula in the 1860s.

Jacques LePique's wigwam. The image was taken by A. G. Emery and appeared in illustrated form on September 16, 1865 in Harper's Weekly, *along with five other Emery images of the Great Lakes area. The illustrated version slightly differs in terms of the people and their placement so there may have been another similar photograph from which the illustrated version was created. The image's caption is "Jack La Pete's Sugar Camp." LePique is standing on the left. Kawbawgam is seated at the far right. Others in the photograph are unidentified. The short article accompanying the images refers to LePique as "Chief of the Chippeway Half-Breeds," a dubious title. The other images in* Harper's Weekly *are of landscapes except one portrait of "Old Thunder, a Chippeway Indian," of whom nothing more is known.*

Chapter 7
The Kawbawgams in the 1860s

By the 1860s, Marquette was no longer a village but a thriving city of more than 1,000 people. With the outbreak of the Civil War, Marquette County's iron industry began to boom, and amid this boom, the Ojibwa found themselves marginalized to the edges of the community. During this time, Kawbawgam's role as a local Ojibwa leader became more substantial.

Marquette in 1857

Becoming a Chief

Exactly when or how Kawbawgam became a chief has been lost to time, but by the 1860s, when he was well into his thirties, he was certainly recognized as a leader among his people. The passing of his father-in-law, Chief Marji-Gesick, about 1862 may have had something to do with this. In an 1891 speech, Peter White referred to Kawbawgam as "heir apparent" to Marji-Gesick when he first met him in 1849.[1] Bourgeois, Kidder's editor, however, states, "Kawbawgam's chieftainship derived from his claimed succession to Madosh (Kawgayosh), a head-chief recognized by the U.S. Government."[2] Bourgeois does not provide a source for this statement, but he appears to be referring to Marji-Gesick's brother, Chief Madosh. I suspect Bourgeois got the information from Ray Brotherton's 1945 statement that Kawbawgam "became chief upon the death of Ma-dosh,"[3] although there is no evidence that this is true.[a] Plus, this inheritance seems unlikely since Madosh had many sons to succeed him, and while titles were not hereditary among the Ojibwa, it was not uncommon for sons to be chosen to succeed their fathers, as Kawbawgam's stepfather Shawano had chosen his son Edward as his successor. Furthermore, it is unknown when Chief Madosh died, but his son George Madosh was also considered a chief by his people, so Kawbawgam did not likely inherit chieftainship from his wife's uncle. Another possibility is that Bourgeois is confusing Madosh (Kawgayosh) with Kawbawgam's uncle Chief Kaygayosh who became head chief at the Sault after his brother Shingabawossin died. No reason exists to think Madosh and Kaygayosh are the same person since Kaygayosh migrated to Canada and was probably considerably older than Madosh. Plus, we know Shingwaukonse succeeded Kaygayosh.

Furthermore, a tribe had several chiefs. Being a chief was not an official position so much as a title of honor and respect given to an elder or someone recognized as a leader by the tribe or clan. In whatever way Kawbawgam became a chief, by the 1860s if not earlier, he was giving advice to his fellow Ojibwa, possibly officiating at marriage ceremonies, and probably walking a fine line to keep peace between his people and the white Americans.[4b]

a. Brotherton often made unsubstantiated claims, creating a sort of pseudo-history. For more examples of his unreliability, especially concerning identification of Native Americans in photographs, see the appendix.

b. The statement of Kawbawgam officiating at marriage ceremonies comes from a 1970 article by Deborah Bruner, but she provides no source for this information. It has been repeated by later authors who used her as their source. Since Kawbawgam was Catholic and most of the Ojibwa at Presque Isle likely also were, it seems unlikely, though not impossible, that he would officiate at marriages.

We know from Kawbawgam's own words that by 1855 he was an underchief among his people, and he was listed as a headman when he signed the 1855 Treaty of Detroit. In the 1890s, he told Homer Kidder about his participation in 1855 in the League of the Four Upper Algonquian Nations, which consisted of the Ojibwa, Ottawa, Potawatomi, and Menominee tribes. These four tribes would come together in peace to hold a council, and as stated earlier, they all claimed to be closely related. Kawbawgam told Kidder that the pipe and belt of wampum used at the council were now in the possession of his brother Wabememe (Waubmama) at the Sault.[5]

Kawbawgam stated that 1855 was the last time the four nations assembled. The council was held at Manitou Island on the Canadian side of the St. Mary's River, and several thousand Native Americans were present. Representing the Ojibwa were his stepfather, Shawano, the head chief, his father Black Cloud (Muk-kud-day-wuk-kwud), another chief, and himself as an underchief.[6]

This assembly was called to settle a problem brought by the Menominee. One of its young men had disappeared the year before in the Red River country. The missing man's sister said he had gone on a buffalo hunt to the prairies, but the Menominee accused the Ojibwa of killing him. The council was called to determine the truth of the allegation. During the council, the Ottawa orator spoke in favor of the Ojibwa, saying, "the Ojibwa whip was not easy to break," meaning that to accuse them could be detrimental. The Potawatomi orator also spoke in favor of the Ojibwa and said that since the Menominee were the youngest of the brotherhood, they should be reasonable. In the end, the council resolved that peace would be maintained. The following spring, the missing Menominee man returned from Red River.

Chiefs did not have actual power to enforce laws; rather, they were seen as founts of wisdom who could guide their people and who were shown respect. How much power Kawbawgam had by this point is questionable. Outside of his tribe, he likely had none since he was not white. The Ojibwa basically lived by the goodwill of the whites, so Kawbawgam's only real power would have come from recognition by them. The US Government never had reason to recognize him as a chief since no more treaties needed to be made. Fortunately, Kawbawgam had the friendship of some prominent white men in his community, most notably Peter White.

Fatherhood

As mentioned earlier in Captain Kelley's memories of Marquette's first year, Charles and Charlotte Kawbawgam had a son who died in 1849. Kelley built the coffin for the child. Where this child was buried has been lost to history as has the child's name, if it were given one. Sadly, most information about the Kawbawgams' other children has also been lost.

We know Charlotte had at least two, and possibly more, children who were stillborn or died in infancy. The only child whose name we know for certain is Elizabeth. According to the 1860 Marquette County census, the Kawbawgam family consisted of Charles, age forty; Charlotte, age thirty-six; and Elizabeth, age one. The ages of both Charles and Charlotte are incorrect in the census; they would have been closer to forty-three and twenty-nine at this time. Also interesting is that Kawbawgam is listed as being worth $40 (about $1,238 in 2020 dollars).[7] As for Elizabeth, she is not listed on the 1870 census where, oddly enough, Kawbawgam is listed by himself. We can assume Elizabeth was dead by 1870 and probably soon after the 1860 census. The 1880 census lists Charles and Charlotte living with Charlotte's nephew Frederick Cadotte and his wife, and also Francis Nolin (Jacques LePique), so we can assume Elizabeth was long dead by this point. Marquette County did not keep death records until 1867 and no death record exists for Elizabeth, although it is possible her death would not have been reported. Elizabeth was likely named after her father's half-sister Lisette (Elizabeth) who married Honorable John Logan Chipman.

A photo exists of a woman holding a baby. The woman has often been identified as Charlotte. Arthur Bourgeois used the photograph in *Ojibwa Narratives* in which he identifies the woman as Charlotte and the baby as Monee (Mary).[8] However, I don't know where Bourgeois got this name for the child, and more likely, if the photograph is of Charlotte, the child would be named Elizabeth. Bourgeois may have thought the baby was Charlotte's great-niece, Mary Tebeau, but Charlotte would be too old to be the woman in the photograph by the time Mary was born in 1876. This photograph, discussed in detail in this book's appendix as Photograph 2, is almost certainly not of Charlotte and her child.

While the Kawbawgams' children all died young, the Kawbawgams also raised the children of Charlotte's sister Amanda and her husband Pierre

Cadotte, a member of the Cadotte family that resided at the Sault.[c] Pierre was the brother of Achille Cadotte whom Captain Kelley mentioned in his reminiscences.

Pierre was not an ideal husband. On October 9, 1851, he murdered Auguste La Ponce, another métis, when both were intoxicated. According to the *Lake Superior Journal* on October 22, 1851:

> Peter Cadotte, a half-breed Indian, was brought down in the Manhattan, on her last trip, in charge of an officer, for the purpose of being lodged in jail at this place, charged with the murder of

---

c. The Cadottes were métis, of French-Canadian and Ojibwa extraction. The first Cadotte at the Sault had been Jean-Baptiste Cadotte, Sr., a partner in the fur trade with Alexander Henry, survivor of the 1756 massacre at Fort Michilimackinac. Jean-Baptiste Cadotte, Sr. was the son of a Frenchman whose surname had been Cadeau and who had come to Lake Superior in the late seventeenth century on a French exploratory mission (https://en.wikipedia.org/wiki/Michel_Cadotte). Eventually, Alexander Henry would sell his interests to the Northwest Company, but Jean-Baptiste, Sr. continued to trade on his own; he even became one of the first eight people on Michigan's board of trade. Cadotte's wife, Athanese, was Ojibwa, and together they became the most prominent métis family at the Sault, other than the Johnstons who arrived there in 1793 (Magnaghi, *Upper*, p. 49; Magnaghi, *Native*, p. 69; Arbric, *City of the Rapids*, p. 44-46).

Jean-Baptiste Cadotte, Sr. would die in 1800, but his sons would remain active in the trade. One of his sons, Michael Cadotte, would work for Johnston (Lewis p. 42). Johnston's son Lewis Saurin Johnston would twice get Mrs. Cadotte pregnant, creating scandal at the Sault (Hambleton and Stoutmire p. 25). Another child of Jean-Baptiste Cadotte, Sr. was Lieutenant Joseph Cadotte, who worked in the fur trade and served with the British in the War of 1812. Joseph was the father of five children: Achille, Alfred, Pierre, Charlotte, and Lucy. We met Achille previously as one of the settlers of early Marquette. Pierre, who was born about 1827 or 1828 in Canada, likely met Charlotte Kawbawgam's sister Amanda at the Sault when Marji-Gesick's family traveled there, or he may have met her in Marquette since he either came there with Achille or to visit him. We know from Captain Kelley's reminiscences that Achille was in Marquette in 1849, so Pierre probably arrived at the same time or soon after.

According to John Tanner's captivity narrative, Joseph Cadotte may also have been the half-brother of Louis Nolin, father to Jacques LePique, which would have made LePique and Pierre Cadotte not only brother-in-laws, since each married a daughter of Marji-Gesick, but also first cousins (Tanner, Chapter 12).

> Auguste La Ponce, a half-breed. It appears from the testimony at the examination that they were both intoxicated in their lodge at Marquette, on the 9th inst. and, in an altercation respecting the fire, Mr. Cadotte caught up a stick of wood and struck Mr. La Ponce on the head, and immediately after struck him several times with an axe, causing his immediate death.[9]

This may have been Marquette's first murder. Pierre was brought to the Sault to be jailed. What happened after that is unclear. In 1852, the Marquette Supervisors' board met and agreed to reimburse Jeremiah Crane, former sheriff of Chippewa County, the sum of $64.88 for keeping Cadotte in jail for 173 days.[10] This may mean Pierre was released after serving a nearly six-month sentence for murder. In her 1852 travel journal, Juliette Starr Dana mentions traveling from the Sault to Marquette. On August 4, she writes, "There was an Indian on board who was being carried to Marquette the county town, to be tried for murder. His poor mother was with him, & looked sad enough."[11] It is possible this man was Pierre Cadotte, returning to Marquette for his trial. Also on board was Judge Daniel Goodwin who had recently been elected the first district judge for the newly formed Upper Peninsula Judicial District. Dana notes that the next morning when the ship arrived in Marquette, the judge and prisoner left the ship. That day, Judge Goodwin held his first court in Marquette County in a small office building adjoining the Northwestern Hotel. There he presided over the Indian's murder indictment and other indictments for forgery and larceny.[12] Unfortunately, I have been unable to find records concerning this murder trial or any additional information about Pierre Cadotte's sentence. Whatever punishment Pierre Cadotte received, by the 1860 census, he was again in Chocolay Township near Marquette with Amanda and their children.[13] Both Amanda and Pierre would die sometime between 1860 and the 1870 census, leaving behind two children, Fred and Angelica (sometimes listed as Angeline or Angelique), whom the Kawbawgams adopted.

Fred Cadotte may have been named after his uncle Alfred Cadotte, who appears to have died as a child.[14] The source for Angelica's name is unknown. These children would play a significant role as their grandfather Marji-Gesick's heirs in Charlotte's landmark lawsuit against the Jackson Iron Company as will be seen in Chapter 8.

Marquette County Migrations

The Kawbawgams, true to their Native American heritage, rarely stayed in one place long, although as they now entered middle age, that was not always by choice. As mentioned before, Kawbawgam had lived at Grand Island, at the Sault, in Ontario, and at Tahquamenon. In the Marquette area, he had resided near where Gaines Rock is today when he greeted Marquette's first visitors, though other reports say Boggam House was at the foot of today's Baraga Avenue, a few blocks north of Gaines Rock. Once Marquette's downtown began to grow, Kawbawgam could not remain there, presumably because downtown property was at a premium and he had no money. By the 1860s, he and the local Ojibwa, who by now apparently acknowledged him as their chief, moved to Lighthouse Point on the north end of Iron Bay where a lighthouse had been built.

The locations of all of the Kawbawgams' residences are not known today, and none of their structures have survived. At some point, also in the 1860s, the Kawbawgams moved back to the Carp River where Marji-Gesick had frequently resided. Ben Mukkala (1930-2013), a popular Upper Michigan author, recalled a family story about Kawbawgam from this time. While Kawbawgam had been living at the mouth of the Carp River, he had rescued a woman and her young daughter. The mother and daughter had found themselves in peril while trying to cross the river. Their wagon was swept downstream, but Kawbawgam helped the women back to shore. The daughter was Mukkala's great-grandmother.[15]

From the Carp River, Kawbawgam seems to have moved to Chocolay Township where he lived beside the lake that today bears his name: Lake Kawbawgam.[16] Then he moved to Cherry Creek. When his cabin in Cherry Creek burned down, he moved to Presque Isle.[17] He is also said to have resided at Green Garden Hill, also known as "Kawbawgam Hill." Since 1876, the hill has been the home of the Heitman farm.[18] According to *Chocolay Township History*, "Legend has it that Charlie Kawbawgam lived near the top of the hill. Remnants of the foundation of his cabin remained until recent years when a new home was built on the site."[19] All these locations are close to each other and in Chocolay Township, so some references to his residences may refer to the same property.

How long Kawbawgam resided in Chocolay is unknown. He seems to have resided in Marquette and its immediate vicinity the majority of the time. According to *The Mining Journal*'s lengthy article about Kawbawgam after he died in 1902, "Up to the time he moved to Presque Isle, about twenty years ago, [circa 1882], he lived with the exception of a couple of years he spent somewhere in the Chocolay valley, on the site of the present South Shore freight depot."[20d]

These moves were not always Kawbawgam's decision. Like other Native Americans, he believed the land belonged to everyone; you couldn't own the land any more than you could own the sky. However, the early white settlers did not view things this way. Kawbawgam would no sooner build a house than someone would inform him that the property had just been purchased and he was now a squatter, causing him to have to move again.[21]

Kawbawgam's move to Presque Isle did not occur until the 1880s. The reason it became his permanent home dates to the winter of 1865 when he was trapping in Humboldt Township west of Ishpeming and Marquette. He had a small shack there to live in while trapping. Peter White, for whatever reason, was in the area alone and got trapped in a snowstorm. After a few hours floundering about, he came upon Kawbawgam's shack. Kawbawgam let him inside and took care of him for a few days until the storm ended. White was eternally grateful to him. While White was not the impetus for Kawbawgam later moving to Presque Isle, since the Ojibwa had long resided there, he would be instrumental in making it Kawbawgam's permanent and final residence as we will see in Chapter 9. White also reportedly made sure Kawbawgam never wanted for food or clothing for the rest of his life.[22]

But Kawbawgam's most comfortable years at Presque Isle were still in the future. For now, the bustling little town of Marquette was about to be involved in a national crisis. Many of the Ojibwa were ready to serve the same nation that less than half a century before they had fought against with the British—a nation that had forced them to sign away their land and continued to threaten them with removal from the Upper Peninsula.

---

d. Mrs. Emma Everett Ball also mentions that the Native Americans were encamped at the location of the present South Shore freight depot, as cited in Chapter 4. This location is hard to pin down, however, in terms of Marquette's current geography. The reference is to the Duluth South Shore and Atlantic Railroad. No listing has been found for a "freight depot" on the Sanborn maps or in the city directories of the time. However, the "freight office" was located at the foot of Jackson Street on Lake Street and the shipping office was at Main and Lake Streets. The storehouse was at the foot of Baraga Avenue near what is today known as the Customs House. In any case, the Native Americans were clearly encamped along the lakeshore in Iron Bay.

The Tragedy of Edward Oshawano

Edward Shawano

While the Kawbawgams were migrating about Marquette County, and the events leading to the Civil War were brewing, Kawbawgam's younger half-brother, Edward Oshawano, had grown up and gone off to college, intent on becoming a lawyer like his brother-in-law, John Logan Chipman. Earlier, we saw that an agreement was made with the US Government, possibly in connection with the 1855 treaty, that Edward would be educated. Edward was already seventeen in 1855 and attending Detroit public schools, so the government must have been agreeing to pay for his college education. Edward did attend college and then prepared to become a lawyer, but tragedy struck before his career could commence. The tragic incident probably occurred in the early 1860s. Upon Edward's death in 1899, it was recalled in the *New York World* and then repeated in newspapers throughout the United States, including the *Fall River News* of Fall River, Kansas, the *Seattle Post-Intelligencer* of Seattle, Washington, and *The Phillipsburg Mail* of Granite, Montana. The full article follows:

> FIGHT BLASTED HIS CAREER.
>
> ---
>
> Indian Lost His Nose in a Melee and Gave Up His Ambition.
>
> Edward O'Shawano was the name, not of a descendant of Irish kings, but of a noted Indian chief who has just passed away at his home on Sugar island, near Sault Ste. Marie. Sometimes O'Shawano was called the "Indian Chesterfield[e] with the Wax Nose." For he had a wax nose. His own original nose was chewed off in a fight. Yet, notwithstanding the bright and youthful tendencies which led him into it, O'Shawano was quite entitled to his name of the Indian Chesterfield. He was polished and courteous in speech, dignified in

---

e. The reference is probably to Philip Stanhope, 4th Earl of Chesterfield, who was famous for the 1774 publication of *Letters to His Son on the Art of Becoming a Man of the World and a Gentleman*. The book became a guide to many young men on how to maneuver through society and achieve worldly success with appropriate manners.

> bearing and always faultlessly dressed. His language was excellent and clearly indicated the good education he had. For, notwithstanding his father and mother were full-blooded Indians, Edward in his youth was one of the brightest students in the Detroit public schools and afterward in Albion college. His natural quickness as a boy and his ambition to live as white men do drew attention to him, and Rev. A. M. Leach and D. C. Fitch of Detroit became his patrons and helped him on. After leaving Albion college he read law, and it was expected he would make his mark at the bar. But, unfortunately, at this epoch in his career he got into a terrible fight over a game of cards with deckhands of the steamer Dubuque. O'Shawano had taken passage on the steamer, which was caught and held for a time in the ice on St. Mary's river. The game of cards began to while away the time, and one of the deckhands, in the course of a dispute, struck O'Shawano in the face. The latent savage in his blood broke loose at this, and the Indian ran for a bowie knife, with which he murderously attacked his assailant. In the melee that followed O'Shawano's nose was chewed off. Always inordinately proud of his personal appearance, his disfigurement quite broke his spirit. From that time on he lived the life of a wanderer, but making his home often on lonely Sugar island. He got a wax nose made, and it fairly well concealed his disfigurement, but O'Shawano never regained his lost ambition. He was 61 years old when he died. O'Shawano's sister became the wife of Judge J. L. Shipman [sic] of Detroit, who did all he could for his Indian brother-in-law. But the lost nose meant a lost career for the proud-spirited Edward. And no influence could restore his old spirit. He was the son of a noted Ojibway chief.—New York World.[23]

We can only imagine how Edward felt about this blow to his vanity and aspirations. We also must wonder how the Kawbawgams felt about it. Since the article also suggests that John Logan Chipman stayed involved in Edward's life, we have to wonder how much contact Kawbawgam had with his brother and his brother-in-law and whether they visited one another at the Sault and in Marquette.

The Ojibwa During the Civil War

As the 1860s arrived, the Ojibwa were no closer to being satisfied over the treaty of 1855 and its aftermath. In 1861, the Ojibwa at L'Anse were uneasy because of rumors of minerals on their lands. They were told that because of the 1854 treaty, they could be removed.[24] Fortunately, minerals were not discovered on their property. Despite continuing removal threats, in 1862, the government appointed a farmer to instruct the Lake Superior Ojibwa in farming.[25] This farmer likely operated chiefly on the Eastern end of the Upper Peninsula, aiding those who lived near the Sault and on reservations.

In 1864, the Ojibwa complained when Indian Agent Dewitt Clinton Leach gave them paper money as their annuity payment (they had probably received gold before). They felt this change was influenced by the Confederates,[26] a sign that many Ojibwa did not have a good understanding of the Civil War. The Ojibwa may have also had reason not to trust Leach since in September 1863, he recommended that scattered bands of Native Americans throughout Michigan be moved to one large reservation in Western Michigan because it was too difficult to deal with them when they were scattered about.[27] The Lake Superior Ojibwa would have opposed any such move. These and similar removal threats would continue for many years. In Leach's defense, he did try to help the Native Americans by stressing that they should have patents to their lands according to the 1855 treaty.[28]

Despite their problems with the US government, many Native Americans from Upper Michigan would answer the call to fight for the Union cause. They were certainly interested in the Civil War even though they didn't always seem to understand it. When Leach distributed payments at Mackinac Island, he was asked many questions about the war.[29] Some Ojibwa hoped that by volunteering in the Union Army they would be granted American citizenship, but this did not happen.[30]

Many white men from Upper Michigan served in the Union Army, although many others did not enlist because they were needed to work in the iron mines. It has been said that "iron ore won the Civil War" because the ore being shipped out of Marquette's harbor was made into cannons, ships, bullets, and many other items needed for the Union Army to gain the upper hand against the Confederacy. No documentation exists of how many Ojibwa and métis may have worked in the mines, though no doubt some did, and perhaps that number increased during this time of national crisis. We do know that in June 1864, several Ojibwa and métis worked as packers in surveying for the Marquette and Ontonagon Railway.[31] The railroads were just as important as the mines for aiding the Union cause; they transported ore from the mines to the lakeshore where ships then carried the ore to Cleveland, Buffalo, and other cities where it could be made into various weapons.

Three grandsons of John Johnston from the Sault, the sons of George Johnston, enlisted and would give their lives for the Union.[32] They were, of course, métis.

Robert Graveraet died in 1861 just as the Civil War was in its infancy. However, his brother Henry Graveraet, Jr. and Henry's son Garret, both of Mackinac Island, were among the métis who enlisted. Both were wounded in battle and died in a Washington, DC hospital.[33]

Among the white men from Marquette who enlisted was Nelson Truckey, who became a Captain in the Michigan 27th. Truckey had been the lighthouse keeper in Marquette until he enlisted. In a rare situation, his wife, Anastasia "Eliza" Truckey, was left to tend the lighthouse. During this time, many Ojibwa were encamped about Lighthouse Point. Eliza developed a close relationship with them and a Truckey family legend says they called her "mother of the light." That relationship proved invaluable when one of Eliza's relatives was disrespectful to a Native American and she had to intercede on his behalf. According to a Truckey family historian, the relative "was allowed to keep his hair."[34]

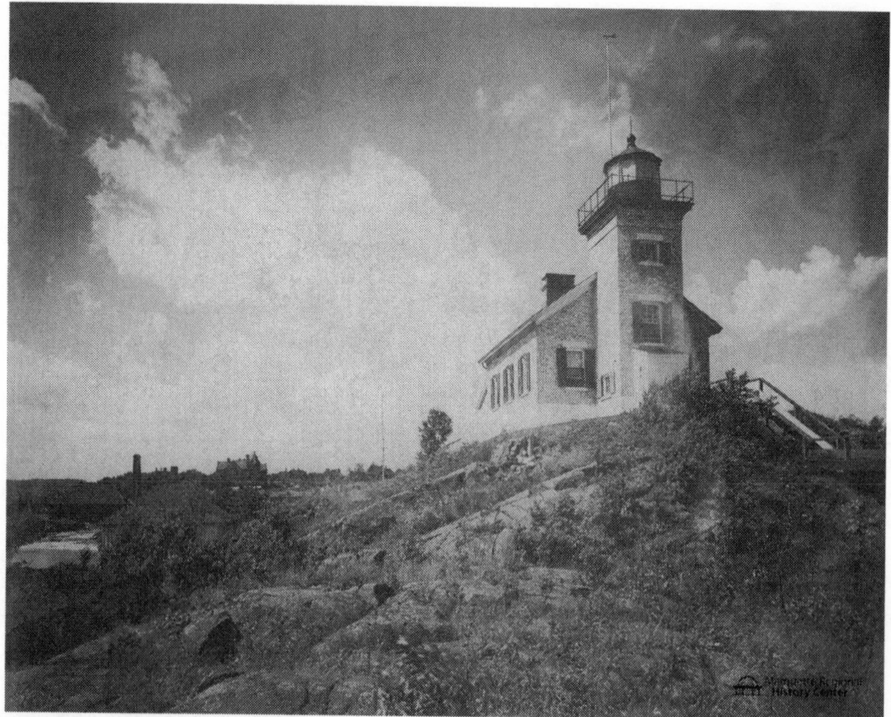

Marquette lighthouse taken from the point about 1895. This lighthouse replaced the lighthouse where the Truckeys had lived.

One of the most notable services by Native Americans during the Civil War was the formation of Company C of the 1st Michigan Sharpshooters, established in April 1861. Many Ojibwa joined this company, coming from such places as Grand Island, L'Anse, and Sugar Island. They saw action in the Battle of the Wilderness, Cold Harbor, Spotsylvania, the Crater, and Petersburg.[35]

In 1863, Company K of the 1st Regiment Michigan Volunteer Sharpshooters was formed. It would be composed almost completely of Ojibwa, Ottawa, and Potawatomi.[36]

By 1865, 196 Native Americans from Michigan were identified as fighting for the Union Army.[37] The number was probably significantly larger since not all of them may have been recorded from not wishing to identify themselves as Native American.

As for the Kawbawgams, they were not left untouched by the war. Kawbawgam's brother-in-law John Roussain would be among those who enlisted. As previously mentioned, he was residing in Marquette in the 1850s based on letters he wrote from there. He enlisted at Marquette on November 18, 1862, which suggests he may have been residing in the area still or have traveled from the Sault to enlist. He enlisted for three years in Company L as a corporal. He mustered on January 22, 1863, and on May 1, 1864, he was transferred to the Veteran Reserve Corps.[38]

Even closer to home, the Kawbawgams had an adopted son who enlisted. This son is one of the great mysteries of their history, especially since Kidder suggests he may have been white, although more likely he was métis.[39] The only reference to him in association with the Kawbawgams is in an 1887 *Mining Journal* article that, in mentioning the children the Kawbawgams adopted, states:

> They have adopted several children who had lost their parents, and have shared their all with them until they were able to take care of themselves. One served throughout the war and sent his pay home to his foster parents regularly. After going through the war he came back, only to meet his death by the accidental discharge of his gun while he was getting out of his boat at Au Train.[40]

We can only imagine how difficult it must have been for the Kawbawgams to know this adopted child of theirs was away fighting in a war they may not have understood, and since they could not speak or read English, they could not even follow the war in the newspapers. Since their adopted son sent pay home, however, he may have also written to them and they may have found someone to read his letters. Unfortunately, extensive efforts to learn his identity have not determined his name.[f] *The Mining Journal*'s reference to him makes it seem he and his tragic death were well known in the community even though his name wasn't given. In 1903, *The Mining Journal* reported that the Kawbawgams had "adopted a boy, who died,"[41] which may also refer to this Civil War veteran since the only other boy we know they adopted was Charlotte's nephew Fred Cadotte, unless we count Frank Perreau, who will be discussed in Chapter 10.

Charlotte's cousins, the Madoshes, also enlisted. Chief Marji-Gesick's brother, Chief David Madosh, may have been among the enlisted. Some confusion exists because he also had two sons, George and David, who definitely enlisted. George Madosh was an Indian Scout in the Civil War.[g] David (either the father or son) would receive a medal for his bravery from President Lincoln and be granted 160 acres of land of his own choosing.[42] The land he chose was northwest of Marquette at the mouth of the Little Garlic River. The Madosh family would reside there for decades.

To commemorate the Madosh family's presence on this land, in 1994, six historical plaques were placed on top of Sugarloaf Mountain, a popular

---

f. This mysterious adopted child would have died between 1865 when the Civil War ended and 1887 when *The Mining Journal* mentioned his death. Since he died at Au Train, a death record should exist in the Alger County Death Records, but those records only date to 1884 since Alger County was part of Schoolcraft County prior to that, and Schoolcraft County's death records only date back to 1880. Since he was from Marquette, it seemed likely his death would be recorded in Marquette County, so I looked through all the Marquette County death records from 1867-1887 to try to identify him, but without success. Many people who died outside Marquette County were listed but none who died at Au Train. A few deaths at nearby Munising were recorded but they were all females or children. Furthermore, causes of deaths when not listed as specific illnesses or diseases simply say "accident" which could mean anything, including a gunshot wound. Consequently, the chance of ever learning his identity seems slim.

g. In *Superior Heartland*, Fred Rydholm refers to David Madosh as being a soldier, but Madosh family records at the Marquette Regional History Center, donated by descendants, state it was George. However, the land grant from President Lincoln, a copy of which is in Madosh folder BF 920 at the Marquette Regional History Center, definitely has the name David Madosh upon it, so either the father or the son named David may have received the land grant.

hiking destination that overlooks the Madosh land. They were placed by the Keweenaw Bay Band of Chippewa Indians, the Madosh Family, and the Marquette County Historical Society, in cooperation with the Michigan Department of Natural Resources. Unfortunately, by 2018, the plaques had disappeared, probably removed by vandals. Fortunately, Matt Madosh took photographs of the plaques and shared them with me. Two plaques showed maps outlining the various land formations viewable from the top of Sugarloaf. The other four provided history. Although not originally numbered, I have numbered the historical plaques below to separate each one and put them in chronological order.

1

Noquet Tribe

For many years before the arrival of Europeans on Lake Superior, there was an Algonquin tribe of Indians who called themselves the Noke (today known as the Noquets) who lived in the central Upper Peninsula. A small number of this tribe summered along the shore of Lake Superior between the Big Huron River and Grand Island. They lived mostly in family groups at the mouths of rivers. In the fall, they moved to their hunting grounds and in the winter they migrated from Au Train south to Bay de Noc (Bay of the Noquet) on Lake Michigan and in the spring they returned north to their various maple groves in time to make maple sugar.

The Cass Treaty (1820) at Sault Ste. Marie was between the Chippewa and the U.S. Government, consequently, the Noquets, a sub tribe of the Chippewas, went by that name from then on. The Lake Michigan group merged with the Menominee, another sub-tribe.

The descendants of Chief Madosh appear to be the last remnant of the Lake Superior Noquet. They were living at the mouth of the local rivers in the 19th and 20th centuries when the first Europeans arrived.

2

Early Area History

In the mid-1840s entrepreneurs traveled the south shore of Lake Superior searching for minerals and their fortunes. When they arrived in this area, they met three Otchipewa (Ojibwa-Chippewa)

Chiefs who were related by blood or marriage. Their bands were descendants of the Noque or Noquet tribe (sub-tribe of the Otchipewa) and were first encountered by Father Marquette in the late 1660s. They summered at the mouths of the rivers along their shores and wintered on the Bays of the Noquets (Bay de Noc) on Lake Michigan.

Chief Mah-je-ge-shik led Philo Everett of the Jackson Iron Company to the rich iron deposits of the Marquette Range. Mah-je-ge-shik's daughter, Charlotte (c. 1830-1904) married Chief Kawbawgam (Nawaquay ge-zhik), who died in 1902. Kawbawgam provided wild game and lodging for many early visitors to the region.

Chief David Madosh (Maw-Dosh) had several sons. During the Civil War, Chief Madosh and two young sons volunteered as scouts behind enemy lines for the Union Army. For his services, Madosh was awarded a medal and 138 acres of land at the mouth of the Garlic River. Several Madosh families lived at that location until 1902.

County of Marquette
Marquette County History Museum
The Madosh Family

3

Little Garlic River Mouth

138 acres of land was granted to David Madosh in 1865 by the U.S. Government for service in the Civil War. The deed was signed by Abraham Lincoln. The Madosh families lived there for 40 years.

Harlow Plains

After timber was cut in the 1880s and 1890s, the ground was covered with blueberry bushes. During the period of World War I, the Marquette and South Eastern Railroad (1906-1922), and later the Lake Superior and Ishpeming (1922-1957), ran a "Blueberry Special" to the Harlow Plains. The local Native Americans and others picked crates of blueberries, which were sent to a blueberry packing plant in Marquette.

Harlow Creek Mouth

Tom Madosh, son of David, built a cabin north of the mouth of the Harlow in the late 1880s.

Little Presque Isle

George Madosh, another son of Chief David Madosh, built a cabin on the point south of the Harlow and raised a family of ten children there.

In the 1880s, Amos R. Harlow, one of the original founders of the City of Marquette, purchased this property from the U.S. Government. He gave the Madosh family permission to live there as long as it was in his ownership. Harlow built a water-powered sawmill upstream on Harlow Creek.

The George Madosh family was the last Native American family to be born at the mouth of a river in this area. August (Gus) Madosh, one of the children, was born here in 1881 and died in 1963. Many Madosh descendants live in the area today.

4

Partridge Bay

Chief Mah-je-ge-zhik became ill while living with the Madoshes at the mouth of the Garlic in the late 1860s. Francis Nolan (known as Jacques LePique) was bringing him to Marquette in a sailboat when he died in Partridge Bay. He was buried near the two falls of the Carp River.

Presque Isle

Presque Isle was obtained from the federal government through the efforts of Peter White in 1886. Kawbawgam came from Sault Ste. Marie with Robert Graveraet in 1845 and remained in this area. He and his wife Charlotte provided food and lodging for the first party of settlers in the 1840s. Kawbawgam is known as the last Chief of the Chippewa in the Marquette area. He and Charlotte are buried on Presque Isle.

Despite good intentions, the plaques have numerous errors, notably the late date for Marji-Gesick's death and that he died in a sailboat rather than a canoe. Other items such as the date Kawbawgam came to Marquette are questionable, but overall, the plaques provided a fair summary of the Ojibwa in the area and especially the Madosh family.

Once Chief David Madosh acquired his property, he cut down, with the help of several wives,[h] enough trees to build a log cabin. For many years, this spot was known as Madosh's Clearing. It became a favorite place among lumberjacks because they would stop there for refreshments when traveling up the old state road from Marquette to Big Bay. In the hills near the clearing was a forest of maples where, every spring, Madosh and his band would make maple syrup and candy so sticky it could pull out your teeth. They would place this candy in birchbark baskets and then sell it door to door in Marquette.[43] Once again, the Ojibwa were exercising their entrepreneurial spirit to make a living off the whites who had encroached on their ancient lands.

Later, the Madoshes would sell their land to Ernest and Carroll Watson Rankin and to William S. Hill. Mrs. Rankin, as previously mentioned, was the popular children's author of *Dandelion Cottage* (1904). William S. Hill was a Marquette lawyer, best known for being one of former president Theodore Roosevelt's defense attorneys when Roosevelt sued George S. Newett, editor of the Ishpeming newspaper, the *Iron Ore*, in Marquette County in 1913 after Newett called Roosevelt a drunkard in an editorial. Hill would give his half of the property to his secretary, Mrs. Tom Gowling. Twenty years later, the Rankins wanted to sell their property to the Gowlings, but the Keweenaw Bay Community objected, saying Indian lands could not be sold. An investigation ensued, and the Marquette city attorney, Waldo McCree, determined the land could be sold because it was not granted as Indian land but as a special land grant to David Madosh.[44] Years later the land grant given to David Madosh was found in the Rankin home. The original had been signed by President Lincoln's secretary.[45]

In 1878, Amos Harlow had also bought several sections of land from the government in the area where the Madosh cabins stood. He built a sawmill on what became known as Harlow Creek and cut timber there, but he let the Madosh family remain on the land. It is not clear whether the Madosh family had sold this property to Harlow or they were squatting on property adjacent to their own and Harlow let them remain. In the 1930s, Frank Russell, owner of *The Mining Journal*, leased the Echo Lake property from Cleveland-Cliffs

---

h. This statement in the Madosh folder at the Marquette Regional History Center is the only I have seen suggesting Chief Madosh had multiple wives. His wife Maria seems to have been his primary and maybe only companion. However, we must not forget that Susan Gesick had a child with one of Marji-Gesick's brothers, and it's possible Madosh was the brother. As previously stated, polygamy was accepted but not widely practiced by the Ojibwa.

and ordered the Madosh family off the property.[46] Russell was married to Ellen Shiras, daughter of George Shiras III and Frances White, making her Peter White's granddaughter. Despite this family background, Russell obviously did not share Shiras and White's fondness for the Ojibwa.

The entire area north of Marquette where the Madoshes resided was heavily logged; as a result, blueberry bushes flourished there. During blueberry season, daily blueberry trains would operate from Marquette to Big Bay and Birch for Marquette residents to come pick berries. The Madosh family was a major part of the blueberry-picking force during this time.[47]

George Madosh would die on February 26, 1926, reputably having lived to age 102. He is buried in Holy Cross Cemetery in Marquette. His grave includes a Civil War marker, and his stone includes his Ojibwa name "Naw-key-way."[48]

Living in a Post-Civil War, White American World

Despite Native Americans' support of the Union during the Civil War, the US Government did not improve its treatment of them. In 1866, it was reported that a "better class" of whites was taking advantage of the Native Americans in the Upper Peninsula, especially at annuity time. Whites also continued to trespass on Native American lands, creating problems for the Indian agent. In 1866-67, the Michigan legislature recognized the Ojibwa as fully qualified citizens of the state. However, this recognition and the extension ultimately of state citizenship was not helpful until after 1900. In 1867, the Ojibwa of Minnesota and outlying regions met at L'Anse to choose representatives to go to Washington, DC to complain to President Andrew Johnson about unpaid annuities and unkept promises.[49] These issues probably continued until 1874 when the last of the twenty annual annuity payments was made in accordance with the 1855 treaties.[50]

In Marquette, the Ojibwa had been pushed to the outskirts of the community, both north and south of the city. In 1868, "Native American Town" was located in South Marquette along Lake Superior. The Ojibwa there lived mainly in log cabins with a few still residing in lodge houses. They maintained maple groves to the west of them and tapped the trees in the spring. An Indian trail ran from Lake Superior to the Dead River. West of Marquette, in the vicinity of today's Grove and Homestead Streets, was an Indian sugar camp.[51] By 1869, a sizable Ojibwa settlement was at the neck of Presque Isle where Kawbawgam would eventually reside.[52]

In 1867, Alice Sutton Ross moved to Marquette. She was interviewed in the early 1920s by Lew Allen Chase, who interviewed more than one hundred of Marquette's early residents. Ross recalled: "The Indians used to come to Marquette once a year for their government money, and I saw them many times line up on Baraga Avenue, then known as Superior Street. They would dance various dances."[53] Another early resident, Mrs. Emma Coles, recalled that about 1864, "There were about 1,500 people here at that time, and the first year, I remember the Indians had their last powwow on Front Street. Their faces were all painted [and] they were dressed in full Indian costume."[54]

Carroll Watson Rankin also recalled the local Ojibwa in the 1860s and 1870s in an article in *The Mining Journal* in 1935:

> In the early days there were many Indians in Marquette and the white people knew them all by name. There was old Mahgegeswick, the Kawbawgams, the Madoshes, Lame Jane, the Katticbes and many others. Marjigeegies, the famous Indian, who in 1845 led Mr. P.M. Everett to the site of the Jackson mine and the discovery of iron ore, once brought me a fawn, tied up in his red bandanna handkerchief.
>
> **Lived In Wigwams**
>
> As a rule the Indians were great beggars. Even one's chewing gum wasn't safe in one's mouth if there happened to be a squaw any place around.
>
> They congregated in the stores to enjoy the heat from the stoves and to beg for cookies, candy and provisions. Most of them lived in wigwams in south Marquette, where there was a regular Indian village of wigwams. And it seemed to me that every wigwam held a vast number of Indians.
>
> I have seen them roasting squirrels on horizontal sticks over small outdoor fires. They brought vast quantities of maple sugar and maple wax to town and even if it was true that they strained these products through their blankets, their sugar and their wax had a flavor that you don't find nowadays.[55]

By this point, the Ojibwa were becoming a curiosity to the whites who no longer felt threatened by them. In fact, the Ojibwa had become part of Marquette's tourist industry. In 1869, T. Meads was advertising that he was selling "Indian Curiosities, Indian- Tanned Deer Skin, Indian Photographs."[56] Obviously, Native American items were in demand and the Ojibwa were not above providing such objects to whites as a way to earn a living. Meads, whose shop was located on the northeast corner of Baraga and South Front Street, continued to offer such items at least through 1876, adding to the list moccasins, snowshoes, and furs.[57] In 1875, even the Marquette postmaster was selling Native American curios as a sideline to "visitors who were anxious to carry souvenirs back home with them to exhibit as testimonials that they had been in the wilds of Marquette and vicinity."[58]

Meanwhile, the Ojibwa tried to continue to live their traditional lifestyle as much as possible while making a living the white man's way. Local fishing companies like Peterson's hired some of the males, who were paid in netting material so that in their free time they could fish for themselves. Surplus fish were sold from door to door, as were blueberries, maple sugar, and moccasins. In 1878, during the berry season, a considerable number of Native women and children gathered blueberries for commercial shippers who operated out of Ishpeming and shipped to Chicago. Native American women would also continue to weave baskets and make snowshoes to sell well into the 1920s.[59]

While living on the outskirts of Marquette and other Upper Peninsula communities, the Ojibwa found themselves financially reliant upon the whites, and in the process, slowly assimilating, probably more out of financial need than direct desire. In a November 29, 1864 letter, Bishop Frederic Baraga wrote, "It is a pleasure to see how the Indian missions are growing, whereas the pagan Indians in the woods, who will not hear about conversion, are remarkably decreasing in numbers."[60] Notably, where once there were Indian villages in the forests, now there was not a single Indian living there.[61] The Natives might not be living among the whites, but they were living close by. Similarly, in 1871, the Indian agent reported that the Upper Peninsula's Native Americans had nearly all ceased to be "blanket Indians," and to a greater or lesser extent, they had adopted white customs, including Christianity.[62] In 1872-3, the annual report of the Commissioner of Indian Affairs went so far as to claim that tribal organizations had now dissolved and the Native Americans were Michigan citizens.[63]

Such claims come from the mouths of whites, not the Ojibwa, who may well have viewed the situation differently. Certainly, with a few exceptions, most whites were not ready to accept the Ojibwa as their equals even if they were citizens. Charlotte Kawbawgam's efforts to claim her father's share in the Jackson Iron Company proves this point, as the next chapter illustrates.

Chapter 8
Charlotte Kobogum et al. vs. The Jackson Iron Company

A STRICT CHRONOLOGY OF THE KAWBAWGAMS' lives is nearly impossible since they did not keep track of time with calendars like their white neighbors. Therefore, Charlotte's lawsuit against the Jackson Iron Company is the only real source we have for dating Chief Marji-Gesick's death. Some sources claim he died as early as 1856, but most accounts suggest he died about 1862. He was definitely dead by early 1865 when Philo Everett, as we will see, tried to help Charlotte collect on the money originally promised to him.

Marji-Gesick's son-in-law, Jacques LePique, was with him when he died. LePique would testify during the lawsuit that Marji-Gesick died in his canoe on Lake Superior between Middle Island Point and Presque Isle.[1] LePique was trying to bring Marji-Gesick to Marquette for medical care. Marji-Gesick was buried in a small Indian cemetery on a hill southeast of the two falls of the Carp River, near the old Carp River forge, five miles east of Negaunee. The grave had a wooden marker, but it has long since deteriorated so the exact location of Marji-Gesick's final resting place is unknown.[2] The Michigan Supreme Court would later state that he died "at a time not ascertainable by reason of the inability of the Indians to fix it definitely by our methods."[3]

After her father's death, Charlotte found a little birchbark box in his canoe in which he had kept the certificate stating he had a right to shares in the Jackson mine.[4] Before his death, Marji-Gesick may have made some efforts to claim compensation through the shares, but the Jackson Iron Company had struggled during his lifetime and been unable to do anything for him. One day, sometime after Marji-Gesick's death, the Kawbawgams and Jacques LePique were talking about the iron location. Charlotte then showed LePique the certificate she believed stated her father had a share in the Jackson mine. Neither LePique nor the Kawbawgams could read, but Charlotte knew her father had valued the paper.[5] To be certain of the certificate's content, some sources say that in May 1864, Charlotte went to Philo Everett to ask him about the paper and whether she could, as her father's heir, obtain compensation for the shares in the Jackson mine.[6] However, during the trial, Charlotte would confirm that she actually gave the paper to her husband, who then brought the paper to Everett.[7] This inquiry began a twenty-seven-year struggle for Charlotte and Marji-Gesick's other descendants to obtain their rights to their share of the mine's profits.

Everett knew Marji-Gesick had never received any compensation for his services to the Jackson party. During the ensuing trial, when Everett was pressed by the mine's defense attorneys to confirm that Marji-Gesick had already received compensation, he stated that at one point Marji-Gesick had stolen some corn from the company that Everett felt he had been "entitled" to since he had not been compensated in any other way.[8] Everett agreed to help Charlotte receive compensation, so in early 1865 when he traveled east to attend President Lincoln's second inauguration, he stopped in New York to see David Stewart, president of the now reorganized Jackson Iron Company.[9] Everett asked Stewart to settle the agreement, but Stewart initially denied the claim was legitimate. After he found the company records pertaining to it, Stewart offered to give the Kawbawgams a $100 charitable contribution. Everett refused this contribution because he knew it would not be fair compensation. In response, Stewart stated the company had been reorganized since the shares had been issued, so the claim was no longer good.[10]

The Jackson Iron Company had known its share of difficulties since its founding in 1845. By the 1850s, it was in the hands of absentee owners who knew nothing about the agreement with Marji-Gesick. In 1854, the forge had been shut down, and no dividends would be paid by the company until 1861.[11] In the 1850s most of the original shareholders had sold out, unable to afford the continual financial assessments, although they knew the mine had the potential to make them wealthy.[12] Since Marji-Gesick had never received dividends in 1861 when they were finally paid, three possibilities exist: 1) the company chose to ignore him at that time, 2) it no longer had knowledge of the agreement, or 3) Marji-Gesick had already died by 1861 and no effort was made to find his heirs. In any case, Everett's initial inquiry for Charlotte resulted in no compensation for her.

By this point, Marji-Gesick's daughter Amanda and any other children of his had died, leaving Charlotte his only surviving child. During the case, in 1883, Judge James V. Campbell would state that "Charlotte Kobogum was a lawful heir of her father," and "It appears that his other children all died, and…the testimony indicates they all died before him."[13]

While the Jackson Iron Company's early years were difficult, by the 1860s, the company was decidedly profitable,[14] which may have motivated Charlotte to make a concerted effort now to receive her rightful share. On January 16, 1870, she sold, assigned, and set over all her rights and shares in the property to Jeremy Campau.[15] Campau, whose name was listed as Compo in the first case, was a prominent local métis and a family friend. Little else is known about him and his relationship with the Kawbawgams. An obituary in 1930 exists for "Jerry Campeau," likely Jeremy's son, while none seems to exist for him. Jerry's obituary says he was born in 1850 in Canada and came to Marquette in 1867.[16] Jerry's wife's obituary tells us he was a fisherman and the family lived in Chocolay at the time of her death in 1913.[17] The Compeaus may have lived near the Kawbawgams in Chocolay in the late 1860s when they arrived in the area, which is how the Kawbawgams got to know them. I assume Jerry is the son since he would have only been twenty in 1870, so he probably wouldn't have had the means to sue a mining company. I have been unable to find out anything about Jeremy himself beyond his involvement with the trial. No Marquette County death record or local obituary exists for him.

Because Charlotte could not afford the legal expenses for the case, she handed over the rights to Jeremy Compeau in exchange for an agreement that he receive 25 percent of future settlements.[18] In 1871, Charlotte hired Egbert J. Mapes, a Marquette lawyer, to represent her. Mapes, who had come to Marquette in 1868, had a prominent career, including serving as village attorney and prosecuting attorney.[19] Mapes contacted Fayette Brown, the Jackson Iron Company's general agent and business manager. Brown did not offer to buy Marji-Gesick's certificate, but he was willing to offer $300 as a settlement.[20] The settlement was refused, and later, when the case went to trial, it was determined that Brown had not been in a position to make such an offer. Once again, Charlotte failed to receive compensation. The refusal of $300 was likely due to it being considered inadequate. In 2020 dollars, it would be the equivalent of $6,319.03, hardly sufficient for a mine that had been paying out dividends for ten years. As *The Mining Journal* reported in 1888, the amount at stake was not only the value of twelve shares of stock, but the accounting of all the mine's earnings since its origin.[21] By the time the trials concluded, the Jackson Iron Company had earned a 1,900 percent dividend.[22] Obviously, the Jackson Iron Company was unwilling to pay out such a large sum of money.

In 1877, after the Jackson Iron Company's thirty-year charter expired, it was reorganized again. The new corporation succeeded to all the assets of the old organization, but it would once again express ignorance of Marji-Gesick and his heirs' claims.[23]

In 1879, Charlotte hired a new lawyer, Frederick Owen Clark (1843-1905). Clark had been practicing law since 1870, first in Escanaba, and then in Marquette from 1876 on. He had also served in the state legislature in 1874. In 1877, he had married Ellen Harlow, daughter of Marquette founding father Amos Harlow. Clark would later become mayor of Marquette twice.[24] Charlotte may have picked Clark because he was not involved with the mining companies like so many other Marquette lawyers.

Frederick Owen Clark

Witnesses expected to testify on Charlotte's behalf included her husband Charles Kawbawgam, Edward Shawano (Kawbawgam's half-brother), John Busha, Louis Cadotte (a cousin of her brother-in-law Pierre Cadotte), and John Gurnoe. These men were all relatives of the Kawbawgams or their friends from the Sault. In the end, however, only Charles Kawbawgam would testify.[25] Although not all testified, their willingness to do so showed

Native American witnesses for Charlotte Kawbawgam. Left to right: Edward Shawano, John Busha, Charles Kawbawgam, Louis Cadotte, and John Gurnoe.

that Charlotte had the support of the Native American community in her efforts. Paul Pine, a local métis who resided in the Marquette area, acted as interpreter for the Ojibwa who testified.[a] Several surviving partners from the original formation of the Jackson mine would also testify on Charlotte's behalf, perhaps feeling they had also been cheated out of their rights.[26]

The case went to trial in March 1881 as Jeremy Compo v. The Jackson Iron Company in the local circuit court in Marquette.[27] The company's legal team used the concept of laches as its strongest defense. In other words, the

a. Paul Pine was the son of Chief Ogista of Garden River in Ontario and grandson of Chief Shingwaukonse (meaning Little Pine, hence the use of Pine as a surname by his descendants). Shingwaukonse had established the Garden River community in Ontario and had been the chief who tried to placate Kawbawgam's Uncle Sassaba when Cass had come to the Sault in 1820 (Chute 259, n. 12). Paul Pine would also serve as a guide to Lewis Henry Morgan when he visited Marquette. He was fairly well educated, having attended schools at the Sault and L'Anse (Chute 291, n. 2). I refer to Pine as métis because his grandfather Shingwaukonse had a white father (Chute 21-2). On his mother's side of the family, Shingwaukonse was related to the Crane clan (Chute 10) so the Pines would have been Kawbawgam's distant cousins.

complainant had failed to pursue the matter in a reasonable time frame so a settlement would now be unfair to the defendant because of changes in the value of the property over time. Therefore, the claim had gone stale.[28] This argument provoked debate over whether Native Americans should be held to the same standards of judicial promptness as Euro-Americans. Clark asserted the legal responsibility of the current company to acknowledge Charlotte Kawbawgam's rights. Judge William Williams then issued a write of subpoena upon the company's local manager, but the company's attorney, Matthew Maynard, another prominent Marquette lawyer, filed a demurrer to block litigation by asserting the claim was late or insufficient. Judge Williams granted the demurrer but gave Clark and Campau time to amend the complaint. However, in January 1882, the new circuit court judge, Claudius B. Grant, dismissed the complaint, though he gave the defense time to amend its petition. At this point, Clark and Campau decided to appeal directly to the Michigan Supreme Court. This meant posting a $500 bond, which would be lost if the appeal failed.[29] However, the Michigan Supreme Court refused to hear the case and sent it back to the circuit court.[30]

Ultimately, Charlotte's legal team had to prove three important points to win the case:

1. The Jackson Mining Company had the authority to make the original agreement and its successor, the Jackson Iron Company, was liable for the obligations of its predecessor.
2. Charlotte was Marji-Gesick's rightful heir.
3. The claim had not gone stale.[31]

The third point required proving Marji-Gesick and his family had made several attempts to receive compensation over the years, and it was the easiest point to defend. Susan Gesick, Charlotte's mother, testified that she had known of "the paper," stating "I did not see it at the time it was given, but…I knew about the giving of it." Charlotte testified that her father had tried to collect on his claim, stating that she had seen him remove "the paper" from a trunk "and present it to the company, or some one that was acting for the company," and that "they had some argument about" the paper.[32] Jacques LePique testified that he was present when Charlotte's husband, Charley, "gave the paper…to Mr. Everett to take down to New York." At this point, Everett; Charlotte's former lawyer Mapes; Mr. Stewart, who had made the earlier offer of $100; and Lloyd, the Jackson Iron Company's secretary and treasurer, all confirmed that Charlotte had made several unsuccessful attempts to resolve the claim.[33]

The second point—that Charlotte was Marji-Gesick's rightful heir—received the most contention from the Jackson Iron Company. It tried to claim Charlotte was not the rightful heir because she was illegitimate. She was deemed illegitimate because her father had had multiple wives and she was born to the second wife. In response, Charlotte's lawyer argued that it was unfair to judge Native Americans by Anglo-American practices, and consequently, testimonies were given about the marriage habits of the Ojibwa and the acceptance of polygamy among them. Charlotte's attorney, Clark, tried to construct a serial monogamy argument about Marji-Gesick's lifestyle, but it was clear Marji-Gesick had simultaneously had more than one wife.[34]

Among those who testified about Ojibwa marital relations was Jacques LePique. He explained that when an agreement of marriage was made, the groom gave gifts to the bride's family and this was regarded as a lawful bargain without a ceremony. At most, a few words would be said and there would be a feast. He also outlined how the Ojibwa divorced, "When they didn't like one another, they didn't tie them up like you do; they had a better way of marrying in them days."[35] Kawbawgam confirmed what LePique said. When asked "What was the custom of getting married among the Indians fifteen or twenty years before you were married to Charlotte?" he replied:

> I was familiar with their ways and customs of living and getting married, always, up to that time, and I don't know but it is so now; the young man and young woman agreed to marry and live together; if they made a bargain they was to live together; if they did not get along very good they parted, but so long as they kept their bargain and was using one another all right, they lived together all their life time, otherwise they parted; that was marriage.[36]

Reading between the lines, we can see that Charles and Charlotte Kawbawgam had by this point been married more than thirty years, so they must have gotten along well and loved each other. Although, being Catholic, one wonders whether they, or other Ojibwa, if they had not gotten along, would have bothered to get an annulment.

As the testimony continued, Charlotte clarified that she was not married in the traditional way her husband had described, but that by the time she had married, there were more whites in the area so she was able to be married by a priest at the Sault.[37]

Philo Everett testified that he had known at the time that Susan was Marji-Gesick's wife. He also had known that Margaret, Marji-Gesick's first wife, had lived in the area, and he stated that he had heard when he was in L'Anse in February 1849 that Marji-Gesick (referring to him as "the old major"[b]) had just gotten married again, presumably to wife three, although he could not remember her name. When Everett returned from L'Anse, he stopped at the cabin of Margaret, who was eager to hear the details of Marji-Gesick's marriage.[38] Testimony about Susan as Marji-Gesick's second wife (or possibly third since there is confusion about whether Marji-Gesick married Susan or Odonebegan first), was not needed since she was one of the witnesses at the trial.

Further clarification was also desired regarding Charlotte's sister Amanda and her descendants and whether they should also be considered Marji-Gesick's heirs. The defense tried to argue that Marji-Gesick was a philanderer (because he had multiple wives), but Susan explained how the death of their son Kennedy had caused problems between them (which may have led him to seeking a third wife). In fact, it was testified during the trial that part of Marji-Gesick's agreement with the Jackson Mining Company was that his son would be educated by the company, but their son Kennedy's drowning prevented it.[39] In addition, numerous previous cases from the US Supreme Court and state courts were cited stating that no state laws had any force over Indians in their tribal relations.[40] In addition, Marji-Gesick's marriages had all taken place either before Michigan achieved statehood or before the land he lived on in the Upper Peninsula was ceded to the United States, so he could not be expected to live by American laws or customs, and if his marriages were to be deemed invalid, all Native American marriages would be invalid.[41]

Notably, at this time none of Marji-Gesick's grandchildren were included as defendants. Judge Campbell of the Michigan Supreme Court, during one of the appeals of the case before it was sent back to the circuit court, doubtless referring to Charlotte's nephew Fred Cadotte, stated:

> There is some testimony concerning the existence of a son of one of his daughters but there is no testimony that she was married, and his name would seem to indicate a mixed origin. He has set up no claims and we do not think there is enough to disturb the condition of Charlotte Kobogum as sole heir. The circuit judge was

b. In Chapter 9, we will again see Marji-Gesick referred to as "major" by *The Mining Journal* on January 8, 1887. I do not know if this is a nickname and just a sign of respect for him, or if he had some military background; perhaps he fought with the British against the Americans in the War of 1812, although no tradition has come down that he had such military service.

of opinion that there was not sufficient evidence that this young man's grandmother was wife of Marji-Gesick. There is certainly no evidence that he is a legitimate descendant, or that he has any claim."[42]

In February 1883, Judge Grant of the circuit court issued a decision that was a victory for Charlotte. He rejected the idea that she was not the legitimate heir, saying she was "born in lawful wedlock" and the "legitimate heir of Marji Gesick." Grant then instructed the court registrar to determine an equitable settlement.[43] However, in June of that year, the Michigan Supreme Court overturned this decision. Justice Cooley in the Supreme Court's majority opinion included that Charlotte was not the sole heir to Marji-Gesick, and using the idea of laches, he rejected the "ignorant Indian" argument, stating Charlotte had not made her claim in a timely manner. Justice Graves concurred, but Justice Campbell dissented, though he was in the minority.[44]

This injustice by the Michigan Supreme Court did not go unnoticed by the community. In January 1887, *The Mining Journal* went so far as to remark that "by a quibble of the law the poor Indian woman was cheated out of the million which was her due, the supreme court deciding her claim lost through laches. The Jackson Iron Co. goes on rolling up its millions, while Charlie and his blind wife live alone and in poverty, depending upon the assistance of friends."[45] Such a statement by *The Mining Journal* must reflect the greater outrage felt by the community. This remark is also our earliest indication that Charlotte was going blind. She would have only been about fifty-six at this time.

A new case was filed in March 1887, and the issue returned to court in June 1887. By this point, Jeremy Campau had lost all the money he'd posted for the court costs so he withdrew from the case and reassigned the rights to Charlotte.[46] Because the case had failed partly because Justice Cooley decided Charlotte wasn't the sole heir, this time, Marji-Gesick's other heirs, the descendants of his daughter Amanda, were included in the case. Amanda's son, Fred Cadotte, now in his thirties, became the second plaintiff. Amanda's daughter, Angelica Cadotte, born in 1858 in Chocolay Township, had married Frank Tebeau (born 1834 in Ontario) on June 18, 1875, in Marquette—they were actually married by the Catholic bishop, Ignatius Mrak, successor of Bishop Baraga. Angelica would have two or more children with Frank Tebeau before she died.[c] By the time of the trial, only the daughter, Mary Tebeau (born October 1876), who was ten at the time, was still alive.[47] Mary, therefore, was the third plaintiff, with her father, Frank Tebeau, cited in the court documents as her natural guardian. Charlotte may well have decided to try the case again to provide for her younger relatives, since by this point, she and her husband were growing old.[48]

This third time trying the case did not result in any changes to the case itself or the arguments to be made other than the addition of the new plaintiffs. However, this time, the Michigan Supreme Court saw fit to rule in favor of Charlotte and her fellow plaintiffs. It declared that "the rights of a holder of a certificate entitling him to a paid up interest in a corporation, which has been recognized on its records, which is non-assessable, and which has never been surrendered, cannot be barred by laches until they are repudiated by the corporation, as the latter is the trustee for the certificate holder," and "marriages between Indian tribes in tribal relations, valid by the Indian laws, and contracted at a time when there was no law of the United States on Indian marriages, must be recognized by the state courts, as Indians in tribal relations are not subject to state laws."[49]

After more than twenty years, Charlotte had won a notable battle for Native American rights. Today, the lawsuit is considered a landmark case and "a Michigan Milestone" because it ruled that practices such as polygamy prohibited by state law but permitted by tribal law must be regarded as valid.[50] The case also set two important precedents:

---

c. According to https://www.myheritage.com/names/mary_tebeau, Mary Tebeau had a sister named Mary Josephine Wherry (perhaps a married name?), a sister named Angelique Tebeaux (Thibeault—which may be a form of Tebeau or vice-versa), and three other female siblings, but apparently all of them had died by the time of the trial. These may also have been half-siblings since her father appears to have been previously married and lost his wife in 1870 according to https://www.ancestry.com.au/boards/SearchResults.aspx?dir=back&sortKey=CIAAIf0BHMvy&pOff=19&_F0002BF1=&csn=Localities&cst=category&db=mb&gskw=tebo&gss=ancMB&p=localities&period=&rank=0&hc=50. Therefore, these children would not have been Marji-Gesick's heirs. However, FamilySearch.org (https://www.familysearch.org/tree/pedigree/fanchart/K4YW-P93), the genealogy site of the Church of Latter Day Saints, says Mary had two older siblings, Julin Petrus Thibault (1875-?) and Joannes Thibault (b.&d. 1876). In any case, Mary was Amanda's only surviving child by the time of the trial.

1. The Native right to self-government was valid as set forth in the treaties, including traditional family practices.
2. Corporations have responsibilities to their stockholders despite the passage of time or changes in corporate ownership.[51]

These precedents would help other Native Americans with inheritance cases.[52] *The Mining Journal*, reporting on the Michigan Supreme Court's decision by Judge Campbell, stated the decree should be affirmed as the court stated, and went so far as to say that the Native American tribes "were placed by the constitution of the United States beyond our jurisdiction, and we had no more right to control their domestic usages than those of Turkey or India" and "We cannot interfere with the validity of such marriages without subjecting them to rules of law which never bound them."[53]

Marji-Gesick's heirs had won their case. While some sources claim the Kawbawgams received nothing because the company had no profits, this is a mistake since the successor to the original company was clearly profitable. Still, it is unclear if the Kawbawgams and the other plaintiffs did receive their money. Charlotte's attorney, Frederick Clark, accepted the $10,000 appeal bond posted by the Jackson Iron Company and bound unto Charlotte Kobogum, Fred Cadotte, and Mary Tebeaux (by her father Frank Tebeaux) on September 18, 1888. This suggests the money would be split three ways between the plaintiffs.[54] However, Charlotte would receive half as Marji-Gesick's daughter, and the descendants of her sister Amanda would each receive a quarter, in lieu of Amanda receiving half if she had been alive. Clark opted to accept this bond rather than pursue a separate settlement, although he calculated the sum rightfully owed was closer to $30,000.[55] In 2020 dollars, $30,000 would be worth about $811,496.84. What the three plaintiffs actually were to receive was closer to $270,498.94 in 2020 dollars.

In 1890, the settlement had not yet been received. Mary Tebeau's father had died by then so Charlotte petitioned to have Frederick Clark named Mary's guardian. This was done so Clark could legally sell Mary's shares of the Jackson mine. Charlotte and Fred had already agreed to sell their shares but could not do so until Mary had a legal guardian. To ensure Clark would not use the funds for himself, his father-in-law, Amos Harlow, put up a bond for $3,000 to cover the value of the shares, valued at approximately $2,375.00, plus interest. It was to be a limited "special guardianship," giving Clark control only over Mary's settlement monies.[56]

Kawbawgam and Mary Tebeau
at the Kawbawgam Home at Presque Isle circa 1888

What happened next is unknown. No records have been found proving that Marji-Gesick's descendants received the money.[d] However, if they did not, Charlotte would likely have returned to court since she seemed determined. Charles and Charlotte Kawbawgam would each live more than a decade after the presumed settlement. Given that they were raising Mary and later the Perreau children and were likely kind to their Ojibwa neighbors, it is easy to see how quickly the $5,000 they received would have been used up.

As for Fred Cadotte, in 1880, he had married Eliza (Lydia) Thibault (Tebeau), who may have been some relation to his brother-in-law, Frank Tebeau. Lydia was only thirteen at the time of the marriage. Since their daughter Annie was born the year of the marriage, it's possible the couple had to get married. They were married at St. John the Baptist Catholic Church in Marquette, a church founded by the local French-Canadian Catholics. By 1890, Fred had three children and three more would come. He owned a farm in Chocolay Township, though when he purchased it is not known.[e] Possibly he used his share of money from the lawsuit to purchase it, or if he already possessed the farm, certainly the money helped support his growing family.

Many questions remain about the settlement. Unless further documentation is found, they will likely never be answered.

---

d. Rumors exist that the money was deposited in the First National Bank and overseen by Peter White for the Kawbawgams, but this cannot be verified. A phone call to Flagstar Bank, which bought out Wells Fargo in Marquette, which in turn had acquired First National Bank in 2000, resulted in my being told that no nineteenth century bank records remained at the main branch of what had been First National Bank, and if any had been found, they would have been given to the Marquette Regional History Center. However, the Marquette Regional History Center does not have any such records, nor are they among the Peter White papers in the Burton Historical Collection at the Detroit Public Library. It is possible such records exist in the Bentley Historical Library at the University of Michigan. However, a preliminary look by the research staff at the library found nothing. Peter White's papers at the Bentley are extensive, and unfortunately, I was unable to explore the records in depth.

e. I have been unable to find Fred Cadotte listed as Fred Bawgam or Fred Cadotte in Marquette County's property or mortgage records between 1870 and 1900 so how and when he purchased his property remains unknown.

Chapter 9
Moving to Presque Isle

DURING THE LATER YEARS THAT Charlotte and her family were fighting in the courts with the Jackson Iron Company, the Kawbawgams had begun to make Presque Isle their home.

Presque Isle, meaning "almost an island," is a peninsula jutting out into Lake Superior just north of Marquette proper but within the city limits. Today, it is Marquette's best-loved city park. Roughly three-hundred acres in size, Presque Isle is marked by stunning sandstone cliffs, remarkable rock formations that include the geographically impressive Black Rocks, and many hidden little glades and coves that make it a tourist attraction and favorite place among locals for picnicking, hiking, biking, and relaxing. However, for most of Kawbawgam's life, Presque Isle was barely connected to the mainland because a swamp at its neck made it largely inaccessible except by boat. For some time, the property had belonged to the United States Government.

In the 1860s and 1870s, the Kawbawgams had lived either at the mouth of the Carp River or in the Chocolay area, but about 1885, the Kawbawgams' cabin in Cherry Creek burned down,[1] so they moved to Presque Isle where other Ojibwa were already residing. About this time, the Ojibwa had been pushed out of other areas in Marquette, including Lighthouse Point and South Marquette, where they had resided in the area of Whetstone and Orianna Creeks near Gaines Rock. The South Marquette community was forced to relocate in the early 1880s when the Detroit, Mackinac & Marquette Railroad developed in Marquette and later merged with the Duluth, South Shore and Atlantic Railroad. Because land was needed for the railyard, the Native

Charles (center standing) and Charlotte Kawbawgam (seated second from left) with unknown friends. Date and location unknown.

Americans were driven out and their land filled with twenty feet of rubble to lay the railroad track. Today, below the track's surface lie the remains of the untouched Ojibwa village.[2]

The Ojibwa had lived at Presque Isle for centuries. In Kawbawgam's time, the peninsula was far enough removed from Marquette that the Ojibwa were not encroached upon by the whites. However, the Ojibwa continued to associate with the whites in Marquette, and by 1880, it was reported that the Native Americans at Presque Isle were gradually being assimilated.[3] That same year, the Ojibwa, dressed in their native clothes, would dance in Marquette's streets to entertain passersby and collect donations.[4] Depending on how one wishes to look at the situation, the Ojibwa might be described as demeaned from their previous state of independent living since they desired white money, or capitalizing upon the white presence by using their unique culture as a way to support themselves (assimilation via capitalism).

By 1880, Kawbawgam was definitely recognized as a chief among his people. He would have been in his early sixties by now, and he had become well-respected by both whites and Native Americans. Being a chief at this time must have been difficult for Kawbawgam, who was seeing his people gradually become more and more assimilated into white society while still not treated like equals. For example, in 1881, few physicians were available to the Native Americans of the Upper Peninsula.[5] We can speculate that some physicians may have had racist reasons for not ministering to Native Americans, but also, some Native Americans may not have trusted white medicine. Doctors also probably made more money treating white than Native American patients. Alcohol and its accompanying problems also remained an issue of concern among Natives, although in 1884, Indian agent Edward P. Allen stated drunkenness among the Lake Superior Ojibwa was declining.

By this point, Allen had also established three schools in Upper Michigan for Native children at Munising, Iroquois Point, and Hannahville. A total of eleven Indian schools were in the Michigan Indian Agency.[6] Despite these improvements and efforts toward assimilation, Allen wasn't above proposing in 1885 that all the Native Americans of Michigan (apparently regardless of which tribe they belonged to) be placed on one large reservation where they could be protected from encroachment by white Americans, a suggestion previously made in 1863 by Indian Agent Leach.[7] Allen also predicted that within fifty years, the Native American race would disappear in Michigan.[8] Allen's wish to put Natives on reservations may have been to protect them, but such intentions did not take into account Native American culture or tribal or regional differences. Fortunately, in December 1885, Mark W. Stevens took over as the Indian agent; he does not seem to have proposed removal.[9]

In Marquette, the Ojibwa had an additional reason to fear being removed from their lands when Peter White, generally considered their friend, proposed just before 1886 that Presque Isle be preserved as a city park. White's suggestion was not surprising since he was interested in beautifying Marquette, and at least since 1875, he was park commissioner for Marquette.[10] Because Presque Isle was government property, White traveled to Washington, DC to convince the government to sell the property to him. He purchased it for $65,000 and then presented it to the City of Marquette as a gift. The city government, however, wanted nothing to do with it. The city fathers believed it was too far away from the city so no one would ever want to use it. As a result, Peter White said he would build a road out to it to make it accessible. That road became today's Lakeshore Boulevard.

The Kawbawgam wigwam at Presque Isle, circa 1885

The Ojibwa concluded that if Presque Isle were to become a city park, they would no longer be welcome there. For this reason, the Kawbawgams moved again, this time to Green Garden Hill, called Kawbawgam Hill today. From the hill, the Kawbawgams had a beautiful view of the countryside. However, they lived in a small shack in dire need of repair. By this point, Kawbawgam had become so well-respected in Marquette that white residents felt bad about his living situation. In the fall of 1886, after the matter was brought to his attention, Peter White and his neighbor, Alfred Kidder, built the Kawbawgams a house at Presque Isle.

The Mining Journal gave a long description about how the building of the house came about in its article "The Guardian of Presque Isle" on January 8, 1887, stating:

> There are gentlemen in Marquette who have known Charlie for nearly forty years and in that time they have never known him to drink or steal as Indians usually do. He has never been arrested, something that can be stated of few Indians. Last summer Mr. Kidder met Charlie on the street and stopped him to talk of the old days when he used to go hunting and stop at the Baw-Gam cabin. Charlie told him how he had been burned out near Cherry Creek, losing everything, and that since the fire, Charlotte was nearly blind and that he himself could not see the sights on his gun any more, the fire and smoke having injured his eyes. In broken English he spoke of his "paper" and wondered why the white men never paid him for the iron, disclosing such a pitiable state of affairs that Mr. Kidder vowed then and there that something should be done for him. He at once spoke to Hon. Peter White on the subject and the latter drew up a paper which Mr. Kidder circulated for subscriptions, the plan being to build the old couple a house on Presque Isle. When the sum needed was almost obtained Mr. Kidder returned the paper

to Mr. White asking him to secure the rest if possible. Mr. White had already subscribed $50, but said he knew of one man he could approach without fear of a rebuff and at once put down his name for the $60 still needed. The following is the paper:

Marquette, MI, July 19th, 1886.

> Before any white people lived in Marquette county, Charley Kaw-Baw-gam and Charlotte his wife lived here where the city of Marquette stands, and have lived here continuously ever since. They are good honest people and have worked hard all their lives; each is now over seventy-five years of age. They are both too old to hunt or trap for wild game and too blind to be able to pick berries or do any other work to obtain a livelihood. Charlotte's father, Major Madji Geshick, discovered the iron mines of this county and showed them to the first white men that came here. He never received any reward and died poor. The first settlers in Marquette had fish, venison, rabbits, ducks, partridges and other wild game from Charlie Kaw-Baw-Gam when starvation was staring them in the face. A little over a year ago, the Kaw-Baw-Gam's [sic] lost all they possessed by the burning of their log dwelling. It is proposed now to build them a small house, plain but warm and comfortable, and furnish it with a few necessary articles of furniture. It is estimated that it will cost five hundred dollars to do it, and buy a small supply of provisions for them for the next winter. Surely it should be done. The undersigned promise to pay to Mr. Alfred Kidder, treasurer of the fund, the sum opposite our respective signatures below, to be expended by him for the purpose indicated:

Peter White	$50.00
A. Kidder	50.00
H. C. Thurber	50.00
Cash	10.00
C. H. Call	20.00
F. B. Spear	10.00
Watson & Palmer	10.00
J. M. Longyear	25.00
A. Mathews	5.00
A. R. Harlow	10.00
F. W. Read & Co	68.97
Peter White	60.00
Total	$368.97

> The house cost, complete $368.97. A good cook stove was placed in it, and a complete set of dishes. The house was very warmly built, two thicknesses of tarred paper being used inside and out. Charlie and his wife find their new home very comfortable, and take great delight in it. Nearly every day Charlie can be seen coming into town, his figure as erect as ever, despite the years which have whitened the long locks which were once as dark as night. He can still fish, trap rabbits, securing plenty of game for food. The new park could certainly have no more fitting tenants than this aged Indian and his wife.[11]

It is believed the Kawbawgams' new home stood about where the current Presque Isle Ice Cream Store Pavilion stands, just to the left of the park's entrance.[12] This location agrees with James Jopling's recollection in 1933 that Kawbawgam's house was "near the end of the street car track."[13] However, the *Iron Ore* reported in an article following Kawbawgam's death that the house was on the road to Presque Isle, but before getting to the island.[14] In either case, it would be Kawbawgam's last home. He and Charlotte would live in it for sixteen years. Numerous other Ojibwa would also live at Presque Isle in a small community with the Kawbawgams.

We may consider the building of his house at Presque Isle as the start of Kawbawgam's golden years. He was now highly respected in Marquette and someone everyone knew or at least recognized. By this point, the

This photograph gives the best perspective of the Kawbawgam home from a distance, although it is hard to tell whether it was truly where the ice cream pavilion is today.

The Presque Isle Ice Cream Store Pavilion in 2019

Kawbawgams were as assimilated as they were going to become, and once they received money from winning the lawsuit—if they did receive it—they must have settled down to what was a fairly comfortable life by late nineteenth century Native American standards.

Even in their new home, the Kawbawgams still had a primitive refrigeration system. Bob Hume, Presque Isle Park's caretaker in its early years, once pointed out to local historian Kenyon Boyer a large stump beside the road at Presque Isle. He stated the stump marked a deep hole that led down to roots; the hole had served as Kawbawgam's ice box or cooling cellar. Part of the stump was visible there for many years.[15] The Kawbawgams did have delivery services. A grocery wagon drove out to Presque Isle at regular intervals to make sure they wanted for nothing.[16]

The event depicted in this photo is unknown, but it reflects a large number of Marquette's white residents at Kawbawgam's house. Perhaps it was a ceremony for the dedication of the house. Oddly, Charlotte does not seem to be in the photograph.

Kawbawgam also continued to provide for his family through the traditional ways of fishing and trapping,[17] although this became more difficult for him as he grew older, and especially when people robbed him, as reported in *The Mining Journal* on January 29, 1887:

> An Outrage.
>
> When last fall some of the generous hearted citizens of whom Marquette is justly proud, put their hands in their pockets and built on Presque Isle, the city's new park, a home for Charlie Baw-Gam and his wife everyone applauded the deed and thought that the deserving old couple were well cared for in the time of their need. Charlie was very happy over his good fortune and said that though his eyes were too poor for him to hunt any more still he could trap rabbits and catch plenty of fish so that there was no fear about his not finding enough to eat for himself and for his wife.
>
> He set his traps this winter and it now comes to the knowledge of *The Mining Journal* that his traps are being systematically robbed, and sometimes not only the game is taken from them but the best traps are also carried off. In one day recently eight rabbits were stolen from his traps and Charlie was forced to make complaint that if they'd only be fair and leave half he wouldn't mind it so much. No man could be mean enough to steal in such a petty way from a poor Indian, and if boys are doing it they will soon be taught a much needed lesson, for Charlie has powerful friends who will spare no effort to have the offenders ferreted out and punished as they deserve.

No further stories ran in *The Mining Journal* on this situation. Perhaps the story was enough to scare off the thieves, who seem never to have been caught. In any case, to our knowledge Kawbawgam did not make further complaints.

Despite not being able to hunt anymore, Kawbawgam must have still been nimble and fast with a gun because nearly two years later, on December 20, 1888, *The Mining Journal* reported:

> Charles Baw Gam a day or two since killed a genuine catamount [wildcat] on Sugar Loaf mountain. The first citizen of Marquette is still as good as the best of them in the woods, although his hair is white with the snow of many winters, and he is not the Indian that he was.[18]

The reference to Kawbawgam being the first resident is interesting and references his coming to Marquette with Graveraet and settling here long before the city was established.

Identified as Charles and Charlotte Kawbawgam and Mary Tebeau at Presque Isle home circa 1890s. However, the man looks rather short to be Kawbawgam.

Meanwhile, Peter White had been busy with the process of turning Presque Isle into a city park. When the famous landscape artist Frederick Law Olmsted visited Marquette, Peter White took him to Presque Isle to get his opinions on the park and what improvements he thought should be made to it. Olmsted recommended Presque Isle be left in its natural state save for a road being placed around it. In 1887, Peter White hired Native Americans to construct the road, which was completed in September. It is unlikely Kawbawgam helped in the construction of the road given that he would have been about seventy at this point, but many of his wife's relatives and their friends and neighbors were probably involved in its construction.[19] In addition, to make Kawbawgam's residence at Presque Isle official, he may have been made park warden. In 1887, *The Mining Journal* referred to him as "The Guardian of Presque Isle," and the following year, it referenced him as "Charlie Kobogun, who has charge of the National park, at Presque Isle."[20] Given Kawbawgam's advanced age, it was likely only an honorary title, and Presque Isle was only a city park, not a national one. No known records exist to verify Kawbawgam ever officially held such a title, but since Peter White was Marquette's park and cemetery commissioner,[21] it would not be surprising if he gave Kawbawgam a job as "park warden" or caretaker and paid him a salary out of the city government's funds or out of his own pocket.

Once Presque Isle was officially a park, people came regularly to see its many attractions, including a zoo begun in 1887. Makeshift cages housed

Kawbawgam and Mary Tebeau at Presque Isle with visitors who appear to be white citizens, but notice the unidentified Native boy in the doorway.

a small menagerie that included partridge, coyotes, wolves, and bears.[22] Perhaps Kawbawgam or some of the other Native Americans living at Presque Isle were responsible for caring for the animals. While most of Presque Isle's other attractions were natural and scenic, Kawbawgam was a definite added attraction for many visitors and locals. According to *The Mining Journal*, writing in 1902 after Kawbawgam's death:

> It was about twenty years ago[a] that he [Kawbawgam] settled down at Presque Isle in a cabin built for him by Peter White and Alfred Kidder. Up to that time he spoke little English, and intercourse with him had to be in Chippewa. He picked up English at Presque Isle, and finally came to have a fairly large vocabulary, which he increased from year to year. However, at no stage was Charley a fluent speaker of English, and he always used Chippewa when he could.[23]

a. It was sixteen years. *The Mining Journal* was about as good at exaggerating the passage of time as Kawbawgam.

Charles Kawbawgam (far left), Charlotte (seated on steps), Jacques LePique (far right), and unknown friends at Presque Isle home

Nevertheless, with so many white people coming to see him, Kawbawgam probably learned quite a bit of English. Artists who visited Presque Isle wanted to draw or paint his portrait, and Peter White had a portrait of Kawbawgam in his home.[24]

During this time, Peter White was first and foremost in providing Kawbawgam with accolades. In 1889, White gave a speech at the Guild Hall in Marquette, in which he recounted his 1849 arrival in Marquette and his first meeting with Kawbawgam. During the speech, he made a point of praising Kawbawgam's moderate behavior of never "striking, drinking."[25] In other words, Kawbawgam was acknowledged as a "good Indian" with all the connotations that term held for white people—including that he had assimilated enough not to be a threat to them.

With the winning of their lawsuit, the Kawbawgams ended the 1880s on a high point, but that was not the case for their people. The Dawes Severalty Act of 1887 would dismantle most reservations and traditional forms of tribal government throughout the United States, including in Upper Michigan. The act gave the United States permission to divide up Native lands and offer individual land allotments to Native Americans. Those who accepted the land and did not live among their tribes would receive American citizenship. The act's intention was to give Native Americans a faster assimilation by not providing them with their own lands. This law would wreak havoc upon Native culture. Not until the Indian New Deal legislation of the 1930s would reservations in Upper Michigan be reconstituted, and then the Ojibwa and their fellow Natives would have to rebuild their traditions.[26]

Chapter 10
Family and Troubles

While life for the Kawbawgams may have been more comfortable once they settled at Presque Isle, they would still have their share of problems. Two troublesome incidents would happen in 1888 and 1893 that would threaten to tarnish their good names and could have increased racism by whites toward Native Americans. Both incidents must have been very upsetting for the Kawbawgams now that they were in their golden years. During this time, they also coped with the loss or moving away of loved ones as well as raising new family members.

Kawbawgam's Brush with the Law

Throughout his life, Kawbawgam's white contemporaries frequently referred to him as a "good Indian."[1] By definition, a good Indian was one who did not get drunk, did not get into fights, and was not rude to white people. Kawbawgam did not seem prone to any of these faults. He was obviously highly intelligent since he had achieved chief status among his people, and he was respected by some of the most prominent men in Marquette. Most importantly, he had learned how to walk a fine line to keep the peace between his people and the whites who had all but stolen their land.

However, about 1888, when Kawbawgam was probably in his early seventies, he broke the law.[2] He was apprehended by an overly zealous game warden who cited him for setting a sucker net, possibly in the Dead River. Kawbawgam was fishing out of season, and Ojibwa chief or not, the game warden decided Kawbawgam was not above the law and gave him a citation. Kawbawgam may have seen things differently from the game warden. After all, the 1820 treaty had granted the Ojibwa "perpetual" fishing rights at the Sault, although the 1855 treaty had overturned this. No doubt, Kawbawgam was aware of this since he signed the 1855 treaty, but he was not living anywhere near the Sault now. We can only speculate whether Kawbawgam intentionally broke the law. At his age, now in his early seventies, he may have been confused or ignorant about the dates of fishing seasons, or he may have just been trying to provide for his family. I am skeptical he was at all senile at this time since five years later he would begin sharing his Ojibwa stories with Homer Kidder, recalling a fair amount of detail in them. Perhaps Kawbawgam simply loved fishing so much he could not resist setting his sucker net.[a]

Kawbawgam may have gone to court over the citation. Fortunately, according to Peter White's biographer, Ralph Williams, Justice Leonard P. Crary[b] had "a strong enough sense of the fitness of things to peremptorily order his release." This statement suggests Kawbawgam was actually arrested. Williams says Kawbawgam was "put in durance" but that he would be placed in jail seems extreme. Obviously, the judge didn't think the matter warranted a fine or any other punishment; he may have felt Kawbawgam, as an Ojibwa chief, should be allowed to fish when and where he wanted. The game warden's name has been lost to time, but Williams refers to him as "a miserable game warden."[3] Williams likely discussed the situation with Peter White, who probably knew the game warden personally since Marquette was a small city of about 9,000 at the time.

We do not know whether Kawbawgam felt guilty over the situation. Was he apologetic, angry, or frustrated by it? He was likely relieved that the case was dismissed. As a chief, his status was equal or greater among his own people to that of the mayor of Marquette, so to be treated in

---

a. I have been unable to pinpoint the date of this event or find any court records about it. Peter White's biographer, Ralph Williams, states it happened in Kawbawgam's ninety-third year, which would likely make it in 1892 or 1893 if Kawbawgam had been born in 1799, as White believed. However, White, in his 1889 address to the Marquette YMCA, titled "My Recollections of Early Marquette" states that it happened the previous year in Kawbawgam's 94th or 95th year" (p. 4), which would push Kawbawgam's birth back to 1793 or 1794, another example of how White liked to exaggerate Kawbawgam's age. Since White mentions it in 1889, the game warden incident likely did happen in 1888.

b. Williams refers to the judge as Creary but this is no doubt a typo. Justice Crary will figure again in the next trouble to strike the Ojibwa community.

View of Marquette looking northwest from downtown circa 1883

such a manner must have been humiliating. Fortunately, it was a minor infraction and did no real harm to the esteem in which most people held him.

Such was not the case for Charlotte's cousin, Thomas Madosh, who would be at the center of the next crisis in the Ojibwa community.

"A Bad Indian"

Charlotte's uncle, Chief Madosh, had a large family. By all accounts, the Madoshes were law-abiding people who resided north of Marquette near Sugarloaf or at Presque Isle and never seemed to cause trouble, with one exception—Chief Madosh's son Thomas Madosh.

About 1891, Thomas became prone to taking things that did not belong to him. When his thievery was finally discovered in May 1893, its full extent was astonishing. The list of his victims reads like a who's who of Marquette history and, consequently, Thomas earned from Chief Kawbawgam the shameful appellation of being "a bad Indian." No doubt Kawbawgam thought even more of the situation than this simple statement, but it is his only recorded comment on the case. Kawbawgam may well have worried that Thomas' behavior would have repercussions on the Ojibwa community so he had to reprimand him publicly through this comment to *The Mining Journal*.

The sheer audacity of Thomas Madosh is so astonishing that *The Mining Journal* reported on the story for five days as various details came to light. The first day, Wednesday, May 17, 1893, *The Mining Journal* reported:

ACQUISITIVE MR. MADOSH

Tommy Had Gathered In a Good Share of North Front Street.

AN ENORMOUS COLLECTION OF PLUNDER FOUND YESTERDAY

Brussels Carpets, Doors, Window Frames, Rugs, Clocks, Tinware, Etc., Etc., In One Huge Pile

---

ALTOGETHER TOO INDUSTRIOUS.

The elegant and debonair Mr. Thomas Madosh, descendant of innumerable Chippewa chieftans [sic] and for a number of years one of Marquette's most interesting Indian exhibits, in that he toiled not, neither did he spin but no Broadway dude was more elegantly attired, the neat, natty little Tommy is in the hands of the law and Chief Kobawgam pronounces him very emphatically "a bad Indian."

Tommy's misfortune has been overshadowing him since last Friday, though he was in blissful ignorance of the fact and *The Mining Journal* was careful not to disturb his serenity until his arrest, which was determined upon Saturday evening, was an accomplished fact.

For some months Mr. Lovejoy has been on the lookout for material, fittings, etc., stolen from houses which were erected under his superintendence. On Friday Ransom Manhard happened to pass Tommy's new house, on the street railway track about half way between the Dead river mill location and Oudotte's boat house, and thought he recognized some of the fixtures on the door as those stolen from his father's new residence while it was being completed. He notified Mr. Lovejoy who immediately went out to make a friendly call on Tommy. He was admitted cheerfully and at once recognized one of the doors in the house as a cypress door stolen from its hinges, with all its hardware, from F. H. Brotherton's new residence on Front street. Looking about him he recognized the window easings as those stolen from E. J. Sink's new residence, the material being cypress and the detail something gotten up by Mr. Lovejoy himself and found in no other house in the city. Tommy's name was Dennis from that hour.

Mr. Manhard took the matter up and the necessary papers were given to Jake Dolf who proceeded to gather in the unregenerate scion of an illustrious family yesterday morning. Tommy professed entire ignorance of any cause for complaint against himself but in the afternoon a searching party was organized among those who had been the greatest sufferers in the past year from the organized raid on new residences. Messrs. Lovejoy, Manhard, Connolly and others and Mrs. Brotherton were in the party while Mr. Dolf took the unfortunate Mr. Madosh along to do the honors. On entering the house the party was met with disappointment, nothing being found apart from the stolen woodwork already noted. Finally Mr. Lovejoy noticed a small hole in the ceiling and getting up there with some difficulty at once discovered that he was in the Madosh treasure house and a treasure house it was indeed. First he stumbled over a whole Brussels carpet rolled up in a pile which it was all he could do to lift—down stairs this went. Rugs, portieres, bedquilts, tidies, curtains, elegantly embroidered fancy work, teakettles, saws, planes and miscellaneous carpenters tools, etc. etc., followed, while the search revealed lamps, watch chains and jewelery, clocks, tinware, clothing, chair covers, and every variety of bric-a-brac and household goods, useful or ornamental. A bureau at one side was found packed full of the choicest linen, gentlemen's night shirts, handkerchiefs, pillow shams, hem-stitched sheets, etc., etc., all of the finest quality, attesting Tommy's good taste but—alas for Tommy's reputation!—every article marked with the name of some well-known Marquette family. Mr. Manhard found the hardware stolen from his house, Mrs. Brotherton her door, lamps and a large and varied assortment of goods, Mr. Connolly the marble slab and brackets stolen from his house, a whole new Brussels carpet and a few other odds and ends of similar nature, then Mr. Lovejoy picked out a choice assortment of tools stolen from carpenters whom he had employed, naming the owner of each tool, besides discovering stuff stolen from the Schwalm and Sink residences as well as those already noted. Then there was clothing with F. E. Hixson's name on it, a rubber coat, etc., stolen from some one else, a lot of stuff stolen from Pine street residences and—awful testimonial to Tommy's gall—a pocket book containing cards bearing the name of Constable Michael Foard.

The hour was growing late, however and the party did not linger to make a thorough inspection of the great find but concluding that what Tommy hadn't lugged off must have been well spiked down, they prepared to return to town. Old Mrs. Madosh, by some alleged to be over one hundred years old, was in the house and could not be left alone there. A council of war was held and finally the old lady was tumbled into a chunk of carpet and with one man ahold of each corner, the procession moved over to the house of Dave Madosh back of the Dead River mill, the third son, George Madosh, assisting in the removal. The party then returned to Tommy [sic] house where a man was placed in charge and then all returned to the city with the champion connoiseur in house furnishing and interior woodwork, who bore himself with all the dignity and calmness due to his untainted Indian blood. He professed entire ignorance as to the wonderful collection discovered in the loft until Mr. Lovejoy named the owner of the carpenter's tools and told him that he had stolen them by getting into the house through a basement window. Tommy cheerfully owned up then that the diagnosis was entirely correct and endeavored to do up the man who was "onto him" with a couple of stolen handsaws but was at once disarmed.

How on earth this industrious pilferer managed to lug a whole door out of his house or a big Brussels carpet or half a dozen other bulky objects discovered in the collection passes all understanding. One thing is certain, if any one has lost a house and lot, a barn or a front sidewalk, they now know where it is. Today a more complete search of the premises will be made and it is thought that another storehouse will be found under the floor. The loud complaints made during the last two years by parties building new houses and especially those moving into new houses and having no one on guard until they became settled under the new roof, will now come to an end.

The Lovejoy Home, circa 1896. One of Tommy's victims.

Ironically, this story was followed by a story about "Another Beautiful Residence," referring to the home of Mr. A. W. Lovejoy who was robbed by Tommy. Lovejoy was an architect in Marquette and his beautiful home still stands today at 1025 N. Front Street in Marquette. Jacob Dolf was an early policeman in Marquette as may be determined by the story. It is shocking that when apprehended Tommy tried to attack Mr. Lovejoy with a saw.

What are we to make of this story? Obviously, Tommy's behavior was reprehensible, but *The Mining Journal* was relatively kind about the reporting, its tone implying it saw the situation as comedic. While it might not have been out of line for a newspaper in those days to refer to Tommy as "a no good, thieving Injun," *The Mining Journal* instead makes a point of referring to his descent from "innumerable Chippewa chieftains" and stating that he is from an "illustrious" family, showing the esteem the Madosh family, and by extension, the Kawbawgams and the rest of the Ojibwa population, may have been held in by Marquette residents.

Also of interest is the mention that Tommy's mother, Mrs. Madosh, is about 100 years old. This is a clear sign of how ready white people were to attribute great ages to Native Americans as we have already seen in regards to Chief Kawbawgam.

The next day, Thursday, May 18, 1893, *The Mining Journal* updated its readers on the continuing investigation:

TOMMY TAKING INVENTORY.

Marquette's Champion Kleptomaniac
Parcelling Out His Spoils
Among His Victims.

MANY PROMINENT EX-RESIDENTS
COME IN ON THE DIVVY.

Plunder Being Brought in by the
Wagon-Load—Another Big Batch
Found Yesterday

TOMMY'S GRAND DIVVY

Great was the commotion in the city yesterday when *The Mining Journal*'s description of the collection discovered in Tommy Madosh's house was read at the breakfast table. Within a few hours a large number of Marquette housekeepers had visited the Madosh house and had proved their claim to property on exhibition there, carpets, rugs, lace curtains, china, silverware, lap robes, etc. etc.

By afternoon a whole wagon load of goods had been claimed and was sent into the city around by the Collinsville bridge and distributed among the owners. Mr. J. J. Conolly received his carpets, marble slabs and other household goods, M. R. Manhard secured his house finishing hardware. F. H. Brotherton his cypress door, oak interior finish, lamps and other goods, while Mrs. N. D. Hodgkins identified a lot of china and silverware stolen from her over two years ago and Mrs. W. C. Brandon recovered some silver spoons. Another big load was sent into town later and will be on display at Justice Crary's office today.

Tommy takes a very cheerful view of the situation and has kept an officer busy most of the time since the arrest writing down the names of those to whom property is to be returned. This is a sample of the conversation between Justice Crary and the Indian Boss Tweed:

"Now, Tommy, where did you get that quilt?"

Tommy stops picking his teeth and walks up and down the office once or twice, then answers, "That's mine."

"Oh come now, where did you get it?"

"I bought it."

"Where did you buy it?"

"Well, I forget now."

"See here, Tommy, this won't do. If you want us to make this as light [as] possible for you you've got to do the square thing by us. Where did you get that quilt?"

"Well, you can put that down to Louis Vierling. Yes, I got that out of Louis Vierling's yard—put that down to Louis Vierling."

Next came a lot of framed engravings and after having his memory jogged in the same way Tommy decided that they could be "put down" to Judge Grant and, once started, he ennumerated [sic] a lot of other things stolen from the upper peninsula's representative on Michigan's supreme bench. Another fortunate inquiry brought out a long list of things belonging to the former rector of St. Paul's church, Rev. Dr. Wyllys Hall, and to his brother, W. Toote Hall. Another batch was put down to George N. Conklin at Tommy's request, a few carpets and other household goods to Hon. Wm. P. Healy, an oil stove to F. H.

St. Paul's Episcopal Church, which Tommy actually entered to steal from

Gooding and a vapor stove to S. S. Ormsbee and several marble table and bureau tops to Mr. Draper of Pine street, together with a caddy of tea and other supplies which Tommy enumerates accurately, but which long since disappeared from the Madosh larder.

The Dead River Mill company yesterday recovered one or two cross cut saws and a whole stack of other tools from the Madosh house. Somebody's front gate is still out there awaiting an owner, while there is a supply of tinware big enough to fit out several good-sized households. Eight valises of different sizes and descriptions were found in the house, most of them packed and with a full traveling outfit of combs, brushes, etc. in neat cases. Besides several new suits of clothes there was a roll or two of silk on hand, a case or two of silver, including knives, forks and spoons; a lot of picks, shovels and other tools unearthed from under the floor yesterday, a suit of clothes identified by M. H. Forard, etc., etc.

The queerest thing about the business is the way in which Tommy remembers exactly to whom the articles belong. One lady enquired for her lace curtains and he at once called her by name and told where the curtains were to be found, neatly wrapped up in newspapers and entirely uninjured by their two years or more in the Madosh storehouse. Every collection seems to have been kept by itself and Tommy can at once tell to whom the collection belongs and enumerate the articles in it.

Another strange thing about the matter is the fact that there is every probability that sixty days in jail will be all the punishment that can be given the noted little Indian dude. While he has robbed half the town it is doubtful if any of his victims can show up a loss exceeding $25 and unless someone can come forward with a complaint charging a greater amount he can only be tried for petty larceny. In any event it does not appear that he can be charged with housebreaking for he seems to have confined his depredations almost entirely to houses which were unoccupied, either those into which the owners were just moving or those which were closed through the absence of the owners.

Tommy had lived high for years. He had a partiality for canned fruits and kept his table supplied with the choicest varieties put up by Marquette housewives. To many it will seem very strange that he was never caught in his rascality or unmasked before this but the fact is

> that he is as cunning a little rascal as was ever turned loose in a city. It was impossible to keep an eye on him at night for he could elude the quickest and sharpest with ease and this fact, together with the general belief that he was a nice little fellow and entirely harmless, accounts for his long immunity from suspicion, let alone arrest.

This article is quite interesting for its treatment of Tommy, making him out to be a rather comical but clever character, a "rascal" and "a nice little fellow." From this last comment, we can gather that he was a small man, not tall and imposing like Kawbawgam or Kawbawgam's stepfather Shawano were said to be. There are some references to his being Native American, including his being called an "Indian Boss Tweed," which is a reference to William M. Tweed (1823-1878), known as the "Boss of Tammany Hall," the Democratic Party's political machine. In 1877, Tweed was charged with political corruption and stealing from New York taxpayers between $25 and $45 million (in 2020, it would be valued between $713 million and $1.3 billion). Tweed escaped from jail, but he was caught and died the following year. Tommy Madosh's thievery is, as the article notes, minor by comparison. Nothing Tommy stole was worth more than twenty-five dollars. However, twenty-five dollars in 1893 would be the equivalent of $713 in 2020, so certain items like a Brussels carpet would have been considered valuable by their owners.

The reference to Tommy being a "noted little Indian dude" may seem surprisingly modern, and recalls that in the first article, he was compared to a "Broadway dude." The word "dude" was fairly new at the time, dating to 1880-1885. While today it is used to refer to a male in general, at the time, it referred to someone from a big city, especially someone well-groomed or a bit of a dandy. The first article also mentioned that Tommy was "natty," another reference to his being well-dressed.

That Tommy could afford to dress well and keep such a good table raises questions about how he did so given that no mention is made of his trying to sell or pawn the items he stole; he simply preserved them, and sometimes used them, as seen with Mr. Draper's caddy of tea and other supplies that have "long since disappeared from the Madosh larder." Perhaps he also stole money to live on that could not be traced as stolen. Or perhaps he did sell some stolen items but did not confess to this so *The Mining Journal* never reported on it. No mention is given of his occupation, and it sounds like he did not have one for some time, which makes it all the more surprising that he was not under suspicion much sooner but managed to carry on his thievery for at least two years. One also has to wonder, since he was able to cart away Brussels carpets, whether he had an accomplice.

The next day, Friday, May 19, 1893, *The Mining Journal* continued its report, giving a full list of items discovered. As stated earlier, the list of Tommy's kleptomania victims reads like a who's who of Marquette's most prominent east side residents. Even so, the story was no longer breaking news so the headline was less prominent and the article much shorter.

> Madosh's Inventory.
>
> *The Mining Journal* gives herewith Tommy Madosh's inventory of the goods brought in from his house and stored in Justice Crary's office yesterday. He sorted out the goods himself and named the parties to whom each pile belonged. There were many other things whose rightful ownership he could not remember, but which are held in Justice Crary's office to await identification.
>
> Tommy's old house on Presque Isle is to be overhauled today when it is expected that another lot of goods will be discovered.
>
> The solid silver teapot stolen from Mr. T. J. Millen's residence was part of a set presented to Mr. and Mrs. Millen by a party of Cleveland hunters to whom he showed many courtesies near Seney. Tommy set it in the stove and tried to make tea in it, the result being that part of the base was melted off.
>
> The following is Tommy's list, five or six five-gallon cans of oil and two or three loads of truck not yet brought in not being referred to in it.
>
> J. J. Connolly 1 large bracket, 1 lock, ½ doz. bronzed hooks, 2 carpets, 3 weight cords, marble slab, 1 Sargent lock, ½ pair butts; Peter Patenaude, 2 heavy curtains; T. J. Millen, 2 marble tops, 1 umbrella, 1 rug, 1 silver tea pot, 1 satchel with clothes; W. P. Healy, 1 carpet; Thos. E. Foard, 1 lady's umbrella, 2 comforters, 1 purse; A. J. Draper, 2 silver knives and forks, 1 rug, 1 shirt, 2 white curtains, 2 boxes cigars (smoked), tea; Everett house, 3 ½ heavy curtains, 1 towel, (Adams); Brotherton 1 cypress door, 1 quilt, 1 lamp, 1 tea kettle; 4 tin pans, 1 tin cover; Ormsbee, 1 oil stove, 2 knobs, 2 locks; Frizelle, 1 brass lamp, 1 bottle perfume; C. Van Iderstine, 3 rolls building paper; F. Hixson, 1 table cloth; W. H. Wheatley's house, 1 Norway pine door, (Lovejoy): Manhard & Co., 2 locks sets, 1 rubber rug; J. M. Longyear, 2 bed spreads, 1 towel, (lost one); W. C. Brandon,

> 6 tea spoons, "B," 7 gilt saucers; N. D. Hodgkins, 5 tea spoons marked "Maria," 4 tea spoons, bird pattern, 5 towels; Dead River Mill Col., 1 claw hammer, 2 paint brushes; Schwalm's house, 1 deer head, 1 can varnish, 1 brush, 2 hand saws, 1 rubber coat, 1 basket with tools; Belanger, 1 screen door, Third street; Arch street, 1 rubber rug, 1 cocoa rug; Pine street next to J. Pendill, 4 picture frames, 2 pieces of carpet; back of Episcopal church; Louis Reidinger, 6 towels; bishop's room, St. Paul's rectory, 1 towel, 2 sheets, 2 pillow cases, 1 scarf; Dr. Northrup, 1 white blanket; D. H. Merritt, table cloth and towels; C. A. Payne, 4 towels; A. Kidder, 1 curtain; St. Paul's Rectory, 1 lot of sheets, 2 carpets, bed spread.

Besides listing the amazing inventory, the article makes clear that Tommy resided at Presque Isle, so he must have been a close neighbor to the Kawbawgams. It is amazing that Tommy was able to carry all these items north of Marquette without being noticed or that none of his fellow Ojibwa realized what was happening. If they did realize it, perhaps they kept their mouths shut from fear of the authorities coming out to their little "Indian town" and causing trouble. Did Kawbawgam know of the thievery, and did he also keep his mouth shut to keep the authorities away? Or did any of the Ojibwa know

The Merritt House, circa 1890s. Notice its tennis court.

The Longyear Mansion, Marquette's most impressive home in Tommy's day

and plead with Tommy to no avail to quit stealing? Tommy appears to have been so delusional about his crimes that it's possible if anyone knew, they had given up on trying to reason with him. All we can do is speculate since we have no real indication, beyond Kawbawgam's statement that Tommy was "a bad Indian," of how the Native American community felt about the matter.

The following day, Saturday, May 20, *The Mining Journal* continued to detail Tommy's additional plunder.

> **More Madosh Plunder.**
>
> Justice Crary, Deputy Sheriff Dolf and a representative of *The Mining Journal* made another search of Tommy Madosh's house on the Presque Isle road yesterday afternoon and collected another wagon load of plunder which had been stored away by the gay and festive Thomas. In the lot was a large amount of clothing, the blankets from the bishop's room in St. Paul's rectory, a cloak stolen from the Baptist church, some silverware, a lot of carpenters' tools, a window from J. E. Sherman's house, A. Westlake's oil can and another fountain can,

> a lot of china and the usual collection of handkerchiof [sic], napkins, towels and other fruits of clothes line raids. Fully 200 empty fruit cans, quarts and pints, were found under the floor and a bushel or two of empty jelly and jam glasses were found in the shed back of the house. Handkerchiefs, towels and stockings by the hundreds were left in the house, as no distinguishing marks could be found upon them. That Tommy's taste in literature was varied was shown by the collection of papers, novels and books unearthed. Among the books were volume 1 of Tolstoi's "War and Peace" "Natural Laws in the Spiritual World" by Drummond, "Gospel Hymns," "The Army of Cumberland" by H. M. Cist and "New York to the Orient" by Emerson. The names could not be found in any of the books, the artful Tommy having torn the fly leaves out. In nearly every case where missing property had been described by the owner it was found in Tommy's collection, among other items being enough paint, oil, varnish and putty to start a good sized paint shop.

This passage is fascinating particularly for the books stolen. While it is likely Tommy stole items for the sake of stealing them, that he stole books suggests he had an interest in literature or at least was literate, or they may have been very decorative books that simply attracted him. Considering that Charles and Charlotte Kawbawgam were both unable to read, if Tommy Madosh could read, that would be quite impressive, although Tommy was born in 1847 and grew up surrounded by whites, unlike Charlotte, so he may have had some opportunities for education.

On Monday, May 22, *The Mining Journal* reported on the final result of Tommy's thievery.

> GOT A TEN-YEAR SENTENCE
>
> ———
>
> Mr. Tommy Madosh and Marquette
> Clothes-Lines Dissolve Partner-
> ship for Ten Years.
>
> ———
>
> Saturday Tommy Madosh changed his residence from North Marquette to South Marquette, from his shingle-clad cottage by the Presque Isle drive to the brownstone Castle Van Evera by the sounding Carp. At the same time Mr. Madosh decided to change his occupation from stripping Marquette clothes lines to stripping broom corn for the state whose servant he will be for the coming

> ten years, having pleaded guilty to the charge of burglary preferred because of his forced entrance into the rectory of St. Paul's church in the night time about two years ago, on which occasion he cleaned out "the bishop's room" completely, from window curtaius [sic] to towels and bed-clothing.
>
> Tommy was arraigned Saturday and was sentenced immediately after entering his plea of guilty. The sentence imposed by Judge Stone caused general surprise but is explained by the fact that the charge on which the now notorious Indian was arraigned was a much more serious one than it was supposed could be brought against him.

This last entry is surprising—both that Tommy had not only robbed a church, but that he did so by breaking and entering. The reference to "Castle Van Evera" refers to the Marquette Branch Prison, built in 1889 and just south of Marquette, where John R. Van Evera was the warden.

No mention is made of Tommy's attorney. We can assume he received a fair trial despite the hefty sentence. I have been unable to determine whether he remained in prison until 1903 or got time off for good behavior. One has to wonder whether Charles and Charlotte Kawbawgam attended his trial. Surely at least some of the Madosh family did. The embarrassment the family must have felt can well be imagined. Since many of them probably spoke limited English and did not understand it perfectly, they may have thought the courts were against Tommy. Obviously, Chief Kawbawgam's comment that Tommy was "a bad Indian" has to be taken in context. He may have felt he had to say something when *The Mining Journal* reporter asked for a comment. By this point, Kawbawgam may also have spoken English well enough to have said more that was not recorded.

Tommy's mother, Mrs. Madosh, apparently lived with him until the time of his arrest when she went to live with her son David. When Chief Madosh died is not known, but he must have been long dead by this time, especially if it's true that Kawbawgam "inherited" his position as chief from him. *The Mining Journal* at the time of Tommy's arrest said Mrs. Madosh was about one hundred, but when she died the next year, her obituary stated she was more than 100 and died of old age at home near the Dead River mill. It also stated she came many years before from Sugar Island (near the Sault).[4] From this we can gather that Marji-Gesick's brother Madosh and his family lived near the Sault or at least on the east end of the Upper Peninsula for a significant time. In addition, George Madosh's obituary in 1926[5] says he was 102 years old and that he came to Marquette from Drummond Island in the St. Clair

The Marquette Branch Prison, aka Castle Van Evera, where Tommy spent his prison sentence

River when there were only a few houses in Marquette.

As for Tommy, he would die in 1907 at age sixty from cancer. He was buried in Park Cemetery in the potter's field. His death record states he was a tailor,[6] which may help explain his fine clothes. No record exists that he ever married or had children. That he was buried in Park Cemetery is surprising since Catholics were buried in Holy Cross Cemetery and his brother George and George's wife Jane were buried in Holy Cross.[7] However, Tommy's brother David and nephew George (Oscar) would also be buried in Park Cemetery.[8] Either way, Tommy did not seem to have a fear of God when he broke the commandment not to steal; perhaps religion did not matter to him.

More About Jacques LePique

Jacques LePique was involved in two other important events in 1893 that affected the Kawbawgams, both of which will be discussed in Chapter 11. First, however, we will catch up on his life since 1862 when Marji-Gesick died in his canoe on Lake Superior.

As previously stated, after LePique and his wife Mary's house burnt down in L'Anse, the couple moved to Presque Isle where they resided until about

Jacques LePique

1866.[9]

One day, during this time, LePique and Mary traveled by train to Negaunee to sing in a choir. During the train ride, a cinder flew into LePique's eye, causing him to be nearly blind for ten years. The couple then moved near the Marquette Rolling Mill on Lake Street at the base of the bluff.[10] They resided in the Carp House, built by Hiram Burt for the Rolling Mill's employees, although by then the mill was abandoned.[c] Mr. Burt hired the LePiques to be the house's caretakers. Later, the LePiques spent their winters at Lighthouse Point and their summers at the Green Garden German settlement where LePique would buy forty acres and build a house near the Kawbawgams.[11]

LePique's eyesight was restored by a strange chain of events. He related to Kidder that one day Ed Sawonon's squaw[d] began to suffer from fits. Colonel Winslow Kidder, a cousin of Alfred Kidder, was able to calm her by putting his hands on her head. She then said she needed a medicine man, so one from L'Anse, named Bush-quay-gin (Leather), was sent for. He built a medicine lodge at Green Garden which was, according to LePique, "like a round screen, shaped like a barrel about eight feet high and open at the top, having six poles and six hoops. It was two fathoms around, that is about four feet in diameter and the poles were covered round with a sail. Bush-quay-gin wanted scarlet cloth to cover the frame but could not get it."[12]

---

c. The chronology here seems a bit confused since the mill operated from 1868 to 1884. LePique must have remembered some of these details incorrectly if the mill was closed when he resided there, or else the mill had a down year. Since LePique's wife Mary died in 1874, it is likely the mill was temporarily closed.

d. I have been unable to identify this family, but they were doubtless part of the Ojibwa community in Marquette. Perhaps it is a reference to Kawbawgam's half-brother Edward Shawano. Later Kidder references Shawanong as Kawbawgam's brother, translating the name as "from the South," a translation also often applied to the name of Kawbawgam's stepfather, Chief Shawano.

Once the lodge was finished, the ceremony was to take place at dusk. Because it was getting dark, LePique could not see, so his wife Mary led him to the ceremony. Once they sat down near the medicine lodge, LePique heard a voice above say: "We can do nothing for this woman. She is not pure." Next he heard the sound of a robin, and then the voice said, "But the man sitting there holding his wife's hand, we can help him."[13] It's not clear whether this voice was the voice of a disembodied spirit or of the medicine man himself (though the voice supposedly came from above). It's also not clear whether Mary heard the voice or LePique told her about it, but he managed to get her to lead him beside the lodge and spread a blanket beside it. He then lay down on the blanket and put his head into the lodge, under a flap near the ground. Kidder continues by saying:

> His head lay close to the medicine man who sat inside. For a good while there was no sound. Then he heard a voice above saying: "Now is the time to go and blow on him." Another voice answered: "Then why don't you blow on him?" With that Jacques heard a noise like that of claws coming down the pole next to his head. He then felt a cold wind blowing on his head, it seemed as if his eyes would freeze. The water ran from them and he felt as if they were being pulled out. Then the noise of scratching claws went back up the pole.
>
> As the spirit went up, a voice above asked, "What did you do for him?"
>
> The spirit answered: "This man once got a piece of iron in his eye but now I have taken it out. He will see very well all day tomorrow."
>
> The other spirit said: "I wouldn't thank anyone to give me my sight for one day."
>
> "Well," said the first, "that's all I can do for him. If you can do so much more, you'd better go down and try."
>
> Jacques heard the other coming down and felt the same cold wind. When this spirit went back up the pole, the first one said, "What did you do for him? You don't seem to have anything in your bill?"
>
> They sounded like birds talking. What they said was interpreted by another spirit that was invisible except for a light like sulphur which went out when he ceased speaking. His voice was no bigger than a baby's. In interpreting, he addressed each spirit as his grandfather.
>
> "Well," said the second, "I have done enough so that this man's sight will get better from this time forth, to the end of his life."

> Jacques then got up, and accordingly his sight steadily improved till he could see perfectly. At present (1895) he has remarkably good vision. As he told me this, he pointed to a vessel lying about a quarter of a mile off and said: "I can see every rope and halyard on that schooner." His hearing, as I have found in hunting deer with him, is more acute than mine.[14]

The truth of this remarkable story cannot be known, but it reflects that LePique firmly believed in the Ojibwa traditions and the medicine man's power to heal him with the help of the spirits. Although we do not have any statements from LePique about Christianity, the Kawbawgams clearly were Christians, yet this story shows that even in the late nineteenth century, the Ojibwa retained their traditional religious beliefs.

This event occurred sometime between 1860 and 1874 when Mary died. Although LePique stated he resided at Presque Isle for ten years, it may have been for a shorter period. His statement he was blind for ten years may also be unintentionally exaggerated. Nor do we know the full extent of his blindness; his vision seems to have been problematic primarily at night. The event probably occurred after 1863 since it references Alfred Kidder's cousin, Winslow, and we know LePique first met Alfred Kidder in the spring of 1863. LePique went exploring with Kidder on the head waters of the Salmon Trout and Yellow Dog, going inland from Big Bay. He was in the woods with Kidder off and on all that summer and winter and into 1864. He often served as Kidder's cook on these trips.[15]

Alfred Kidder

One of the most entertaining stories about LePique dates from a winter trip with Alfred Kidder in the 1860s. Homer Kidder related the following tale as told to him by his father, saying it showed "the tenacity of Ojibwa concepts among the more or less Christianized half-breeds of Lake Superior."

> One morning late in the winter, when they were breaking camp for a long tramp along the coast, a thaw promised to make for heavy

> snow shoeing. Before they left, Jacques took some moist snow and fashioned a rabbit standing on its haunches on the shore facing the north.
>
> The rabbit had an absurd, rakish air, and my father asked Jacques what it meant. Jacques said that the rabbit was intended to make the north wind blow, for Ka-bi-bo-na-kay (the north wind) would think the rabbit was making fun of him and would try to blow him down, but, of course, the colder it blew the harder the rabbit would freeze.
>
> Captain Joe Bridges, who was of the party, asked Jacques if he really believed that nonsense. Jacques said: "Just wait and see." As a matter of fact, when they had gone several miles, it came on to blow from the north and began to freeze. Jacques was elated. He said to Bridges: "Didn't I tell you? It never fails."
>
> Jacques afterwards told my father that this was an old practice with the Ojibwas to stop a thaw at sugar making time.[16]

This story illustrates once again a belief in the spirit world and in pantheism in the sense that all things, even the wind, have personalities.

During this time, while still living at Green Garden, and according to Kidder, helping Kawbawgam build his house there, LePique also helped to build a club house for Mr. Ripka.[e] Kidder tells us that at this clubhouse he also used to see Huey Fay and Walton Duane, who was called Bay-be-wah-kun-see-gah-dayd (Slim Legs). LePique and most Ojibwa clearly liked to give nicknames to their white friends.

On November 3, 1874, Jacques would face the greatest tragedy of his life when his wife Mary drowned off the northwest point of Presque Isle.[17] *The Mining Journal* gave a brief notice of the event:

> On Tuesday evening last, as Jack LaPique [sic] and a party of four or five other Indians were coming around Presque Isle Point, their boat struck a rock and capsized, throwing the whole party into the water. Two men and a woman, the latter Jack's wife, were drowned.

---

e. Kidder refers to him as Ripca, but this is surely a typo. A. A. Ripka lived in Marquette in the large sandstone house at 430 E. Arch Street, built in 1875 and still standing. The location of the clubhouse and its purpose are not known.

The bodies were recovered the following day.[18f]

This story, curiously, has two different versions based on how LePique told the story differently to two different friends, Homer Kidder and George Shiras III.

Kidder, in a letter to Helen Longyear Paul that was published in *The Mining Journal* on March 12, 1937, describes the event:

> Jacques and Mary after provisioning at Marquette for a trip up the lake—imbibing rather too copiously as Indians were likely to do when 'treating' among friends at the moment of taking leave—started off in a bark canoe. They may have struck choppy seas on rounding Presque Isle or it may be that they were, by that time, too drunk to sit up. Anyway the canoe capsized in the shallow water that lies on those shelving rocks at the northwest point. Jacques scrambled ashore and not till then, though I don't know how soon, noticed that Mary wasn't with him. This seems to have brought him to his senses. He saw her in the water and dragged her out, drowned. He told me it pretty nearly killed him when he found she was dead. He didn't tell me that he had been drinking—that I learned from my father, who was evidently informed of the circumstances, though I think all this happened a good while before he went to Lake Superior in 1861. Jacques was no drunkard and I have understood was devoted to Mary. She seems to have been a good woman, a good wife to Jacques.[19]

This statement is very surprising since we know Mary drowned in 1874 (the year of Homer Kidder's birth), yet Kidder assumes it happened before 1861 before his father first came to Marquette or at least before his father knew LePique; elsewhere Kidder says LePique and his father met in 1863.[20] Whether LePique was a drinker to the extent of getting drunk is unclear. That he didn't mention alcohol to Homer Kidder may show his guilt over the event, or it may suggest Alfred Kidder heard rumors that were simply not true. Given that Native Americans were stereotyped as having a tendency to get drunk, it's possible rumors circulated without basis.

The other interesting possibility here is that Jacques had two wives and

---

f. Despite *The Mining Journal* covering this story, I have been unable to locate a death record in Marquette County for Mary Nolin or for any of the other Native Americans who drowned during this incident. Apparently none of their deaths were recorded.

both drowned, but more likely, Kidder did not think through the comments about how his father could have known about the story or that it happened before his arrival in Marquette.

Also missing from this story is that, as *The Mining Journal* reported, four or five Native Americans were in the canoe and two others drowned besides Mary.

George Shiras III

The second version of Mary's death comes from George Shiras III. Here, it is worth making a short digression to explain how well Shiras and his family knew LePique. Shiras claimed his grandfather, George Shiras I, was the one who had given LePique the nickname Jack of Spades (English for Jacques LePique) in 1860. Shiras' grandfather had first come to Marquette to go fishing in 1849, and the family had annually returned to Marquette on fishing trips. Shiras' father, George Shiras II, would become a justice of the United States Supreme Court. Shiras' mother was Lillie Kennedy, one of the four Kennedy sisters who all married prominent men with Marquette connections; consequently, once George Shiras III married Peter White's daughter, he could claim to be related by blood or marriage to most of Marquette's prominent Ridge Street families. Shiras served as a congressman for his native Pennsylvania, and after he introduced a bill against the shooting of migratory birds, President Theodore Roosevelt befriended him. Although in his youth Shiras hunted and fished, he later developed an interest in photography and became the first photographer to learn how to set up cameras in the wilderness that were triggered by wildlife themselves to take their own photos. His wildlife photographs would earn him prizes at the Paris Exposition of 1900 and World's Fair in St. Louis in 1904. He would later author the two-volume work *Hunting Wild Life with Camera and Flashlight*, in which he described his many adventures in photographing wildlife and provided depictions of those who assisted him, including LePique and several other Ojibwa guides.

Shiras describes the death of LePique's wife as follows:

> In his earlier years Jack married one of his race, but never had any children. He appeared to have great affection for his wife, Mary, but when I condoled with him over her death by drowning in Lake Superior he said he had won a bet, though it was a poor kind of bet to make. He had bet his wife she couldn't swim, and now she was gone, but he couldn't collect the bet.[21]

It may be that LePique was simply trying to hide his grief by joking about the situation. Shiras goes on to say that LePique's "unconscious humor" was also shown in how he described the death of his mother-in-law, Susan. He told Shiras: "Do you know when I was driving her home in a cart she fell off the back end and broke her neck, and the funny thing about it is, she never even kicked."[22] The date of Susan's death is unknown. There is no death record for her in Marquette County but one contributor to Ancestry.com has guessed it to be 1884.

Sadly, we have no record of how Charles or Charlotte Kawbawgam responded to these family tragedies. LePique was apparently in no way blamed by the family for Mary's death since he remained close to the Kawbawgams until he chose to leave Marquette. It's also notable that he testified for Charlotte in her lawsuit against the Jackson Iron Company. Since Mary was dead by the time of the trial, and she was not Marji-Gesick's child but Susan's by one of Marji-Gesick's brothers, she was never listed as one of his. Plus, since LePique and Mary had no children, LePique could have no claim on money from the trial, so his willingness to testify was solely out of goodwill toward Charlotte and her family.

At some point in the 1880s or 1890s, LePique moved again, this time to "Whitefish Lake," which may refer to Laughing Whitefish Lake in Onota Township in Alger County, about twenty-five miles southeast of Marquette. Shiras describes LePique during this time as still hunting, and although unable to help on expeditions, he still assisted at "our camp," which probably refers to Peter White's camp on Deer Lake, about five or so miles from Laughing Whitefish Lake, just east of Deerton. Shiras states:

> As Jack became old and decrepit, he passed much of his time in his cabin on a hill at the south end of Whitefish Lake, a habitation that was a great improvement over the one occupied by us when he first conducted us to this beautiful body of water. Unable to do any hard work, such as rowing, paddling, or packing, he depended upon little contributions given him for work done at our camp, such as weeding [the] garden or killing potato bugs. During the season of

open water, Jack always had fresh meat, for a deer could be killed at almost any hour in the slough just below his cabin. His failing eyesight demanded that he get within close range of his quarry.[g]

I remember once climbing an overhanging tree in the south end of the slough, where seated on a comfortable platform, I could pull one of several strings that led across the water to cameras set on the opposite shore. I had been seated on my convenient perch only a few minutes when I saw old Jack enter the slough in his dugout and knew that he was after fresh meat.

AN AGED HUNTER USES CUNNING

At a certain spot on the opposite shore was a locally famous large pine log that lay parallel to the bank, with a salt spring behind it. Many large bucks were killed at the spot each year. I had placed two of my cameras a short distance from each end of this log, and Jack's presence blocked any chance I might have of getting a picture.

Since I could not be seen, I concluded to watch his *modus operandi* in killing a deer only a few feet away. With some effort, Jack shoved his old water-soaked dugout [boat] through the mud and shallow water until he was about 10 feet away from the "buck log." When the dugout was in position, Jack made ready for a shot by placing his old musket athwart the canoe, and then he lay back quietly in the stern in a comfortable position.

Some 10 minutes had passed when I saw a deer in the reddish-yellow summer coat coming down the wooded hillside on one of the many runways that converged at this point. The deer looked up and down the shore and along its back track fearful of the possible presence of a timber wolf, but did not see Jack in his old weather-beaten canoe, that looked like a log, floating in the water, a place where danger was not ordinarily expected.

The hunter did not see the deer until it began drinking at the spring, and then he slowly reached for the musket. In pulling it toward him, however, he discharged it, and the deer bounded away, having learned that the quiet waters of the slough also demanded examination for possible enemies.

Disappointed by this outcome and probably having no more

g. This remark is not in keeping with LePique's claim to excellent eyesight after being healed from his temporary blindness.

> ammunition for his muzzle-loader, Jack slowly backed out and paddled off down the slough, quite unaware of having had an eye witness to his misadventures.[23]

From Shiras we have also learned about LePique's pride in his age. Shiras states:

> After he had faithfully served three generations of my family, I once asked him how old he was. "I am old enough," he said, "to know better than to answer such a question." But in his later years he took pride in his age and always added a few years for good measure.[24]

We must wonder from this comment whether age exaggeration was a conscious tendency among the Ojibwa given that so many claimed to have lived to a hundred and beyond.

Finally, from Shiras we learn of Jack's desire, despite his old age and the tragedies he had faced during his life, to still have a good time.

> During the later period of his stay in this region Jack led a simple and temperate life. Once a year, however, he had a grand celebration in town.
>
> He would put on his best clothes and, with his long black locks glistening with bear's grease, go to a livery stable and select the best looking buggy and a horse that seldom went out of [sic] a walk. Then he would choose some good-looking young girl, red or white, as a companion, and traverse every street in town, repeating his appearance on the more crowded thoroughfares. He held the reins listlessly in one hand and used the other to wave greetings. He often rested his feet on the dashboard.
>
> During these appearances Jack excited as much attention as a Lord Mayor of London. At that time Marquette was so small and self-contained that every one knew old Jack and gave him a cordial reception. On returning to the stable, he would pay the bill for his rig and hand a five dollar bill to his young companion. The girls always took pride in being selected for this occasion by the kindly old Indian.[25]

Notably, LePique's celebration included imbibing alcohol once a year, which he may otherwise have sworn off after Mary's death, especially if alcohol had been involved in the accident that caused her death. This story also shows that whites took kindly to and were proud of the Ojibwa who resided among them, or at least the notable ones like Kawbawgam and LePique, especially since even white girls were willing to go for a ride with LePique.

In 1894, while LePique was living at Whitefish Lake, Shiras took a party of people on an expedition. A camp log was kept, and in it the entry for July 8 reads:

> As we came home we stopped at Jack La Pete's cabin and got some maple sugar. McClay had some doubt about the cleanliness of the sweet stuff, but Jake [Brown] assured him that it was all right, since he had seen Jack strain it through an old blanket.[26]

Of course, living among the Ojibwa, LePique would have been well-versed in the ways of maple sugar production, despite what any finicky white man would have thought.

One final story of LePique during this time concerns how he was always accompanied by a small dog. He may have had multiple dogs, but one named Toodley was said to provide almost as much amusement to people as his master. LePique would often tell it to "Laff a leelte" and it would turn up its lips to give an expressive grin.[27]

In the next chapter, we will look at LePique and the Kawbawgams' recording of Ojibwa legends and also LePique's decision to leave Marquette. First, however, it is worth noting that by this point, Fred Cadotte, also known as Fred Bawgam, was grown up and also working as a guide for Shiras.

When LePique's old dugout boat was no longer serviceable, LePique was given a small-bottomed boat, perhaps by Shiras who took this photo. The dog may be LePique's dog Toodley.

Fred Cadotte

Shiras writes of Fred Cadotte, Marji-Gesick's grandson:

Among the guides we had for many years along the south shore of Lake Superior was Fred Cadotte, a full-blooded Ojibway Indian, often called Fred Bawgam because of his relationship to a notable Indian chief of this region. Fred was a packer and assistant guide who in more than 30 years accompanied us on many hunting trips.

FRED CADOTTE BEGAN HIS SERVICES YOUNG

His services began when he was a slender boy of 14 [circa 1866] who spoke only Ojibway. Later he grew to a height of 6 feet and 3 inches but never filled out in proportion. He was a quiet, good-natured woodsman who could always be depended upon....

Fred excelled any man I have ever known, either Indian or white, in his extraordinarily accurate sense of location, or, as it is termed, orientation. Often he accompanied me on deer hunts about Whitefish Lake when the forest, extending away for many miles, was an untracked wilderness. When he was along, I never considered it necessary to carry a compass.

On some of these hunts we would be out all day, and when the time came to return I would tell Fred that it was up to him to find camp. I had gained such complete confidence in his woodsmanship that I had paid no attention to landmarks, as I would have done if by myself, or even with another guide.

Without any hesitancy Fred would turn and make a bee-line through the heavy forest, often for miles, and with unerring certainty would bring us to camp. At times on the way back we would cross the course we had followed on the way out, as shown by some notable landmark.

Even darkness failed to confuse this sense of direction. Once in the fall of 1882 we left the railroad track for Whitefish Lake Camp less than two hours before dark. The only route had been traversed so few times that no trail was visible. We left Fred at the railroad to make up a pack of our camp outfit, all of which he insisted on carrying.

Being unencumbered, my companion and I made fast time and arrived at camp just before dark. It was evident that it would be much later before Fred could come in with his heavy load, and we built a fire to serve as a beacon when he came near.

About an hour after dark the light of the camp fire revealed Fred's tall, gaunt figure as it appeared on the edge of the clearing. As he came into the open he continued for a few yards the curious high-stepping gait he had been using in the woods in order to clear as much of the tangled brush underfoot as he could in the pitch-black darkness of the forest.

Approaching the fire, he threw down the pack with the remark, "Gosh, you fellers must be hungry," and at once set about preparing some of the food he had brought. He took his trip through the woods at night as a matter of course.

A PERSISTENT WEASEL

After a successful deer hunt the following day we were seated about the camp fire before our lean-to in the evening. A weasel was seen on top of our rude table, helping himself to some of our venison hanging just above it. The intruder was within about 6 feet of us.

We drove it away repeatedly but it persistently returned. It was so bold and intent on getting at the meat that once I inserted my toe under its body and tossed it 10 feet away. Even this failed to discourage it, for it immediately returned to the meat.

Finally, to discourage the little beast, which we did not wish to kill, we placed the venison on a narrow shelf over one of the balsam beds in the lean-to. Soon after this we went to bed and within a few minutes the light of the camp fire showed the weasel climbing up to the shelf to renew its interrupted feast.

Fred was lying below the shelf and we told him to frighten the weasel away. He sat up and seizing a heavy shoe hurled it at the intruder. The weasel in its alarm crowded itself into a narrow crevice between an upright sack of corn meal on the shelf and the wall of the lean-to. The bag was so nicely balanced that some slight jar of the shelf made it tip forward.

The top of the bag was open, and as it turned down over the edge of the shelf the meal poured in a cascade over Fred's head and shoulders, giving him an extraordinary appearance in the flickering firelight. After the excitement of this amusing occurrence had subsided, we hung the meat where it could not be disturbed, and soon forgot the persistent little carnivore in sleep.

Fred's skill in orientation may have been aided by his remarkably keen eyesight, quite the best I have seen in a man, and a subconscious memory of topography. His acuteness of sight was a constant source of wonderment to me. With my long years in the woods and training in observation my powers of seeing and distinguishing birds or animals were insignificant when compared with his.

When we were passing through the woods, ruffed grouse often flew up and disappeared into the thick top of a tree. Almost without hesitation Fred would point out the perching bird in its fancied concealment. Along the way he constantly drew my attention to grouse perching quietly high in the treetops.

His ability to distinguish standing deer up to 100 yards or more away in the undergrowth was almost uncanny. Apparently, as we walked along, only a patch of the animal's side needed to be exposed for him to spot it by a casual glance. Frequently it required some time for me to distinguish the form of deer that had so instantaneously caught his eye.

Although Fred served as my camp helper and guide from the age of 14 years, his contacts with other white people were few, and his vocabulary was limited. Most of his emotions were expressed by the one word, "gosh."

One night we were seated by a camp fire beneath a big pine at camp when we heard some strange sounds from the treetop, "Gosh!" said Fred, "an owal."

IT RAINED OWLS

Looking up we saw the pale breast of a barred owl perched high on a limb. Taking a rifle, which was close at hand, I stood in front of the fire and, aiming upward, fired. A moment later three feathered objects came tumbling down nearby.

"Gosh!" exclaimed Fred, "three owals."

In mock disappointment I said, "only three? I expected six."

"Gosh!" said Fred, as he picked up the game.

Then the unexpected result of the shot was revealed. The big bullet had cut the bird I shot at into two fragments, and had killed its mate which was sitting behind it concealed by the leaves.

On coming out of the cabin early the next morning, I saw Fred carefully searching the ground among the bushes under the big pine tree.

> To my inquiry as to what he was doing he replied, "Gosh! I am looking for dem oder three owals."
>
> He had taken literally my jocular little remark of the night before.
>
> Fred lived until his seventy-third year and died in a small cabin near Chocolay River, where he had a little farm. After his death, in memory of his faithful services and my many pleasant days with him in the woods, I had a small granite slab placed to mark his last resting place.[28]

Fred Cadotte and Shiras were obviously good companions, being fairly close in age. That Shiras paid for a gravestone for Fred shows his esteem for him. Fred would die on April 19, 1926 and be buried in Marquette's Holy Cross Cemetery.[29]

Despite Shiras' remark above, however, Fred was not a full-blooded Ojibwa. Such assertions of Natives being full-blooded is curious since it means that whites did not always take the time to inquire into Native Americans' ancestries and possibly they found some pride in referring to Natives as such, still clinging to an idea of the "noble" and hence, pure, "savage." Language barriers also would have made it difficult to gather genealogical details, but we know Fred's father was of both Ojibwa and French-Canadian descent so Fred was not a full-blooded Ojibwa but métis, just like LePique and Kawbawgam. Shiras should have known better given that Fred had a French surname. Furthermore, Shiras' father-in-law, Peter White, likely had known Fred's father, having been Kawbawgam's close friend, and since Fred's father had committed murder in Marquette, it's unlikely White didn't at least know of him. One would think White would have given Shiras more information on Fred, especially since we know White also spent time hunting with him, and White spoke fluent Ojibwa. By the time Shiras published his book in 1935, however, Fred had been dead for nine years and

Fred Cadotte

Peter White for twenty-seven, so Shiras was relying on memories decades old and may simply have forgotten certain details he knew about Fred's background.

One has to wonder where Fred Cadotte learned his skills. Did Kawbawgam teach him much that he knew? Since Fred's father died while he was still a boy, we don't know how much influence he may have had on Fred. It is also interesting that Fred spoke only Ojibway up until the time he was fourteen, which suggests the Ojibwa largely kept to themselves in Marquette's early years rather than associating much with the whites, or perhaps children were not encouraged to be around adult whites.

Peter White's own experiences hunting with Fred led to a surprising incident that almost became a serious accident. Shiras recounts the event as follows:

Fred Cadotte,
photo taken by George Shiras III

> During a several days' hunt about Whitefish Lake our companion was Peter White, the "grand old man" of northern Michigan. Although one of the founders of Marquette in 1849, and a pioneer in the development of that region, he did not become interested in hunting until late in life.
>
> Usually he was successful in getting a deer, but had been disappointed up to near the end of this hunt. To give him another chance, I suggested that on our way out we follow a part of the old trail that passed close by a small slough to which deer often came to feed on water plants.
>
> As we approached the place, we heard splashing in the water, resembling the noise of a deer wading about.

> The elderly hunter was told to go ahead and look carefully through the alders bordering the water. Very soon he raised his gun and tried to find a small clear opening for it through the brush.
>
> Before he had succeeded in getting a good sight, Fred Cadotte, our Indian guide, and the most experienced deer hunter of his race I have ever met, tiptoed up close behind the shooter and suddenly said in a low, tense voice, "Don't shoot! It's a man."
>
> Flustered by this, the hunter drew back his gun and through the opening we saw the indistinct figure of a man, bending over, scooping up water with his hands and washing his face. He wore a yellowish brown canvas coat, about the color of the deer at that season. While he was bending over the water behind the screen of bushes, he bore a striking resemblance to a deer feeding in the water. We silently hastened by without being noticed.
>
> Later we learned that the man we had seen was a young Mr. Robert Dollar, who was engaged in land-looking, or timber-cruising, and was camped near by. Since then he has become an international figure as the organizer of the Dollar Steamship Line. One of the most successful of our merchant fleets. Unless he sees this printed page he will probably never know of his narrow escape at that time.[30]

Shiras didn't realize, apparently, that by the time his book was published in 1935, Dollar had been dead for three years. Robert Dollar was born in Scotland in 1844. His family migrated to Ontario in the 1850s, and from the age of fourteen, he worked in lumber camps that produced timber for the English market. Then in 1882, he came to Marquette. He built a house at 433 E. Arch, which still stands today. He only remained in Marquette until 1888 when he moved to San Rafael, California, due to ill health. In California, he became a prominent lumberman and ship owner and pioneered trade between North America and the Orient, becoming known as the "Grand Old Man of the Pacific." In 1914, he was considered one of the fifty greatest men in the United States. He died in 1932 at the age of eighty-eight. Dollarville, Michigan, where he once worked as the general manager of a logging camp, is named for him.[31] That Fred Cadotte saved his life is just another instance of unsung Native American heroes.

Photo of Hunting Party at the old Peter White Camp. 1884. Left to right: "Fred Bawgam, seated; Samson Noll, facing left; Jack La Pete—all guides; and young Brassey, afterward Lord Brassey; McLean, stroke oarsman in the Oxford, England, crew; Peter White and Charley, an Indian guide."[32] *Photo taken by George Shiras III.*[h]

Not a lot more is known about Fred Cadotte, other than that he lived on his farm and took care of Charlotte after Kawbawgam died. That he was known as Fred Bawgam by many speaks of the closeness of his relationship with Kawbawgam as his adopted son.

---

h. Noll was an African-American guide often employed by Shiras, a sign that Shiras was not at all racist in the people he employed. Noll was an escaped slave who had hit his master over the head with a wagon stave. More details about Noll can be found in Valerie Bradley-Holliday's book *Northern Roots: African Descended Pioneers in the Upper Peninsula of Michigan*. Lord Brassey (1836-1918) was an English baron and later the first Earl of Brassey. In his book *Voyages and Travels of Lord Brassey, 1862-1894*, he mentions his 1886 visit to Marquette (Vol. 1. p. 241-44), including visiting the Titan mine, but no mention is made of a hunting trip with Shiras. Shiras dates the picture to 1884 and refers to his guest as "Young Brassey" so this may be Lord Brassey's son, the second earl (1863-1919). Why either English lord visited Upper Michigan is unclear. It may simply have been out of curiosity, or they may have had investments in the iron mines (McCommons p. 33). Most likely Brassey and McLean, the Oxford stroke oarsman pictured, were friends and traveled together to Upper Michigan. McLean is Douglas Howard McLean (1863-1901) which makes it likely Brassey is the second earl. Perhaps he and McLean were at Oxford together, being the same age.

The Kawbawgams as Grandparents

Although the Kawbawgams' children died young, because they adopted Fred and Angelica Cadotte, a multitude of young children would eventually look up to them as adoptive grandparents.

Angelica had a daughter, Mary, who would have been the first of the Kawbawgams' "grandchildren." Mary would have been especially precious to them since they raised her as they had her mother. However, some confusion exists about other children the Kawbawgams raised, who may have even been Mary's children. By 1893, at about the age of sixteen or seventeen, Mary may have married a man named Perreau or Perrot because the 1900 census shows her living with the Kawbawgams and the two "Parrow" children Elizabeth (Lizzie b. 1893) and Frank (b. 1895).[33] However, these may not be Mary's children but children the Kawbawgams simply adopted, although it seems strange that they would have adopted children at their advanced age who were not related to them.[i] Who Mr. Perreau was remains a mystery; if he was involved with or married to Mary, he likely died or possibly abandoned the family not long after Frank's birth. Frank and Lizzie's father may have been a son or other relation to "Old Perreau," an old man identified in a photograph taken with Kawbawgam. He was likely métis, of French-Canadian and Native blood, but nothing else is known about him.

In 1900, at about age twenty-four, Mary married Peter Mendosking (Mandosking/Moduskee/Mandoski), who was twenty-seven and from the Sault. She may have had a son named Richard with Peter, but it is also likely Richard was Peter's son by a previous marriage since at least one record states Richard was born at Sugar Island at the Sault in 1894, six years before Mary

---

i. I am uncertain whether the Perreau children are Mary's children. That Mary was their mother is the most logical reason for why they were living with the Kawbawgams, but the Kawbawgams may simply have adopted them because their parents had died or were unable to care for them. The only source suggesting the Perreau children are Mary's comes from Homer Kidder, who stated that Frank was "Mary Cadotte's child" (Kidder, *Ojibwa*, p. 36)—perhaps Mary Cadotte was a completely different person than Mary Tebeau, but more likely Kidder may have confused the surnames. That said, he might also have confused the relationship. I have not found any marriage record for Mary to a Perreau. I did find a Marquette County birth record for a Lizzie Perreau born on April 17, 1892, whose mother is named Kittie and Swedish, but we cannot be sure this is the same Lizzie Perreau, especially since no birth record for a Frank Perreau has been found to compare the names of the parents.

and Peter married.[34j] Where Mary lived while married is not known—it may have been Marquette or the Sault. Peter, however, died not long after the wedding because on her death certificate, Mary is listed as a widow. Mary would herself die in Marquette in 1903, the year between Kawbawgam and Charlotte's deaths.[35]

Meanwhile, Fred and Eliza Cadotte's family was quickly growing. By 1898, they would have six children: Annie (1880-1905), Charles (1884-1960), Alfred (1887-1948), Alice Mary (1893-1972), Clifford (1895-1965/6), and Wilfred (1898-1960).[36] Although the Cadottes lived on Fred's farm in Chocolay Township, no doubt the Kawbawgams saw them and their children frequently and would have considered all of their children as their grandchildren.

By this point, the Ojibwa and métis world of the past had all but vanished. The Kawbawgams, seeing how the world had changed since their youth, may have felt the need to preserve their people's traditions for the young generations springing up around them. Consequently, when Homer Kidder approached them with the idea of recording their traditions and stories, they agreed, as our next chapter will explore.

---

j. In 1903, *The Mining Journal*, in "Kaw-baw-gam: Interesting Facts Regarding the Old Chippewa's History," states the Kawbawgams adopted a girl, "who married a man named Tebe, who died later, when she afterwards married Peter Moduskee." This suggests Tebeau was Mary's married name and not maiden name but it is an error since the lawsuit documents list her as Mary Tebeau, daughter of Frank Tebeau. This article also says the Kawbawgams adopted a boy who died, presumably referring to the unidentified Civil War veteran they adopted. This means the Kawbawgams adopted four children altogether, including Charlotte's nephew and niece, Fred and Angelica Cadotte. That does not mean, however, that Mary, and perhaps even the unnamed adopted boy, were not near-relatives like the Cadottes. Nor are newspapers to be relied on to get family relationships correct. Adoption also probably means the Kawbawgams raised the children as their own and not that any formal legal adoption took place. The appointment of Frederick Clark as Mary Tebeau's legal guardian appears to be the only time the Kawbawgams felt the need to legalize any aspects of their relationships with the children they raised, and this was to protect Mary's financial settlement from the lawsuit.

Old Perreau and Kawbawgam at Presque Isle

Greenewald Cigar Store at 115 Washington St. in 1886

Chapter 11
Preserving Ojibwa Culture

THE KAWBAWGAMS AND JACQUES LEPIQUE grew up in a time when the United States controlled Upper Michigan. They had no living memory of the French or British days, much less of the golden days before the white man came. During their lifetimes, they had seen Ojibwa lands signed over through treaties. They had themselves dealt closely with the white men—Kawbawgam being involved in signing treaties, LePique having traveled to Washington and met with President Polk to interpret for Native Americans trying to retain their land, and Charlotte Kawbawgam having sued a mining company to get her father's rightful share of the profit. These had not been easy efforts, and while neither LePique nor the Kawbawgams had engaged in warfare against the white men as their ancestors had done, they had still fought their battles, fighting by the white men's rules. Now, as the nineteenth century came to a close, they were watching their culture die because of the white Americans. At the same time, the Americans were largely the ones writing their history, and as the many cigar store Indians throughout Marquette's downtown illustrated at this time, it was not always an accurate or a complimentary one. Even whites who were sympathetic and friendly to Native Americans tended to write about them in broad, vague, and often derogatory terms with a hint of nostalgia for a past that had been largely brutal.

The time had come for the Kawbawgams and LePique, if not to sit down and write the elegies, to ensure their history and cultural traditions be preserved for future generations. The children of their community were becoming assimilated by whites—they worked for whites, lived among whites, wore white clothes, worshipped in white churches, and were forgetting Native American ways. Oral traditions were also starting to be forgotten, so the Kawbawgams and LePique knew if their culture were to be preserved, it would need to be written down.

The Ojibwa had their own type of writing—pictograms more akin to Egyptian hieroglyphics than written English. When Johann Georg Kohl visited the Lake Superior Ojibwa in 1855, he had been very curious about the birchbark books they kept, books of pictograms that told stories. Yet even these books relied on oral traditions to remember what the pictures meant, and by the time of Kohl's visit, many of the birchbark books that had been kept had been lost or destroyed. In fact, Chief Shingwaukonse had possessed a large library of such books but chose to destroy them all before his death, not long before Kohl's visit.[1] The days of birchbark books had clearly passed. If the Ojibwa wished to preserve their history, they would need to record it in the white man's languages in the form of the white man's books.

Since Chief Kawbawgam was probably illiterate, we don't know how aware he was of the power of the written word, although he certainly would have understood that the whites valued it, especially since he was present for the signing of the 1855 treaty. LePique would have been even more knowledgeable. Equally unknown is how aware the Kawbawgams and LePique were in 1893 of previous attempts to record Ojibwa history. Some seventy years earlier, Henry Schoolcraft had sought to record Ojibwa tales. Nearly forty years earlier, in 1855, Henry Wadsworth Longfellow had popularized Ojibwa culture through *The Song of Hiawatha*. In 1847, William Warren, an Ojibwa from Wisconsin (his mother was a Cadotte from the Sault), at a public council of chiefs, declared it was his desire to write down all important events of the Ojibwa so they wouldn't be lost forever, a task approved by his grandfather.[2] However, Warren's death in 1853 resulted in his book not being published until 1885. Certainly, the age of writing had come to the Ojibwa, and when those like Kawbawgam could not write for themselves, they found people to do so for them.

That is not to say the Kawbawgams consciously sought to record their tales; more likely, when the idea was presented to them, they agreed to the task. Fortunately, Homer Kidder was interested in preserving their lore.

Homer Huntingdon Kidder (1874-1950) was the eldest son of Alfred Kidder, the mining engineer whom LePique had worked with for many years and who, with Peter White, had constructed the Kawbawgams' home at

Presque Isle. From an early age, Homer was interested in Native Americans and their lore. While attending school in the East in 1890, he composed a lengthy short story in the school magazine, *The Vindex*, about three boys who go on adventures in the Huron Mountains northwest of Marquette, including visiting Pine Lake, Ives Lake, and Trout Lake. In the story, the boys' guide is the Indian "Marji Gesick."[3] The story is definitely fictional since Margi-Gesick died about 1862, a dozen years before Kidder was born, but Kidder had no qualms about using the famous chief's name for his fiction.

Homer was still a teenager in 1893 when he recorded LePique and the Kawbawgams' tales. He was attending Harvard University when illness forced him to leave. He returned to Marquette for the next two years, spending his summers at the Huron Mountain Club. He would later return to Harvard and graduate in 1899.[4] During those two years in Marquette, Kidder became interested in preserving Ojibwa tales, probably having heard several of LePique's tales from his father and maybe having already heard some from LePique himself.

When Kidder approached LePique with the suggestion of collecting the tales, LePique was open to the idea and suggested Kawbawgam be included. Perhaps because Kawbawgam was acknowledged as the local chief, LePique felt he should be involved in this important project. LePique may have also thought Kawbawgam knew more or better stories than he did.

Kidder probably already knew of Kawbawgam, but he does not seem to have known him well because LePique instructed him on how to make his request to Kawbawgam properly, including bringing him a gift of tobacco. This gift was part of the Ojibwa convention of storytelling; Kawbawgam would smoke the tobacco in silence between the telling of the stories.[5] Kidder tells us that LePique described how, on a previous occasion, he had "cut some tobacco from a stick, mixed it with a little Kinnikinnick, and lighting a pipe with fire steel and punk, gave it to Shawonong ["From the South," Kawbawgam's brother] because he was going to tell a story." Shawonong smoked slowly, then related the story as he had heard it. Kidder goes on to say, "This seems to have been the custom. When I arranged with Kawbawgam to tell me the stories of his people, Jacques LePique, who was to interpret, suggested the first day that I should take a pipe and tobacco to Presque Isle, to present to Kawbawgam. This I did, and Kawbawgam would always smoke in silence between stories."[6]

During this storytelling process, the Kidders may have been given their Ojibwa nicknames. Alfred Kidder became known as Te-quah-bit (Glass

Eyes) and Homer Kidder as Te-quah-bince (Little Glass Eyes).[7] Obviously the names refer to the Kidders' glasses, though curiously, a photograph of Kawbawgam from about this time shows him also wearing glasses. Spectacles certainly weren't new to the Ojibwa, and Kawbawgam's eyesight was failing by this point.

Kawbawgam wearing glasses

How formal this process of requesting Kawbawgam to tell stories was, how Charlotte became included in the process, or whether regularly scheduled appointments were made is not known. We do know the process had to be laborious. Kawbawgam's English was still not good and Charlotte's was probably no better. Kidder did not know enough Ojibwa to understand the Kawbawgams. Therefore, the Kawbawgams told their tales in Ojibwa and LePique translated them into English for Kidder. Consequently, every story had to be told twice, and the retelling by LePique would have been done slowly so Kidder could record everything by hand. Furthermore, LePique spoke in a heavy accent and had his own peculiarities of dialect. In translating the Kawbawgams' stories, he also may have embellished or added his own details.[8] Kidder briefly describes the process as follows:

> The stories related in Ojibwa by Charlotte and Kawbawgam, at their house at Presque Isle, were interpreted for me by Jacques LePique, and I took them down with a pencil as he slowly translated. His English was that of the Canadian French, marked by an accent but fluent and sometimes surprisingly adequate. I have not tried to reproduce the peculiarities of his dialect but have tried to express his thoughts as accurately as I could in readable English. It has proved anything but an easy task and I am far from being satisfied with the result. The lore of any folk should, if possible, be recorded in their

> own language. I am well aware that the use of an interpreter is a makeshift. Still I have felt it was worthwhile to record these tales as carefully interpreted. In the case of such as have been recorded, the versions in this collection may present local variations of interest.[9]

The process certainly would have required a patience that few nineteen-year-old boys possess. But Kidder seems to have been a deeply sensitive young man with the determination of a true scholar. Furthermore, it is telling that the Kawbawgams and LePique were willing to trust such a young white man with their precious history. Kidder was well aware of his task's importance, and also how important his informants found it, stating:

> My informants realized that their ancestral lore was passing from the memories of their people, and they gave me the tales with the understanding that these should be preserved in writing if not in print. I regret that other concerns have so long delayed the completion of this task.[10]

Kidder wrote this statement in 1910, several years after the Kawbawgams had passed away. His introduction to the collection of the tales shows that in that year he probably planned to publish the material after arranging and retranscribing it. How much work he put into the manuscript over the years is not known, but the bulk of the stories were collected between 1893 and 1895.

Kidder labored over rewriting the stories as evidenced by him giving more than one version of two of the stories, showing that he reworked the material to cut redundancies and strengthen them for dramatic effect.[11] In other words, like Schoolcraft before him, Kidder was making the stories more accessible for a white audience and a future Ojibwa audience that might only speak English.

Although Kidder's intention, as reflected in his original title *Ojibwa Myths and Halfbreed Tales*, may have been to capture Ojibwa mythology, unlike most myths, the stories collected are not timeless works but largely reflect the early years of his informants' lives in the 1820s and 1830s when the fur trade still existed, Ojibwa culture was still largely intact and migratory, and few whites resided in the Upper Peninsula other than at the Sault.[12] Mixed in with the historical incidents is a deep belief in the old ways of Ojibwa culture. Kidder describes Kawbawgam's beliefs as follows:

> Kawbawgam was a pronounced conservative and lamented the transformations which had come over his country and the life of the

> Indians. The stories he gave me, even those that recite incidents in his own experience, are uniformly concerned with the ancient lore of his people, in which he retained unquestioning faith. They represent a stage of Ojibwa culture that has now quite disappeared in that part of the tribe. His wife was even less influenced by American life than he.[13]

That Kawbawgam clung to his people's beliefs is remarkable given that he had been married and probably baptized as a Catholic and later would have a Catholic funeral. Unfortunately, we have no record of whether he regularly attended Mass. However, it was not uncommon for the Ojibwa to practice a blend of Christianity and traditional Native beliefs. For example, when Chief Ogista, son of Chief Shingwaukonse, died in 1890, *The Sault Express* quoted him as saying he would reappear "as a sturgeon in a small lake at the back of the houses." Reverend James Irvine, the resident missionary at Garden River, the community Shingwaukonse had established, insisted the newspaper was mistaken because Ogista was a Christian and once "saved" no Christian chief could hold Native beliefs, but the newspaper's editor responded that his information had come from a "reliable" source and "had been corroborated."[14]

It's possible that white Christians and white people in general could not fully understand the Native American mindset and Kawbawgam was aware of this. That may explain why, notably, while he told many stories about Nanabozho, the Ojibwa trickster hero, not all the stories from the Nanabozho cycle are included among those Kawbawgam told. Bourgeois, Kidder's editor, notes that other well-known women's stories and some bawdier stories are also not included. Bourgeois theorizes that their absence may reflect Kawbawgam's Christianity or his respect for Kidder.[15] Possibly, Kawbawgam was conscious that a white, Victorian, and Christian audience might not appreciate such stories. Certainly, after half a century of living in or near white communities, Kawbawgam may have developed a sense of what whites would like or dislike. We have to wonder whether he had already told some of these stories in Ojibwa to Peter White or other whites who spoke Ojibwa and how those versions may have differed from those recorded or those he may have told his fellow Ojibwa.

One example of Kawbawgam's belief in the truth of the stories comes from a statement he made after he told the tale of the Great Skunk and of the Great Bear of the West. Kawbawgam said: "These things must have happened before the Flood, for although the bones of monstrous animals are sometimes found in the ground, no one knows when these animals lived and there are now no more of them in the world."[16] Kidder explains that Kawbawgam meant such animals would have had descendants as large as them still living, and then adds:

> I (H.H.K.) answered that I knew it was true as he said, that once there had been monstrous animals in the world and I mentioned that their bones had been discovered by scientists.
>
> On hearing this, as interpreted by Jacques LePique, Kawbawgam smiled and said with his usual gentleness but with fine scorn: "The scientist thinks he understand[s] these things, but the man who knows is the Jessakid"—the Indian soothsayer.
>
> Nothing that Kawbawgam ever said tickled me so much as this, for it proved his unquestioning faith in the ancient lore of his people and in the stories that he was relating.[17]

The Flood story is noticeably absent from Kawbawgam's stories, but Johann Georg Kohl recorded it when he visited Lake Superior in 1855. It tells how following the Flood, Nanabozho created a new earth out of three grains of sand that a muskrat dove into the waters to get. The muskrat drowned but floated to the top and Nanabozho found the grains of sand in his hand and created the earth from them. Kohl goes on to state that unlike other spirits, Nanabozho did not go up to heaven but stayed on earth to live among the Indians as if an Indian himself.[18] This tale of the Flood and Creation and even a god-type character walking among men may suggest a Christian influence on the legends; however, it should be noted that many ancient cultures besides the Hebrews, including the Greeks and Sumerians, had their own tales of the Flood so there's no reason why the Ojibwa could not have their own Flood stories independent of Christian influence.

As Kidder recorded the stories, he continually wondered how they might have already been colored by the Kawbawgams and LePique's experiences with whites. For example, the story "Nibawnawbé" is named for Charlotte's grandfather. The name Nibawnawbé means merman, or someone half man and half fish. When Kidder suggested to LePique that the Ojibwa got the idea of a merman or mermaid from whites, LePique said no, mermaids had always existed in Lake Superior and Charlotte herself had seen one.[19] Charlotte then told her experience, although she said she saw the mermaid in Pickerel Lake (later renamed Harlow Lake), not Lake Superior. LePique then said he had heard a story from Kawbawgam's brother Shawonong of seeing two mermaids.[20] Kidder states that he later found a passage in the Jesuit Relations 1669-1670 in which Father Claude Dablon recalled hearing a fable about marine people who lived in water, and one of the "savages" had even told Dablon he had seen such a creature.[21] Therefore, the Ojibwa already had a mermaid tale tradition before their encounter with the Europeans.

The "Nibawnawbé" story is also of interest because Kidder provides two versions of it, showing that Kidder revised the stories. The stories' content is very similar, but the word choice is different. In the second version, Charlotte's story is told in her own voice rather than summarized in third person, reflecting Kidder's effort to make the story more dramatic and enjoyable to readers.

Another story with two versions tells how Sauks Head, along Lake Superior, got its name. First Jacques LePique told his version and then Charlotte told the version she had heard from her father, Marji-Gesick. Kidder later published Charlotte's version in *The Mining Journal*.[22] The story's publication reflects that local white Americans had an interest in the stories.

Another interesting story is "Our Brother-in-Law's Adventures." In this story, Kawbawgam pokes fun at Jacques LePique, but in doing so, he is drawing on an Ojibwa tradition of telling humorous stories that mock brother-in-laws much like today we disparage mother-in-laws.[23] Despite the title, the story actually concerns Kitchi Nonan (the Great or Wise Nolin), a nickname for LePique's grandfather, Louis Nolin, Sr.[24]

This story is of personal interest to me because my great-uncle, Roland White (1910-2007), told it to me in the 1990s, only he said the main character was not Kitchi Nonan but my great-grandfather, Jay Earle White (1880-1963), whom he had previously told me had known Kawbawgam. Both my great-uncle and great-grandfather were lifelong Marquette residents, so it is very likely my great-grandfather knew Kawbawgam, although given the differences in their ages, it's questionable how well he knew him.

The story, as Kawbawgam told it, is:

> In the spring, Kitchi Nonan took a walk to another lake, and there he saw several swans. Wanting to catch them but not knowing how in the world to do it, he finally dove under the water and swam around till he found where the swans were; then tied all their feet together with a line and gave it a jerk. Away went the swans through the air, with Kitchi Nonan hanging on to the line. After being carried for miles, he lost his hold and fell. As luck would have it, he landed right in the top of a hollow pine just as a bear was coming out. Nonan tumbled on the bear and surprised it so it scrambled out of the tree and ran away.[25]

Kidder says of this story:

> The form of these yarns, as told by Kawbawgam, largely disappears in taking them down as interpreted. Kawbawgam more or less acted out each episode and the Indians present were once or twice convulsed with laughter, as for example, when he showed how Kitchi Nonan bent the barrel of his gun to make it shoot in a curve, and so killed all the ducks with a single charge.[26]

That my great-uncle appropriated this story for his own purposes, or perhaps his father appropriated it, suggests that people in Marquette in the early twentieth century were familiar with Ojibwa tales, perhaps sometimes forgetting their origins, but adapting them into their own oral storytelling entertainment in the age before radio and television. For all I know, given how small Marquette was in those days, my great-grandfather may have heard the story from LePique, Kidder, or another Ojibwa who spoke English.

Also note that Kawbawgam acted out the story. Kidder also states that while telling the story of "Nanabozho in time of Famine," Kawbawgam's pantomime of one of the scenes caused the Ojibwa present to roar with laughter.[27] This comment tells us that other Ojibwa came to hear the stories as Kidder recorded them. Were the stories already familiar to these listeners, or were they seeking to educate themselves in their people's culture? Perhaps they simply sensed the importance of a young white man wanting to preserve their lore so they wanted to be part of the experience.

Altogether, Kidder collected just over fifty stories from the Kawbawgams and LePique between 1893 and 1895. Then, in 1901, he collected one final one. That year, Kidder decided to create a bust of Kawbawgam so Kawbawgam traveled to the Kidder home at 461 E. Ridge Street (just across from Peter White's home) to pose. During these visits, Kidder heard the story of "The Diver," another Nanabozho story. Because LePique had moved away from Marquette by this point, Kidder had Paul Pine serve as his interpreter. Pine had been the interpreter during the Jeremy Compo vs. The Jackson Iron Company hearings in 1881 in Marquette. Kidder states:

> The story was elicited by my asking the meaning of 'Amiksago' as a nickname for the little boy, Frank Perrot (Mary Cadotte's child[a]) who lived with the Kawbawgams and used to come to my

---

a. As previously stated, this is the only reference to suggest that Mary Tebeau, whom Kidder may have mistakenly called Cadotte here, was mother to the Perreau children.

> father's with the old man [Kawbawgam] when I was modelling a bust of the latter in 1901. It seemed that as a baby, the boy had a way of bobbing his head up and down like a diver, and the old man gave him the nickname for Shingebiss [a water bird, the pied-billed grebe or dabchick].[28]

Today, Kidder's 323-page, handwritten manuscript is at the American Philosophical Society of Philadelphia.[29] A microfilm copy of it is available at the Marquette Regional History Center. In 1994, Wayne State University Press published the manuscript in book form as *Ojibwa Narratives of Charles and Charlotte Kawbawgam and Jacques LePique, 1893-1895.* The book was edited by Arthur Bourgeois, who upon learning of the manuscript's existence realized the need to publish it. Bourgeois, when interviewed by *The Mining Journal* about the book's publication, spoke of the manuscript's importance, saying the "transformation tales" were the most interesting aspect "where people turn into animal guardians and change back." He stated that in other collections of Native American tales, the supernatural side was often downplayed or sanitized while in *Ojibwa Narratives*, "There's nowhere else so many tales of this belief or world view are collected."[30]

Why Kidder never published the manuscript himself is unknown since in 1910, when he wrote the introduction to it, he must have intended to. He apparently felt he needed to do more research, so he delayed publication. He visited Marquette in 1949[b] with the intent to do research into the spelling of Ojibwa names for the manuscript. At that time, when a reporter from *The Mining Journal* asked if the manuscript would be out in book form anytime soon, Kidder said he didn't know, but his wife said it would be out as soon as he had time to complete it.[31] Kidder's many other archaeological interests, in Europe especially, had apparently been taking up his time. During his 1949 visit to Marquette, he also reminisced

b. *The Mining Journal* article announcing Kidder's death, "Archeologist Kidder, Native Of Marquette, Dies In East," December 8, 1950, says he visited in 1948, but this is clearly a mistake since *The Mining Journal* ran an article on July 3, 1949 about his visit at that time titled "Visitors Do Research on Indian Lore." We also know the Kidder home was torn down in 1949 by its then owner George Spear, which may have been connected with Kidder's visit, although it is not mentioned in any sources.

about Charlotte Kawbawgam, stating, "Charlotte was a fine woman. She reared three white[c] orphans and adopted an Indian girl. In her later years she was totally blind but she kept her house at the entrance of Presque Isle very clean. I have never been able to understand how she did it."[32]

That Kidder never got around to publishing the manuscript is not surprising given what a busy life he led. After graduating from Harvard in 1899, he taught English composition as a teaching assistant at both Harvard and Radcliffe. In 1904, he joined the excavation staff of Rafael Pumpelly, Sr. and made a caravan journey across Russian Asia to China. Later, he would be employed on the newspaper staff of *The Bellman* in Minneapolis, then with the Brown-Burt Lumber Company, and then as an apple rancher on the Columbia River in Washington state. During World War I, he was an ambulance driver in Europe for the Red Cross and conducted relief trains as a Red Cross major. He then studied physical anthropology in Zurich and did archaeological research of the Dordogne cave deposits in central France, receiving the Legion of Honor for his work. He remained in France, and when Germany invaded in 1940, he moved to Nice where he and his second wife, Lilia Moreno, engaged in war relief activities. After World War II, Kidder moved to Berkeley, California, where he suffered from a stroke. When he visited Marquette in 1949, he was a semi-invalid. He died in Cambridge, Massachusetts, on December 5, 1950, at the age of seventy-six and was buried there.[33] Clearly, Kidder never forgot Chief Kawbawgam nor his goal to publish the Ojibwa tales.

Kidder's work in collecting Ojibwa folklore and his archaeological interests may have also inspired his younger brother. Alfred V. Kidder, Jr. (1885-1963) would become the foremost archaeologist of the southwest United States and Mesoamerica area (central Mexico to Honduras and Nicaragua) in the first half of the twentieth century.[34] Alfred Kidder, Jr.'s son, Alfred 2nd (1911-1984), and a grandson, Tristram Randolph Kidder (b. 1960), (nephew to Alfred 2nd), would also become archaeologists.[35]

We don't know when Homer Kidder first became interested in archeology and Native American lore, but his encounters with the Kawbawgams and LePique certainly fueled his interests and may have helped create an

---

c. By white, Kidder may mean métis children. The three "white" children he refers to are probably Fred and Angelica Cadotte and the unidentified boy who fought in the Civil War and later died of a gunshot wound at Au Train, Michigan. The Indian girl is probably Mary Tebeau, who would have been métis also.

archaeological family dynasty. According to a short online biography of Alfred V. Kidder, Jr.:

> During Kidder's younger-years he liked to sit in his father's small library and read. Mostly about books that related to American Indian-history and topics that were related to archeology.... In 1904 he enrolled at the University of Harvard wanting to major in pre-med., which would change once Kidder realized that chemistry would soon crush that dream. During his campaign at Harvard Kidder grew a strong interest in the field of Anthropology. Kidder graduated from Harvard in 1908, with a strong passion for anthropology....
>
> In 1914 Kidder went on to become the sixth person in the United States to receive a Ph.D. in archaeology, after the Harvard University accepted his thesis entitled, "Cliff Dwellers and Basket Maker."[36]

This statement suggests that Alfred Kidder, Sr. was interested in Native American history and passed that interest on to both of his sons. Adam Berger of the Marquette Regional History Center sheds additional light on the Kidders' interests in prehistoric and Native American history:

Brothers Howard, Alfred, and Homer Kidder, circa 1890

> As boys, the Kidder brothers were fascinated with the writings about Native American cultures collected in their father's library. They read *North American Indians* by artist George Catlin, the publications of the Bureau of American Ethnology, and articles about North American indigenous peoples compiled by the Smithsonian Institute.
>
> Though they moved back east, to Cambridge, Massachusetts, when Alfred Vincent Kidder was a boy, their time in the Upper Peninsula influenced the Kidder brothers. The boys' father worked as a guide in Marquette County for eminent anthropologist Lewis Henry Morgan. As children, the boys hunted arrowheads with their father, who submitted artifacts found in the Dead River area to the Peabody Museum at Harvard.[37]

Alfred Vincent Kidder also noted in a letter to Dr. Leslie A. White at the University of Michigan that both his uncle Walter Kidder and his father knew Lewis Henry Morgan well and guided him on his trips to study beaver in the Upper Peninsula.[38d] Obviously, the entire Kidder family had an interest in the Ojibwa whom they frequently associated with while living in Marquette. In 1901, Alfred Kidder, Sr. retired and the family left Marquette soon after.[39] The Kidders had really only been summering in Marquette for several years prior to that; we know from letters Alfred Vincent Kidder wrote to Ernest Rankin that he never went to school in Marquette but was only there in the summers and spent the winters in Cambridge, Massachusetts, although his older brothers, Homer and Howard White Kidder (1877-1899), went to school in Marquette.[40]

Today, Alfred Vincent Kidder is revered as a leader of modern anthropology while Homer Kidder's name seems to have been forgotten outside of Upper Michigan. Regardless, the big brother's influence should

---

d. Lewis Henry Morgan (1818-1881) made numerous trips to Marquette to study beaver. His journals are housed at the University of Rochester, and Volumes 2, 4, and 6 detail his trips to Marquette. The journal entries are almost exclusively about beaver habits, the many beaver dams he saw, and drawings of the dams, which seem to have been numerous in the area in the 1860s. Morgan mentions Kidder and LePique in his journals, and he may have met Kawbawgam, though he never mentions him. He did meet Kawbawgam's brother Edward Shawano at the Sault, but he only recorded a list of Ojibwa vocabulary from him. As an anthropologist, it is a shame Morgan missed the chance to record any biographical information about the Ojibwa and métis he met in the Upper Peninsula.

not be overlooked, nor that of Chief Kawbawgam, the most prominent Native American Alfred Vincent Kidder would have known in his childhood. Unfortunately, the only biography of Alfred Vincent Kidder, Richard B. Woodbury's *Alfred V. Kidder* (1973), makes no mention of Alfred's life in Marquette, his brother Homer, or Chief Kawbawgam.

Jacques LePique Moves Away

As noted earlier, in 1893, Jacques LePique went to George Shiras III with a strange story that led to his leaving Marquette. He wanted to move to Canada, but Homer Kidder tells us LePique continued to live in his little cabin at Whitefish Lake from 1893-1895, where Kidder often went to visit him and record more of the Ojibwa stories, though the majority were recorded at the Kawbawgams' home.

Although LePique remained in the area for two more years, he still desired to move away, as Shiras states:

> In the summer of 1893 Jack visited camp one morning and said he wanted to talk to me on an important matter. He was always very voluble, but never had much to talk about except events of past decades.
>
> JACK LA PETE TELLS A QUEER TALE
>
> This time he opened the interview by saying, "I want to go to Manitoba, in the Red River country, so that when I die I will be buried there."
>
> No statement from him could have been more puzzling or astonishing, for Jack had lived with his Indian brethren on Lake Superior for some 80 years.
>
> His proposal to make such a trip evoking inquiry, he explained, "I have carried a secret unknown to anyone but my mother since I was 15 years of age. She told me then that I ought to know, but should conceal the fact, that she had been abducted on a raid made by Ojibway warriors on a Sioux camp near the Red River in Canada and that she had been brought to an Indian settlement of the Ojibways on Sault Sainte Marie River, where some years later she married a French trapper. 'Therefore,' she said, 'the Indian blood in you is that of the Sioux, and yet you have lived all your life with the Ojibways, their traditional foes.'

"Ever since I learned this, long ago as it was, I have kept in my mind that when the time came for the Great Spirit to call me I would die and be buried in the land of my forefathers. This time has now come, but unless you and your friends provide the means for making the trip my last wish must be denied."

For several weeks after this we tried in every possible way to dissuade Jack from his intention to go among total strangers, where such relatives as he may have had must have passed away, but his answer was always the same: "You are denying my last wish."

Mr. S. P. Ely, a pioneer business man of the community and a friend of Jack's, agreed to raise the necessary money to send him on his journey, and also to provide an annuity for the remainder of his life. Mr. Ely, who in addition to having a kind heart was something of a humorist, got a sheet of paper one foot wide and two feet long. In the first column he entered the names of some 15 subscribers who agreed to pay a small sum annually as long as Jack lived; but, to impress Jack with the generous character of these pledges, at the head of the ruled columns he had noted the succeeding years. The last pledges, if paid, would have made Jack 110 years old.

This seemed to some of the subscribers a rather clever joke, but, after reaching his new home, Jack continued to live on year after year, until toward the end only a few of the original subscribers were left.

The impression finally got around, after some 10 years had passed, that Jack's paper must have got into the hands of unscrupulous persons after his death, who were drawing his pension. In consequence of this suspicion I wrote Jack, asking a number of questions which he alone could answer.

In due course a reply came from a friend who customarily wrote Jack's letters, answering all of them and giving other facts from Jack that I had forgotten all about. Five years more passed, and the subscribers were reduced to three, when the suspicions arose again that Jack had died. He would then be nearly 100 years old.

HE OUTLIVED HIS BENEFACTORS

Another test letter was sent, written partly in Ojibway, requesting information which he alone could give. The reply to this was conclusive and indicated that only one or two of the contributors

> would live to see Jack exhaust the last year's pledge on the two-foot sheet of paper.
>
> However, two years later I received a letter from St. Boniface, Manitoba, signed by a Roman Catholic priest who had watched over Jack for many years. It was dated November 30, 1911, and read as follows:
>
> "It is a duty to me, as I promised my old friend Jack La Pete, to write you when he would be dead. He died on the 28th inst., in the morning, seated on his chair; he passed as a child, without suffering. Funeral to-day."
>
> Thus there came to a peaceful end a centenarian who, always frail in body, showed ever an unbroken spirit in looking forward to rest in the country of his forefathers, even though the fulfillment of his wish deprived him of his old home and friends. His was a fidelity that bespoke a soul ready to make personal sacrifices for the assurance of a future life with his ancestral tribe.[41]

Shiras, like so many others, succumbed to the desire to call an elderly Native American a centenarian, although Jacques was likely closer to ninety-one when he died.

LePique's leaving Upper Michigan must have been saddening to Shiras and Samuel Ely, and perhaps more so to Homer Kidder, who could no longer collect stories from him, but LePique's decision must have been hardest on the Kawbawgams, who had known him since childhood and been his brother-in-law for more than forty years. LePique would ultimately outlive both of them. One wonders if Shiras or anyone else in Marquette wrote to tell LePique when the Kawbawgams themselves passed away.

Marquette has had its share of eccentric characters, but few have been as colorful and good-natured as Jacques LePique. Thanks to his willingness to assist Homer Kidder, we have a great deal of information about the Kawbawgams, the Lake Superior Ojibwa, and even Upper Michigan history that otherwise would have been lost.

Chapter 12
A Local Celebrity

As Kawbawgam entered his last decade, his celebrity status grew. Homer Kidder was just one of numerous people who called upon him out of curiosity or to pay their respects. However, the primary promoter of Kawbawgam's celebrity status during this time was Peter White.

White and Kawbawgam—an Enduring Friendship

As Kawbawgam grew older and became more of a celebrity, Peter White became prouder of their friendship. White had, to some extent, taken on the role of the Ojibwa community's benefactor and protector by this point. Levi Lewis Barbour (1840-1925), a prominent Detroit lawyer and philanthropist, would give an address about Peter White in Ann Arbor, Michigan in 1909, a year after White's death. The address spoke to White's kindness toward Native Americans and especially toward Kawbawgam. Barbour stated:

> He [White] supported many of the Indians who lingered in the neighborhood of Marquette. He felt that they had not been treated fairly, and was rejoiced when he could in some measure from his own bounty liquidate the debt that the white man owed to his copper-colored brothers.... To the most influential and exalted in the land, however, he was no more courteous than to the blind and helpless Kaw-baw-gam who was entirely dependent upon him for food, clothing, and shelter. He was more attentive to others than himself. He saw that Charles had every comfort and contentment—a ticket to the concert or play or lecture. He bought him a paper when he bought one for himself.[1]

View of Marquette Harbor from Peter White's residence in 1887. White had built the first home on Ridge St. in 1868, thus establishing Marquette's most fashionable neighborhood.

This statement is somewhat surprising since Kawbawgam probably couldn't read, but he may have understood English better than he spoke it so he could attend public events. It also suggests the Kawbawgams still needed some financial support, despite any money they may have received from the lawsuit against the Jackson Mine, or perhaps if White did administer the funds from the lawsuit settlement for the Kawbawgams, he was using their funds to provide for their needs.

White himself spoke out against how the Native Americans were treated in his 1889 address to the Marquette YMCA titled "My Recollections of Early Marquette." This forty-five page history of Marquette includes his first meeting with Kawbawgam. It was quoted in Chapter 4 as it ran in *The Mining Journal* as a tribute to Kawbawgam after his death in 1902. However, *The Mining Journal* did not see fit to include White's diatribe against how Americans had treated Native Americans. In a digression from his history, after describing how Graveraet, he, and their companions were royally entertained by the Kawbawgams upon their arrival on Iron Bay, White states:

> Most of you are probably aware that Charley Bawgam and Charlotte his wife are still living; The woman totally blind, the man so far so, that he can no longer hunt with a gun.
>
> They live in a cottage built for them on Presque Isle;
>
> They are not overstocked with clothing or food.
>
> It is a fact worthy of notice that Charlie KawbawgGam [sic] [several illegible words here that seem to say he never drank] never struck a man or woman, never was accused of stealing, never committed a crime. Never was arrested but once and that was last year.—in the 94th or 95th year of his age by the Deputy Game Warden of this County, for setting a sucker net in a sucker pond.
>
> This vigilant Game Warden drew this poor old blind Indian's piece of a fish net from the pond and destroyed it.
>
> Justice Crary was easily convinced that this Indian had rights which the white man's laws could not deprive him of; that his title to these lands and these rivers, and the game and the fish could not be called in question under laws which were not framed by his people or with his consent.
>
> He was told to go and succor some more.
>
> Let your thoughts for a moment dwell on the patent fact that the Indians occupied and owned all this region for hundreds of years before the white man came to it.
>
> Their title to the soil was absolute, in fee simple. The game, the fish, and the furs were plenty and it was easy for them to live well and always be comfortable.
>
> The white people came and drove them from their lands and now enact laws that in certain months of each year they shall not fish or hunt. It follows that they must starve!
>
> Cruel white man![2]

White's kindness and sympathy toward Native Americans was well known even at the White House. Peter White was a frequent visitor to the White House during Grover Cleveland's first administration (1885-1889). He entertained the president with stories of life in Upper Michigan and French dialect stories, making the president aware of White's kind attitude toward and acquaintance with Native Americans. Cleveland eventually offered White the position of Commissioner of Indian Affairs. White, however, declined the position, writing to Mr. Dickinson[a] on August 18, 1888 that he could not move because his wife's parents, Dr. and Mrs. Morgan Hewitt, were now eighty-one and eighty and "both very infirm and likely to 'drop off' any day." He adds, "My knowledge of the Indian character derived from a life-long acquaintance with them, and my great sympathy for an injured and illy understood people, make me keenly regret that I have to decline such an opportunity, which Providence would seem to have thrown in my way to do just the thing that I would have liked."[3] Later, as Cleveland was preparing to commence his second administration (1893-1897), White was offered the position of first Assistant Secretary of the Treasury or to be ambassador to any nation he chose except England, France, Germany, or Russia. On March 1, 1893, White wrote to thank President Cleveland for the offer, but again declined, this time stating that he was too busy as World Fair's Commissioner for Michigan, which would have its own pavilion in Chicago.[4]

About 1893, an incident occurred that showed Peter White was still heavily involved with the Ojibwa. According to White's biographer, Ralph D. Williams, Judge Matthews[b] was visiting Marquette and decided he wanted a canoe. Williams relates what happened:

> The Indians were adepts in making models of birch bark canoes, but the gradual elimination of the Indian has also eliminated their handiwork. Birch bark canoes are becoming very scarce but the judge was anxious to obtain one. Seeing a beautiful little model of one in the First National Bank, he asked Peter White where he might get one.
>
> "You may have this one," said Mr. White.
>
> "I do not want that one," answered the judge. "Where will you get another?"

---

a. Mr. Dickinson's first name is not given on the letter, but he is likely Donald M. Dickinson (1846-1917) who was serving as United States Postmaster General at the time. He must have presented the offer to Peter White on the president's behalf and White expected him to inform the president that he had declined the offer. Notably, Dickinson, who was from Detroit, would be present for the unveiling of the Father Marquette statue in 1897 as we will soon see.

b. Williams does not give the judge's first name. He was probably Thomas Stanley Matthews, Supreme Court Justice (1824-1889). However, Williams dates this story to 1893, four years after Judge Matthews' death.

> "The Indians may as well make me one," replied Mr. White. "I've got to support them anyhow."

Williams goes on to state that the judge took the model and later repaid White by recommending him as master in chancery for the Pewabic Copper Co.[5c]

White's remark in this story, "I've got to support them anyhow," shows that White may have felt some irritation about his relationship with the Ojibwa. Certainly, White had worked hard his entire life and acquired a sizeable estate, so the Native Americans' lack of understanding about property as held by the whites and their desire to retain their Native customs may have frustrated him at times. However, we cannot doubt he respected them, especially Kawbawgam. He had traveled with the Ojibwa through the forests to collect the mail in his youth, relying on them as guides. Plus, his friendship with Kawbawgam must have caused him to be held in respect by the other Ojibwa, and the White and Kawbawgam families' friendship continued to the next generation, as we have seen, between White's son-in-law, Shiras, and Kawbawgam's adopted son, Fred Cadotte. That White was able to get the Ojibwa to make canoes for him probably resulted from his friendship with Kawbawgam.

At the same time, while it seems Kawbawgam and White's was a true friendship, we can't neglect to think Kawbawgam must have recognized early on that White was becoming a person of importance in Marquette. Perhaps Kawbawgam was a wise enough leader to know to ally himself with Peter White as a community leader to protect his own interests and those of his community, especially in these later years when he and several of the local Ojibwa resided at Presque Isle.

---

c. The confusion over who Matthews was is further compounded here because the Pewabic had a lawsuit before the Supreme Court in December 1889, but Matthews died in March of that year. Furthermore, Williams seems to have the company's name wrong. He calls it the Pewabic Copper Co. but it was the Pewabic Mining Co. as noted in the court case of Mason v. Pewabic Mining Co. Williams also says White later sold the Pewabic to Mason & Smith of Boston for $710,000, but I have been unable to verify this. The Pewabic Mine was actually bought in 1891 by the Quincy Mine in Hancock, Michigan. Nor did White own the company. Being the master of chancery suggests White was only involved in the company's sale. The title refers to a senior official or clerk of a court of chancery who assists the chancellor in such duties as inquiring into matters referred by the court, examining cases, taking oaths and affidavits, hearing testimony, and computing damages.

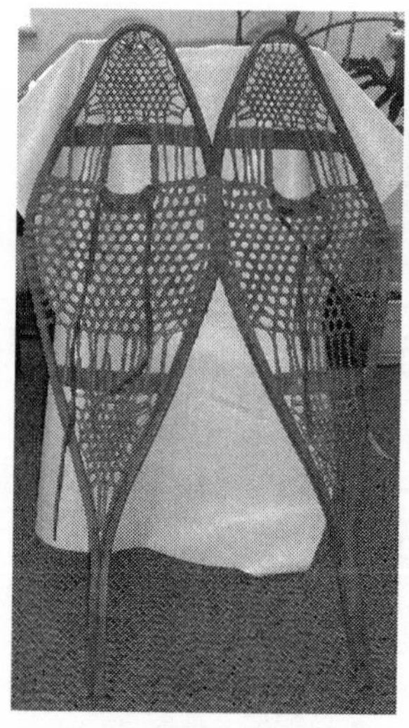

Snowshoes Kawbawgam made for John B. Ferguson, in the Marquette Regional History Center collection

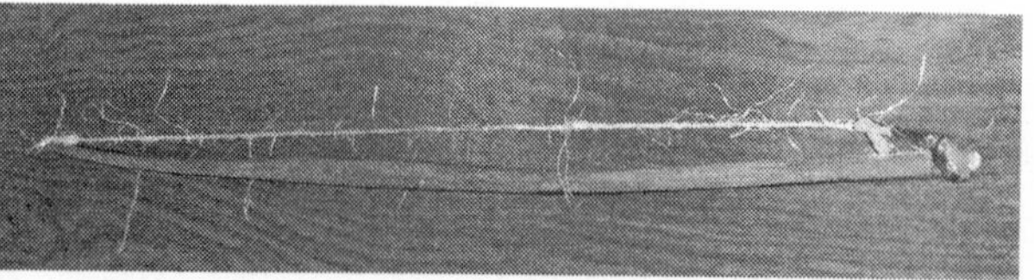

Toy bow reputedly made by Kawbawgam

Kawbawgam may have been one of the Ojibwa who made birchbark canoes. In 1898, he made a pair of snowshoes for John B. Ferguson of Marquette. Ferguson took the snowshoes with him when he left Marquette, and later in 1964, his son Gerald M. Ferguson donated them to the Marquette County Historical Society. For a time after that, the snowshoes were on display in the lobby of the First National Bank on the corner of Washington and Front Streets.[6]

Kawbawgam also reputedly made a bow donated in 2019 to the Marquette Regional History

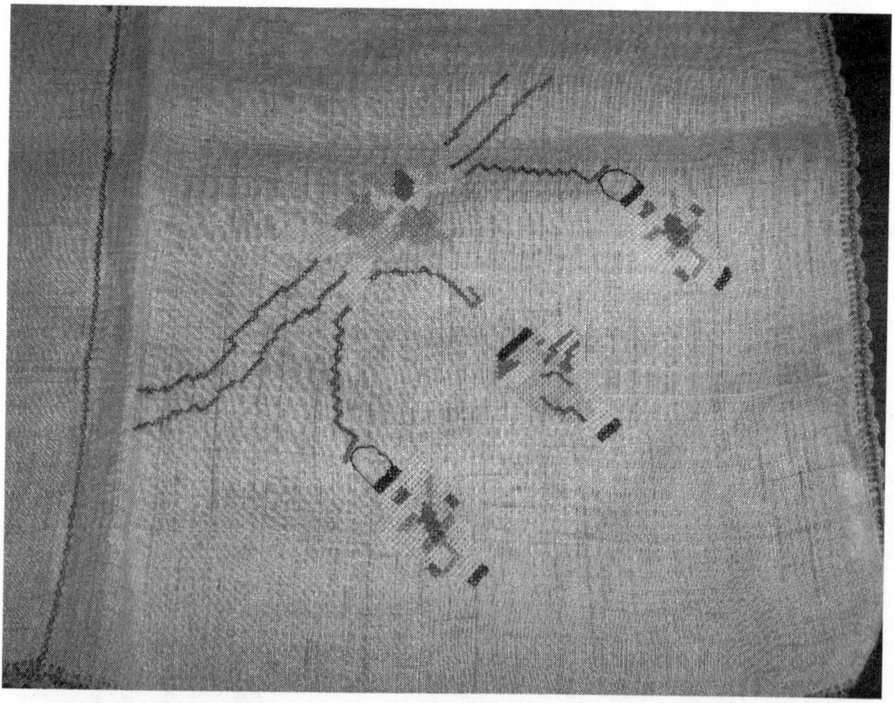

Detail of tablecloth reputedly embroidered by Charlotte Kawbawgam

Center. It looks like a toy bow, made for a child. The Marquette Regional History Center also has a tablecloth Charlotte reputedly made for Mrs. John Pearson, said to have had the first house on Presque Isle Avenue. It is made of natural linen with a blue and lavender crocheted edge and cross-stitched with Asian lanterns. It measures 36" x 37". It is not known if Charlotte gave it as a gift or was paid for it. It was donated by the estate of Mrs. John Pearson's granddaughter, Edith Barkow.

In these last years of his life, however, Kawbawgam was respected as far more than just a craftsman of Native American souvenirs. He had become someone of such importance and stature that his image would be captured repeatedly in both art and photographs.

The Father Marquette Statue

The Ojibwa of Lake Superior had first come into contact with Christianity through French-Canadian Jesuit missionaries in the seventeenth century. One of the most prominent Jesuits was Father Marquette. Tradition says he preached at Lighthouse Point and converted many of the Ojibwa. Consequently, Marquette was chosen as the city's name in his honor. Because of the Ojibwa's connection to Father Marquette, Kawbawgam would play a significant role when the city decided to erect a statue to its namesake.

The idea that Marquette should have a Father Marquette statue began in the early 1890s when the State of Wisconsin commissioned a marble statue of Father Marquette for Statuary Hall in Washington, DC. The statue was sculpted by Gaetano Trentanove (1858-1937), an Italian sculptor who lived in Milwaukee.[7] Upon learning of the statue, people in Marquette felt the city should also have a statue to honor its namesake. Consequently, Alfred E. Archambeau, the president of the Society St. Jean Baptiste, an active Catholic organization in Marquette, wrote to Trentanove to inquire what it would cost for Marquette to have a similar statue. Trentanove had created Wisconsin's marble statue for $10,000, but he said he could use it to make a

Gaetano Trentanove

mold for a bronze copy for $6,000. The Society St. Jean Baptiste agreed to these terms and began a city-wide campaign, viewing the statue as a monument for the entire city rather than just for the society or for Catholics.[8]

Of course, Archambeau approached Peter White for his support. White was one of the wealthiest men in Marquette and a prominent Episcopalian, so his support would ensure the society's success in raising funds among non-Catholics. Usually, White was generous, and he often backed causes for other churches, but because of the 1893 financial panic, he felt it was a bad time to ask people for money, so he declined, thinking the campaign would not succeed. Archambeau was disappointed, but he did not give up. He approached Episcopalian Bishop G. Mott Williams, who enthusiastically gave fifty dollars. The society continued to raise money until January 1895 when Trentanove visited Marquette to meet with community leaders and discuss the project. By this point, White had decided to support the statue since Trentanove took photographs of both him and Kawbawgam, having heard a good deal about them. Trentanove decided his statue would include two bronze reliefs on its base: one of Father Marquette leaving Lighthouse Point following his 1669 visit and the other of him preaching there in 1671.[9] *The Mining Journal* reported on January 7, 1895 that Trentanove was also in Marquette to "make some studies of the Chippewa Indians here, near Ashland and Superior for the bas-reliefs" and that "While here he will get a portrait of Charles Kobogum as material for the purposes indicated."[10] The statue would be cast in Italy and then transported to the United States.[11] The sandstone base would be donated by John H. Jacobs, who owned the South Marquette sandstone quarry. It was decided to place the statue beside the waterworks building, just off Lighthouse Point, where tradition said Father Marquette had preached. Debate ensued about whether the statue would face the town or the lake. Peter White said it should honor the explorer priest and, therefore, face Lake Superior, but others argued that people passing by the statue on Walnut Street would then see its back. Only when the statue was unveiled did people discover it had been made to face the lake.[12]

The statue's unveiling took place on July 15, 1897. A story exists that Peter White bought Kawbawgam a new suit to wear to the ceremony. Kawbawgam wore the suit jacket but refused to wear the new pants and instead wore an old pair—presumably because they were more comfortable. Unfortunately, photographs of Kawbawgam at the ceremony do not provide a good enough look at his pants to know if this story is true.

Kawbawgam (seated second from left) and other Ojibwa posing at the base of the Father Marquette statue

During the ceremony, speeches were made by Honorable Donald M. Dickinson (the former US Postmaster General), James Russell (owner of *The Mining Journal*), Peter Primeau (who spoke in French), Father Connolly of the Sault (the only Jesuit in the Upper Peninsula), and eighty-seven-year-old Catholic Bishop Mrak (who spoke in Ojibwa). Historian Fred Rydholm claimed Kawbawgam also made a speech that day, but the program flyers that have survived and the reports of the events in *The Mining Journal* do not reflect this.[13] Rydholm also stated that when Trentanove spoke, he said he had used Kawbawgam's likeness twice in the bas reliefs, once as a young man in the canoe and once as an elderly person listening to the Mass.[14] However, the speeches were all reported in the "Pere Marquette Edition" of *The Mining Journal*, published that same day, and Trentanove's speech does not refer to Kawbawgam specifically. Nor does *The Mining Journal* make any reference to Kawbawgam in the days following the celebrations. Furthermore, in the frieze depicting a canoe, Father Marquette is clearly with two voyageurs and no Native Americans.

Charles Kawbawgam at unveiling of Father Marquette statue

The highlight of the festivities was a reenactment by some local Ojibwa of Father Marquette's landing at Lighthouse Point. *The Mining Journal* reported that "Over fifty Indians have been secured to take part in this spectacle and to ride in the procession."[15] A 1968 article states that even some white men and boys came dressed in Indian costumes and smeared with paint and riding ponies while some of the actual Native Americans arrived by canoe.[16] Later, a grand ball was held at midnight at the Hotel Superior.[17] The event was in many ways a celebration of early contact between the whites and Native Americans. That the Ojibwa were included in the ceremonies to such an extent shows the goodwill that existed between them and Marquette's white citizens. How the Ojibwa felt about white people dressing up like them, we can't know, but it was a different time, and may have been done to show respect for the Ojibwa, even though it rankles our modern-day sensitivities.

Bronze relief of Native Americans listening to Father Marquette. At least one was supposedly modeled on Kawbawgam.

Bronze Relief of Father Marquette with voyageurs

Despite the festivities' success, Alfred Archambeau was not completely happy. At the banquet, he allegedly told several people the statue was actually of Peter White and not Father Marquette.[18] This rumor has been perpetuated in Marquette ever since. Is it true? Since Wisconsin's statue was not completed until 1896, after Trentanove visited Marquette and took White's photo, it is possible Trentanove used White as his model for Father Marquette, although the resemblance is questionable. Of course, the statue could not resemble Father Marquette since no one knew then what Marquette had looked like. Consequently, Trentanove took artistic license and gave Father Marquette a beard and a full head of hair. Ironically, the year the statue was dedicated, an oil portrait of Father Marquette was found in Montreal, depicting what he looked like in 1666 before he left France; it shows a balding and beardless man.[19] Later in 1937, John Alexander Nielsen was commissioned to paint a portrait of Father Marquette based on the dilapidated seventeenth century portrait; this portrait was reprinted thousands of times thereafter and is the best known image of Father Marquette today.[20]

Whether or not the statue resembled him, Peter White was so pleased with it that he ordered another version to be placed in Father Marquette Park on Mackinac Island. This statue would be dedicated in 1909 after White's death.

The Father Marquette statue and Trentanove's bust of Peter White show little, if any, resemblance.

White's friends and family also secretly had Trentanove make a marble bust of White which was unveiled at a public ceremony in the Marquette Opera House in 1898. Some sources, however, say that White commissioned this bust himself. Today, the bust resides at the Peter White Public Library.[21] In this author's opinion, there is no notable resemblance between the bust of White and the statue of Father Marquette, so the theory that White was the model for the statue seems unlikely.

The Nielsen reproduction of the only known portrait of Father Marquette made during his lifetime

One must wonder what Kawbawgam thought of all this activity surrounding the statue's dedication. This event was probably the day Kawbawgam was most in the limelight in Marquette, recognized as a leader at an event of city-wide importance.

In 1912, several years after both White and Kawbawgam had passed away, the Father Marquette statue was moved to its present location in Lakeside Park near Marquette's current Chamber of Commerce building. Over the years, the statue has experienced some damage from the elements and from vandals, but in 2018, it was restored, and today, it continues to be a landmark and a symbol of the city that bears Father Marquette's name.

Family Losses

In the 1880s and 1890s, the Kawbawgams were experiencing the passing away of their family members from their generation and the preceding one. As noted earlier, Charlotte's mother Susan probably died about 1884. Chief David Madosh, Charlotte's uncle, likely died around this time too. A listing at Ancestry.com states 1880 as his possible death date but nothing is recorded to verify this.

We do not know the date of death for Kawbawgam's biological father, Muk-kud-de-wuk-wuk, but in 1880 Kawbawgam's mother and stepfather were still living at the Sault. The 1880 Federal Census lists Robert Roussain, age twenty-three, and his wife Frances, age twenty-four, living with Robert's grandparents, Frank Chavinane (Chavineau?—the handwriting isn't clear) age ninety-five who was formerly a chief, and Charlotte age ninety. This is no doubt Chief Shawano, whose name is often given as Francis, and Kawbawgam's mother, Charlotte Sayre. Robert is the son of Kawbawgam's half-sister Mrs. Jean (Charlotte) Roussain.[22]

Kawbawgam's mother would live until 1889, dying at the advanced age of about ninety-nine. We do not know if the Kawbawgams traveled to the Sault for the funeral. The date of Chief Shawano's death is not known. However, William B. Cady, a Detroit lawyer, interviewed both Kawbawgam and his half-brother Chief Edward Shawano in 1897 regarding litigation affecting the title to lands claimed by Chief Shawano's heirs, so we can assume Chief Shawano died that year or soon before.[23]

Chief Edward Shawano's daughter, Lizzie Shawano (Kawbawgam's niece), would die at the young age of thirty-two in 1897. The funeral was described in picturesque terms in the *Sault Sainte Marie News* on Saturday, September 18, 1897:

> Lizzie Shawano, age 32 and daughter of Chief Shawano, died Friday of last week, at the home of her father on Sugar Island. On Saturday the remains were conveyed to the Soo in a canoe, followed by the relatives and friends in similar conveyances.
>
> The funeral procession of canoes, as it came up the river, formed an interesting spectacle. At the head of Little Rapids the remains were taken charge of by Undertaker Ryan & Co., and conveyed to St. Mary's church, where funeral services were held. The remains were interred in the Catholic cemetery.[24]

Kawbawgam's half-brother Edward Shawano would also precede him in death on September 20, 1899. A newspaper article from the time described him as "a real and not a manufactured chieftain, being regularly descended from a line of chieftains, but he was a chief without a nation and without a country. He was one of the few of his race left in his native place."[25] A 1974 article states Edward died a tragic death, apparently of alcoholism, and that "he was one of the few remainining [sic] Chippewas in the Sault Ste. Marie region and despondently watched the settlers dig ship canals through his tribe's sacred Indian burial ground and transport his people to other locations—leaving him and his fathers as chieftains without a tribe."[26] One wonders how Kawbawgam felt upon his younger half-brother's death.

Edward was buried in Sault Sainte Marie's new Riverside Cemetery "among his pale faced contemporaries; but near the spot where his father lived so long, and through which the great ship channels were built, was the Indian burying ground where were laid the remains of his dark faced ancestors."[27]

With the world he knew disappearing around him, Kawbawgam must have been feeling his own years, but it did not stop him from continuing to play an important role among his people and in the Marquette community.

Kawbawgam's Fame Continues

The unveiling of the Father Marquette statue was not the only time Kawbawgam was included in city festivities in the 1890s. Arthur Bourgeois, who would edit Kidder's manuscript, recalled that his grandfather said Kawbawgam made annual appearances in the Independence Day parades, usually riding on horseback.[28] Kawbawgam was a rather ironic addition to the parade since his ancestors, though not involved in the American Revolution itself, had fought against the Americans in the War of 1812. But most late nineteenth century Marquette citizens probably had no clue that the Ojibwa had ever been the United States' enemies in war. To them, Kawbawgam may have seemed as American as apple pie, an integral part of Marquette's history, and thus, a symbol of community pride.

Kawbawgam's appearance in the 1891 Independence Day Parade is especially noteworthy since that year marked one of Marquette's biggest Fourth of July celebrations. On July 6, *The Mining Journal* gave a full account of the day's activities, including a list of everyone in the parade. Kawbawgam rode in a carriage with Peter White, Reverend J. B. Bonar (the Presbyterian minister), and Alfred Swineford (former publisher of *The Mining Journal* and current Governor of Alaska).

This 1899 newspaper image of Kawbawgam is the only known one of him with short hair.

Peter White gave one of the speeches to celebrate the day, offering a recollection of past Fourth of July celebrations in Marquette. He stated that in 1849, there was no celebration because there was "no real Marquette" then, noting that the first iron bloom was struck on July 10 that year. However, he went on to describe briefly what Marquette was like then, praising his friend Kawbawgam in typical European and American language used to refer to chiefs and their children:

> At Marquette, which was then called "enemabine Sebing," or "Carp River," there lived the great chief "Madja Geshic," who ruled his small tribe hereabouts with wonderful dignity and justice. The prince and heir apparent to the throne was my friend Charley Bawgam. He, with the Princess Charlotte, his wife, lived in a cedar bark palace covered with birch bark and lined with curly maple.[29]

Interestingly, White says Kawbawgam was the "heir apparent," which suggests he was destined to become chief upon Marji-Gesick's death, although other, later sources claim he inherited his chieftainship from Marji-Gesick's brother Chief Madosh.

Besides the Fourth of July parade, Kawbawgam also participated in at least one parade to celebrate St. John the Baptist's Day on June 25, 1894. This parade provides us with the only known photograph of his presence in a parade. He is seated in a canoe on top of a float. The back of the photograph identifies the woman beside him as Charlotte Kawbawgam, but she does not resemble her. Also identified in the canoe is Jerry Compo, son of Jeremy, who had been the plaintiff in the lawsuit against the Jackson Iron Company on Charlotte's behalf, and Henry St. Arnold, a local Indian guide.[d] *The Mining Journal* mentioned the parade both in its June 23 and June 26 editions, but neither article mentions Kawbawgam. The event was highly popular, however, with numerous activities at Presque Isle Park following the parade through Marquette. About 3,000 people turned out for the activities.[30]

By this point, Kawbawgam's fame had extended across the Upper Peninsula and below the Straits of Mackinac. His advanced age, along with his height and stately figure, made a great impression on those who met him. Many visitors to Marquette sought him out at Presque Isle. There he would sit on his porch and talk with them as best he could since he was still not completely fluent in English.[31]

In the next chapter, we will see how Kawbawgam's image was appropriated after his death, but already, people were interested in using his image, which was closely associated with Marquette. In September 1891, just two months after White's Fourth of July speech, the fifth annual meeting of the Michigan Bankers' Association was held in Marquette. Peter White was probably responsible for arranging to have the meeting in Marquette and

---

d. Henry St. Arnold, also known as Santinaw—the Americanized spelling of his name based on its French pronunciation—was a métis who worked for John M. Longyear as a wilderness guide. He eloped with a wealthy young white woman, Mary Seymour, the full story of which can be found in my books *My Marquette* and *Haunted Marquette.*

St. John the Baptist's Day parade. Seated in canoe, left to right are Charles Kawbawgam, Charlotte Kawbawgam, Jerry Compo, and Henry St. Arnold.

getting members of the association from as far away as Detroit to attend. The meeting was held in the "old Masonic Hall" and Peter White gave the annual address. Most notably, the steel plate menu cards for the dinner "bore views of Marquette and portraits of Charles Kobawgam, the old Chippewa chief, still living here."[32] No doubt, White was also responsible for authorizing the use of Kawbawgam's image.

Sometime between 1897 and 1902, J. Everett Ball, grandson of Philo Everett, decided to photograph Kawbawgam with his 1893 Eastman camera, which allowed him to develop the film himself. We can date Ball's photographs to after 1897 since Ball also took photographs of the Father Marquette statue. Ball had known Kawbawgam all his life, their families having long been friends, ever since Kawbawgam's father-in-law Marji-Gesick had first led Philo Everett's party to the iron ore more than a half-century earlier. Ball was sure Kawbawgam would be receptive to being photographed, so he rode his bicycle out to Presque Isle. When Ball arrived, Kawbawgam agreed to be photographed, but he wanted to dress properly for the photo. However, Ball first took a photo of Kawbawgam in his everyday work clothes. Then Kawbawgam changed into a long black jacket with a white shirt and a hat and was photographed with a little girl, who was probably Elizabeth (Lizzie) Perreau.[33]

Kawbawgam posing for Ball in his work clothes in front of his house. Note Ball's bicycle to the left.

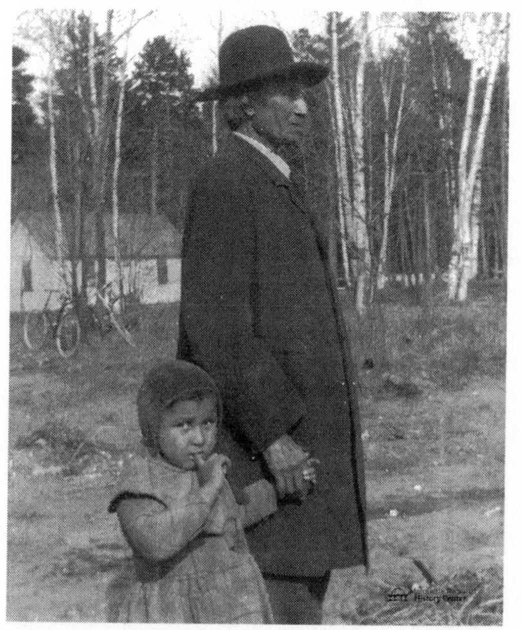

By this point, Kawbawgam was also included in the city directories. The 1895-6 Polk Directory lists him as "Baugum, Charles" with his occupation as laborer,[34] although the 1899 Polk Directory lists him with his occupation as "Chippewa chief."[35] Neither lists him as a park warden so that title may not have been official.

Ball's more formal photo of Kawbawgam and Lizzie Perreau

This image, in the Marquette Regional History Center's possession, is believed to be Mrs. Hambleton Kirk's sketch of Kawbawgam.

In 1900, Mrs. Hambleton Kirk, a visitor to Marquette, made a sketch of Kawbawgam. In 1939, she donated the sketch to the Marquette County Historical Society. With the sketch she sent a letter to Helen Longyear Paul, daughter of John M. Longyear and director of the society. In the letter she described the sketch's creation. She stated that Charlotte Kawbawgam had been pleased that she wanted to sketch her husband. Mrs. Kirk also remarked that Kawbawgam must have had "some good French blood" in him because he impressed her as being somewhat aristocratic with the countenance of a "French marquis."[36] Mrs. Kirk's sketch shows Kawbawgam in a somber black suit but wearing his Indian headdress. While Mrs. Kirk may have been impressed by Kawbawgam, her suggestion that his noble countenance reflects French blood shows her own racism in the implication that white blood is needed to be noble. Of course, Kawbawgam had no French blood, but he did have Scottish blood through his mother.

Kawbawgam's headdress has been lost to time but a beaded sash he owned as part of his Native American regalia survives. When the sash was made is not known, but it was made on a loom with very small beads. Kawbawgam eventually gave it to his friend, the Honorable Dan Harvey Ball, son-in-law of Philo Everett. Ball later gave it to his granddaughter, Mabel Smith Spalding, who gave it to John H. Burt in 1965. Burt was the son of the Rev. Bates Burt of Marquette's St. Paul's Episcopal Church and also an Episcopalian bishop. The sash has been on loan to the Marquette Regional History Center since 2013.

Kawbawgam's beaded sash

In 1901, as noted previously, Homer Kidder made a bust of Kawbawgam. Kawbawgam likely rode the streetcar from Presque Isle to the Kidder home for the sittings, during which time he was accompanied by Frank Perreau. In fact, a story has circulated in Marquette that he was given a free lifetime streetcar pass. Maude (Brown) Breer recalled that one time she sat near Kawbawgam on the streetcar, and when she dropped her purse, he picked it up and handed it back to her.[37]

Kawbawgam in his full regalia

Kidder must have been highly impressed by Kawbawgam to want to

The Kidder House at 461 E. Ridge St. where Kawbawgam posed for his bust. The house was demolished in 1949.

make a bust of him. He had graduated from Harvard in 1899 but now taught there, returning home in the summer, at which time he made the bust.[38] It was only the second bust he had ever made, the first having been a smaller one of his father.[39] We don't know how many sittings there were, but Kidder, who had never received instructions in art, was tremendously successful at it, as the bust reveals. He later made a smaller bust of Kawbawgam. It is nice to imagine how young Alfred Vincent Kidder, who would have been fourteen at the time, must have been in awe of Chief Kawbawgam when he came to his home to sit for his older brother. Perhaps that was the moment when this future famous anthropologist's interest in Native American studies was truly sparked.

The completed bust was put on display in the window of Stafford's Drug Store in downtown Marquette where it attracted a great deal of attention, as reported by *The Mining Journal* on December 1, 1901. People, amazed by how true to life the likeness was, praised Kidder's skill.[40] In 1949, when Kidder visited Marquette, he was interviewed by *The Mining Journal* and stated regarding the bust, "I had never had any instruction in sculpturing, but I just felt that a bust should be made of Kawbawgam so I did it, working on it every day of my vacation, and—I still like it! It looks just as he did." In the same article, *The Mining Journal* refers to two busts at the library as reproductions of the busts Kidder made.[41] In 1950, in an article announcing Kidder's death, *The Mining Journal* again stated the "pair of statues" housed at the Peter White Public Library were "reproductions" of a bust Kidder had made.[42] However, the smaller bust, made of plaster by Homer Kidder, was actually given to the Marquette County Historical Society in 1933 by Duane North (how he got it is unknown).[43] Today, the larger bust, which resembles

The Kawbawgam bust at the Peter White Public Library

The painted Kawbawgam bust at the Marquette Regional History Center

photographs of Kidder's original, making it likely the original, can be seen at Peter White Public Library. The smaller bust is on display in the classroom at the Marquette Regional History Center. Oddly, the smaller bust has been painted. It is not an exact replica of the larger bust. Kidder apparently modeled it after his earlier one but took some liberties with it.

Blindness

Despite his growing fame, Kawbawgam's last years were marred by the loss of his eyesight. One of the last people to document anything about Kawbawgam during his lifetime was Ralph Williams, Peter White's biographer, who states:

> The writer saw Bawgam in the spring of 1902. He was living with his wife Charlotte in a little cabin on Presque Isle which had been built for him by Peter White. The framework of his great figure was erect, gaunt and giant-like and indicates clearly what a powerful man he must have been. He spoke of the blindness which had come upon him in 1899 with touching simplicity. His large grief was not that he could not read or view the myriad delights of nature, but that his remaining solace had been taken from him. "I can no longer fish," said he; and there was a world of meaning and of sorrow in the words. For it bespoke the great love of outdoor life and the Indian's inherent right to wrest his living from nature.[44]

Because Kawbawgam could no longer support himself due to the loss of his eyesight, he was made a public charge and given an allowance from the county.[45e] During these last years, he always wore somber black clothing—white men's clothing, as he had worn most of his life—although he still had a feathered headdress and other Native American garments that he would occasionally don.[46]

Because of his blindness, Kawbawgam was constantly led about by Frank and Lizzie Perreau. Several photographs exist of the children with him, the most famous being that of Kawbawgam and Lizzie taken by Ball as mentioned earlier.

---

e. I have been unable to find documentation of Kawbawgam receiving a county allowance, but it is likely true since *The Mining Journal* mentioned it in the article reporting his death. This statement raises questions about whether the Kawbawgams ever received money from the lawsuit against the Jackson Mine, or whether they had simply spent it all by this point, more than a decade later.

Charles and Charlotte Kawbawgam at their Presque Isle home with Frank and Lizzie Perreau

That Kawbawgam was being led by children while blind was recorded in *The Mining Journal* on July 25, 1902, in an article published just five months before his death. It offers the most complete picture of how he declined in his last years.

Kawbawgam with children in boat who are likely Frank and Lizzie Perreau

IS 102 YEARS OLD

KAWBAWGAM WAS ENTERTAINED AT WEDNESDAY'S PICNIC.

CHIEF IS BLIND AND FEEBLE

OBJECT OF GREAT INTEREST TO VISITING NEWSPAPER MEN.

He Came to Pavilion Clad in All His Native Finery, But Partook Only Sparingly of Food and Drink

---

Charles Kawbawgam, the last simon pure relic of the magnificent race of Chippewas, with slender form as straight and true as an arrow, with immobile face and set eyes, sat at the west end of the Presque Isle pavilion Wednesday afternoon, while the visiting newspaper men and their Marquette friends discussed Peter White's punch and danced to the merry music.

Chief Kawbawgam was present at the festivities as the particular guest of the association and his old friend and protector, Hon. Peter

White. The old man, leaning on the arm of a young Indian friend and guided by the little Indian lass who always accompanies him on his jaunts, tottered into the pavilion just as the guests were rising from the picnic dinner. His steps were short and feeble, but he walked as erect as if he were in the prime of his youth, with his handsome Indian face retaining all its strong character lines.

The chief was clad in the relics of his old finery, and a feather head dress surmounted his long, thin white hair. He tottered along the pavilion, evidently feeble to the last degree, to the end of the picnic tables, where Mr. White was busy. He, having been seated, ate very sparingly of the food placed before him and drank as sparingly of the liquid refreshment.

For a couple of hours he sat in one position, as immovable as if he were lying in wait for a forest deer. No burst of music or laughter caused any expression of attention or pleasure to flit over his worn features. With eyes fixed, he stared into empty space.

Kawbawgam Is Blind.

For this there was good reason. Kawbawgam is blind. His eyes have gone to sleep, tired with their long service of upwards of 102 years, for this, so says Peter White, is now the old patriarch's age.

The chief was the center of many eyes. Most of the visiting newspaper men had heard of Kawbawgam and there was much curiosity to see him. Seeing him was as far as anyone got in the direction of making an acquaintance. The old man is too feeble to undergo the ordeal of a handshaking reception, and introductions would now be unintelligible to him.

Baffled of getting any satisfaction from the old man himself, the visitors turned to Mr. White, who submitted to a regular fusilade of questions, which he answered to the best of his ability, about the chief.

The presence of the old man, recalling the days when he was at the head of a magnificent race which held undisputed possession of fields and forests now owned by the white man, was a pathetic incident in the festivities. His century of years is weighing old Kawbawgam down. His tottering steps are directed toward the grave. Only his marvelous vitality has sustained him to this day to be pointed to as the "last of the Chippewas", but now this is sapped and exhausted. Kawbawgam's race is almost run. One day, and it cannot be far distant now, his life will go out without fear or pain in the humble cottage that has sheltered him, in the kindly shades of Presque Isle, for so many years. Then a noble red man will have departed for his cherished happy hunting grounds.

A Second Daniel Webster.

Mr. White related a story at the picnic Wednesday which is apropos. A couple of years ago he was dining Dean Hutchinson [sic][f], of the law department of the University of Michigan, then acting president in the absence of President Angel [sic] in Turkey, at his home here. In Mr. White's dining room hung a magnificent portrait of old Kawbawgam, in which the native serength [sic] and nobility of his features were adequately brought out.

Mr. White observed that his guest gave the portrait very close attention. His eyes were rarely off it during the lulls in the conversation. He appeared to be finding an unusual fascination in the savage countenance and to be endeavoring to study out something that puzzled him.

Finally, when they were leaving the table and the dean was casting one last, lingering glance at the portrait, Mr. White said: "Dean, you are greatly interested in old Kawbawgam. You will certainly know him when you see him. What do you think of the portrait anyway."

"Mr. White," solemnly responded the dean, "if that old savage, with the character attested to by those features, that head and noble bearing, had been a white man, with a white man's advantages, he would have been a second Daniel Webster."

While this article does make Kawbawgam sound "pathetic," it also offers many points of interest. It should be noted that the article refers to Kawbawgam as "the last simon pure relic of the magnificent race of Chippewas," another example of how whites sought to make him noble and to purify him in some way, ignoring his mother's Scottish blood, although

f. *The Mining Journal* reporter was not good at fact checking. He is referring to Harry Burns Hutchins who was acting president of the University of Michigan from 1897-1898 while President James Burrill Angell was serving as US Minister to Turkey. Hutchins must have, therefore, visited Peter White in 1897 or 1898, four or five, not a couple of, years prior to the picnic described in this article. (See https://en.wikipedia.org/wiki/President_of_the_University_of_Michigan#List_of_Presidents_of_the_University_of_Michigan) also recognizing that by this time, few of the younger Native Americans were pure-blooded due to more than two centuries of intermarriage with whites. The article plays on other clichés about Native Americans from the time, such as that in death they go to "happy hunting grounds." However, the dean's remarks are of interest because they acknowledge not only Kawbawgam's strength of character but also that if he had known a white man's advantages, he could have been an even greater man (though it is questionable Kawbawgam would have seen it that way). It's also worth noting that by this time, "Kawbawgam" was accepted as the standard spelling of his name. From this point on, all other spellings, including hyphenated ones, gradually fell into disuse. Perhaps most importantly, the article again testifies to Kawbawgam and White's friendship—White admired Kawbawgam enough to hang his portrait in his dining room. Kawbawgam cared enough about White to attend a picnic where he obviously did not enjoy himself and may have even felt it a hardship to attend. One wishes the portrait from White's dining room still existed, and also a photo of the picnic at the Presque Isle pavilion that Wednesday afternoon, perhaps Kawbawgam's last real public appearance.

Death

During the fall of 1902, Kawbawgam became ill and was admitted to St. Mary's Hospital in Marquette. We can imagine Charlotte and the Perreau children possibly taking the streetcar there each day to visit him. He remained in St. Mary's until his death at about 2 p.m. on Sunday, December 28.[47] The cause of death was typhoid fever. His death record states his age as 103, his occupation as Indian chief, his father as Charles Makadoagun, and his color as Indian.[48] It is unknown who gave the information for the death record. That Kawbawgam's father is accurately listed suggests Kawbawgam held veneration for his father despite being raised by his stepfather; he had obviously made certain his friends and family knew who his real father was. His age was likely inaccurate as previously discussed. Although Kawbawgam's occupation is listed as chief, Peter White, upon Kawbawgam's death, remarked that Kawbawgam "would have been a chief but for the fact that his tribe were so widely dispersed that they needed none."[49] White's statement is surprising given how Kawbawgam is always referred to as a chief in most books and articles that mention him. It makes one wonder whether he was acknowledged as such by whites more than by the Ojibwa, or if the role of chief was really one given to him out of respect rather than in any way official among his people. Regardless, the sign beside Kawbawgam's grave, though placed decades after his death, refers to him as "the last chief of the local Chippewa."

Kawbawgam's body was available for viewing at the Tonella Funeral Home in Marquette until 9 a.m. on Wednesday, December 31, the day of the funeral. Then it was taken to St. Peter's Cathedral for a Catholic funeral complete with a High Mass being sung.[50] His funeral was treated with all the pomp and circumstance he deserved as a chief. *The Mining Journal* stated, "The old Indian will be given decent burial, his faithful friend, the Hon. Peter White, having arranged all the details," including his being buried in a fine coffin with good clothes. We may assume Peter White paid for everything.[51]

Peter White delivered the funeral speech. In it, he stated Kawbawgam was not materialistic and ended his life owning only a gun, a fishing pole, and a blanket. White recalled his generosity, stating it was a misnomer to call the Boggam House a hotel since Kawbawgam had never charged his guests. Marquette residents referred to Kawbawgam as a "good Indian,"[52] which to them probably meant he didn't drink or cause trouble, but to Kawbawgam probably meant living his life as an Indian chief, a model and source of

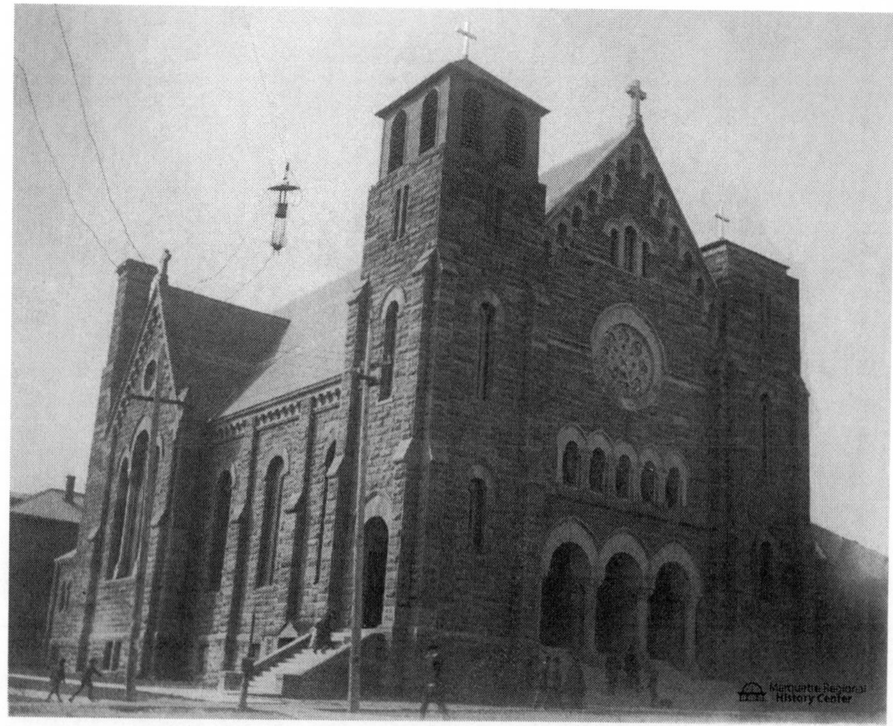

St. Peter's Cathedral at time of Kawbawgam's funeral

wisdom and instruction for his people, as well as having a reverence for the land and other natural resources, and respecting all forms of life.[53] St. Peter's Cathedral, in its own register of his death, states of Kawbawgam, "He is the *last* chief of Sault Chippewa Band between Marquette and Sault Ste. Marie."[54]

Following the services, a funeral cortege processed from St. Peter's to Presque Isle Park. The casket was carried down Superior Street (today's Baraga Avenue) to Front Street where it was met by a train of streetcars that took the casket and the mourners to Presque Isle Park. Peter White had gone to the city aldermen with the suggestion that Kawbawgam be buried at Presque Isle, for which they "all gave hearty approval."[55] *The Mining Journal* noted that "no one but Charles, who has any desire to be buried there, has the slightest right to such a resting place."[56] The body was buried "about the middle of the east front of the resort, on the high bluff o'er looking the waters that Kaw-baw-gam loved so fondly."[57] Father Joseph of St. Peter's Cathedral blessed the gravesite and presided over the burial.[58] Already there was talk of building a monument to Kawbawgam that would "record the main facts of his life and the single fact of great local interest, that he was the longest continuous resident of the site of Marquette" and it would "commemorate the memory of one of the best Indians that ever trod the shores of Lake Superior."[59] What made Kawbawgam one of the best Indians, as repeatedly mentioned in such articles, was that he did not drink or steal, or as *The Mining Journal* stated in reporting on his funeral, "His abstinence from liquor was always remarked, inasmuch as his friends and fellow tribesmen were notorious offenders in this respect."[60]

Not long after the funeral, Peter White gave the following memorial text that was published in "Memorial Reports Marquette County 1902," in the Michigan State Historical Society's *Michigan Historical Commission* Vol. XXXIII. Here White repeated the story of Kawbawgam as well as some other details. It is not known if this text was part of the eulogy he gave at the funeral, although it may well be.

Kaw-baw-gam 1902

> Charles Kaw-baw-gam, aged 104 years. I came to Marquette on the 18th of May, 1849, and found him here. He was a noble specimen of his race, a full-blooded Chippewa, and stepson of the great chief Shan-wa-non, and would have been a chief but for the fact that his tribe were so widely dispersed that they needed none. Kaw-baw-gam was a good man, a good citizen, a good hunter and a good fisherman. He always took good care of his family, and was never idle or lazy.

> Did not drink, never was arrested, and never fought his own race or any other. He was generous and helpful to all about him. He walked so erect, and looked so vigorous and strong up to the time of his fatal illness, only a few weeks before his death, that many people expressed doubts about his being a hundred years old. All the proof that I have to offer that he did reach this age is that on the 18th of May, 1849, the first time I ever saw him, I asked him how old he was. He replied in his own language, "Just fifty," and he explained just where he had lived in those fifty years. He looked to be fifty and I believed him implicitly, and since that day fifty-four long years have rolled around. I feel sure that he was 104 when he died. The citizens are just now making a contract for a bronze statue of heroic size of him, to be erected over his grave on Presque Isle, to be unveiled in July, 1904.

As mentioned, this statement is interesting since it raises the question of whether Kawbawgam was technically a chief. It also repeats the mistake that he was a "full-blooded Chippewa," a statement the white men seemed to take delight in. White has now also stretched Kawbawgam's age to 104 when, if Kawbawgam had been fifty in 1849, he could not have been more than 103 when he died in 1902. More likely he was about eighty-six.

Whatever Kawbawgam's age, his death would mark the end of an era for the Ojibwa of Marquette.

This photograph of Chief Kawbawgam beside Marquette resident Joe Flannigan was taken in the late 1800s. It shows, as Peter White said, that Kawbawgam walked erect and looked vigorous and strong until the end.

Chapter 13
Legacy

Soon after Kawbawgam's death, Peter White spearheaded the effort to erect a bronze statue in his friend's memory. White engaged Trentanove, who had previously built the Father Marquette statue and the bust of White, to produce the statue. White circulated a subscription list for the statue dated June 1, 1903, that stated:

> It is proposed to erect a statue by Signor Trentanove, to the memory of Chief CHARLES KAW – BAW – GAM, at Presque Isle over the spot where he was buried. It is estimated it will cost when ready to unveil, the sum of Twenty Five Hundred Dollars. It can be ready to unveil about the middle of July next.
>
> We, the undersigned, do each promise and agree to pay the sum opposite each of our respective signatures below. This pledge is pending or to be binding unless the whole sum named above as necessary is not subscribed.

White himself pledged $500 and Nathan Kaufman, a local banker, the former Mayor of Marquette, and the nephew of Robert Graveraet, also pledged $500. However, the only other two subscribers were J. R. Van Evera (warden of the Marquette prison) for $25 and an illegible name that looks like Claude W. Case for $25.[1] Apparently, there were difficulties raising the needed funds.

Regardless, plans for the statue went ahead during the summer of 1903. Milwaukee's *Evening Wisconsin* stated that Trentanove currently had two commissions, the Milwaukee Kosciuszko monument and the Statue of

Kaw-Baw-Gam.[2] Trentanove was traveling to Italy to do the work for the statues. The statue of Kosciuszko was for General Thaddeus Kosciuszko, a Polish national hero who had also served in the American Revolution. It would be completed and placed in Milwaukee in October, 1904.[3] Regarding the Kawbawgam statue, the *Evening Wisconsin* notes that the commission came from Peter White, who previously led the movement to give the city the Father Marquette statue. It states that Kawbawgam was an Indian chief of the Chippewa respected by all of Northern Michigan's early settlers and recounts White and Kawbawgam's first meeting. It goes on to say how they had a friendship that lasted until Kawbawgam's death and that Kawbawgam carried mail through the woods to Negaunee and the Soo. Finally, it praises Kawbawgam because "He never failed in courtesy to the whites or in the faithful execution of any task he undertook to perform. He never stole. He never was arrested." Next follows a subtitle "Was a Good Indian" and the mistake that he died in 1888 at age 104.[4] These statements show that Kawbawgam's legacy continued to be determined by white notions of what makes "a good Indian."

Another article, probably from *The Mining Journal*, noted that White was commissioning the statue, mentioned Trentanove's past work in Marquette, and recalled that Kawbawgam died the previous winter at about age one hundred. It said the statue would likely be placed near Kawbawgam's grave at Presque Isle and stated:

> Signor Trentanove studied Indian types in connection with the bas reliefs of his statue of Father Marquette, and as there are many admirable photographs of Kawbawgam, in all manner of poses, available he should be able to make a fine statue. Kawbawgam's face was distinctive and should prove an easy and admirable study for the sculptor. There will be much pleasure here with the knowledge that the memory of Charley is to be thus preserved, as the old fellow was always a favorite, even though he stalked his path through life alone and aloof, in latter years, at least. In this connection it may be remarked that there is an admirable bust study of Kaw-baw-gam's head and features in clay in the Peter White library at present, the work of Howard [sic] Kidder, who made no pretense of being anything but a dabbler in modeling. However, people generally will comment that if Trentanove catches the old Indian's face with the same fidelity shown in the study referred to he will have done everything that can be asked.[5]

Two letters about the statue from Trentanove to Albert F. Koepcke exist among Peter White's papers. Koepcke lived in Marquette and was working with White upon the statue. The first, dated June 11, 1903, thanks Koepcke for his kindness during Trentanove's brief stay in Marquette and requests he send to him the photographs of Kawbawgam promised to him by a gentleman whose name he can't remember that they met at the Nester Block.[6] The second letter, dated August 12, 1903, thanks Mr. Koepcke for sending the photo of Kawbawgam standing opposite his cottage at Presque Isle, which he thinks very beautiful. Trentanove says he is preparing a model of the statue and will send a photograph of it to share with Mr. White for approval. He then asks to be remembered to Mr. and Mrs. White and requests any correspondence be sent to him in Florence, Italy.[7]

What happened in regards to the statue after that date is not known. If a model was ever created and photographs of it were sent, record of them has been lost. Peter White probably never raised the money for the statue so the project was put aside. White's death in 1908 apparently ended any plans for such a monument, although it should be noted that White went on to work with Trentanove to have a statue of Father Marquette placed in Marquette Park on Mackinac Island, which happened in 1909.[8]

The Kawbawgams' grave remained without any substantial marker for nearly a decade. Then on October 1, 1912, Robert Hume, the caretaker at Presque Isle, found a large granite boulder washed up on the shore following a storm. The boulder had an unusual diagonal stripe of red across it (today it has faded to more of a white color). Hume said it reminded him of the chest sash Kawbawgam had worn.[9] Because of the stone's uniqueness, a visiting geologist offered Hume $1,000 for it, but Hume refused, saying it was to mark the Kawbawgams' grave.[10] A couple of days later, *The Mining Journal* reported that the stone would be placed at the Kawbawgams' grave, adding:

> Across the smooth, twelve inch face of the red band of granite, the names of both Kaw-baw-gam and his wife will be carved, together, with an emblem of their Catholic religion, a suitable inscription, and some design, such as an Indian head, in relief. It will be impossible to include the dates of the two last full-blooded Chippewas, in the engravings, for their ages are unknown, although Kaw-baw-gam was estimated to be considerably over 100 years old.[11]

Kawbawgam's Grave circa 1940

The boulder was placed on a base of stones gathered from Presque Isle's beaches. John Miller, a stonecutter, was involved in creating the grave according to a tradition in his family, although it is unknown whether he carved the base or the inscription.[12] Initially, a stone pattern on the ground also outlined the graves, although over time the vegetation around the stones became overgrown and the stones sank into the ground or were removed.

Eventually, a sign was placed beside the grave. I have been unable to determine the sign's date, but it appears in photos from 1957 onward. It reads:

CHARLEY KAWBAWGAM (1799-1902)
THE LAST CHIEF OF
THE LOCAL CHIPPEWA INDIANS
CHARLOTTE KAWBAWGAM (18—1904)
THE DAUGHTER OF CHIEF MARJIGESICK
PRESQUE ISLE WAS THEIR HOME FOR MANY YEARS
AND INTO ETERNITY.

The sign repeats the notion that Kawbawgam was 103 at his death. It also calls him "the last chief of the local Chippewa Indians." No other Ojibwa was considered a chief in the Marquette area after him, although there were certainly other Ojibwa chiefs in the Great Lakes area who outlived him, including his half-brother Louis B. Shawano, who died in 1910 in his late eighties or early nineties at the Sault, and Chief John Smith (Gaabinagwiiyaas) who died in 1922 in North Minnesota at the alleged age of 137. (Historians believe he was more likely in his nineties.)[13]

The sign does not clarify the Kawbawgams were husband and wife, but perhaps it is implied. According to historian Rebecca Mead, the grave is often covered with offerings of feathers and tobacco,[14] although I have never seen this myself. A 1997 article claimed the stone is covered with Catholic and Ojibwa symbols,[15] doubtless because the article's author copied from *The Mining Journal*, which had said the stone would be so carved in 1912, but no sign exists of any carving done to the stone.

Despite the long delay in a marker being placed beside their grave, the Kawbawgams were not easily forgotten by the people of Marquette or the Upper Peninsula. The month after Kawbawgam's death, the *Lake Superior Journal* ran the following memorial story, drawing largely upon information from Peter White:

WAS A FAMOUS CHIEF

KAW-BAW-GUM [sic] OF THE CHIPPEWAS IS DEAD.

Was Probably Over a Century Old and the First Man of Great Peter White

---

Charley Kaw-baw-gam's long life was brought to a close about 2 o'clock Sunday afternoon, when the old chief passed peacefully away at St. Mary's hospital at Marquette, where he had been lying ill for the past couple of months.

Charley was one of the best known figures in Marquette, and he enjoyed this distinction from the first day when white men began to frequent the spot where the city was to grow.

Charley's reputation was not local alone. He was known throughout the upper peninsula and even below the straits his name and fame were familiar to many people.

He was an excellent type of the original owners of the soil, and an unusually creditable speciman [sic]. He was a full blooded Chippewa and a chief by blood. What is more he was a good Indian, and he lived a good life, according to his lights.

Over 100 Years Old

Kaw-baw-gam was also remarked upon time and again for his great age. It is believed that he was over 100 years old at the time of his death.

In 1849 when Peter White first landed on the shores of Iron bay it is well known that the first Indian to greet him and the party of which he was a member was the same chieftain. In the same year 1849, Mr. White, in carrying on a conversation in Chippewa with Charley asked him, for the sake of having something to say, "How old are you, Bawgam?" Charley replying said: "I am fifty. I spent twenty at the Soo; twenty years on the Tonquomenon bay and ten years on the Canadian side." If Charley spoke the truth on that occasion he was about 103 years of age when he died, and there was no reason to doubt that this was the case. The Indians of his day were a notoriously long lived race and Charley was a fine Indian physically, strong, tireless and healthy. Furthermore his countenance was that of a patriarch.

Seeing Kaw-baw-gam, and perchance talking to him has always been one of the inevitable experiences for visitors to Marquette. He has been accessible at Presque Isle for the past twenty years, and during that time hundreds of curious eyes have beheld him in his last home.

An Interesting Figure

He was always an interesting man to see, if only to look upon. Intercourse with him was always difficult first on account of his limited knowledge of English, later on account of his failing mental powers, but there was always a great charm in beholding his tall, absolutely straight and strangely spare form prowling around his cabin home at Presque Isle or busied with the little tasks for which he had the inclination and strength. His face, too, was always worthy of study. Seared and lined to a degree, it expressed Indian refinement and it always seemed that such a face could only have developed on a man who had somewhere, in some state of repression or immature development, a refined, noble and upright soul. It expressed more spiritually and fineness than is common to the Indian type and confirmed all beholders in the belief that Charley was no ordinary Indian.

Kaw-baw-gam is survived by no children, but Charlotte, his faithful wife of fifty-four years that are recorded, still lives, but she is helpless and stone blind. This Charlotte welcomed Peter White and his friends that beautiful May morning in '49 when they first landed on the shore of the bay where Marquette was destined to grow.

Early History Vague

Charley's early history is largely unknown. His own account of the first fifty years of his life is given above. How far is correct is impossible to say. It appears certain that he had been living here for some time before Mr. White met him, but just how long he had been in the neighborhood is not known, nor is the date when he united his fortunes with those of his wife, Charlotte. After '49, however, there is a pretty good record of Charley's life.

He lived continuously in Marquette. In '49 he was tall, strong, straight, resourceful and brave, a typical Indian of the best class. He lived by hunting and fishing. In the early years he supplied the companies with fresh fish and meat. Up to the time he moved to Presque Isle, about twenty years ago, he lived with the exception of a couple of years he spent somewhere down in the Chocolay valley, on the site of the present South Shore freight depot.

Moved to Presque Isle

It was about twenty years ago when he settled down at Presque Isle in a cabin built for him by Peter White and Alfred Kidder. Up to that time he spoke little English, and intercourse with him had to be in Chippewa. He picked up English at Presque Isle, and finally came to have a fairly large vocabulary, which he increased from year to year. However, at no stage was Charley a fluent speaker of English, and he always used Chippewa when he could. Charley had no children who survived. The little Indian tykes whom Marquette people were accustomed to see in his train were not relatives of his, but it is believed that he was firmly convinced that they were his grandchildren.

Public Charge for Years

For many years past Kaw-baw-gam was a public charge. He had no friends or relatives to work for him. He had an allowance from the county most of the time that he was not able to support himself, and this was eked out by contributions from a couple of old residents of the city. Peter White has always had a warm place in his heart for Charley, and has been one of the links that has bound Mr. White to his early days in Marquette. And, besides, Kaw-baw-gam has always

> had much of his regard and admiration for his own personal worth. To Kaw-baw-gam, Mr. White has been a great chief whom he was always ready to consult and honor and come to in hour of need. It is needless to say that Kaw-baw-gam's passing is greatly regretted by his benefactor.
>
> **Their First Meeting**
>
> Mr. White gives the following account of his first meeting with Kaw-baw-gam and the hospitality the chief dispensed on that occasion, it being taken from an address which Mr. White delivered before the Y.M.C.A. at Marquette in 1889.[16]

The remainder of the article quotes the speech, which had also been printed in *The Mining Journal* at Kawbawgam's death and was previously quoted in full in Chapter 4.

Another article in *The Mining Journal*, "Kaw-Baw-Gam: Interesting Facts Regarding the Old Chippewa's History," besides recounting events of his life said that he was probably born about 1819, a surprisingly late date given Peter White's continual insistence that Kawbawgam said he was fifty in 1849. It is surprising *The Mining Journal* would give such a date, and with no explanation for it. Regardless, it is probably two or three years too late. More importantly, whatever year Kawbawgam was born, he had seen dramatic changes no one could have imagined during his lifetime.

Kawbawgam's Family and Band After His Death

After her husband's death, Charlotte Kawbawgam left Presque Isle to live with her nephew Fred Cadotte (Bawgam) and his family until her own death. If she had wanted to remain at Presque Isle, the City of Marquette probably would have allowed her to. But according to Kenyon Boyer in a 1955 radio talk, an old resident told him that not long after Kawbawgam's death, the rest of the Ojibwa colony that had lived on Presque Isle was moved off the island, some going to South Marquette.[17] With their leader gone, they may not have wanted to remain, but more likely, they had been allowed to remain out of respect to Kawbawgam during his lifetime, and now the City felt it was time for Presque Isle to be a true park and not a residence for anyone except the park caretaker. When Kawbawgam's house was torn down is not known.

Up to this time, the Native American population in Marquette had experienced a rather unique situation compared to other Native American communities in the Upper Peninsula because, unlike at the Sault or L'Anse, they were not on reservation land. Nor did Kawbawgam have to deal with government interference or negotiations like those on the reservations. The level of respect the Marquette community showed him may be considered remarkable to some degree, and consequently, he was able to hold his band together during his lifetime.

In the early twentieth century, the Ojibwa who remained in the area were largely relegated to North Marquette, west of Presque Isle Avenue. This area would become known as "Indian Town." It would have a segregated school, which today is part of the St. Vincent de Paul complex. In the 1960s, the situation at the school was so bad that the Federal government came close to bringing the Marquette School Board to court to close the school. However, the school was already in the process of closing and incorporating the Native children into the city schools. Many streets in this area—the North Marquette Addition—also remained unpaved until as late as 2010, probably the last streets in Marquette to be paved.[18]

Mary Tebeau would outlive Kawbawgam by less than seven months. She died on July 24, 1903 after an illness of about three weeks. Her death certificate lists her as Mary Mandoski. The cause of her death was tuberculosis. According to her death certificate, she was twenty-two, although she was more likely twenty-six or twenty-seven. She is listed as a widow who was married at age twenty and had no children. Oddly, her parents are listed as Frank Tebo and Mary Codotte. While a doctor, registrar, and undertaker are named, none of them likely knew her well enough to give accurate information. She was buried on July 25, 1903 in the Old Catholic Cemetery in Marquette on Pioneer Road.[19]

As for Charlotte, she died on Tuesday, May 24, 1904. Although she died less than two months before Kawbawgam's monument was to be unveiled, her death did not motivate efforts to make it a reality. In fact, *The Mining Journal* could hardly be bothered to mention her. Her obituary, in the Saturday, May 28, 1904 issue, consisted of a small paragraph in the "City Brevities" section as follows:

> Mrs. Kaw-baw-gam, wife of Charles Kaw-baw-gam, died early this week at the home of her son, Fred-Kaw-baw-gam, in the Chocolay valley. The remains were buried Tuesday beside those of the old chief, on Presque Isle, at the eastern side of the park. Mrs. Kaw-baw-gam was a very old woman.[20]

Since Charlotte died on Tuesday, it is unlikely she was buried the same day. Nor was she a "very old woman" but only about seventy-four. As the daughter and wife of chiefs, and a brave woman who stood up for Native

American rights when she sued the Jackson Iron Company, she deserved a front page headline.

Fred Bawgam/Cadotte would live to age seventy-nine, dying on April 29, 1926 after a month's illness at St. Mary's Hospital. His funeral was held at St. John the Baptist Catholic Church and he was buried in Holy Cross Cemetery.[21] Today, his innumerable descendants live in the Marquette area, including the descendants of his daughter Alice and her husband Raymond George Trevillion. The Trevillion clan has spread throughout the country but remains largely represented in Marquette County. Alice and Raymond's son Raymond G. Trevillion (1929-2001) would marry Clara Hilliard, whose first husband was Leander Madosh (great-grandson of Chief Madosh). According to Raymond G. Trevillion's obituary, he had fourteen children and numerous grandchildren, great-grandchildren, and great-great-grandchildren.[22] They are all the descendants of Chief Marji-Gesick.

Fred's sister Angelica's descendants did not fare as well. Her only daughter Mary died childless, unless as previously noted, Lizzie and Frank Perreau or Richard Mandosking were her children. Whether or not these three children are descendants of Angelica Cadotte, their histories have been largely lost. Richard married Anna Oller and they had four children including David (1924-2004), Raymond, and two children whose names I have been unable to find.[23] In any case, this family is likely not directly related to the Kawbawgam/Cadotte family. I have not been able to find any further records for Richard Mandosking.

According to the Durant Roll, in 1909, Lizzie and Frank Perreau, listed as ages sixteen and twelve (more likely sixteen and fourteen), were enrolled at the Mount Pleasant Indian Industrial Boarding School.[24] The school, established by act of the US Congress in 1891 in Mount Pleasant, Michigan, had the purpose to educate Native American children off reservations, which was, of course, a way to separate Native American children from their families. The school was run in a paramilitary fashion with students required to wear uniforms and march to and from school activities. The children received basic instruction in kindergarten through eighth grade with a strict schedule focused on vocational training and religious education. Classes included English, arithmetic, woodworking, farming, baking, sewing/tailoring, laundry, housekeeping, farm work, and basic first aid. The coursework included learning how to fit into white culture.[25] While some children seem to have enjoyed the school atmosphere because it removed them from impoverished reservation life, it served both to destroy Native

George Madosh family home, 2204 Wilkinson Ave. Marquette, circa 1900

traditional culture and to strengthen their identity as Native Americans, especially when the school's sports teams usually defeated other teams of non-Native children.[26] One has to wonder how the Kawbawgams would have felt knowing the young children they had loved and cared for would have such a future. Unfortunately, I have been unable to determine what became of Frank and Lizzie later in life. However, records show that Aylmer and George Roussain from the Sault, being one-quarter and one-half Ojibwa, and possibly descendants of Kawbawgam's sister or related to her husband's family, also attended the school, as did Genevieve and Nellie Madosh of Marquette, both being three-quarters Ojibwa.[27] In other words, attending the school was common among the Kawbawgams' relatives and the Ojibwa in general.

The Madosh family has continued to flourish in Marquette County. They are too numerous to list here, but Charlotte's first cousin, Civil War veteran George Madosh, had among his children Augustus, who was born in 1881. Augustus had six children: Nellie, Leander, Richard, Jeanne, Peter, and Mary.

Richard (1914-1985)[28] and his wife Elsie had twelve children in Marquette born in the 1950s and 1960s; many of them and their descendants still live in Marquette or Upper Michigan.[29]

As noted above, Leander (1912-1961) was married to Clara, who later married Raymond G. Trevillion.[30] Clara and Leander had three children: Gerald, Judy, and Leander August "Lee." Lee (1949-2011) himself had four children and his descendants continue to live in the Marquette area. According to his obituary, "Lee was proud of his American Indian heritage and received the name 'Muh-Koons' meaning 'Little Bear.'"[31]

Leander and Richard's brother, Peter (1916-1998), known as "Mandolin Pete" married Helen Hocking. They had three children: Margaret, Peter, Jr., and Patricia. Peter, Jr. had three children: Summer, Matt, and Mike. Matt Madosh provided me with information for this book.[32]

Aftermath of the Treaties

Throughout Kawbawgam's life and long after, disputes continued over the treaties that had been signed in his youth. An entire book could be devoted to this topic, but a brief overview will suffice here. Part of the controversy resulted from the discovery in the early twentieth century that many of the Ojibwa and Ottawa had money owed to them from the 1855 treaty, due to government investments. As a result, Horace Durant was commissioned to create what became known as the Durant Roll. This roll was a census taken in 1907-1910 that listed everyone of Ojibwa or Ottawa descent, the degree (percentage) of Native blood they had, and their ages.[33] It included information from the bands at Mackinac Island, Sault Sainte Marie, Grand River, and Traverse. Today, it is a wonderful genealogical source for Native Americans, although how effective it was in getting Native descendants their money is questionable.[a]

A few articles from Sault Sainte Marie's *The Evening News* illuminate how long this battle for payment of money continued. In 1916, *The Evening News* reported that William M. Johnston was going to Washington, DC regarding a partial payment made to some Native Americans because few of them had received the whole amount they should have. He claimed some names on the list of those to receive payment were stricken off and others on the list had received no compensation.[34] This issue doubtless led to *The Evening News* reporting in 1925 that descendants of the six bands of Native Americans in the Sault area needed to enroll to establish their rights. Plans had been made to present claims to the government arising out of the guarantee given by the United States under the 1820 treaty. Johnston, along with the Cadreau

a. The Durant Roll is available online at http://www.mifamilyhistory.org/mi-mack/native_american/miller/durant.asp.

Brothers, was on the committee to present the claims. They warned that anyone not enrolling at this time might have difficulty establishing their rights later.[35]

A fascinating document from 1935, the full purpose of which I have been unable to determine, is an official form from the Chippewa County probate court. It contains the testimony of Kawbawgam's nephew, Charles Shawano, the son of his half-brother Edward. (Perhaps Charles Shawano was named after his uncle.) The document suggests that as soon as the 1855 Treaty of Detroit was signed, it was controversial.

STATE OF MICHIGAN

COUNTY OF CHIPPEWA

At a session of the Probate Court for said County, held at the Probate office, in the City of Sault Ste. Marie, on the twenty-first day of August, in the year one thousand nine hundred and thirty-five,

Present, Charles H. Chapman, Judge of Probate

In the Matter of the Treaty between the United States of America and the Chippewa and Ottawa Indians of the Sault Ste. Marie band, held in the city of Detroit, Michigan, July 31st. and August 2nd., 1855.

Charlie Showano, first being duly sworn, says:

My grandfather, O-shaw-waw-no-Ke-wan-ze, attended and aided in executing the treaty on July 31st., 1855. My said grandfather, together with nearly all of the Indians returned to their homes on Lake Superior, and two days later, on August 2, 1855, the treaty was re-enacted by two or three who had remained, and they signed the names without any authority, signing away the most valuable rights of the Indians of the Lake Superior country. The treaty of August 2nd., 1855 was a well known fraud perpetrated upon the Indians, one of the greatest crimes ever committed under authority of a great nation, and all this without the knowledge of the head officials at Washington, but through the manipulation of some of the irresponsible representatives sent to procure a treaty of the kind that was made. I solemnly state upon my oath that my grandfather, the said O'shaw-waw-no-Ke-wan-ze, made a statement to me in the presence of my father, Ed Showano, that he did not sign the treaty of August 2, 1855, here alluded to, and that his signature was a forgery and was signed by someone for the purpose of defrauding the Indians of their rights. I heard my grandfather repeatedly saying that he never signed the treaty, and these statements were made in the presence of my father, Ed Showano.

And further, deponent says that it was well known that Indians from Canada signed the treaty of 1820, and some of the same names were signed to the treaty of August 2, 1855, and it was known at the time that some of these Indians had been dead for some time when their names were attached to the second treaty.

I make this statement with my full faculties and understanding, being well preserved at my age, which is now seventy-seven years, and I reside at the Bay Mills Indian Mission, in Chippewa County, State of Michigan.

Witnessed by:

his

Kathryn E. Smith Charlie X Shawano

Bernice Frost mark

Subscribed and sworn to me this 21st. day of August, A.D. 1935.

Charles H. Chapman

Judge of Probate

As late as 1969, *The Evening News* was reporting that the local Native American community was still contesting the treaties. A January 7, 1969 meeting was attended by 100 people of Native American descent. Eighty of them voted to reject an offer to settle the treaty of 1820 for $12,000, saying the settlement proposed was based on 1820 values and because they were also contesting the 1836 treaty for $10.8 million, so they did not want to set a precedent that could hurt that contention by accepting a settlement for the 1820 treaty.[36]

Contentions have continued into more recent years, including over protecting Native American fishing rights.

Marquette National Bank Card and Coin

Numerous tributes have been made to Kawbawgam in the one-hundred-plus years since his death, both through the naming of various places and objects after him and by fictionalizing him and his family in literature. Most of the rest of this chapter provides a chronology of such items.

In 1903, the Marquette National Bank issued a "statement of condition" card that contained a drawing of Kawbawgam on its cover.[37] This appears to have been the second time Kawbawgam's image was appropriated by an organization for commercial use (the first having been by Peter White at a Michigan Bankers' Association meeting in 1891 as mentioned in Chapter 12). No doubt the card was intended to honor Kawbawgam. Surprisingly, Peter White had no connection to the Marquette National Bank, which was short-lived. The use of Kawbawgam's image can be interpreted either as his endorsement of the bank (it's unlikely he would have endorsed it) or that Kawbawgam's long life and good moral character were representative of the bank's own good standing and longevity. More likely, it was done simply to honor Kawbawgam since he had died less

Marquette National Bank card

Kawbawgam commemorative medal

than a year previously. The bank also issued and sold a special medal honoring Kawbawgam. The front bears his image, the words "Kawbawgam, Last Chief of the Chippewas," and the word "integrity." The back depicts the bank building, its name, and the word "lucky."

Uses of Kawbawgam's image since his death are too numerous to mention in full here, but it should be noted that postcards of his photograph, of his grave, and also of Jacques LePique's wigwam have been sold throughout Marquette's history. The Marquette Regional History Center has a collection of some of these.

Iron Ore Discovery Historical Marker

In October 1904, just months after Charlotte Kawbawgam's death on May 24, the Jackson Mine erected a pyramid to mark the place the iron ore was discovered in Negaunee. The marker was later moved to Jackson Park, about a mile and a half from the actual site. The marker reads:

> This monument was erected by the Jackson Iron Co. in October 1904, to mark the first discovery of iron ore in the Lake Superior region. The exact spot is 300 feet North Easterly from this monument to an iron post. The ore was found under the roots of a fallen pine

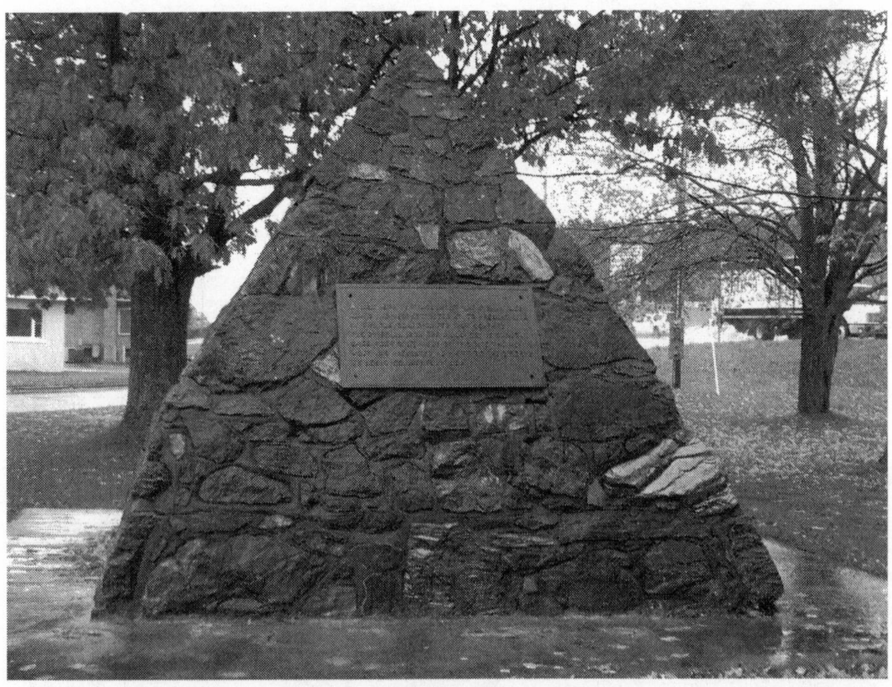

Jackson Iron Company historical marker

> tree, in June 1845, by Marji Gesick, a chief of the Chippewa tribe of Indians. The land was secured by a mining "permit" and the property subsequently developed by the Jackson Mining Company, organized July 23, 1845.

Interestingly, the marker repeats the false story of the ore being found under a fallen pine tree. That the marker gives credit to Marji-Gesick shows any contention by the Jackson Iron Company over Marji-Gesick's contributions had now been put to rest.

Kawbawgam Poem

On July 17, 1905, *The Mining Journal* printed a curious anonymous poem titled "Charley Boggum Reminiscitur." The poem is one of several that appeared beginning the year the Father Marquette statue was dedicated that depicted Father Marquette and Peter White, referred to usually as Pierre Le Blanc, conversing. They are humorous poems written in French-Canadian dialect. Some of them pretend that Peter White was alive and living in Marquette's current location when Father Marquette first came to Iron Bay; Peter White then agreed to build a city in the priest's name. Others depict the Father Marquette statue coming to life and visiting Peter White. This specific poem, however, while written in this vein, does not mention Kawbawgam at all, despite its title. Instead, the speaker seems to be Kawbawgam, remembering the past, but oddly speaking in a French-Canadian dialect. The other remarkable thing about this poem compared to the others is that it references Jacques LePique.[b]

CHARLEY BOGGUM REMINISCITUR[38]

Aiee yass! I well remember me
  Does happy tam of ole
Wen Pere Marquette he come on lac
  For save sauvages his soul.

---

b. At least five other poems appeared in this vein in various publications. One first appeared in the *Detroit Free Press* on September 27, 1897 and was reprinted in Ralph Williams' *The Honorable Peter White* (p. 194-95). The others exist in newspaper clippings in the second volume of Peter White's scrapbooks at the Marquette Regional History Center. Surprisingly, White did not seem to save a copy of this poem referencing Kawbawgam. In issue 4 of *U.P. Reader* (2020), I published a short story I wrote, "The Many Lives of Pierre LeBlanc," which draws upon this poetry tradition.

Eet wasn't auny one here dose days,
Only me and Pierre Blanc,
He live way up on top the hill,
Wile me—I stay down on the bank.

Zat Pere Marquette he varry good man;
He arrive in bark canoe,
He build chapelle for crucifix
And preach long serment, too.

Zees place all b'long to M'sieu Blanc,
But eit ain't got a name, not yet;
So M'sieu Blanc he regard it good ting
For call cit by ze name "Marquette."

Zis mek le bon Pere tres content
An' he say to M'sieu Pierre:
"S'il vous plait I mek you archeveque
For all ze sauvages bout here."

But M'sieu Pierre he mek gran' bow
And to Pere Marquette he say:
"Tanks beaucoup for grand politesse
But I b'long to l'eglise Anglais."

All doze oder sauvages an' me
We soon get good Catholique.
Except one tam bad Injun man
Wat call himself Jack le Pique.

He live in cabine on White Fish Lac
An' steal everyting he see.
'Specialment ze boards from M'sieu Blanc's fence
Also sugair out of his tree.

Een summaire tam he kill red deer,
Of ze law he 'ave no respec
So Pere Marquette he give 'im hell
Till he learn to be'ave currec."

Helas! Dose bon tam ancien
  Dey don't come anny more back
Wen Pere Marquette he come on shore
  From batteau on Superior Lac.

Camp on Chingoochickee Lake
  July 24th, 1903

Peter White Dies

Peter White would die in 1908, never seeing a monument erected to his friend Kawbawgam. However, to the end, he was a supporter of the Native Americans and interested in carrying on their culture, regardless of how we might view his efforts today. In the summer of 1907, White, who had a national reputation by that point, agreed to teach Ojibwa war dances to a group of young men who belonged to the Episcopalian Church. They were to perform the dance at a church anniversary event in October. Numerous newspapers in Michigan carried the story, with various titles, including the *Vassar Times* ("Peter White Will Teach a Bunch of Young Men Chippewa War Dance"), the *Calumet News* ("Aged One to Dance"), the *Kalamazoo Telegraph* ("Peter White as Dancing Teacher"), and the Wesley Newspaper Bureau ("Teaches Indian Steps"). One article even speculated that White might actually take the stage himself. Ernest Rankin was one of the young boys who performed at the event who remembered how Peter White went hopping about the stage showing the boys how the Ojibwa made their war whoops.

Northern Michigan Normal School Yearbook

From 1924-1932, Northern Michigan Normal School (today's Northern Michigan University) named its yearbook *The Kawbawgam*. While it had various themes each year (e.g., the 1932 issue was devoted to George Washington), in 1928, the issue was devoted to an "Indian theme" and included an image of Kawbawgam in the front pages (the same image used by the Marquette National Bank), illustrations of teepees (used by Plains Indians, not the Ojibwa) and Native Americans throughout, and the following Foreword:

> We live in a land of past romance, where once the wild bear leisurely turned the stones on a sunny hillside, seeking for ants; where once the Indians hid behind the trees to trap the wily deer; where men have hewn away the forest and made history. This is all before us, about us, meeting our eyes at every step. With this in mind

> the Editors of the Kawbawgam decided to use an Indian theme in this book, perpetuating the Indian traditions.[39]

Notably, while the Northern students intended to honor the Native Americans who had once resided on the land, they hardly took a realistic view of history, viewing it as "past romance."

The Marquette Redmen

In 1928, Marquette's Graveraet High School opened. It was funded by Louis Kaufman, nephew of Robert Graveraet, and named to honor his mother, Julia Graveraet. The school's team was named the "Redmen," which may have been in honor of Kaufman's Native American heritage. Later an Indian in a headdress was added as the team logo. Ironically, the team name and logo led to a major controversy that began in the late 1990s with opponents saying the school appropriated a Native American image and that "Redmen" is a derogatory term. Nor was Marquette the only school to use Native American imagery. Nationwide, schools, universities, and professional athletic teams have used such images. By the early 1990s, more than 100 Michigan high schools and colleges had Native American logos, often featuring angry Native faces or warriors brandishing tomahawks and weapons. These logos also promoted racial stereotypes through their references to skin color, such as "Redmen" and "Redskins."[40]

Once the controversy arose, numerous Marquette school board meetings were held regarding changing the logo, and *The Mining Journal* was flooded with Letters to the Editor on the issue. On January 11, 1999, the school board voted to phase out the logo by the end of the year but to keep the Redmen/Redettes name.[41] The community was appalled by this decision after having been very proud of its logo for many years. Meanwhile, new logos were proposed, including one designed by Dan Pemble, which resembled a male superhero. When the student body voted on three logo options, out of 1215 votes, 620 were for the superhero logo and 500 were against any logo. Despite the superhero logo winning the vote, the schoolboard decided it was too macho for the school. Pemble offered to draw a female counterpart, but he also said he was surprised by the gender controversy over his logo since gender had never been raised as an issue by the Indian headdress logo.[42] Another vote was taken in which 1179 students voted. This time, 227 voted for the muscular superhero while 729 voted for the Indian headdress logo as a write-in candidate.[43] Ignoring the students' wishes, the schoolboard considered the muscled Redman superhero the winner.

The public was so angry at the logo being changed that it voted out the school board. Fred Rydholm, Marquette's most recognized historian at the time, wrote a letter to the editor of *The Mining Journal*, published July 16, 1999, arguing that the school mascot was a tribute to Kaufman and Marquette's Native American heritage and that all of the students, citizens of Marquette, and "Indian members of the community" were "very proud of their logo."[44] In another letter, Rydholm and Rob Dupras stated that when Graveraet High School was established, Coach C.C. Rushton had asked student athlete Henry "Hank" Jackson to select an appropriate logo and he had picked a Sioux Indian in full headdress.[45] Other origin stories of the name have included that Louis Kaufman picked it to honor his mother's Native American heritage, and that it was chosen by an early superintendent of the school after Harvard University's crimson-red, and only after the logo was chosen years later did the name take on a Native American meaning.[46] I have been unable to find historical documentation of these origin stories—and there are more—I suspect some are borderline myths created to justify the logo and name. More research needs to be done to determine the truth of them and the reasons for the choice of name and logo.

When the new schoolboard decided to reinstate the Redmen logo, a civil complaint was filed, the plaintiffs being Lisa Boyd, Jodi Potts, and Lisa McGeshick of Marquette and Michael Haney of Urbana, Illinois. However, by May 2000, the lawsuit was dismissed when the plaintiffs failed to prepare a joint status report as required by court order.[47]

While the Redmen name was retained, in the years that followed, the Indian headdress logo was discontinued, although school football helmets with two feathers next to the M continued to be worn by players at least as late as 2016, although the students may have done so against school policies. Pat Lynott, one of the board members who initially voted to change the logo, had stated that Native Americans consider eagle feathers sacred and she was "not for using someone's religious symbol for a high school logo."[48] Meanwhile, the school logo was changed to a red M for Marquette.

In 2019-2020, the controversy again erupted. This time it was claimed that the Redmen name was creating "an adverse learning environment" for some of the students and once more hearings were held about changing the name. Local residents, most of them graduates of Marquette Senior High School, were again furious. A Facebook group "Save the Redmen/Redettes" quickly garnered more than 2,300 members in a couple of weeks and a petition that circulated online received more than 2,500 signatures. Unscientific polls by *The Mining Journal* and the local TV station, WLUC TV6, showed overwhelming community support for retaining the logo.

Several Native Americans spoke out to say they were not offended by the logo and those in favor of saving the logo used this Native response as an argument to preserve it. However, opposing arguments suggested that Native Americans who spoke in favor of retaining the logo in some cases may have felt intimidated and even fearful of repercussions if they spoke in favor of changing it. On February 5, 2020, the Great Lakes Area Tribal Health Board unanimously passed Resolution No. 20-001 stating that "sports team logos, mascots, and names degrade and diminish American Indian and Alaska Native (AI/AN) people throughout the history of the United States as documented in various studies and relayed by personal experiences and first-hand accounts by AI/AN people" and they argued that the negative effects were long-lasting and detrimental to positive self-esteem, exposing "generation after generation to these stereotypes, and indoctrinating them with the idea that it is acceptable to stereotype an entire race of people." Numerous other individuals and organizations spoke to both sides of the issue, those in favor of keeping the logo arguing it was a longstanding tradition and even that it could be used for educational purposes to raise awareness of Native American issues. The Episcopal Diocese of Northern Michigan advocated for changing the logo with Bishop Rayford Ray, drawing upon discussions with local Native Americans, stating:

> The 'Redmen' and 'Redette' nicknames are not only hurtful to indigenous members of the community, but to all who believe in human dignity, freedom and justice. We are called to recognize an injustice, to educate each other about the nature of this injustice and to follow the lead of local indigenous leaders who recognize how to heal this unnecessary trauma.[49]

The issue of Native American team mascots is not limited to Marquette but has been a nationwide issue for thirty years now. Numerous organizations have come forward to add their voices to the cry to end the use of Native American team mascots, logos, and nicknames. A complete list would take up far too much space, but it includes Michigan's State Board of Education, The National Council of American Indians (the nation's oldest and largest Native American advocacy group), the Sault Sainte Marie Tribe of Chippewa Indians, Little League International, the National Collegiate Athletic

Association, the Michigan Education Association, and the Michigan Civil Rights Commission.[c]

Adam Berger of the Marquette Regional History Center, in a letter to the editor of *The Mining Journal* on February 14, 2020, argued that the use of stereotypical team logos serves to obscure our historical record of Native Americans:

> Much of the material that is in our collection comes from pageants, scripted performances featuring idealized, costumed Native people. These pageants, popular in Marquette County around 1920, were literally plays with inauthentic costumes and props. We have some beautiful photos of Native Americans. Unfortunately, many are based on plains-influenced imaginings of what Native people should look like. Some performers are not Native at all. It leaves us with a confusing photographic record.
>
> We are a serious historical society and it looks like someone erased our understanding of local Native history and drew cartoons instead.[50]

The Redmen logo adds to this confusion since it is a Sioux headdress and the Sioux were the natural enemies of the Ojibwa who were the predominant tribe in Upper Michigan.

As a historian, I do believe the Marquette Redmen name and logo was established with good intentions, and I certainly understand why many people wish to maintain a logo and name that have been a tradition for nearly a century. However, no one benefits by a distortion of history. As I stated in this book's introduction, I grew up assuming Native Americans welcomed white settlers to Upper Michigan and it was a peaceful settlement. Only in researching this book did I learn how the Ojibwa were coerced into surrendering the Upper Peninsula to the US Government or how they were constantly threatened with removal or forced assimilation. That white people usurped Native American images for their own purposes, including school team names, logos, and mascots, is only additional injury heaped upon the

---

c. An impressive list of organizations that has spoken out particularly against the use of the Washington Redskins name can be found at https://www.changethemascot.org/supporters-of-change/. Besides organizations, it lists many famous individuals who support changing the team's name, including President Barack Obama, musician Gene Simmons of the band Kiss, radio personality Howard Stern, political activist Ralph Nader, and boxing champion Mike Tyson.

many injuries Americans have already inflicted on Native Americans, from stealing their land to committing genocide. No one is served well by presenting a distorted historical record—it perpetuates falsehood, dishonesty, and distrust from generation to generation, preventing us from moving forward together. Even if racism is done unintentionally or with the best intentions, it is still racism.

Ultimately, I ask myself, "What would Chief Kawbawgam say about this matter?" Given the time in which he lived, I suspect he would have stayed out of the discussion from fear of repercussions to his people. I suspect many Native Americans today continue to have the same fears. Anything that breeds—or has the potential to breed—fear, pain, misunderstanding, and distortions of the truth needs to be changed.

At the time of this book's printing no decision regarding the Marquette Redmen name has been made, although the logo has been officially retired. With numerous local Native American organizations and tribes calling upon the Marquette public schools to change the name, I think it is time we respect their wishes.

Kawbawgam Hotel Company

In 1917, George Shiras III, Peter White's son-in-law, decided it was time for Marquette to have a new, high quality hotel. He approached the Marquette Rotary Club and sold shares of stock to fund building the hotel. However, delays kept the hotel from opening until 1930. In the meantime, the effort continued under the name of the Kawbawgam Hotel Company, which was an unsurprising name choice since Shiras would have known Kawbawgam, who had been his father-in-law's great friend, and had hired Fred Cadotte (Bawgam) as a guide. However, when the hotel opened in 1930, it did so as the Northland Hotel. Perhaps the shareholders felt hotel patrons, who would not be from Marquette, would find the name Kawbawgam too hard to pronounce or too foreign-sounding.

In 1982, the hotel closed. It remained vacant until 1995 when it reopened as the Landmark Inn. Various rooms in the restored hotel were named for Marquette's most famous people and various celebrities who had stayed there. One room is named for Chief Kawbawgam. Other rooms were named for Fred Rydholm, John Voelker, and George Shiras III.

Marquette Bottling Works

The Marquette Bottling Works was begun in 1919. About the 1920s, it issued a commemorative one-pint bottle with Kawbawgam's image on it.

Kawbawgam Bottle

Chief Bottle

The bottle says "Marquette Bottling Works" on the top, "The Chief of All Beverages" on the bottom, and has Kawbawgam's image and name "Kawbawgam" in the middle.

Later, about the 1950s or 1960s, the Marquette Bottling Works issued a quart-size bottle that said "Marquette beverages" on it and had the image of a Native American chief inside an arrowhead graphic with arrows behind it. This image is not likely to be Kawbawgam, although it may have been intended to reflect the Marquette Redmen logo.

Examples of both bottles are in the Marquette Regional History Center's collection.

Kawbawgam Lake

In 1933, Pickerel Lake in Chocolay Township was renamed Kawbawgam Lake. It is reputed that Kawbawgam resided along the lake during the time he lived in Chocolay Township. The name change was partly made because of there being two Pickerel Lakes in Marquette County. The other Pickerel Lake also had its name changed. It became Harlow Lake to honor Marquette city father Amos Harlow.[51]

Grave Desecration at Grand Island

Not everyone in Upper Michigan was as ready as people in Marquette to honor Native Americans. In the 1930s, a road crew was hired to build a road to the life saving station on Grand Island, where Kawbawgam was likely born and where many of his relatives may have been buried. The road crew dug up the Ojibwa cemetery. By then, the spirit houses the Ojibwa had built over the graves were long gone, but many skeletons were found below the sand. Some members of the road crew brought home

Ojibwa spirit houses at cemetery in L'Anse. Those at Grand Island would have been similar.

skulls as souvenirs while the rest of the bones were thrown in a heap in a ditch.[52]

Kawbawgam Lodge

The Negaunee *Iron Herald* noted on May 2, 1947 that an improved road had been built from Highway 490 to the Darch's Kawbawgam Lodge, several miles southeast of Marquette. This lodge was likely on Kawbawgam Lake, although I have been unable to find out more information about it or the Darches.

Boy Scout Pageant

In September 1965, twenty-three members of Marquette's Boy Scout Troop 361, Hiawathaland Council, presented a pageant honoring Chief Kawbawgam at the Presque Isle bandshell. The boys were in "full costume."[53] It is not known whether "full costume" refers to the Boy Scouts' uniforms or whether they donned Native American costumes. Regardless, it shows that Kawbawgam's role in Marquette's history was still remembered and being passed on to younger generations.

Laughing Whitefish by Robert Traver

Also in 1965, local author John Voelker (1903-1991) published *Laughing Whitefish*, a novel featuring Charlotte Kawbawgam. Voelker had become nationally famous nearly a decade before for writing the bestselling novel *Anatomy of a Murder* (1956) under the pen name Robert Traver. The book was made into a major motion picture of the same name starring James Stewart and Lee Remick.

John Voelker

Now Voelker was following up his previous success with *Laughing Whitefish*, also published under his pen name. *Laughing Whitefish* is based on Charlotte Kawbawgam's lawsuit against the Jackson Iron Company. However, Voelker took many liberties with history, grossly distorting the trial's events and who Charlotte was. Consequently, the novel is far more fiction than history. Those knowledgeable about the trial will quickly see the many differences in the novel. As Matthew L. M. Fletcher, in his 2011 Foreword to the novel, states, it is only "a tad accurate."[54]

Because of Voelker's novel, many people mistakenly assume Charlotte's Ojibwa name meant Laughing Whitefish, but that was actually the creation of John Voelker, and only the first of many liberties he took. Voelker stated:

> I also wanted to name my Indian girl after the river she was born by, but which history alas said was the Carp, so one night I stealthily crept over to adjoining Alger County and stole one of its more romantically named rivers—and instead called her Laughing Whitefish.[55]

No historical lawyers are referenced in the novel. Instead, Charlotte goes to an elderly gentleman lawyer named Cassius "Cash" Wendell. An alcoholic, Cassius decides he can't handle the case so he convinces the new lawyer in town, young William Poe, to take it on. William is from Detroit. He was on his way to Copper Harbor, Michigan, wanting to live somewhere exotic, when the boat stopped in Marquette. He decided to stay after witnessing how the local Indians in Marquette were mistreated. When two Indians canoed past William's ship, the ship's passengers started whooping out Indian war cries and throwing pennies at the Indians. William realized his shipmates hated Indians, but he felt that whatever faults the Indians might have, it was the white man's fault they were that way. Consequently, William is very happy to take Charlotte's case; it doesn't hurt that he's attracted to her.[56]

Since the novel takes place in 1873, the real Charlotte Kawbawgam would have been in her early forties by that year, but Voelker uses extreme poetic license with Charlotte's age and with many other details of her life. In the novel, Charlotte/Laughing Whitefish is only twenty-one. She has just reached the age of majority, which is why she now decides to sue the Jackson Iron Company. She is also single, attractive, and a teacher at her own school for Indians at Presque Isle. Chief Kawbawgam is completely written out of the book, although Charlotte's last name is still Kawbawgam. That's because her father is Marji Kawbawgam instead of Marji-Gesick. Perhaps Voelker decided Kawbawgam was the more familiar name so he retained it even though he eliminated its namesake.

In the novel, Charlotte's father has had three wives: Blue Heron, whom he apparently divorced in the Indian manner; Charlotte's mother, Sayee; and Old Meg, a drunken Indian woman who met an untimely death. Sayee also died when Charlotte was small so Charlotte was adopted by Blue Heron and raised by her. Blue Heron is dead when the novel opens.

Charlotte's father had showed the white men where the iron ore was on the Haunted Mountain. Voelker makes extreme changes about finding the iron ore. He says Marji was working with William Burt when the ore was discovered. Philo Everett (one of the few historical people retained in the novel) heard of the ore and wanted to find it, so Marji led Everett's party to it, resulting in them giving him shares in the mine. Voelker repeats the pine tree story, saying Marji found pieces of ore under the uprooted stump of a white pine tree that was the victim of a lightning strike on the Haunted Mountain.

Charlotte grew up rarely seeing her father. Marji ended up working as a miner for the Jackson Iron Company until he was fired. Then he worked in a traveling medicine show with a quack doctor. He was also a drinker. Superstitious, Marji believed the gods who lived on the Haunted Mountain cursed him for revealing the iron ore's location. He later died from a lightning strike when he was on the Haunted Mountain.

Voelker also makes interesting changes in regards to Presque Isle. First, it never contained an Indian school. Second, the Indians live in the interior rather than at Presque Isle's entrance. Several Indians are also buried at Presque Isle, including Charlotte's parents, her maternal grandparents, and her uncle Sassaba, whom we are told was once chief of the Marquette Chippewa. Of course, Sassaba was really Charles Kawbawgam's uncle and a chief at the Sault. It is odd that Voelker did not, instead, use Madosh or Mongoose, Charlotte's real uncles. I also suspect Voelker did not realize Sassaba was any relation to the Kawbawgams.

Some characters are radically changed from their historical counterparts. Since Charlotte's mother is Sayee and Charlotte's maiden name is Kawbawgam, Voelker introduced an old Indian woman named Susan Gesick (Charlotte's real mother's name) to testify at the trial about Charlotte's parents' relationship. Another witness Voelker creates is Octave Bissonette, who seems to be based on Jacques LePique since he says his father was a trader for the American Fur Company at Grand Island and he knew Charlotte since she was a baby. However, Bissonette turns out to be an unsavory character who has romantic notions about Charlotte and at one point tries to force her to kiss him.

The trial follows the same course as in history, although Voelker has William use different arguments before arriving at the one that wins the case. At first, William believes he must work under American legal and social assumptions, so he wants to prove Marji divorced Blue Heron and then married Sayee, which would make Charlotte legitimate. At the same time, if he cannot prove Charlotte is legitimate, he can prove that Blue Heron, not Sayee, is the legal wife. In that case, Blue Heron would have been Marji's heir, and then because Blue Heron adopted Charlotte, he could argue that Charlotte is Blue Heron's heir. However, the circuit court rejects these arguments and decides illegitimate children cannot inherit. This ruling leads to William appealing the case before the Michigan Supreme Court and changing his argument. This time he argues that the case cannot be judged by American standards because the treaties say Native American tribal customs must be respected by the American government. By this argument, William is able to win the trial. The result is Charlotte will receive a large payment, although she wants to split it with William and Cassius to thank them for their assistance.

In *Laughing Whitefish*'s postscript, Voelker discusses the novel's historical background and the changes he made in depicting the lawsuit. For example, he notes that Henry Schoolcraft left the Upper Peninsula by the time of the trial, but he couldn't help bringing him back for the story. (Voelker omits mentioning that Schoolcraft died in 1864, many years before the trial took place.) Voelker also notes that Schoolcraft's wife was not a full-blooded Ojibwa as depicted. Furthermore, in the novel the case only goes to Lansing once, not three times.[57] Voelker's postscript is strange since Schoolcraft is not a character in the novel and barely referenced, and Voelker omits to mention the far more significant changes he made. Perhaps Voelker did not want people to realize how much he had changed the truth, trying to pass it off as relatively accurate local history, and he didn't want people disillusioned about the love story—especially since Charlotte is two decades younger than she really was at the time of the trial and William Poe never existed.

The final and most surprising change made is that after Charlotte wins the trial, she and William confess they love one another and plan to marry. Although interracial marriages between whites and Native Americans had been common during the French-Canadian and British occupations of the Great Lakes, they were frowned upon by nineteenth century Americans, and even in Voelker's time, they may not have been easily accepted, so this is quite a radical decision. Of course, even historical fiction is a product of the time when it was written, and Voelker, writing during the Civil Rights

Movement, may have felt an interracial marriage would make his novel feel progressive. In some ways, the novel is ahead of its time in its statements about Native Americans and how they have been wronged, but in other ways, it is stereotypical. The most offensive stereotype is the sexualization of Laughing Whitefish, who becomes the exotic female Other in the novel. Not only is she described as "exotic," but when William first meets her, he describes her eyes as "dark and smouldering,"[58] and overall, she is "withdrawn and aloof but strangely exciting."[59] She is a type of male sexual fantasy who kisses William on the cheek soon after he starts helping her with her case, and later at the start of the trial, lightly kisses him on the lips. One can't help but remember that Voelker wrote in the immediate wake of film noir with detectives like Philip Marlowe (played by Humphrey Bogart) being hired by sexy women like Lauren Bacall, and Mickey Spillane's sexy detective novels featuring Mike Hammer. Although Voelker keeps the sexual overtones to a minimum compared to these contemporary works, he is clearly trying to sell sex, or at least romance.

Today, *Laughing Whitefish* is Voelker's best-known and most read book after *Anatomy of a Murder*. More than fifty years after its publication, it is still chosen by local book clubs in Upper Michigan as a monthly read. Despite the novel's continuing popularity, however, it is a product of its time. According to historian Rebecca Mead, the novel and other depictions of the Kawbawgams in recent years do a disservice to the Kawbawgams because they contain a hint of "imperialist nostalgia," celebrating Indians as relicts of the past while ignoring those living in the present.[60] Voelker's treatment of Charlotte and her family is demeaning even though Voelker did not intend it to be. Certainly demoting Marji Gesick from being a chief and making him a drunk and an actor in a traveling medicine show is not complimentary. Furthermore, while the novel has several speeches about how Americans have mistreated Native Americans, the assimilated Charlotte also speaks ill of her people in a somewhat veiled way. Having attended a white-established missionary school, she now is working to educate her people, which she realizes is necessary for them to survive in a white man's world. However, part of that education, she tells William, must include "common hygiene, teaching the grownups as well as the children to keep themselves clean—their bodies, their teeth, their hair—to decently prepare and eat their meals…." These sound more like assumptions by a white person about Native American hygiene than actual issues an Ojibwa woman would be concerned with; they reflect the belief that Native Americans are inferior to whites by not following their ways.[61]

Understandably, a novelist must make many difficult decisions in writing historical fiction, and Voelker himself stated the novel was "the toughest job of writing I ever tackled."[62] Regardless, he did not feel he should let facts get in the way of telling a good story, stating, "The better a book is as a novel, the poorer it simply must be as history…the one seeks to create illusion, the other deals with sober fact."[63] Being a writer of historical fiction myself, I understand that difficulty but believe Voelker could have still produced an effective and powerful novel while adhering more closely to the facts; still, some concession can be made to Voelker for being a product of his time; like Schoolcraft, Longfellow, and many other authors who have adapted Native American stories, he was clearly writing for a white audience, and appropriating Native American stories for his own purposes—including to write a novel that would sell and that he and his publisher would make a profit from. Voelker may have feared that if he were more accurate, his publisher would reject the work. Had he lived today, he probably would have written a more historically accurate novel. Regardless, this reader feels let down by the book.

In 2011, Michigan State University Press reissued *Laughing Whitefish* with a foreword by Matthew L. M. Fletcher, a sign that the novel continues to be of interest to a statewide audience. Fletcher is a Professor of Law at Michigan State University's College of Law and director of the Indigenous Law and Policy Center. He is a member of the Grand Traverse Band of Ottawa and Chippewa Indians, located in Peshawbestown, Michigan.[64] That Michigan State University Press would ask Fletcher to write the foreword shows their sensitivity to having a Native American write about the novel. In the foreword, Fletcher primarily writes about the legal aspects of the case the novel is based on, yet he is clearly not knowledgeable about the historical people behind the case. For example, he repeatedly refers to Marji-Gesick as Mr. Gesick, a title the chief would not have adopted, not being a white man or assimilated into white society. Fletcher also remarks that polygamy was only for the wealthy tribal leaders, so people like Marji Gesick could not and did not have extra wives.[65] Fletcher makes this statement despite the fact that, as he acknowledges in his footnote, Marji-Gesick was regarded by the Michigan Supreme Court as an Ojibwa chief. Plus, if Fletcher had perused the trial transcripts, he would see that Marji-Gesick did have multiple wives. Sadly, discussion of *Laughing Whitefish* still overlooks the historical people upon whom it is based.

Kawbawgam Road and Kawbawgam Village

At some point prior to 1967, the road that partially circles Kawbawgam Lake was named Kawbawgam Road. Nearby is Charlotte Trail. Then in 1967, Kawbawgam Village was created in its vicinity just off M-28. A flyer from the time advertising the sale of lots for Kawbawgam Village stated that the project was 830 acres and would feature a mile-long airstrip. Homeowners would be able to fly in and take off on land in front of their houses, then taxi to a hangar-type garage. It would be the first residential airstrip in Michigan and the application for it had already been made. Although the flyer does not have a date, it stated fifteen homes had already been completed and twelve more would be built that year. The flyer included a photograph of Kawbawgam and a somewhat inaccurate history of him.[66] Here we have yet another appropriation of Kawbawgam for commercial purposes.

KAWBAWGAM VILLAGE PROJECT FIRST IN STATE TO FEATURE AIRSTRIP

Development Named For Indian Chief

CHIEF KAWBAWGAM

Pilots Will 'Fly-In' At Home

Marquette Regional History Center

On September 15, 1967, *The Mining Journal* ran a story about Kawbawgam Village, mentioning the airstrip as well as stating that the village would have a commercial district and recreational area and that application for approval of the airstrip had been made to state and federal authorities by developer Leo Glass. Already fifteen homes had been built with twelve more to be completed by the end of the year (the same number mentioned on the flyer so we can date it to September perhaps), and there would be 400 lots total.[67] In addition, Kawbawgam Village would contain Kawbawgam Pocket Park where swings, a basketball court, a restroom, and picnic tables were installed by volunteers.[68]

To the best of my knowledge, the airstrip was never built although I have been unable to determine why.

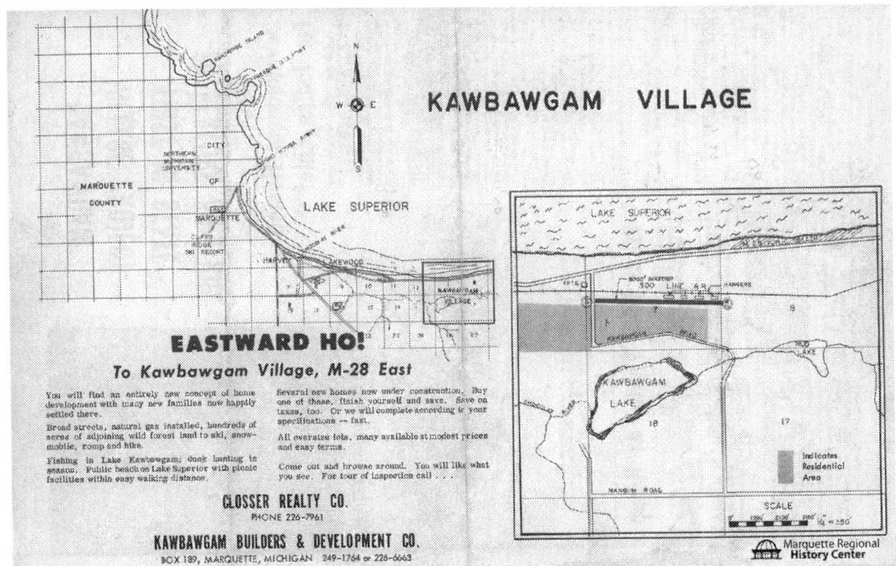

Kawbawgam Cross Country Ski Trail and Ojibwa Casino

Near the location of Kawbawgam Village is the Kawbawgam Cross Country Ski Trail. It is off Kawbawgam Road, but rather than following along Kawbawgam Lake, its parking area is on Lake LeVasseur's public access road. The ski trail has two loops, an easy one of 1.5 miles and a more difficult one of 3.9 miles. It offers forested views of Lake LeVasseur and also crosses with the North Country Trail.[69]

Also off Kawbawgam Road is the Ojibwa Casino, built in the 1990s by the Keweenaw Bay Indian Community, which also operates a casino in Baraga, Michigan. Although not named for Kawbawgam, the casino reminds us of how the Ojibwa have reinvented themselves since his time, finding ways to survive in a white man's world. In December 2019, the casino expanded and now has two restaurants and a concert venue.

Paintings of Kawbawgam

Kawbawgam has been a subject for painters as well. Although the only known painting of him during his life was that of Mrs. Hambleton Kirk, at least three paintings exist of him today, all in the collection of the Marquette Regional History Center.

The oldest is an oil painting from Werner Studio dating to the 1930s.

In the 1960s, an artist who signed their name simply as "White" painted Kawbawgam on Masonite board, depicting him in his regalia. This painting was donated to the Marquette Regional History Center in 1981.

White Painting

Finally, Ida M. Ferguson created a drawing of an elderly Kawbawgam. This painting is inside a wide leather frame. The date of the image is not known but it was donated to the Marquette Regional History Center in 1972.

In addition, a wood burning portrait of Kawbawgam exists in the history center's collection.

In the 1980s, a large mural was also painted on the wall of the Superior View building at the corner of Washington and Third Streets in Marquette. The mural depicted various images from the Marquette area and included a rendition of the famous photograph of an Ojibwa woman with her child, which

Werner Studio Oil Painting

Ferguson Drawing

long has been mistaken as Charlotte Kawbawgam. (See discussion of this image in the Appendix, Photograph 2.)

All of these images were based on photographs of Kawbawgam and Charlotte, or at least what were believed to be photographs of them at the time.

The Mystery of Kawbawgam's Grave by Clifford S. Cleveland

In 1979, the Kawbawgams were again featured in a book, although in a more indirect way. David Goldsmith (1933-2001), an English professor at Northern Michigan University, wrote *The Mystery of Kawbawgam's Grave* under the pen name Clifford S. Cleveland, a play on the name of Cleveland-Cliffs, formerly the Cleveland Iron Company. Ironically, in 1910, the Cleveland Iron Company had taken over the holdings of the Jackson Iron Company, which Charlotte had once sued.

The book is a spoof on the Nancy Drew mysteries, featuring a heroine named Fancy Brew who comes to Marquette because two of her friends have been kidnapped and the kidnappers told her to meet them in Marquette. Fancy arrives in late September to discover there is already two feet of snow on the ground, resulting in her and her companions having to cross-country ski at Presque Isle when the clues lead them to Kawbawgam's grave. Eventually, they learn the kidnappers only abducted Fancy's friends to get her to come to Marquette to solve "The Mystery of Kawbawgam's Grave," though what the mystery is isn't quite clear. However, Fancy and her friends know it concerns the sign at the grave, which we are told was placed there in 1955. After

The Mystery of Kawbawgam's Grave

studying the sign for clues, they realize the clue is in the first letter of each word of the first two lines. Namely:

Chief Kawbawgam	CK
The Last Chief of	TLCO

Of course, there is no logic to how this clue is figured out, and especially not when they decide these letters then refer to the "Clock" at the "Telephone Company." The Telephone Company was, according to the novel, previously in the Savings Bank Building in downtown Marquette which has a clock tower. Fancy goes to the clock tower and there finds "the treasure of Chief Charley Kawbawgam," which turns out to be a beautiful necklace and pair of earrings made of copper with diamonds in them. Since copper is native to Upper Michigan, it isn't unlikely that Kawbawgam may have possessed something made of it, but no explanation is given for how he got the diamonds, which are definitely not among Upper Michigan's mineral resources. Eventually, Fancy learns that when the sign was put in next to Kawbawgam's grave, a worker found the treasure. Because the worker was dying of tuberculosis, he wanted to save the treasure for his son, so he hid it in the clock tower and painted the clue in the sign. His mom had a cigar box that contained the clue, but she died before she could tell her son this, so the cigar box ended up in a garage sale where it was found by Jussi Villainen (the novel's villain, whose name is a play on Finnish names because of the high Finnish immigrant population in Upper Michigan). Jussi couldn't solve the mystery so he kidnapped Fancy's friends to make Fancy solve it. Now that it is solved, Fancy declares the treasure should not belong to Jussi but to the worker's son, Luke Lakewalker (a play on *Star Wars*' Luke Skywalker). The President of the United States, Holly Greer (a real-life Marquette resident at the time who had been mayor), then arrives to give Fancy a citation in her honor and present the treasure to Luke Lakewalker, since it is "rightfully his."

The novel is full of jokes and parodies and great fun to read, but it is also a product of its time. In truth, "the treasure of Chief Charley Kawbawgam" should not rightfully be Luke Lakewalker's but Charley Kawbawgam's, and it should be returned to Kawbawgam's grave or at the very least given to the Ojibwa to place in a museum. The novel does not at all recognize that the real crime committed is stealing from Native Americans.

Murder Near Kawbawgam's Grave

Unfortunately, on September 30, 1988, a real-life mystery occurred near Kawbawgam's grave. In the morning, two people walking around Presque Isle

Park discovered the body of thirty-four-year-old Paul Girard near the grave. Girard had been stabbed dozens of times and his throat slit. Because Girard was gay, police believed his murder was a hate crime. Although suspects were questioned, enough evidence was never gathered to charge anyone, so the crime remains unsolved.[70] Sadly, this murder has become associated with Kawbawgam's grave because of the body's proximity to it.

Michigan Legal Milestone

In 1993, a small legal milestone plaque was erected at the Michigan Iron Industry Museum in Negaunee, Michigan, near both the Carp River and where the original discovery of iron ore was made. The marker commemorates the importance of Charlotte Kawbawgam's lawsuit against the Jackson mine, which in August 1992 had been recognized as the sixteenth Michigan Legal Milestone.[71] The text of the plaque reads:

> MICHIGAN LEGAL MILESTONE
> LAUGHING WHITEFISH
>
> Marji-Gesick, a Chippewa Chief, was hired in 1845 to locate a valuable iron ore deposit about three miles from here. He was paid with a certificate of interest entitling him to stock in the company. That action led to a landmark Michigan Supreme Court decision acknowledging that tribal laws and customs govern the legal affairs of Native American families.
>
> After Marji-Gesick's death, his daughter, Charlotte Kawbawgam, found the certificate. When the Jackson Iron Company refused to recognize her ownership interest, she took the company to court.
>
> The Michigan Supreme Court considered the company's claim that Charlotte Kawbawgam should not be recognized as Marji-Gesick's lawful heir because she had been born to one of the three women to whom her father had been married simultaneously. Polygamy was prohibited under Michigan law, but permitted under tribal laws and customs.
>
> The court concluded that since the marriage was valid under Chippewa law, it must be recognized by Michigan's courts. Charlotte Kawbawgam was declared Marji-Gesick's lawful heir, inheriting his ownership interest in the Jackson Iron Company.
>
> The story of Marji-Gesick, Charlotte Kawbawgam and the Jackson Iron Company was immortalized in "Laughing Whitefish," a book authored by former Michigan Supreme Court Justice John

Voelker under his pen name, Robert Traver.

Placed by the State Bar of Michigan and
The Marquette County Bar Association, 1992

Michigan Legal Milestone Plaque at Iron Industry Museum, Negaunee, Michigan

Ojibwa Narratives Published

The most significant event since Kawbawgam's death in terms of his legacy was the publication in 1994 of Homer Kidder's manuscript by Wayne State University Press. It was retitled *Ojibwa Narratives* by the editor, Arthur Bourgeois, who painstakingly oversaw its publication with the help of several people who transcribed the manuscript. Bourgeois received permission from the American Philosophical Society of Philadelphia to publish it, the manuscript being in its collection. Additional assistance was given by the Marquette County Historical Society (today's Marquette Regional History Center). The result was that Charles and Charlotte Kawbawgam and Jacques LePique, nearly a century after their deaths, were able to speak for themselves. Now it is available for those who want to understand three of Marquette's earliest residents and the Ojibwa who resided along Lake Superior centuries before the white men who built Marquette. As previously discussed in Chapter 11, it also provides a look into Ojibwa myths and legends with several variations on stories that have been retold in other books.

Chief Shawano Chapter of the DAR

In 1996, a Sault Sainte Marie chapter of the Daughters of the American Revolution (DAR) was organized and named the Chief Shawano Chapter, a name suggested by a member who was one of Shawano's descendants. It is an odd name for an organization that celebrates the American Revolution since Kawbawgam's stepfather and his people would have sided with the British during the American Revolution and the War of 1812. Regardless, it shows Shawano is not forgotten.[72]

Center for Native American Studies

In 1996, Northern Michigan University established the Center for Native American Studies. According to its website, it:

> offers a holistic curriculum rooted in Native American themes that challenges students to think critically and communicate effectively about Indigenous issues with emphasis on Great Lakes Indigenous perspectives, stimulates further respectful inquiry about Indigenous people, and provides active learning and service learning opportunities that strengthen student engagement, interaction, and reciprocity with Indigenous communities.[73]

The roots for the center began decades before, and in the nearly quarter of a century since its establishment, besides educating students in its programs, it has done continual outreach to the community from Anishinaabe storytelling at Marquette's Jacobetti Home for Veterans to summer youth programs. Currently, it is under the directorship of Martin Reinhardt, PhD. April Lindala also served as the director for thirteen years. Since 2016, a major, as well as a minor in Native American Studies has been offered by NMU through the center. More information can be found at the Center's website: https://www.nmu.edu/nativeamericanstudies/home-page.

Presque Isle Pavilion Certificates

In 1999, Kawbawgam's image was again appropriated, this time during Marquette's sesquicentennial (150th anniversary). As part of the celebrations, a new pavilion was built at Presque Isle Park to replace the former pavilion built by John M. Longyear. The city raised money for the pavilion and those who donated received stock certificates in "Shares in goodwill to the City of Marquette on the occasion of the 150th celebration of its founding in 1849, a.d. Said shares constitute a gift to the City in the form of the Presque Isle

Pavilion, dedicated to future generations." On the certificates is an 1886 quote from Peter White stating, "The park belongs to the people of Marquette and must be preserved for all who in years to come shall call Marquette 'home.'" At the top of the certificate is a view of Presque Isle as well as photos of Peter White and "C. Kawbawgam," who remain today the two people most associated with Presque Isle.

Peter White

C. Kawbawgam

1849 • MARQUETTE SESQUICENTENNIAL • 1999

PRESQUE ISLE PAVILION

This Certifies that Tyler R. Tichelaar is the holder of One Shares in goodwill to the City of Marquette on the occasion of the 150th celebration of its founding in 1849 a.d. Said shares constitute a gift to the City in the form of the Presque Isle Pavilion, dedicated to future generations.

"The park belongs to the people of Marquette and must be preserved for all who in years to come shall call Marquette 'home'."

1886

Witness, the Seal of the City of Marquette

FOR MARQUETTE SESQUICENTENNIAL COMMITTEE

Common Stock does not constitute an investment in "stock" in the common sense of the term. Purchasers should not purchase common stock with the purpose of making a profit

Pavilion Certificate

***The Time of the Shining Rocks* by Ragene Henry**

Also in 1999, local children's author Ragene Henry (1947-2014) published the first of four children's books celebrating the history of Upper Michigan. *The Time of the Shining Rocks* tells the story of Libby, an elementary school girl in 1999, whose class is studying Michigan history. On a field trip to Negaunee to see the marker commemorating the discovery of iron ore, Libby becomes so interested in the shiny rocks on the marker that she asks her friend to boost her up so she can see them better. The rocks then shine so brightly that, via a magnetic force, Libby is sucked through time.

Before she knows it, she is standing in the forest watching a group of white and Ojibwa men around a fire. Then a young Charlotte Kawbawgam approaches to ask who she is. Libby realizes she's somehow time-traveled back to 1845. Libby then witnesses Charlotte's father, Chief Marji-Gesick, lead the white men to the iron ore.

While the novel educates children about one of the most important events in Upper Michigan history, it takes some historical license. Charlotte and her father both speak broken English, which Charlotte says they learned from fur traders and priests, although they likely did not speak English at all. (Of course, in the novel the characters have to be able to communicate with each other.) The novel also states that the story of the iron ore being discovered under a pine tree is a legend and no one knows if it's true or not; however, when Marji-Gesick leads the white men to the ore, there is a pine tree, which makes Libby realize the legend is true. Charlotte also explains to Libby about her father's three wives, stating that the first died, and then there is Charlotte's mother, and the third wife, O-do-no-be-qua, to whom Marji-Gesick is married simultaneously. Charlotte states that all her siblings have died, which ignores that her half-sisters Amanda and Mary, who are not mentioned, also grew to adulthood.

Despite these literary licenses, Henry does not hold back in making it clear that the discovery of the iron ore was in many ways detrimental to the Ojibwa. Once the ore is found, the white men celebrate, but even young Libby knows the event has its sadness. By the time the novel was written in 1999, a willingness to see history from the viewpoints of people other than the conquerors had become more common. Henry does not shy away from the historical fact that Marji-Gesick was troubled about showing the white men where the ore is or that he was a polygamist. In fact, Charlotte tells Libby:

> "Yes. Father say maybe O-do-no-be-qua have babies. I think she too full of hate for white man. No room for babies inside."
>
> "Why does she hate white men?" Libby asked. Would she hate me, she wondered.

> "She say Ojibwa, all People of the Three Fires, sell souls to white men for guns, traps, kettles, cloth, whiskey. She says we sell souls, forget who we are. She angry." Charlotte paused to take a breath, then continued. "See father's red jacket? He trade white man for canoe O-do-no-be-qua make all winter. She much angry. She say she put jacket in fire. So father wear always." She smiled. "O-do-no-be-qua not want father show white men shining rocks. She say they take land. No more hunting ground. Father say no one can take land. Land belong to all. He say man who shares earth and treasures is great man. Die great man is most best thing. He say it shameful to hide treasures, keep secret. She angry. But he chief."[74]

Despite Marji-Gesick's insistence on showing the white men where the shining rocks are, he still has some qualms about it, so he enters his prayer house, which is so small Libby thinks it looks like a "dog house." There he prays for a sign from the spirits about showing rocks to the white man because his wife has reminded him of the legend that the person who shows the white man the shining rocks will die. We are not told what the spirits tell Marji-Gesick, but he does decide to show the white men the rocks. However, he does not want Charlotte and Libby (whom he thinks is a lost white girl; he plans to help find her family later) to accompany him. When they get close to the rocks, Marji-Gesick walks backwards so the spirits cannot look into his eyes. (In reality, Marji-Gesick refused to approach the rocks but told the Jackson party where they were once they were close enough.) Of course, the white men are thrilled to find the rocks, but afterwards, Libby notices Marji-Gesick's sadness. Charlotte remarks that for the first time her father did not know what the right thing had been to do. Henry then tells us:

> But Libby knew. It made her feel like crying. She knew what would happen to Marji Gesick. And she also knew what happened to the Native Americans and their hunting lands in the next hundred and fifty years. She knew that O-do-no-be-qua was right.[75]

To make matters right with the spirits, Marji-Gesick offers sacred tobacco to the earth to give thanks to the earth spirits for their gifts. Charlotte asks Libby if her people also give thanks.

> Libby thought about that for a minute. As she thought she began to feel ashamed. She felt shame that it wasn't the way of "her people". Maybe if it were, the world wouldn't be in the mess it was now, she thought. She wasn't sure how to respond to Charlotte's question. Finally she said, "Only some of my people."[76]

At this point, Libby tells Charlotte she is from the future since Charlotte and Marji-Gesick want to help her find her parents and get home, but she knows it isn't that easy. Charlotte believes Libby's story of being from the future, saying:

> I believe spirits do many things people not understand. Spirits of all Anishinabe, people who come before and after, are all round. Spirits watch. Protect Anishinabe. Spirits change. One form, then other. One time, then other. Spirits live in all things, in all ways, in all times. Maybe spirits move Libby.[77]

Together, Libby and Charlotte figure out how Libby can return to the future. Once Libby does return, she realizes she really did time travel because she finds in her pocket part of Charlotte's beaded fringe. She then finishes accompanying her class on their field trip to the Marquette County Historical Society's museum where she learns that Charlotte grew up and married Kawbawgam and she sees a beaded stole made by Charlotte. The book concludes with Libby writing her Michigan history report on Charlotte Kawbawgam and receiving an A+.

Despite a few historical inaccuracies, *The Time of the Shining Rocks* provides a realistic approach to the conflict Marji-Gesick and his family must have felt over showing the Everett party the iron ore's location. Both children and adult readers come away with a better understanding of the discovery of iron ore on the Marquette range and the role the Ojibwa played in that discovery. Unfortunately, *The Time of the Shining Rocks* is now out of print.

The Marquette Trilogy by Tyler R. Tichelaar

The Marquette Trilogy: Book One
IRON PIONEERS
a novel

Beginning in 2006, I, Tyler R. Tichelaar, published my novel series, The Marquette Trilogy, consisting of *Iron Pioneers* (2006), *The Queen City* (2006), and *Superior Heritage* (2007). Kawbawgam makes a couple of cameo appearances in *Iron Pioneers*. First, he saves a young boy, Caleb Rockford, from falling off a cliff at Presque Isle. Later, he goes fishing with Caleb's grownup cousin, Jacob Whitman. In the novel I had Kawbawgam speak only a few sentences of broken English to work him into the storyline as a character. In *The Queen City*, Kawbawgam's funeral is depicted.

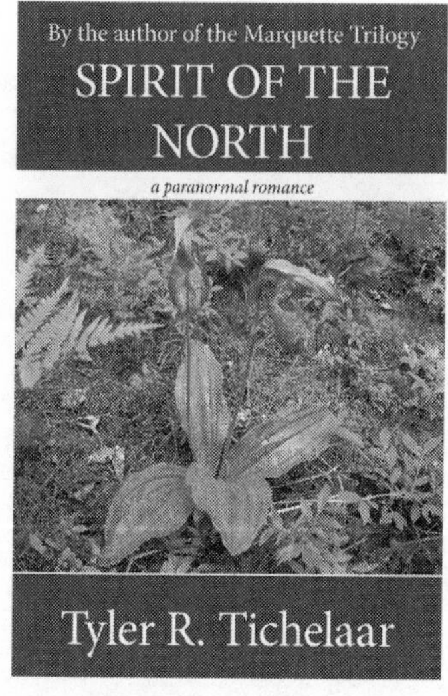

By the author of the Marquette Trilogy
SPIRIT OF THE NORTH
a paranormal romance
Tyler R. Tichelaar

Later, in my novel *Spirit of the North* (2012), Kawbawgam finds the dead body of the little girl Annabella Stonegate, who has been lost in a snowstorm, and brings her home to her family. I also mentioned Kawbawgam in my nonfiction book *My Marquette: Explore the Queen City of the North, Its History, People, and Places* (2011). In 2016, I was selling my books at the TV6 Christmas Craft Show at the Superior Dome in Marquette when a woman told me how much she had enjoyed reading what I had written in my books about Kawbawgam because she knew so little about him. Her comment surprised me because I hadn't really written much about him at all. That conversation sparked the idea to write this book so I could learn more about Kawbawgam and so his story could be shared with a wider audience.

Fall Feast

In October 2008, the Kawbawgams were honored by a fall feast celebrated at their gravesite. Forty Marquette area Native American students and their families gathered for a traditional Native American fall feast. Tanya Sprowl, program director for Title VII Native American studies in the Marquette area public schools, organized the event to educate participants on Native American traditions. The feast began with a "spirit plate" being created so the first taste of food went to the spirit being honored. Foods served were all those traditionally hunted and gathered by the local Native Americans, including wild rice, venison, fish, corn, beans, squash, and strawberries.[78]

Founder's Day Celebrations

On May 18, 2009, at the newly named Founder's Landing—where Peter White and Robert Graveraet first landed on the shore of Iron Bay and were greeted by Chief Kawbawgam—a reenactment was done just after dawn of the famous landing 160 years earlier. The local Ojibwa were invited to be part of the ceremony. I attended the ceremony and heard one of the Native Americans present express gratitude that they had been included, which he said was the first time they had been asked to participate in a city event. This statement is not actually true given the large role Kawbawgam and the local Ojibwa played in the 1897 festivities surrounding the dedication of the Father

2009 Reenactment in Marquette, Michigan of the original Graveraet landing at Iron Bay

Marquette statue. However, that an Ojibwa should make such a remark shows just how little credit has been given to the Ojibwa for their contributions to Marquette's history in the 112 years between these two events.

The reenactment was to become an annual event, and the following year, more activities were held to celebrate it. The ceremonies drew few people (perhaps because they were held at sunrise) and celebrating May 18 as Founder's Day and Marquette's birthday was quickly forgotten. However, in 2019, on Marquette's 170th birthday, I posted a photo on Facebook of the 2009 reenactment and wished Marquette a happy birthday. My post received more than 300 likes and 80 shares. Hopefully, an annual birthday party for Marquette can be revived.

Marji Gesick 100

In 2015, a new bike race began in Marquette. The Marji Gesick 100 has been described as "likely the toughest, most torturous bike and running race in the nation," consisting of one hundred miles of "rugged trails. Rocks. Roots. Extreme climbing. Guaranteed falls. Guaranteed dropouts by superbly well-conditioned athletes." In 2016, the race attracted "500 masochists" and more have been attracted every year since.[79] Two-time winner Jeremiah Bishop called it, "The hardest single-day race in America."[80]

The race's founder, Todd Poquette, explained to me his reasons for naming the race after Marji-Gesick:

> When I was looking for a name for the event, I started to do a bit of research on local history, specifically mining history, and every

> time I found something new or interesting on mining, Marji-Gesick's name was mentioned. He has an incredible story. Before I even knew what the race would be, his story resonated with me and I wanted to honor his past heritage, and especially some of the people who are responsible for paving the way for us to be here today like Marji-Gesick. They had to do a tremendous amount of work for us to have what we have today. The racers have to endure tremendous pain and hardship to finish the race, but if you look at what Marji-Gesick and other people back then had to endure, it pales in comparison. A lot of people didn't know his name until we named the event and that's given us the opportunity to tell his story. We're a non-profit empowering others to discover the best version of themselves through outdoor adventures, and we're trying to make sure his memory is recognized.[81]

The race's website is www.MarjiGesick.com.

Conclusion

I hope this book has provided a new understanding of Upper Michigan history and the role of Native Americans in it. No, the settlement of Upper Michigan by Americans was not ideal. Yes, the Ojibwa were coerced into surrendering their land as a result of the white man's greed for property and the Upper Peninsula's mineral riches. Yes, Native Americans were pushed to the edges of the communities they had helped to found and had served in their early years, and yes, they have had a long journey to achieve their current status as respected members of the Upper Peninsula. Despite predictions in the nineteenth century that they would disappear, the Ojibwa continue to have a strong presence in Upper Michigan.

Currently, the Sault Sainte Marie Tribe of Chippewa has 2,000 employees and is Sault Sainte Marie's largest employer. Although the tribe was not officially recognized until the 1970s, by 1995, its membership had reached 22,000.[82] Today there are nine Native American casinos in Upper Michigan. As of the 1990 census, 943 people of Native American descent live in Marquette—approximately 5 percent of the population. The 2010 census shows that 1.7 percent of the county's population is Native American.

Much more could be written about the Native American experience in Upper Michigan in the twentieth and twenty-first centuries. I see this book solely as a beginning toward acknowledging the Kawbawgams and their people as part of our living history. I hope it will lead people to a greater appreciation of the Kawbawgams, their Ojibwa contemporaries, and the white people who befriended them. I hope it makes all aware of the significant role all of them played in Upper Michigan's history. Hopefully, future historians and biographers will build upon the work I have begun.

Finally, as a white man, I am fully aware that I may have unintentionally erred at times in properly depicting the Native American experience. I apologize for any errors or misinterpretations I have made. I hope the residents of Upper Michigan, regardless of race, can all continue to work together to appreciate and preserve our shared heritage, tell all sides of the story, listen to one another, right any of the past's wrongs, and build a present and future Upper Michigan where all who love this splendid peninsula and contribute to its welfare are welcome and appreciated.

On a beautiful May morning in 1849, Charles Kawbawgam welcomed Peter White and his companions to Iron Bay. Although White and Kawbawgam were products of their time and neither perfect, they developed a friendship that can serve today as a model for us. Each cared for the other in his time of need; each was willing to listen to the other and learn to speak his language; and together they worked to build a community. Let us take up their legacy and do the same.

Appendix
Alleged Photographs of the Kawbawgams and Their Relatives

At least ten photographs over the years have been misidentified as depicting the Kawbawgams or their family members. This appendix is intended to clarify the facts we know about these photographs and why they cannot be whom they have been assumed to depict. Each title assigned to a photograph below reflects the previous incorrect identification because in most cases correct identifications of the people in these photographs has been impossible.

Photograph 1: Rev. John Pitezel and Upper Michigan Ojibwa Chiefs

This photograph (pictured at the end of this section) has long been controversial. Beginning in 1945, it was claimed to represent a group of Ojibwa chiefs from the Upper Peninsula, including Kawbawgam and Marji-Gesick, and the Methodist missionary, Rev. John Pitezel. This identification was given by Ray Brotherton (1883-1960), a member of the pioneer Brotherton family that first settled in Upper Michigan in Marquette and later moved to Escanaba. Brotherton's father Frank and Frank's brothers Charles and August were railroad surveyors in the nineteenth century. Brotherton had a collection of photographs and other memorabilia from them, including this photograph. We do not know if Brotherton or another family member is responsible for misidentifying it.

In 1945, Brotherton gave several presentations about the early history of Marquette County. In conjunction with the presentations, *The Mining*

Journal ran an article on March 24, 1945 titled "Old Pictures Reveal History Of Marquette And Delta Counties." It featured two photographs, this one and Photograph 2 below, both from Brotherton.

This photograph reappeared in the Marquette Centennial issue of the *Mining Journal* in 1949, again with the names listed as being Rev. Pitezel and local Ojibwa leaders and the added statement that it dated to 1846.

In the 1960s, a request by the Michigan Historical Commission to the Marquette County Historical Society for a copy of the photograph inspired Ernest Rankin, a member of the society, to look into the photograph's history. Rankin found several copies of it in the historical society's collection with different identifications written on the backs of them. One image stated it was Benjamin Armstrong with a group of Native Americans from Wisconsin who met with President Abraham Lincoln in 1862. Upon further investigation, Rankin discovered the photograph was first published in Thomas P. Wentworth's 1892 book *Early Life Among the Indians: Reminiscences from the Life of Benjamin G. Armstrong*, and the photograph was labeled as a Wisconsin Native American delegation before President Lincoln in 1862. The names of all the men pictured are given in Wentworth's book along with the various Wisconsin reservations they represented.[1] Rankin published his findings in *The Mining Journal* in a March 2, 1967 article, in which he clarified that the photograph was most likely Armstrong and the Wisconsin delegation rather than an Upper Michigan group.[2]

Fred Rydholm reprinted the photograph in *Superior Heartland* (1989), mentioning the controversy and Rankin's article, while providing both lists of possible identifications. However, he persisted in suggesting the Upper Peninsula identifications could be correct by stating:

> For what it's worth, when the author first saw this picture in the 1950s, the first remark that was made was "The man seated on the left in the front row is Madosh." There were no names on the photo. The man was later identified as Madosh.
>
> Author: at the time I knew August Madosh pictured here [in an accompanying photograph in Rydholm's book] with his son David, August was full-blooded Chippewa, David is one-half. The resemblance of the man in the picture and August Madosh was so striking (when August was younger), that to me they seemed to be the same person. August died in 1987. He was a great grandson of Madosh.[3]

The photograph of August Madosh appears on page 135 of Rydholm's book. There is a resemblance between August in that photograph and the man identified as Madosh in this group photograph. However, one resemblance is not enough evidence to refute the stronger claim to it being Benjamin Armstrong and the Wisconsin Native American leaders.

Identification according to Brotherton:

Back Row, Left to Right: Rev. Pitezel, Mon-go-sid (Loon Foot) of Marquette, Mon-gon-see (Little Loon), brother of Marji-Gesick; Chief Marji-Gesick; Charles Kawbawgam; As-sin-nins (Little Stones) of L'Anse; and Mo-Gwa-da (One Who Creeps) of Marquette.

Front Row, Left to Right: Chief Ma-dosh (Marji-Gesick's brother); Kish-kit-a-wage (Indian With an Ear Cut Off) of what would become Munising Bay; and Match-kwi-wis-ens (Bad Boy) of L'Anse.

Identification according to Armstrong:

Back Row, Left to Right: Rev. Benjamin Armstrong, Ah-moose (Little Bee) of Lac Flambeau, Kish-ke-taw-wa (Cut-ear) of Bad River, Ba-ques (He Sews) of La Court O'Rielles, Ah-do-ga-zik (Last Day) of Bad River, O-be-quot (Firm) of Fond-du-Lac, and Shing-quot-onse (Little Pine) [This is, surprisingly, Shingwaukonse from the Sault and Garden River, Ontario.]

Front Row, Left to Right: Ja-ge-gwa-ya (Can't Tell) of La Pointe, Na-gan-ab (He Sits Ahead) of Fond Du Lac, and O-Ma-Shin-a-Way (Messenger) of Bad River.

Several reasons exist for why this photograph cannot even be from Upper Michigan. First, as Rankin states in his article, a date of 1846 is impossible since photography was in its infancy then and it would have been unlikely there was any photography studio in the Upper Peninsula with chairs, tables, and curtains as depicted in the photograph. Jack Deo, an expert on early Upper Michigan photography, confirms that the earliest photographs from Upper Michigan date to the 1850s and they were taken by visitors to the area. There were no professional photographers residing in Upper Michigan before 1859 when F. W. Hacker set up business in Houghton, save for C. L. Weed, who was only at the Sault from 1850-51.[4] As Rankin also notes, Reverend John H. Pitezel (1814-1906) was only in Upper Michigan as a Methodist missionary from 1843 to 1852, as described in his 1857 book *Lights and Shades of Missionary Life*. There is no evidence that Pitezel ever returned to Upper Michigan after that, much less traveled to Washington, DC with Upper Michigan Native Americans to take such a photograph.[5] Furthermore, the Native Americans referred to Pitezel as "Wa-zah-wah-wa-doong" (Yellow Beard), suggesting he was blonde, not dark-haired, while the man in the photograph appears to have dark hair.[6] Plus, in his book, Pitezel makes no mention of ever being photographed with these chiefs, and the only man in the photograph whom he mentions in his book is Marji-Gesick, as we saw in Chapter 3. Furthermore, if the photograph were taken while Pitezel was in the Upper Peninsula, Marji-Gesick would have been in his mid-forties to early fifties. Kawbawgam would have been about twenty-eight to thirty-six then, yet the man identified as Kawbawgam is clearly older than the man identified as Marji-Gesick in the photograph.

Since Armstrong identified himself as the man in this photograph, I am inclined to think the Armstrong identification is correct.

Photograph 2: Charlotte Kawbawgam

The same 1945 *Mining Journal* article mentioned above includes this photograph from Brotherton of a young Native American woman proudly displaying her papoose. The article says it is "Charlotte Bawgam, daughter of the Chip-ewa Indian chieftain Marji-Gesick and No. 1 wife of Chief Charlie Bawgam." To my knowledge, this article is the only place where it is suggested that Kawbawgam had more than one wife. Possibly, Brotherton or the *Mining Journal* reporter confused Kawbawgam with Marji-Gesick and his multiple wives.

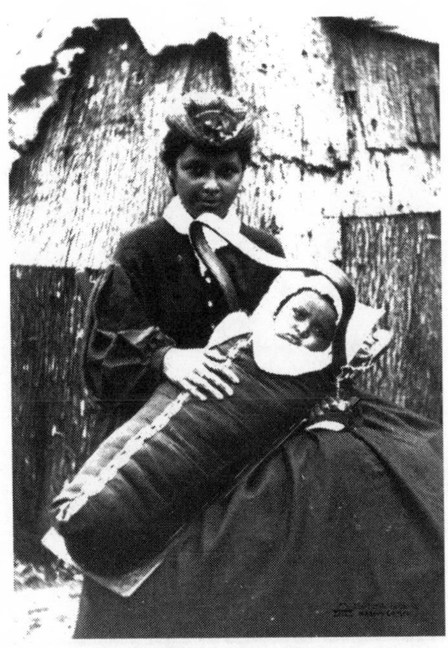

It's highly unlikely this photograph is of Charlotte, but because the 1945 article popularized the image, it has been reused countless times ever since to depict Charlotte.

The gray backing around the photograph indicates it was taken by B. F. Childs and printed at his Ishpeming studio.[7] Because Childs was the photographer, it is impossible that it is a photograph of Charlotte. Childs did not arrive in the Upper Peninsula until 1867.[8] Charlotte Kawbawgam would have been about thirty-six in 1867. The woman in this photograph appears significantly younger. To our knowledge, Charlotte had no children after 1860 and the Cadotte children she raised would have been toddlers or older when she adopted them sometime in the 1860s.

When I told Beth Gruber, research librarian at the Marquette Regional History Center, my reasons for believing the photograph was mislabeled, she did further research and sent me the following email about the three copies of the image in the History Center's collection.

We looked up the donation information on the three original stereoviews of that image.

1. The oldest print (ca. 1867-1871) was donated in 1921. The collection was described as "12 pictures of Charles Kawbawgam, house and family." In the paperwork, the donor is unknown but the name J. G. McCallum is written on the back of the image. There is also a handwritten note "Indian Squaw and papoose, Munising, 1869." There is no printed identification on the front of the image.
2. The second oldest print (ca. 1870s-1880s) was donated in 1925 as part of the J. M. Longyear Estate. It is described as "1 of 7 pictures of Indian canoes, wigwams, and groups." The front lists: "Mrs. 'Lo' and Little 'Negee,'" while on the back "Chippewa mother with baby" is handwritten.

3. The final print (after 1880), was donated in 1975 by Lawrence Robertson as one of four stereopticon slides. The front lists "Sault Ste. Marie - Mrs. 'Loo' and Little 'Niggee.'"[a]

Consequently, I think the most likely identification for this photograph is of Mrs. Lo/Loo and her child from the Sault. A photo of the Loo family wigwam at Sault Sainte Marie verifies there was such a person as Mrs. Loo. Jack Deo believes the photograph of Mrs. Loo's wigwam and this alleged photograph of Charlotte Kawbawgam were taken on the same day and that the same wigwam is in the background due to the upturned flap on the wigwam on the upper right of the door.[9] Given the clothing of the people in the other wigwam picture, one wonders whether the photographer provided the clothes for Mrs. Loo to wear in the photograph with the baby. I think enough evidence exists that we can definitely say this photograph is not of Charlotte Kawbawgam.

Photograph 3: Charlotte Kawbawgam

This photograph appears on page 132 of Fred Rydholm's *Superior Heartland*. It is the only place I have seen it identified as Charlotte Kawbawgam. Furthermore, Rydholm only has the woman's upper body appear in his book, cropping off the bottom of the photograph. Some full image copies of the photograph have written on the bottom "P-157-SOO, MICH - MINNIEHAHA. YOUNG SOO." This identifies Young as the photographer at the Sault. Minniehaha is a misspelling for Minnehaha, the heroine of Longfellow's

a. "Niggee" or "Negee" is probably intended to be the Ojibwa word for "friend," usually spelled "niiji" and pronounced "nee-jee."

The Song of Hiawatha. Rydholm likely did not have a copy of the photograph with this identification, but for him to assume it was Charlotte Kawbawgam still seems rather a leap.

Jack Deo has confirmed that this photograph does not depict Charlotte. Rather it is part of a series of photographs taken at Sault Sainte Marie, circa 1904, during a performance of the "Hiawatha pageant"—a dramatic performance based on Longfellow's poem. Such pageants became very popular in the Great Lakes region in the early twentieth century.[10] The same woman who played the role of Minnehaha appears in several of the photographs in the series.[11] The photographer was probably Andrew E. Young, who operated a photography business at the Sault from 1898 to 1935.[12]

Unfortunately, because Charlotte was born about 1831 and photography was rare in Upper Michigan before 1859, we have no photographs of Charlotte as a young woman.

Photograph 4: Charlotte Kawbawgam

The left photograph has been labeled as Charlotte Kawbawgam as well. However, it in no way resembles the other images of her that exist and that we know are her because she was always photographed with her husband. Furthermore, it appears to depict a quite elderly woman of at least eighty. Charlotte died in 1904 at the age of seventy-three. The right photograph is a closeup of Charlotte, taken from the photograph of her and Kawbawgam that appears in its entirety on page 180. Clearly the women in these two photographs do not resemble each other.

Photograph 5: Chief Marji-Gesick

Because Marji-Gesick died no later than 1862, it is unlikely any photographs of him exist. However, this photograph, donated by A. J. Fontaine to the Marquette Regional History Center in 1966, is labeled as Marji-Gesick.

We know A. G. Emery took this picture; however, Emery did not arrive in the Upper Peninsula until 1862, residing at Hancock until he moved to Negaunee and Marquette in 1864.[13] Marji-Gesick was definitely dead by the time Emery moved to the Negaunee and Marquette areas, and it is unlikely Marji-Gesick would have traveled to Emery's Hancock studio, some 100 miles away. (The photograph was clearly taken in a studio.)

Photograph 6: Charles Kawbawgam

This photograph is clearly labeled as Chief Kawbawgam across its front. However, it looks nothing like other photographs we have of Kawbawgam.

At times, it has also been identified as Marji-Gesick, which is also unlikely. Jack Deo says the photograph was taken by B. F. Childs, so we can date it to the 1870s. It appears to be one of several photographs Childs took at the Sault on the same day in which he used the canoe in this photograph as a background for several photographs. Childs identified the photograph as Chippewa chief K-ga-de-sa (One Who Walks Lame).[14] Who mislabeled it is unknown.

Photographs 7 & 8: The Brotherton Survey Party

This photograph also comes from Ray Brotherton. It depicts a railroad survey crew and identifies Brotherton's father, Frank, as seventh man from the left. Six other men are identified, including the man on the far left as "CHAS BAWGAM."

According to the April 24, 1945 *Mining Journal* article that displayed photographs 1 and 2 above, Kawbawgam "accompanied the Brothertons in locating the North Western between Negaunee and Escanaba." This statement refers to Frank Brotherton and his brothers Charles and August, who were members of the survey party that laid out the route for the first section of the Chicago and North Western railroad line between Escanaba and Negaunee. This is the only claim I have come across that Kawbawgam was ever involved in work with the railroad line.

The photograph's resolution is not good enough that a closeup of this man will allow us to verify his identity; however, neither his build nor height resemble those of Kawbawgam and he also appears to have a beard while Kawbawgam always appears clean-shaven in photographs. The photograph was taken in the winter of 1880-81, at which time Kawbawgam would have been about sixty-five, which seems older than the man in the picture.

It is possible Kawbawgam assisted the Brothertons in surveying, although I believe he would have done so far earlier. The Brothertons grew up in the Rochester, Michigan area and were neighbors of William Burt, who likely recruited them to come to the Upper Peninsula to conduct survey work with him, which they did beginning in 1852.[15] In 1854, Peter White hired Charles Brotherton to survey the land between Marquette and the Menominee River for building a wagon road.[16] Given that the Ojibwa had aided White previously in traveling to Escanaba and that White was good friends with Kawbawgam, it is not inconceivable that Kawbawgam was hired to assist the Brothertons at that time. Diaries exist from Charles E. Brotherton and his son Delavan Brotherton, who assisted his father in railroad surveying from the 1880s on; however, neither diary refers to Kawbawgam, but Charles Brotherton makes passing mention of "Indians" who helped him.[17] Peter Strom, in a manuscript about the Brothertons, states that Charles E. Brotherton worked with William Burt's surveying team and the son of an Ojibwa chief, "Charlie Bawgam" guided him, but Strom does not provide a source and may have gotten this information from sources provided by Ray Brotherton that I have been unable to locate.[18]

A second Brotherton photograph dates to the 1860s when it is more likely Kawbawgam may have worked with the family. The back of the photograph identifies it as: "C&NW Camp Selecting Land. Left to Right-F.H. Brotherton, Henry VanDyke, Henry Brotherton, Charles Brotherton, Charles Bawgam." The source of the identification is not known but Ray Brotherton may have provided it. Distinguishing all five people in the photograph is difficult, but there are two people in the tent, only the legs of one visible and the other clearly a person's torso. However, again it is unlikely Kawbawgam is in this photograph since he is identified as the person on the far right. This person does not look like him, and may even have a beard, which Kawbawgam never had. He also appears to be writing. To the best of our knowledge, Kawbawgam was not literate, so it is unlikely he would have been tasked with any record taking by the Brothertons.

Photograph 9: Jacques LePique or Louis Nolin

This photograph has long been identified as either Jacques LePique (Francis Nolan) or his father Louis Nolin. A *Mining Journal* clipping, date

unknown but definitely twentieth century, states that this photograph depicts Louis Nolin at Chief Island near the Sault. Because the image shows a fairly young man, and Jack Deo dates it to about 1870,[19] an identification of it as LePique or Nolin is unlikely since LePique was fifty by then and his father would have probably been in his seventies. The person's true identity remains unknown.

Photograph 10: Marji-Gesick and His Wives

Three copies of this image exist at the Marquette Regional History Center. The first is the gift of Ray Brotherton from 1919, stating it is Marji-Gesick and his wives. The second copy has no date or donor information but identifies the image as an Indian Camp at Teal Lake near Negaunee in 1845. The third copy, also from Ray Brotherton in 1951, states it is "Indian Village Teal Lake Negaunee 1853 Chief Marji-Gesick Wives (5)."

The 1840s dates are again impossible. The later date of 1853 might be possible, but Marji-Gesick did not usually reside at Teal Lake but along the Carp River. He is associated with Teal Lake only because it is near where he showed the iron ore to the Everett party. Furthermore, we know he had no more than three wives, and by all accounts, he did not live with all of them at the same time. Therefore, it is not likely him or his wives. Just as we probably have no photographs of Marji-Gesick, we appear to have no photographs of any of his wives, not even Charlotte's mother Susan, who lived into the 1880s. The true identities of the people in this photograph remain a mystery.

Acknowledgments

THIS BOOK HAS BEEN THE largest research project of my life, and it would have been impossible to complete without the help of numerous people. My extreme gratitude goes to:

Adam Berger, Fundraising Manager, Marquette Regional History Center: Adam brought overlooked information at the Marquette Regional History Center to my attention, especially concerning Sidney Adams, Lewis Henry Morgan, Chief Marji-Gesick, and Alfred Vincent Kidder. More importantly, I appreciated his continued enthusiasm for this project.

Ann Berman: I thank Ann for several interesting talks as she worked on her book about Louis G. Kaufman and I on this book. Together we unraveled the mysteries of Peter White and Robert Graveraet's relationship and so much more.

Arianna Nolan, Ojibwe Learning Center, Sault Sainte Marie: Thank you to Arianna for allowing me to use the Ojibwe Learning Center's library where I found several relevant books I might have otherwise overlooked.

Bayliss Public Library, Sault Sainte Marie, MI: Meredith Sommers and Megan Kinney were both extremely helpful in aiding me with looking at rare papers in the Judge John H. Steere Collection, particularly the Peter Barbeau papers, and in helping me locate newspaper articles on microfilm.

Beth Gruber, Research Librarian, Marquette Regional History Center: I spent countless hours troubling Beth with requests for various documents and photographs from the John M. Longyear Research Library's collection at the Marquette Regional History Center. Her patience, suggestions, and knowledge were invaluable throughout this process.

Betsy Rutz, Educator, Marquette Regional History Center: For helping me track down information about Eliza Truckey, and for her enthusiasm for the project, including scheduling the book release party at the Marquette Regional History Center.

Bishop Baraga Association: Thanks are due to **Lenora McKeen, Director,** and **Piersan Suriano, Assistant,** for their help in looking through the association's archives and the Marquette Diocese's records for information on the Kawbawgams. Nothing relevant was found, but that, in itself, provided answers to the Kawbawgams' religious practices.

Center for Native American Studies, Northern Michigan University: Thank you to the staff at the Center for their insights and receptiveness to my project and willingness to discuss it with me, especially **Martin Reinhardt** and **Jud Sojourn**.

Chippewa County Historical Society: Thanks are due to **Carolyn Person** and **Bernie Arbric** for their help in locating some newspaper articles concerning Native Americans at the Sault and for providing several photographs for this book.

Christina Rencontre: Chris was the first person of Native American descent I discussed my project with, and she helped me with determining the final title. I am appreciative for all of her advice and support.

Dana Perrow Moran: Dana constantly encouraged me through the writing of this project and listened when I was excited about new information I wanted to share.

Diana Deluca: For reading early drafts of the book; she was invaluable in helping me decide what belonged in the text, what should be a footnote, and the ultimate decision to use both endnotes and footnotes to make the text more readable.

Family History Center, Church of Latter-Day Saints, Harvey, Michigan: The Family History Center is a godsend for anyone who doesn't want to spend time running to every Upper Michigan county courthouse and harassing its employees. I have used it for numerous projects since 1993. I was able to answer many of the questions I had about the Kawbawgams and their relatives through its many records. Thanks especially to **Dewey Jones** and **Andrew Putnam Jones** for their assistance.

Greg Casperson: For listening to me talk about Kawbawgam numerous times and for helping me settle on the title.

Jack Deo: For providing photographs and information on early photography in Marquette. He is the expert on early Upper Michigan photography and this book would have been impossible without him.

James P. LaLone: James generously shared with me his extensive genealogical research into Kawbawgam's family tree as well as that of his stepfather Chief Shawano's family, which provided answers to many of my questions.

Dr. James McCommons: For filling in information about George Shiras III and his photographs.

Jenifer Brady: For her continual willingness to proofread anything I write and her constant enthusiasm for my projects.

Jessica "Red" Bays, Store Manager, Marquette Regional History Center: For insight on book pricing and sales and for carrying my books at the history center.

Jo Wittler, Curator, Marquette Regional History Center: For finding and sharing many of the Kawbawgam-related artifacts in the Marquette Regional History Center's collection, as well as doing additional research on them and keeping me apprised of additional items found.

Karen Lindquist, Archivist, Delta County Historical Society: For helping me with accessing the diaries of Charles E. Brotherton and Delevan A. Brotherton and other information on the Brotherton family.

Larry Alexander, Designer, Superior Book Productions: For the beautiful layout job, including placement of all the photographs, the cover, the creation of the maps and genealogy charts, and especially for keeping his calm over all the endnotes and footnotes. This book would have been impossible without his dedicated help.

Larry Buege: For reading sections of the manuscript and for his insights and testimonial.

Madeleine Bradford, Bentley Historical Library, University of Michigan: For searching the Peter White papers at the Bentley for me.

Marquette Regional History Center and John M. Longyear Research Library: The history center, formerly the Marquette County Historical Society, has been an invaluable resource to me in writing this book. Its staff have always been supportive of my efforts to help promote U.P. history. Many staff members are thanked here individually, but the entire staff and volunteers deserve credit for how this wonderful institution has been preserving our history for more than a century now. Particularly, thanks to

Sarah Niemi and **Ann Hilton Fisher** for their assistance in the Longyear Research Library.

Mary A. June, Shouldice Library, Lake Superior State University: For introducing me to several books I otherwise would have overlooked, especially that of the St. Mary's baptism records, which shed light on Kawbawgam's family's Catholic background.

Matt and Spring Madosh: Thank you to the Madoshes for being willing to talk about their family history with me and especially to Matt, great-great-great grandson of Chief Madosh, for providing copies of the markers about the Madosh family that used to be posted at Sugarloaf, as well as other family documents and information.

Mikel Classen: For sharing the story that Peter White had been entrusted with the Kawbawgams' money gained from their lawsuit.

Northern Michigan University Archives: The staff was most helpful in locating the papers from Charlotte Kawbawgam's various lawsuits with the Jackson Iron Company as well as trying to help me find other information.

Patricia Robb: For the story about her grandmother meeting Kawbawgam on a streetcar.

Peter White Public Library: For assistance with copying Peter White's papers from microfilm, locating items in their research room and biographical files, finding books missing from the shelves, and permission to photograph the Kawbawgam bust.

Rebecca Mead: For answering questions about the Kawbawgam lawsuit and providing additional information, as well as talking over many points of this book that led to new insights and areas to research.

Roslyn Hurley: For reading early drafts of the book. As a resident of the Southwest, she asked me if Homer Kidder was any relation to Alfred Vincent Kidder, the famous Native American anthropologist. I had never heard of Alfred Vincent Kidder before, so this inquiry opened up an expanded interest in the Kidder family for me.

Russell Magnaghi: For his help in locating additional materials of interest, especially the Peter White papers in the Burton Historical Collection. Also for sharing his own work on Native Americans in Marquette County, writing several works that were resources for this book, and his keen proofreading eye.

Todd Poquette: For his willingness to discuss the Marji Gesick 100.

University of Rochester Libraries, Rochester, New York: Thanks are due to **Melinda Wallington** and **Melissa Mead** for providing me with copies of Lewis Henry Morgan's manuscripts that related to Marquette and Kawbawgam's brother Edward Shawano.

I also wish to thank **Shirley Brozzo, Lon Emerick, Anne Metrish, Dianne Patrick**, and any others who were not always able to help me but pointed me in the direction of others who could. My sincere thanks to anyone else I may have forgotten to mention. Your help was more appreciated than you know.

Finally, I want to thank the more than one hundred people who reached out to me following my brother Daniel Tichelaar's unexpected death on September 27, 2019. This tragic event immobilized me so that I was unable to write for several weeks, and dealing with settling his estate, and then the coronavirus pandemic, made the completion of this book extremely difficult and stressful. I appreciate everyone's kind words and gestures of sympathy during this difficult time. It is good to know, especially in times of tragedy, that so many caring people exist.

Bibliography

"Alfred V. Kidder." https://en.wikipedia.org/wiki/Alfred_V._Kidder. Accessed August 27, 2018.

Ancestry.com. https://www.ancestry.com/boards/topics.ethnic.natam.intertribal.mi/666/mb.ashx. Source for Kawbawgam's sister Charlotte's 1828 birth date. Accessed July 14, 2018.

Ancestry.com. https://www.ancestry.com/genealogy/records/john-logan-chipman_34772955. Accessed August 3, 2018.

Ancestry.com. https://www.ancestry.com/genealogy/records/chief-louis-chekatchogemau_99456465. Accessed July 9, 2019.

Anderton, John. *The Jewel in the Crown: An Environmental History of Presque Isle Park*. Marquette, MI: Center for Upper Peninsula Studies, Northern Michigan University, 2009.

"Angel of Death Summons Augustine Gager and Several Others." *Sault Sainte Marie News*. September 18, 1897. Part 1. p. 5. At "Sault Sainte Marie Death Notices." https://sites.rootsweb.com/~wjmartin/dem-deth.htm. Accessed August 4, 2019.

"Ancient Anishinaabek Burial Ground." Plaque at Burial Site, Water Street, Sault Sainte Marie, Michigan.

Anonymous. Article Title Unknown. Publication Unknown. October 13, 1977. Graveraet Family Folders 920 BF. Marquette Regional History Center.

Anonymous. *History of the Upper Peninsula of Michigan: A Full Account of Its Early Settlement; Its Growth, Development and Resources;*

an Extended Description of Its Iron and Copper Mines. Chicago, IL: The Western Historical Company, 1883. Transcribed by Debi Hanes at http://genealogytrails.com/mich/marquette/upperpen.html. Accessed January 31, 2020.

Anonymous. Subject: Jack LaPete. Manuscript. Jack LaPete Folder 920 BF. Marquette Regional History Center.

Anonymous. Subject: Robert Graveraet. Manuscript dated September 21, 1965. Kawbawgam Family Folder 920 BF. Marquette Regional History Center.

Anonymous. Subject: Jack LaPete. Manuscript 977.496 J63M. Jack LaPete Folder 920 BF. Marquette Regional History Center.

Arbric, Bernard. *Sugar Island Sampler*. Allegan Forest, MI: The Priscilla Press, 1992.

Arbric, Bernie and Nancy Steinhaus. "How the Soo Locks Were Made." *Lake Superior Magazine*. July 27, 2015. https://www.lakesuperior.com/the-lake/maritime/how-the-soo-locks-were-made/. Accessed July 18, 2018.

Arbric, Bernie. *City of the Rapids: Sault Sainte Marie's Heritage*. Allegan Forest, MI: The Priscilla Press, 2003.

"Augustus Madosh." https://www.ancestry.com/genealogy/records/augustus-madosh_130619592. Accessed February 14, 2019.

Ball, Mrs. Daniel. Letter to Olive Pendill. April 17, 1921. Jack LaPete Folder 920 BF. Marquette Regional History Center.

Ball, Mrs. Daniel. Letter to Olive Pendill. December 4, 1920. Jack LaPete Folder 920 BF. Marquette Regional History Center.

Banker's Magazine, The. Vol. 46 (Vol. 23 of the Third Series). July 1891-June 1892. New York: Homans Publishing, 1891-1892.

Baraga, Frederic. *The Diary of Bishop Frederic Baraga, First Bishop of Marquette*. Eds. Regis M. Walling and Rev. N. Daniel Rupp. Trans. Joseph Gregorich and Rev. Paul Prud'homme. Detroit: Wayne State UP, 2001.

Barbeau (Peter) Papers. Judge Joseph H. Steere Room, Bayliss Public Library, Sault Sainte Marie, Michigan.

Barbour, Levi I. "Peter White as Man and as Citizen: An Address." Ann Arbor, MI. March 31, 1909. Marquette Regional History Center. 921 W58.

Barney, Mrs. Samuel (Anna Eliza). "Personal Recollections of Mrs. Samuel Barney. Notes taken by O. C. Tuch and transcribed verbatim March 6th, 1915." Manuscript file. Marquette Regional History Center.

Bayliss, Joseph E., Estelle L. Bayliss, and Milo M. Quaiffe. *River of Destiny: The Saint Marys*. Detroit, MI: Wayne State UP, 1955. Reprint by Chippewa County Historical Society, 2018.

Belinsky, Katie et al. (The 3Rs Team). "Who is Marji-Gesick and Why Should We Care?" K. I. Sawyer, MI: The Polar Press, K. I. Sawyer School. n.d. Manuscript. Marquette Regional History Center.

Berger, Adam. "Great American Archaelogist from Marquette." *The Mining Journal*. September 25, 2019.

Berger, Adam. "Historically Speaking." *The Mining Journal*. February 14, 2020.

Berger, Adam. "Mah-je-ge-zhik Was Remarkable Man." *The Mining Journal*. October 2, 2019. p. 7A.

Bieder, Robert E. "Introduction." Kohl, Johann George. *Kitchi-Gami: Life Among the Lake Superior Ojibway*. Trans. Ralf Neufang and Ulrike Böcker. 1859. St. Paul, MN: Minnesota Historical Society, 1985. p. xiii-xxxix.

Blackbird, Andrew. *History of the Ottawa and Chippewa Indians of Michigan; A Grammar of Their Language, and Personal and Family History of the Author*. 1887. n.p.: n.d. Kindle ebook.

Bleck, Christie. "What's in a Name?: Redmen/Redettes at Issue—Divided Community Sounds Off in MSHS Sports Nickname Controversy." *The Mining Journal*. January 7, 2020.

Bond. September 18, 1888. Box John Voelker MSS-39:07018. Folder "Laughing Whitefish"—Jeremy Compo vs. The Jackson Iron Co. #10163, Marquette County Circuit Court (1887-8). Northern Michigan University Archives.

Bourgeois, Arthur. "Editor's Introduction." *Ojibwa Narratives of Charles and Charlotte Kawbawgam and Jacques LePique, 1893-1895*. Kidder, Homer H. recorder. Detroit: Wayne State UP, 1994. p. 11-12.

Boyd, George. 1824 letter to Governor Lewis Cass. Robert J. Graveraet Folder 920 BF. Marquette Regional History Center.

Boyer, Kenyon. "Charlie Kawbawgam." Historical Highlights Radio Talks. Vol. III. No. 43. August 14, 1955. Manuscript. Marquette Regional History Center.

Boyer, Kenyon. "Grand Island." Historical Highlights Radio Talks. Vol. III. No. 44. August 14, 1955. Manuscript. Marquette Regional History Center.

Boyer, Kenyon. "Jack La Pete—Famous Indian Character." Historical Highlights Radio Talks. Vol XI. No. 189. June 15, 1958. Manuscript. Marquette Regional History Center.

Bradley-Holliday, Valerie. *Northern Roots: African Descended Pioneers in the Upper Peninsula of Michigan*. Bloomington, IN: Xlibris, 2009.

Brassey, Lord. *Voyages and Travels of Lord Brassey, K.C.B., D.C.L. from 1862-1894*. Ed. Captain S. Eardley-Wilmot. 2 vols. London, Gr. Brit.: Longmans, Green, and Co., 1895. Vol. 1.

Bremer, Richard G. *Indian Agent and Wilderness Scholar: The Life of Henry Rowe Schoolcraft*. Mount Pleasant, MI: Clarke Historical Library, Central Michigan U, 1987.

Brinks, Herbert. *Peter White*. Grand Rapids, MI: William B. Eerdmans, 1970.

Brinks, J. Herbert. "Peter White." Talk at Historical Society of Michigan. Grand Rapids, MI. September 25, 1964. Marquette Regional History Center.

Brinks, John Herbert. *Peter White: A Career of Business and Politics in an Industrial Frontier Community*. Dissertation. Ann Arbor, MI: University Microfilms, 1965. Marquette Regional History Center.

Brotherton, Charles E. and Delavan A. Brotherton Diary Transcripts. Delta County Historical Society Archives. Escanaba, Michigan.

Brotherton, Ray. "Negaunee Man Compiles Story of Philo Everett's Journey from Jackson to Marquette in 1845." *The Mining Journal*. October 15, 1945. p. 5, 8.

Brotherton, Ray. "Old Pictures Reveal History Of Marquette And Delta Counties." *The Mining Journal*. March 24, 1945. p. 10.

Brotherton, Ray. "Saga of Philo Everett's Trip to Marquette From Jackson Is Ended In Today's Installment." *The Mining Journal*. October 17, 1945. p. 6.

Brotherton, Ray. "This Installment of Everett's Trip Tells Of Storm And Party's Arrival in Marquette In 1845." *The Mining Journal*. October 16, 1945. p. 6, 8.

Bruner, Deborah. "Quiet, Regal Indian Left His Mark on Land That Nurtured a City." *Upbeat. The Mining Journal*. July 30, 1970. p. 8-10.

Cabell, Brian. "Eastside Zoning Dispute, Valle's Facelift, Fat Boyz Closure, and Marvelous Marji Gesick Masochism." *Word on the Street*. May 14, 2017. https://wotsmqt.com/eastside-zoning-dispute-valles-facelift-fat-boyz-closure-marvelous-marji-gesick-masochism/. Accessed November 18, 2018.

"Cadotte (Ancestry and Genealogy)." Madosh Folder BF 920. Contains descendants of Peter Cadotte and Amanda Gesick. Information from Roger and Carol (Trevillion) LeBlanc. Marquette Regional History Center.

Calumet News. "Aged One to Dance." July 23, 1907.

Carter, James L. "Kawbawgam Village Project to Feature Airstrip." *The Mining Journal*. September 15, 1967. Quoted in *Chocolay Township History: Then and Now....* Marquette, MI: Pride Printing, 2008. p. 118.

Census 1860. Marquette County, Michigan.

Census 1870. Marquette County, Michigan.

Census 1880. Chippewa County, Michigan.

Census 1880. Marquette County, Michigan.

Census 1900. Marquette County, Michigan.

Center for Native American Studies. Northern Michigan University. https://www.nmu.edu/nativeamericanstudies/home-page. Accessed September 3, 2018.

"Charles Brotherton." Manuscript. Delta County Historical Society Archives. Escanaba, Michigan.

"Charles Brotherton House." Pamphlet. Delta County Historical Society Archives. Escanaba, Michigan.

Charlie Kawbawgam Death Certificate. #816. Marquette County, Michigan. Michigan Department of State. Lansing, MI. December 28, 1902.

Charlotte Kobogum vs. Jackson Iron Company. Trial transcripts. 345.5 M48j. 2 vols. Marquette Regional History Center.

Chipman Family. https://wc.rootsweb.ancestry.com/cgi-bin/igm.cgi?op=GET&db=mychipmans&id=I2363. Accessed August 31, 2018.

Chipman, Bert Lee. *The Chipman Family: A Genealogy of the Chipmans in America, 1631-1920*. Winston-Salem, NC: Bert L. Chipman Publisher, 1920.

Chipman, Henry C. Wikipedia. https://en.wikipedia.org/wiki/Henry_C._Chipman. Accessed May 17, 2019.

Chipman, John Logan. Wikipedia. https://en.wikipedia.org/wiki/John_Logan_Chipman. Accessed August 31, 2018.

Chipman, Nathaniel. https://en.wikipedia.org/wiki/Nathaniel_Chipman#Family. Accessed May 17, 2019.

Chippewa County Marriage Records. Charles Makatak-wat to Charlotte Madjikijiki. July 12, 1847. p. 70.

Chippewa County Marriage Records. John Roussain to Charlotte Shawono. June 24, 1846. p. 63.

Chisholm, Barbara, ed. *Superior: Under the Shadow of the Gods*. 2nd ed. Toronto, Canada: Lynx Images, 1999.

Chocolay Township History: Then and Now.... Marquette, MI: Pride Printing, 2008.

Chute, Janet E. *The Legacy of Shingwaukonse: A Century of Native Leadership*. Toronto, Canada: U of Toronto P, 1998.

Cleland, Charles E. *Rites of Conquest: The History and Culture of Michigan's Native Americans.* Ann Arbor, MI: U of Michigan P, 1992.

Cleland, Charles E. *The Place of the Pike (Gnoozhekaaning): A History of the Bay Mills Indian Community.* Ann Arbor, MI: U of Michigan P, 2001.

Cleveland, Clifford S. *The Mystery of Kawbawgam's Grave.* Au Train, MI: Avery Color Studios, 1979.

Cutler, William G. *History of the State of Kansas*. 1883. Biography of A. G. Emery quoted by Millie Mowry at http://www.pa-roots.org/data/read.php?5487,732664. Accessed November 4, 2018.

Dana, Juliette Star. *A Fashionable Tour Through the Great Lakes and Upper Mississippi: The 1852 Journal of Juliette Starr Dana*. Ed. David T. Dana III. Detroit, MI: Wayne State UP, 2004.

Danzinger, Edmund Jefferson, Jr. *The Chippewas of Lake Superior*. Norman and London, OK: U of Oklahoma P, 1979.

Daughters of the American Revolution: Chief Shawano Chapter. http://www.shawano.michdar.net/dar2.htm. Accessed September 3, 2018.

"Death of a Famous Chippewa." *Marine Review*. January 8, 1903.

"Death Takes C. R. Everett in Ypsilanti." *The Mining Journal*. October 6, 1951.

Deo, Jack. Personal Email. July 16, 2019.

Deo, Jack. Personal Interview. July 3, 2019.

Deo, Jack. Personal Interview. February 4, 2020.

Dobson, Robert. Possible Burial Ground Folder. Marquette Regional History Center.

Dulong, John P. "Jean Baptiste Cadotte's Second Family: Genealogical Summary-Part 1. *Michigan's Habitant Heritage (MHH)*. 36.4. October 2015. p. 188-96.

Dulong, John P. "Jean Baptiste Cadotte's Second Family: Genealogical Summary-Part 2. *Michigan's Habitant Heritage (MHH)*. 37.1. January 2016. p. 43-56.

Dulong, John P. "Jean Baptiste Cadotte's Second Family: Genealogical Summary-Part 3a. *Michigan's Habitant Heritage (MHH)*. 37.2. April 2016. p. 85-97.

Dulong, John P. "Jean Baptiste Cadotte's Second Family: Genealogical Summary-Part 3b. *Michigan's Habitant Heritage (MHH)*. 37.3. July 2016. p. 156-65.

Dupras, Rob and Fred Rydholm. "Letter to the Editor." *The Mining Journal*. May 28, 1999.

"Early Officers at the Fort Michilimackinac and Mackinac." http://www.mifamilyhistory.org/mimack/military/EarlyMilitary/officerindex.asp?MackinacMilitaryOfficersOrder=Sorter_Given&MackinacMilitaryOfficersDir=DESC&MackinacMilitaryOfficersPage=2. Accessed May 26, 2019.

Edmunds, R. David. *The Shawnee Prophet*. Lincoln, NE: U of Nebraska P, 1985.

EHR [Ernest H. Rankin]/JPW. "Father Jacques Marquette Statue." September 16, 1968. Special article written for Marquette County Historical Society. Marquette Regional History Center.

1855 Treaty with Ottawa and Chippewa (First). https://www.cmich.edu/library/clarke/ResearchResources/Native_American_Material/Treaty_Rights/Text_of_Michigan_Related_Treaties/Detroit_1855/Pages/Ottawa-and-Chippewa.aspx. Accessed July 3, 2018.

1855 Treaty with Ottawa and Chippewa (Second). https://www.cmich.edu/library/clarke/ResearchResources/Native_American_Material/Treaty_Rights/Text_of_Michigan_Related_Treaties/Detroit_1855/Pages/Chippewa-of-Sault-Ste.-Marie.aspx. Accessed July 3, 2018.

Enquirer and News. "Albion's 'copper-colored sons of the forest.'" Battle Creek, Michigan. February 17, 1974. p. H-10.

Escanaba. Wikipedia. https://en.wikipedia.org/wiki/Escanaba,_Michigan. Accessed December 16, 2018.

Evening Wisconsin. "Goes Back to Italy: Chevalier Trentanove Departs for His Native Clime to Execute Commissions." Date Unknown. Peter White Papers. Burton Historical Collection. Detroit Public Library. Box 104. Microfilm Reel 3 of collection at Peter White Public Library, Marquette, Michigan.

Everett, Philo M. Deposition and Testimony. Charlotte Kobogum vs. Jackson Iron Company. Box 70, Voelker Collection, Central Upper Peninsula Archives, Northern Michigan University.

Familysearch.org. https://www.familysearch.org/tree/pedigree/fanchart/K4YW-P93. Family tree of Angelica Cadotte. Accessed October 17, 2019.

Father Marquette Statue. Wikipedia. https://en.wikipedia.org/wiki/Jacques_Marquette_(Trentanove). Accessed August 28, 2018.

Fletcher, Matthew L. M. "Foreword." *Laughing Whitefish* by Robert Traver. East Lansing, MI: Michigan State UP, 2011. vii-xxii.

Gaspar, Angie. "Redmen Indian Logo Gets National Attention." *The Mining Journal*. September 14, 1999.

Ge-shik, Susan. 1884 statement. Marquette Regional History Center. 977.496 J63m.

Gilbert, Mrs. Thomas D. "Memories of the 'Soo.'" October 8, 1899. Publication Unknown. Printed in Grand Rapids, MI. Peter White Scrapbooks. Vol. 1 of 2. Marquette Regional History Center.

Graham, Loren R. *A Face in the Rock: The Tale of a Grand Island Chippewa*. Washington, DC: Island Press, 1995.

Graveraet, Robert J. "Obituary." *Detroit Free Press*. June 15, 1861. Cited at http://www.mainlymichigan.com/Native%20Americans. GRAVERAET-Family-Page.ashx. Accessed December 16, 2018.

Great Lakes Indian Fish and Wildlife Commission. *Treaty Rights*. Odanah, WI: n.d.

Great Lakes Area Tribal Health Board. Resolution No. 20-001. "Elimination of Race-Based Indian Logos, Mascots, and Names."

Gruber, Beth. Personal Email. January 22, 2019.

Gruber, Beth and Ann Hilton Fisher. "Marquette Memories and Yours." *The Mining Journal*. December 13, 2017. p. 6A.

Gruber, Beth, Rosemary Michelin, and Jo Wittler. "The John M. Longyear Research Library & Archives." *Harlow's Wooden Man*. Vol. 54. No. 3. 2018.

Hambleton, Elizabeth and Elizabeth Warren Stoutamire. *The John Johnston Family of Sault Ste. Marie*. Washington, DC: The John Johnston Family Association, 1992.

Hambleton-Kirk, Mrs. Letter to Mrs. Carroll Paul. September 14, 1939. Kawbawgam Family Folder 920 BF. Marquette Regional History Center.

Harper's Weekly. "Views About Lake Superior." September 16, 1865. p. 588. https://archive.org/details/harpersweeklyv9bonn/page/588. Accessed July 26, 2019.

Hearings Before the Committee on Water Power of the House of Representatives Sixty-Fifth Congress, Second Session: March 18 to May 15, 1918. Parts 1, 2, 3 and 4. Washington, DC: Government Printing Office, 1919.

Kirtland, F. W. Deposition and Testimony. Charlotte Kobogum et al. vs. Jackson Iron Company. Box 70, Voelker Collection. Central Upper Peninsula Archives, Northern Michigan University.

Knight, Alan and Janet E. Chute. "In the Shadow of the Thumping Drum: The Sault Métis—The People In-Between. In *Lines Drawn Upon the Water: First Nations and the Great Lakes Borders and Borderlands.* Ed. Karl S. Hele. Waterloo, Ont.: Wilfrid Laurier UP, 2008. p. 85-113.

Hendricks, Kathleen M. *St. Mary's Catholic Church Baptisms: Sault Sainte Marie, Michigan, 1811-1900.* Sault Sainte Marie, MI: Sault Printing Company, 2005.

Henry, Ragene. *The Time of the Shining Rocks.* n.p.: Chickadee Press, 1999.

Hiebel, Kaye. "The Story of Jack La Pete." *The Mining Journal.* January 20, 2016. p. 5A.

Hinsdale, W. B. "Property Rights and Indian Marriage: Two Cases in the Michigan Supreme Court." *Michigan Alumnus.* Vol XL. No. 17. March 1934. Ann Arbor, MI: The Alumni Association of the University of Michigan. p. 154-60.

History of the Precious Blood Cathedral, Part III: The First Catholic Church Is Raised on the Canadian Shore. Available at: https://preciousbloodssm.com/church-history. Accessed January 18, 2020.

Homer Huntington Kidder. Find a Grave. https://www.findagrave.com/memorial/118394847/homer-huntington-kidder. Accessed October 25, 2019.

Howe, Manthei. "Visitors Do Research on Indian Lore." *The Mining Journal.* July 3, 1949.

Hoyum, Kim. "20th anniversary of the Paul Girard Killing." *The Mining Journal.* September 30, 2008.

Husar, Edward. "Quincy Woman Treasures Uncle's Artistic Legacy." *The Quincy Herald-Whig.* September 6, 1987. p. 9D.

"Inspirer of Poems: First Man of Marquette—Unique Record of Hon. Peter White, Jabbers Chippewa and Oneida with W.D. Hoard." Publication Unknown. Date Unknown. Peter White Scrapbooks. Vol. 2 of 2. Marquette Regional History Center.

Interpretive Panel about Mail Carriers. Water Street. Sault Sainte Marie, Michigan.

"In the Matter of the Estate of Mary Tebeau Minor." February 1890. No. 4287, Circuit Court Records, Marquette County, Central Upper Peninsula Archives, Northern Michigan University.

"Jeremy Compo vs. The Jackson Iron Company." State of Michigan Supreme Court. Trial transcripts. Marquette Regional History Center.

Kalamazoo Telegraph. "Peter White as Dancing Teacher." August 5, 1907.

Kappler, Charles J. *Indian Affairs: Laws and Treaties*. Vol. II. Washington, DC: Government Printing Office, 1904. Online at https://web.archive.org/web/20170531182101/http://digital.library.okstate.edu/kappler/index.htm. Accessed July 21, 2019.

Kawbawgam, Charles. "Typed Manuscript of Trial Testimonial." Kawbawgam Family Folder. 977.496 J63M. Marquette Regional History Center.

Kawbawgam-Nolin Manuscript. Kawbawgam Family Folder 920 BF and Jack LaPete Folder 920 BF. (The same manuscript is in both folders). Marquette Regional History Center.

Kawbawgam Statue Subscription Form. Peter White Papers. Burton Historical Collection. Detroit Public Library. Box 104. Microfilm Reel 3 of collection at Peter White Public Library, Marquette, Michigan.

Kawbawgam Village Flier. Kawbawgam Family Folder 920 BF. Marquette Regional History Center.

Kelley, James M. Letter to Peter White. January 11, 1906. Manuscript Case. Marquette Regional History Center.

Kidder, Alfred Vincent. https://web.archive.org/web/20060803221038/http://www.mnsu.edu/emuseum/information/biography/klmno/kidder_alfred.html. Accessed November 23, 2018.

Kidder, Alfred Vincent. Letter to Dr. Leslie A. White. May 29, 1941. Alfred Vincent Kidder Folder 920 BF. Marquette Regional History Center.

Kidder, Alfred Vincent. Letter to Ernest Rankin. February 13, 1962. Alfred Vincent Kidder Folder 920 BF. Marquette Regional History Center.

Kidder, H. H. "Camping on Lake Superior." *The Vindex*. p. 4-6, continued in next issue. St. Mark's School, January 1890. Homer Kidder Folder, BF 920. Marquette Regional History Center.

Kidder, Homer H. *Ojibwa Narratives of Charles and Charlotte Kawbawgam and Jacques LePique, 1893-1895*. Detroit: Wayne State UP, 1994.

Kidder, Homer Huntington. "Charlotte Kobogum et al. vs. The Jackson Iron Company." Manuscript. Possibly written 1948. In Manuscript File. Marquette Regional History Center.

Kienitz, Betty. "Chief Shawano." https://lists.rootsweb.com/hyperkitty/list/nishnawbe@rootsweb.com/thread/25553539/. Accessed September 12, 2019.

Killough, Virginia. "Letter to Editor." *The Mining Journal*. July 28, 1999.

Kilpela, Don. "A Christmas Carol: Reflections on the Cross and Sacred Pipe." *Marquette Monthly*. December 2002. p. 23-26.

Kohl, Johann George. *Kitchi-Gami: Life Among the Lake Superior Ojibway*. Trans. Ralf Neufang and Ulrike Böcker. 1859. St. Paul, MN: Minnesota Historical Society, 1985.

Kosciuszko Monument. Wikipedia. https://en.wikipedia.org/wiki/Kosciuszko_Monument. Accessed June 30, 2019.

LaLone, James P. "Black Cloud—Oshawano Family." Unpublished Manuscript. July 15, 2018.

LaLone, James P. "Graveraet Family." Native Americans in Michigan. Website. http://www.mfhn.com/Native/Default.aspx?Page=-GRAVERAET_Family&AspxAutoDetectCookieSupport=1. Accessed December 15, 2018.

LaLone, James P. "Shingabowossin Family." Unpublished Manuscript. January 17, 2019.

Lake, James. "Logo Debate Boils Over: MAPS Board Votes to Change Logo: Member Resigns in Protest." *The Mining Journal.* January 12, 1999.

Lantz, Raymond C. *Ottawa and Chippewa Indians of Michigan, 1870-1909.* Bowes, MD: Heritage Books, 1991.

Leander August Madosh. https://www.ancestry.com/genealogy/records/leander-august-madosh_130619524. Accessed February 14, 2019.

"Leander August 'Lee' Madosh. Find a Grave. https://www.findagrave.com/memorial/65592793. Accessed February 14, 2019.

Leerhoff, Jennifer. "A New Year's Day Calling Tradition." *The Mining Journal.* December 28, 2016. p. 5A.

Lewis Cass Expedition. Wikipedia. https://en.wikipedia.org/wiki/Lewis_Cass_expedition. Accessed December 10, 2018.

Lewis, Janet. *The Invasion: A Narrative of Events Concerning the Johnston Family of St. Mary's.* 1932. East Lansing, MI: Michigan State UP, 2000.

Lingle, John. "Charlie Kawbawgam." Manuscript. Kawbawgam Family Folder BF 920. Marquette Regional History Center.

List of Presidents of the University of Michigan. Wikipedia. https://en.wikipedia.org/wiki/President_of_the_University_of_Michigan#List_of_Presidents_of_the_University_of_Michigan. Accessed February 10, 2019.

Longtine, Sonny. *U.P. People: Incredible Stories About Incredible People.* Marquette, MI: Sunnyside Publications, 2017.

Mackinac History. Vol III. Leaflet No. 4. 2000.

Madosh Family Folder. 920 BF. Marquette Regional History Center.

Madosh Graves. https://www.findagrave.com/cemetery/1341/memorial-search?firstName=&lastName=Madosh&page=1#sr-124742851. Accessed October 23, 2019.

Madosh, Matt. Personal Interview. December 10, 2019.

Madosh, Peter. Headstone. Holy Cross Cemetery, Marquette, Michigan.

Magnaghi, Russell M. "Native Americans at Marquette." Unpublished manuscript.

Magnaghi, Russell M. *Native Americans of Michigan's Upper Peninsula: A Chronology to 1900*. 2nd ed. Marquette, MI: Center for Upper Peninsula Studies, Northern Michigan University, 2009.

Magnaghi, Russell. "Observations of Marquette by a German Visitor in 1850." *Harlow's Wooden Man*. Vol. 51. No. 3. 2015.

Magnaghi, Russell M. *Upper Peninsula of Michigan: A History*. Marquette, MI: 906 Heritage Press, 2017.

Mail carrier photograph, handwriting on back. 1871. Judge Joseph H. Steere Room. Bayliss Public Library, Sault Sainte Marie, Michigan.

Majher, Patricia. *Ladies of the Lights: Michigan Women in the US Lighthouse Service*. Ann Arbor, MI: U of M, 2010.

"Mapes, Egbert J." http://genealogytrails.com/mich/marquette/biographicalrecord3.html. Accessed August 5, 2018.

Mandosking, David. https://www.myheritage.com/names/david_mandosking. Accessed August 4, 2019.

Marine Review. "James M. Kelley, a Lake Superior Poneer." [sic]. *Marine Review*. Vol. 39. p. 26-28. Accessed at https://books.google.com/books?id=TOA-AQAAMAAJ&pg=RA7-PA26&lpg#v=onepage&q&f=false. Accessed June 12, 2018.

Marji Gesick 100. www.MarjiGesick.com. Accessed November 18, 2018.

Marquette County Death Record. Kawbawgam, Charles. January 4, 1903. Marquette County Courthouse, Marquette, MI.

Marquette Magazine. "Stories of Interest in Marquette History." October 15, 1969.

Marquette National Bank. Advertising Card with Kawbawgam's Image on it. 1903. Kawbawgam Folder BF 920. Marquette Regional History Center.

Marquette, Jacques Statues Folder. BF 920. Marquette Regional History Center.

Mary Tebeau. https://www.myheritage.com/names/mary_tebeau. Accessed November 18, 2018.

Mary Mandoski (Tebeau) Death Certificate. #442. July 24, 1903. State of Michigan. Ancestry.com. Accessed August 3, 2019.

Mason, Philip P. "Foreword." *Schoolcraft's Ojibwa Lodge Stories: Life on the Lake Superior Frontier*. 1962. East Lansing, MI: Michigan State UP, 1997. p. ix-xii.

Mason, Philip P. "Introduction." *Schoolcraft's Ojibwa Lodge Stories: Life on the Lake Superior Frontier*. 1962. East Lansing, MI: Michigan State UP, 1997. p. xvii-xxix.

Mason, Philip P. "Preface." *Schoolcraft's Ojibwa Lodge Stories: Life on the Lake Superior Frontier*. 1962. East Lansing, MI: Michigan State UP, 1997. p. xii-xv.

"Matthew L. M. Fletcher." http://aisp.msu.edu/people1/people/matthew-fletcher/. Accessed March 9, 2019.

Maynard, D. P. "The Life and Times of Charley Kawbawgam: A U.P. Continuum." December 1972. Marquette Regional History Center, 1988.14. Manuscript. Manuscript File.

McCann, Kate. "Charlotte Kawbawgam vs. The Jackson Iron Company. *Marquette Monthly*. May 1993. Part 1 of 2. p. 21-22.

McCann, Kate. "Charlotte Kawbawgam vs. The Jackson Iron Company." *Marquette Monthly*. June 1993. Part 2 of 2. p. 17-18.

McCommons, James H. *Camera Hunter: George Shiras III and the Birth of Wildlife Photography.* Albuquerque, NM: U of New Mexico P, 2019.

Mead, Rebecca J. "The Kawbawgam Cases: Native Claims and the Discovery of Iron in the Upper Peninsula of Michigan." *The Michigan Historical Review.* Vol. 4. No. 2. (Fall 2014): 1-31.

Memorial Addresses on the Life and Character of J. Logan Chipman (a Representative from Michigan) Delivered in the House of Representatives and in the Senate, Fifty-Third Congress, First Session. Washington, DC: Government Printing Office, 1895.

"Memories of Early Marquette by Mrs. Philo M. Everett." *Michigan History Magazine*. Vol. 5. (July-Oct 1921): 571.

"Michel Cadotte." Wikipedia. https://en.wikipedia.org/wiki/Michel_Cadotte. Accessed September 1, 2018.

Michigan Volunteer Sharpshooters. https://en.wikipedia.org/wiki/1st_Regiment_Michigan_Volunteer_Sharpshooters. Accessed September 14, 2018.

Morgan, Lewis Henry. *Journals*. Unpublished manuscripts. 6 vols. Rare Books and Special Collections. University of Rochester, New York. Vols. 2, 4, and 6 include Morgan's visits to Marquette.

Mount Pleasant Indian Industrial Boarding School. https://en.wikipedia.org/wiki/Mount_Pleasant_Indian_Industrial_Boarding_School#The_children. Accessed June 9, 2019.

Mount Pleasant, Michigan Boarding School. Binder. Marquette County Genealogical Society Collection. Peter White Public Library, Marquette, Michigan. 4970.3 MO MCGS.

Mukkala, Ben. "Charlie 'Naw-wa-que-gezik' Kawbawgam." Manuscript. Kawbawgam Family Folder 920 BF. Marquette Regional History Center.

"Negaunee Man Completes Story Of Philo Everett's Journey From Jackson To Marquette In 1845." *The Mining Journal*. October 15, 1945.

Nelson, Henry Loomis. "The Pleasant Life of Pere Marquette." *Harper's Monthly Magazine*. Vol. CXI. No. 661 (1905): 74-82.

Nertoli, Mary C. "Charles Kawbawgam: Fact or Fiction?" 1979.2.13 Manuscript. Manuscript Case. Marquette Regional History Center.

New York World. "Fight Blasted His Career: Indian Lost His Nose in a Melee and Gave Up His Ambition." Reprinted in *The Fall River News*. Fall River, Kansas. December 15, 1899. p. 3.

Niemi, Sara. "Marquette's Ship Fever Epidemic, 1849." *The Mining Journal*. November 20, 2019. p. 6A.

Ontonagon Boulder. Wikipedia. https://en.wikipedia.org/wiki/Ontonagon_Boulder. Accessed December 13, 2018.

Parker, Robert Dale, ed. *The Sound the Stars Make Rushing Through the Sky: The Writings of Jane Johnston Schoolcraft*. Philadelphia: U of Pennsylvania P, 2007. Notes throughout book.

Parker, Robert Dale. "Introduction." In *The Sound the Stars Make Rushing Through the Sky: The Writings of Jane Johnston Schoolcraft*. Philadelphia: U of Pennsylvania P, 2007. p. 1-86.

Parker, Robert Dale. "Preface." In *The Sound the Stars Make Rushing Through the Sky: The Writings of Jane Johnston Schoolcraft*. Philadelphia: U of Pennsylvania P, 2007. p. ix-xv.

Paulsen, David. "Northern Michigan Episcopalians Speak Out in Favor of Retiring High School's 'Redmen' Nickname." January 16, 2020. https://www.episcopalnewsservice.org/2020/01/16/northern-michigan-episcopalians-speak-out-in-favor-of-retiring-high-schools-redmen-nickname/. Accessed February 21, 2020.

Peano, Shirley. "Charles Kawbawgam, Chippewa Chief." *Harlow's Wooden Man*. Vol. VII. No. 4. (Fall 1971): 4-5.

Pendill, Olive. Personal Letter. November 6, 1925. Robert J. Graveraet Folder 920 BF. Marquette Regional History Center.

Pepin, John. "Fall Feast: Cultural Event Honors Kawbawgam." *The Mining Journal*. October 5, 2008.

"Pere Marquette Edition." *The Mining Journal*. July 15, 1897.

"Peter Dougherty of Grand Traverse." *Michigan History*. Vol. 51. No. 3. (Fall 1967): 191.

"Peter White of Marquette." *The Detroit Free Press*. September 24, 1905.

"Peter White's Tales of Early Days in the U.P." Publication unknown. Date unknown. In Peter White's Scrapbooks, Vol 1 of 2. Marquette Regional History Center.

Peter Marksman. https://en.wikipedia.org/wiki/Peter_Marksman. Accessed July 21, 2019.

Pitezel, John H. *Lights and Shades of Missionary Life*. Cincinnati, OH: E. P. Thompson Printer, 1862. Kindle Edition.

Poquette, Todd. Personal Interview. December 27, 2019.

"Proposed Marker Inscription, and Other Writings Supportive of It." Madosh Folder BF 920. Marquette Regional History Center.

Prusi, Renee and Bud Sargent. "Discussion Planned on Indian Logos." *The Mining Journal*. April 4, 2000.

Rankin, Carroll W. "Diverting Incidents of Early Days Form Entertaining Paper Read by Mrs. Carroll W. Rankin." *The Mining Journal*. October 16, 1935.

Rankin, Ernest H. "Accounts of Early Indian Missionary in UP Recalled." *The Mining Journal*. March 2, 1967. p. 7.

Rankin, Ernest H. "Mystery of Graveraet's Death Cleared Up by New Discovery." *The Mining Journal*. July 29, 1968.

Rankin, Ernest H. *The Indians of Gitchee Gumee*. Marquette, MI: Marquette County Historical Society, June 1966.

Rankin, Ernest H. "Untitled Manuscript about Robert Graveraet." April 1, 1959. Robert J. Graveraet Folder 920 BF. Marquette Regional History Center.

Resek, Carl. *Lewis Henry Morgan: American Scholar*. Chicago, IL: U of Chicago P, 1960.

Reuter, Dorothy. *Methodist Indian Ministries in Michigan, 1830-1990*. Michigan Area United Methodist Historical Society, 1993.

Ricky, Donald. *Native Peoples A to Z: A Reference Guide to Native Peoples of the Western Hemisphere*. Hamburg, MI: Native American Books, 2009. Vol. 8.

R.L. Polk & Co's Directory 1895-6. Marquette City Directory.

Robb, Patricia McCombie, granddaughter of Maude (Brown) Breer. Personal interview. October 3, 2019.

Robert Dollar. https://en.wikipedia.org/wiki/Robert_Dollar. Accessed November 15, 2018.

Rupley, Richard M. "Civil War Record of Service of Upper Peninsula Volunteers in Michigan Regiments 1861-1866. Manuscript compiled 2004. John M. Longyear Research Library. Marquette Regional History Center.

Russell, James. "Peter White." *Michigan History Magazine*. Vol. 6. (1922): 296-314.

Rydholm, Fred. "U.P., Indians always got along." *The Mining Journal*. July 16, 1999.

Rydholm, Fred. *Superior Heartland: A Backwoods History in Four Parts*. 2 vols. 1989. Ann Arbor, MI: Braunt-Brumfield, 1999.

Sault Evening News. "Indians Urged to Enroll Now: Chippewa Association Will Present Claims to Govt. W. M. Johnston and Cadreau Brothers on Committee." June 30, 1925.

Sault Evening News. "Johnston to Push Claims of Indians." April 11, 1916.

Samuel Morse. Wikipedia. https://en.wikipedia.org/wiki/Samuel_Morse#Telegraph. Accessed May 10, 2019.

Sault Sainte Marie. Wikipedia. https://en.wikipedia.org/wiki/Sault_Ste._Marie,_Michigan#History. Accessed December 11, 2018.

Schenck, Theresa. "Footnotes" to Warren, William W. *History of the Ojibwa People*. 1885. 2nd ed. St. Paul: Minnesota Historical Society, 2009.

Schenck, Theresa. "Introduction." Warren, William W. *History of the Ojibwa People*. 1885. 2nd ed. St. Paul: Minnesota Historical Society, 2009. p. vii-xxiv.

Schoolcraft, Henry Rowe. *Schoolcraft's Ojibwa Lodge Stories: Life on the Lake Superior Frontier*. 1962. East Lansing, MI: Michigan State UP, 1997.

Schoolcraft, Henry Rowe. *The Hiawatha Legends: North American Lore*. 1856. (retitled from: *The Myth of Hiawatha and Other Oral Legends, Mythologic and Allegoric, of the North American Indians*. Marquette, MI: Avery Color Studios, 1997.

Schoolcraft, Jane Johnston. *The Sound the Stars Make Rushing Through the Sky: The Writings of Jane Johnston Schoolcraft*. Philadelphia: U of Pennsylvania P, 2007.

Shiras, George. *Hunting Wild Life With Camera and Flashlight*. 2 Vols. Washington, DC: National Geographic Society, 1935.

Shiras, George. *Justice George Shiras Jr. of Pittsburgh: Associate Justice of the United States Supreme Court 1892-1903*. Pittsburgh: U of Pittsburg P, 1953.

Showano, Charles. Chippewa County Probate Court Document. August 21, 1935. Native American Affairs, Folder 5. Special Collections. Judge Joseph H. Steere Room. Bayliss Library. Sault Sainte Marie, Michigan.

Smith, Chief John. https://en.wikipedia.org/wiki/John_Smith_(Chippewa_Indian). Accessed November 17, 2018.

Stafford, Morgan Hewitt. *A Genealogy of the Kidder Family*. Rutland, VT: The Tuttle Publishing Co. n.d.

Stanley, Jennifer. "Charles Kawbawgam: Chief of the Chippewa." *Marquette Monthly*. July 1997. p. 14-16.

"Statue of Kaw-Baw-Gam." Publication unknown but likely printed in *The Mining Journal* in 1903. Peter White Papers. Burton Historical Collection. Detroit Public Library. Box 104. Microfilm Reel 3 of collection at Peter White Public Library, Marquette, Michigan.

Stone, Frank B. "The Kawbawgam Pictures." Manuscript. Marquette Regional History Center. September 2001.

Stone, Frank B. *Philo Marshall Everett: Father of Michigan's Iron Industry and Founder of the City of Marquette*. Baltimore, MD: Gateway Press, 1997.

Strom, Peter W. "Three Generations of Brothertons Remembered." Manuscript dated March 15, 2000. Delta County Historical Society Archives. Escanaba, Michigan.

Swineford, A. P. *History and Review of the Copper, Iron, Silver, Slate and Other Material Interests of the South Shore of Lake Superior*. Marquette, MI: *The Mining Journal*, 1876.

Sundstrom, E. J. "Sault Indians Reject Final Settlement of 1820 Treaty." *The Evening News*. January 7, 1969.

Tanner, John. *The Falcon: A Narrative of the Captivity and Adventures of John Tanner*. 1830. New York: Penguin Books, 2003. Kindle ebook.

Terando, Jerry and Genevieve. Correspondence and Manuscripts. Madosh Family Folder BF 920. Marquette Regional History Center.

The Kawbawgam: 1928. Marquette, MI: Northern Normal School, 1928. Marquette Regional History Center.

The Mining Journal. "60 Years Ago." December 1, 1961.

The Mining Journal. "Acquisitive Mr. Madosh." May 17, 1893. p. 8.

The Mining Journal. "A Day in France." June 23, 1894.

The Mining Journal. "Again in the Courts." June 16, 1888. p. 8. col. 2.

The Mining Journal. "A Historic Case Decided." October 19, 1889. p. 4. col. 6.

The Mining Journal. "Alfred Kidder to Leave." November 16, 1901. p. 8.

The Mining Journal. "An Industrial Semi-Centennial." July 16, 1900.

The Mining Journal. "An Outrage." January 29, 1887. p. 1.

The Mining Journal. "Anent Charley Kaw Baw Gam: Detroit Lawyer Presents Some Information Regarding His History." January 8, 1903. p. 8.

The Mining Journal. "Archeologist Kidder, Native Of Marquette, Dies In East." December 8, 1950.

The Mining Journal. "Bust of Koboggam." December 14, 1901. p. 1.

The Mining Journal. "Charley Boggum Reminiscitur." July 17, 1905. p. 5. col. 4.

The Mining Journal. "City Brevities." December 31, 1902.

The Mining Journal. "City Brevities." May 28, 1904. p. 8. col. 3.

The Mining Journal. "Death of Mrs. Compeau." July 5, 1913. p. 1.

The Mining Journal. "Dr. Howard H. Kidder's Letter Gives Echoes of Incidents of Earlier Days in Marquette." March 12, 1937.

The Mining Journal. "Dr. James H. Dawson Read Two Biographies Of Marquette Men At Annual Historical Meeting." October 20, 1938. p. 14.

The Mining Journal. "Ellen J. Clark, Resident Here 89 Years, Dies." April 21, 1938.

The Mining Journal. "Father Marquette." January 7, 1895.

The Mining Journal. "Glorious Fourth." July 6, 1891.

The Mining Journal. "Got a Ten-Year Sentence: Mr. Tommy Madosh and Marquette Clothes-Lines Dissolve Partnership for Ten Years." May 22, 1893. p. 8.

The Mining Journal. "His Features in Enduring Marble: Bust of the Hon. Peter White Unveiled with a Fine Public Demonstration." May 25, 1898.

The Mining Journal. "Indian Marriages." November 2, 1889. p. 4. col. 6.

The Mining Journal. "Indian Motif Will Be Stressed in Winter Carnival; Old Boat Yields Stories About Red Man." January 12, 1940.

The Mining Journal. "Is 102 Years Old." July 25, 1902. p. 8. col. 4.

The Mining Journal. "Jerry Campeau, 80 Years Old, Is Dead." September 3, 1930. p. 3.

The Mining Journal. "Kaw-baw-gam Dead." December 29, 1902. p. 8.

The Mining Journal. "Kaw-Baw-Gam: Interesting Facts Regarding the Old Chippewa's History." February 14, 1903. p. 8. col. 2.

The Mining Journal. "Kawbawgam's Snowshoes Sent to Historical Society, on Display in Bank Lobby." February 24, 1964.

The Mining Journal. "Legendary Account of U.P. Trader Recalled." June 14, 1958. p. 5.

The Mining Journal. "Madosh's Inventory." May 19, 1893. p. 8.

The Mining Journal. "Marji Gesick's Descendants Lost Case Against Iron Firm." Date unknown. Photocopy of article in Kawbawgam Family Folder 920 BF. Marquette Regional History Center.

The Mining Journal. "More Madosh Plunder." May 20, 1893. p. 8.

The Mining Journal. "Mrs. Jacques LaPique [sic] Drowned." November 7, 1874. p. 5.

The Mining Journal. "MSHS Students Vote Again On Logo Decision." June 10, 1999.

The Mining Journal. "Natural Monument to Chippewa Chief: Huge Granite Boulder Found on Presque Isle Set Up at Kaw-baw-gam's Grave." October 3, 1912. p. 8.

The Mining Journal. No Title. Brief Article about Kawbawgam Killing a Catamount. December 20, 1888. p. 5, col. 2.

The Mining Journal. "Obituary: August Madosh." June 17, 1963.

The Mining Journal. "Obituary: Frederick Cadotte." April 29, 1926.

The Mining Journal. "Obituary: George Madosh." February 27, 1926.

The Mining Journal. "Obituary: Helen Marie Madosh." September 4, 2002.

The Mining Journal. "Obituary: Henry Melvin Madosh." July 27, 2017. http://www.miningjournal.net/obituaries/2017/07/henry-melvin-madosh/. Accessed February 22, 2019.

The Mining Journal. "Obituary: John D. Madosh." March 11, 1905. p. 8.

The Mining Journal. "Obituary: Leander A. Madosh." February 24, 1961.

The Mining Journal. "Obituary: Mary Madosh." March 22, 1910. p. 10.

The Mining Journal. "Obituary: Mrs. Madosh." September 27, 1894. p. 8.

The Mining Journal. "Obituary: Mrs. Margaret Madosh." December 1, 1966.

The Mining Journal. Obituary: Michelle Richarda "Madosh" Kohn. July 6, 2018. http://www.miningjournal.net/obituaries/2018/07/michelle-richarda-madosh-kohn/. Accessed February 21, 2019.

The Mining Journal. "Obituary: Raymond Trevillion." March 2001. http://www.genealogybuff.com/mi/marquette/webbbs_config.pl/noframes/read/18. Accessed February 22, 2019.

The Mining Journal. "On Presque Isle: Chief Kaw-Baw-Gam's Remains Will Lie There." December 30, 1902. p. 8.

The Mining Journal. "Ray Brotherton, Prominent Negaunee Resident, Authority on Area History, Dies at 77." October 28, 1960.

The Mining Journal. "Redmen Logo Lawsuit Dismissed." May 3, 2000.

The Mining Journal. "School Logo Too Macho?" May 25, 1999.

The Mining Journal. "Scout Pageant Will Honor Chief Charlie Kawbawgam." September 23, 1965.

The Mining Journal. "Songs of La Belle France." June 26, 1894.

The Mining Journal. "The Guardian of Presque Isle." January 8, 1887. p. 8. col. 1.

The Mining Journal. "Thirty Years Ago." December 29, 1932.

The Mining Journal. "Tommy Taking Inventory: Marquette's Champion Kleptomaniac Parcelling Out His Spoils Among His Victims." May 18, 1893. p. 8.

The Mining Journal. "Voices of the Ojibwa: Once Obscure Manuscript Brings Indian Lore to Life." September 17, 1994. p. 3-4.

Tichelaar, Tyler R. *Haunted Marquette: Ghost Stories from the Queen City*. Marquette, MI: Marquette Fiction, 2017.

Tichelaar, Tyler R. *Iron Pioneers: The Marquette Trilogy, Book One*. Lincoln, NB: iUniverse, 2006.

Tichelaar, Tyler R. *My Marquette: Explore the Queen City of the North, Its History, People, and Places*. Marquette, MI: Marquette Fiction, 2010.

Tichelaar, Tyler R. *Spirit of the North: A Paranormal Romance*. Marquette, MI: Marquette Fiction, 2012.

Tichelaar, Tyler R. *Superior Heritage: The Marquette Trilogy, Book Three*. Marquette, MI: Marquette Fiction, 2007.

Tichelaar, Tyler R. "The Many Lives of Pierre LeBlanc." *U.P. Reader*. Issue 4. Ann Arbor, MI: UP Publishers and Authors Association, 2020.

Tichelaar, Tyler R. *The Queen City: The Marquette Trilogy, Book Two.* Lincoln, NB: iUniverse, 2006.

Tilton, Robert S. *Pocahontas: The Evolution of an American Narrative.* New York, NY: Cambridge UP, 1994.

Tinder, David V. *Directory of Early Michigan Photographers.* Ed. Clayton A. Lewis. Ann Arbor, MI: U of M, William L. Clements Library. Online edition updated December 2013. http://clements.umich.edu/eadadd/tinder_directory.pdf?fbclid=I-wAR0Xba-SoVhuL9TBwX6I6NO24tDdAycxTtmwSrFAaHL-si89Os4BBtpER1L0. Accessed July 16, 2019.

Traver, Robert (pseudonym of John Voelker). *Laughing Whitefish.* New York: McGraw-Hill, 1965.

Trentanove, Gaetano. https://en.wikipedia.org/wiki/Gaetano_Trentanove. Accessed August 28, 2018.

Trentanove, Gaetano. Letter to Albert F. Koepcke. June 11, 1903. Peter White Papers. Burton Historical Collection. Detroit Public Library. Box 104. Microfilm Reel 3 of collection at Peter White Public Library, Marquette, Michigan.

Trentanove, Gaetano. Letter to Albert F. Koepcke. August 12, 1903. Peter White Papers. Burton Historical Collection. Detroit Public Library. Box 104. Microfilm Reel 3 of collection at Peter White Public Library, Marquette, Michigan.

"Tristram Randolph Kidder." Wikipedia. https://en.wikipedia.org/wiki/Tristram_Randolph_Kidder. Accessed August 27, 2018.

"Twice Mayor of Marquette." Article about Frederick Owen Clark. Unknown source but probably *The Mining Journal.* Unknown date. Frederick Owen Clark Folder 920 BF. Marquette Regional History Center.

Untitled Manuscripts. Robert J. Graveraet Folder 920 BF. Marquette Regional History Center.

"Unveiling Day Jubilee." Unknown source. July 1897. Marquette, Jacques Statues Folder. BF 920. Marquette Regional History Center.

Vassar Times. "Peter White Will Teach a Bunch of Young Men Chippewa War Dance." August 16, 1907.

Verwyst, P. Chrysostomus. *Life and Labors of Rt. Rev. Bishop Baraga.* Milwaukee, M. H. Witzius, 1900.

Warren, William W. *History of the Ojibwa People*. 1885. 2nd ed. St. Paul: Minnesota Historical Society, 2009.

"Was a Famous Chief: Kaw-baw-gum of the Chippewas Is Dead. *Lake Superior Journal*. Sault Ste. Marie, MI, January, 1903. Available at http://www.rootsweb.ancestry.com/~michcgs/Kawbawgam.html. Accessed November 17, 2018.

Wentworth, Thomas P. *Early Life Among the Indians: Reminiscences from the Life of Benj. G. Armstrong*. Ashland, WI: A. W. Bowron, 1892.

Wesley Newspaper Bureau. "Teaches Indian Steps." July 1907.

White, Peter. "Address at the Opening of the Escanaba High School." Peter White Papers. Burton Historical Collection. Detroit Public Library. Box 52. Microfilm Reel 3 of collection at Peter White Public Library, Marquette, Michigan.

White, Peter. "Kaw-baw-gam 1902." Published in "Memorial Reports Marquette County 1902" in *Michigan Historical Commission*. Vol. XXXIII. Michigan State Historical Society, 1904.

White, Peter. Letter to Mayor Alfred Swineford. February 1, 1875. Peter White Papers. Burton Historical Collection. Detroit Public Library. Box 129. Microfilm Reel 3 of collection at Peter White Public Library, Marquette, Michigan.

White, Peter. Letter to Mr. Dickinson. August 18, 1888. Peter White Papers. Burton Historical Collection. Detroit Public Library. Box 117. Microfilm Reel 3 of collection at Peter White Public Library, Marquette, Michigan.

White, Peter. Letter to President Grover Cleveland. March 1, 1893. Peter White Papers. Burton Historical Collection. Detroit Public Library. Box 117. Microfilm Reel 3 of collection at Peter White Public Library, Marquette, Michigan.

White, Peter. "My Recollections of Early Marquette: Read Before the Marquette Y.M.C.A., 1889." Peter White Papers. Burton Historical Collection. Detroit Public Library. Box 136. Microfilm Reel 3 of collection at Peter White Public Library, Marquette, Michigan.

Williams, Ralph D. *The Honorable Peter White: A Biographical Sketch of the Lake Superior Iron Country*. 1905. Cleveland, OH: Freshwater Press, 1986.

Wittler, Jo. "Longyear's Landlooking." *The Mining Journal*. September 6, 2017. p. 7A.

Wittler, Jo. Personal Email. January 13, 2020.

Woodbury, Richard B. *Alfred V. Kidder*. New York, NY: Columbia UP, 1973.

Woolson, Constance Fenimore. "On the Iron Mountain." *Appleton's Journal*. Vol. 9. No. 204 (February 15, 1873): 225-30.

Endnotes

Introduction

1. *The Mining Journal*. "On Presque Isle…." p. 8.

Chapter 1: Kawbawgam's Birth and Family Background

1. Marquette County Death Record. Kawbawgam, Charles.
2. *The Mining Journal*. "Kaw-baw-gam Dead."
3. *The Mining Journal*. "An Industrial Semi-Centennial."
4. State of Michigan Supreme Court. Jeremy Compo vs. The Jackson Iron Company. p. 35.
5. *The Mining Journal*. "Again in the Courts." p. 8.
6. Kidder, *Ojibwa*, p. 159; Arbric, *City of the Rapids*, p. 58.
7. LaLone, "Black Cloud—Oshawano Family," p. 1.
8. *The Mining Journal*. "Kaw-Baw-Gam: Interesting Facts…"
9. Chippewa County Marriage Records. Charles Makatak-wat to Charlotte Madjikijiki.
10. Barney p. 6.
11. Kohl p. 275.
12. Tilton p. 91.
13. Kidder, *Ojibwa*, p. 159; Kappler p. 729-30.
14. Kidder, *Ojibwa*, p. 159.
15. *The Mining Journal*. "Scout Pageant." p. 65.
16. Kohl p. 275.
17. Bourgeois p. 14-15.
18. Kappler p. 188.
19. Bourgeois p. 14-15.

20. Nertoli p. 6; Kappler p. 544.
21. Kappler p. 651.
22. Kidder, *Ojibwa*, p. 112.
23. Nertoli p. 1.
24. Warren p. 53, note 30.
25. LaLone, "Shingabowossin Family," p. 1.
26. LaLone, "Shingabowossin Family," p. 2.
27. LaLone, "Black Cloud Family," p. 1; https://www.ancestry.com/genealogy/records/chief-louis-chekatchogemau_99456465.
28. LaLone, "Black Cloud—Oshawano Family," p. 1.
29. Nertoli p. 2.
30. LaLone, "Black Cloud—Oshawano Family," p. 1.
31. Bourgeois p. 15.
32. Maynard p. 7; Kidder p. 15.
33. Verwyst p. 72.
34. Kohl p. 111.
35. Mead p. 20-21.
36. Boyer, "Charlie Kawbawgam," p. 2; *The Mining Journal*. "Anent Charley Kaw Baw Gam."
37. LaLone, "Black Cloud—Oshawano Family," p. 1; Boyer, "Charlie Kawbawgam," p. 2.
38. LaLone, "Black Cloud—Oshawano Family," p. 1.
39. LaLone, "Black Cloud—Oshawano Family," p. 1; Kienitz.
40. Chippewa County Marriage Records. John Roussain to Charlotte Shawono.
41. LaLone, "Black Cloud—Oshawano Family," p. 4-5.
42. LaLone, "Black Cloud—Oshawano Family," p. 4-5.
43. 1880 Census, Chippewa County, Michigan.
44. Ricky p. 142; Knight and Chute p. 267, note 22.
45. Cleland, *Rites of Conquest*, p. 179.
46. Boyer, "Charlie Kawbawgam," p. 2.
47. *The Mining Journal*, "Anent Charley Kaw Baw Gam," p. 2-3.
48. *Enquirer and News*, "Albion's 'copper-colored sons of the forest.'"
49. LaLone, "Black Cloud—Oshawano Family," p. 1.
50. Bayliss et al. p. 226.
51. Hendricks p. 6.
52. Warren p. 18-19.
53. Schenck p. 20, note 5.
54. Cleland, *The Place of the Pike*, p. 5-6.

55. Warren p. 17.
56. Bourgeois p. 12.
57. Cleland, *The Place of the Pike*, p. 6.
58. Warren p. 18-19.
59. Cleland, *The Place of the Pike*, p. 6.
60. Bourgeois p. 13-14.
61. Warren p. 9.
62. Cleland, *The Place of the Pike*, p. 1.
63. Arbric, *City of the Rapids*, p. 21.
64. Bayliss et al. p. 301.
65. Arbric, *City of the Rapids*, p. 17.
66. McCommons p. 2.
67. Warren p. 48.
68. Magnaghi, *Upper*, p. 30.
69. Warren p. 50-51.
70. Warren p. 21.
71. Warren p. 21-22.
72. Warren p. 21.
73. Schoolcraft p. 29-30.
74. Warren p. 224.
75. Warren p. 89, note 6.
76. Warren p. 227.
77. Schenck, "Footnotes," p. 224.
78. Rydholm, *Superior Heartland*, p. 137.
79. Bourgeois p. 15.
80. Danzinger p. 14.
81. Kohl p. 228.
82. Kohl p. 236-37.
83. Kohl p. 238-42.
84. Chute p. 42-43.

Chapter 2: Ojibwa and American Relations at Sault Sainte Marie: 1820-1845

1. Cleland, *The Place of the Pike*, p. 1; Warren p. xvii-xviii.
2. Warren p. 287.
3. Magnaghi, *Upper*, p. 29.
4. Bourgeois p. 12.
5. Magnaghi, *Upper*, p. 29.
6. Magnaghi, *Upper*, p. 29.

7. Cleland, *The Place of the Pike*, p. 7.
8. Blackbird, Chapter 1.
9. Magnaghi, *Upper*, p. 29.
10. Warren p. 72.
11. Kohl p. 244-47.
12. Hambleton and Stoutamire p. 12.
13. Cleland, *The Place of the Pike*, p. 34.
14. Parker, "Introduction," p. 43.
15. Magnaghi, *Upper*, p. 54.
16. Magnaghi, *Upper*, p. 55.
17. Magnaghi, *Native*, p. 72.
18. Magnaghi, *Upper*, p. 56.
19. Edmunds p. 38.
20. Edmunds p. 51.
21. Magnaghi, *Native*, p. 74-75.
22. Magnaghi, *Native*, p. 75.
23. Warren p. 231.
24. Magnaghi, *Native*, p. 77; Blackbird, Chapter 4; Warren p. 228-31.
25. Magnaghi, *Upper*, p. 56.
26. Bayliss et al. p. 134-35.
27. Arbric, *City of the Rapids*, p. 57.
28. Lewis p. 96.
29. https://en.wikipedia.org/wiki/Lewis_Cass_expedition.
30. Arbric, *City of the Rapids*, p. 57; Graham p. 67; Magnaghi, *Native*, p. 82; Williams p. 87.
31. Hambleton and Stoutamire p. 14-15; Cleland, *The Place of the Pike*, p. 16-17.
32. Cleland, *The Place of the Pike*, p. 16-17; Lewis p. 99-100.
33. Lewis p. 99-100.
34. Lewis p. 100; Graham p. 67.
35. Arbric, *City of the Rapids*, p. 56-57; Lewis p. 101; Cleland, *Rites of Conquest*, p. 85.
36. Cleland, *The Place of the Pike*, p. 18.
37. Arbric, *City of the Rapids*, p. 58.
38. Cleland, *The Place of the Pike*, p. 18; Lewis p. 101.
39. "Ancient Anishinaabek Burial Ground."
40. Cleland, *The Place of the Pike*, p. 18.
41. Lewis p. 106.
42. Chute p. 33; Cleland, *The Place of the Pike*, p. 18-19; Lewis p. 101,

106; Graham p. 67.
43. Lewis p. 101; Magnaghi, *Native*, p. 82; Cleland, *The Place of the Pike*, p. 18-19.
44. Chute p. 34.
45. Arbric, *City of the Rapids*, p. 61.
46. Williams p. 87; Hambleton and Stoutamire p. 34.
47. Mason p. xxvi.
48. Lewis p. 107.
49. Magnaghi, *Native*, p. 84.
50. Magnaghi, *Native*, p. 85.
51. Lewis p. 107.
52. Lewis p. 112.
53. Bieder p. xxviii-ix.
54. Arbric, *City of the Rapids*, p. 68.
55. Magnaghi, *Upper*, p. 61.
56. Arbric, *City of the Rapids*, p. 86-88.
57. Magnaghi, *Upper*, p. 61; https://en.wikipedia.org/wiki/Sault_Ste._Marie,_Michigan#History.
58. Lewis p. 113.
59. Schoolcraft, *Ojibwa Lodge*, p. 16-17.
60. Magnaghi, *Native*, p. 87; Schoolcraft, *Ojibwa Lodge*, p. 59.
61. Mason p. xxv; Schoolcraft, *Ojibwa Lodge*, p. 169, note 23.
62. Warren p. 224, note 2.
63. Magnaghi, *Upper*, p. 59.
64. Longtine p. 178.
65. Parker, "Introduction," p. 21.
66. Parker, "Introduction," p. 45.
67. Mason, "Introduction," p. xxiv.
68. Lewis p. 189.
69. Lewis p. 119-20.
70. Lewis p. 122.
71. Parker, *The Sound the Stars*, p. 124-25.
72. Schoolcraft, *Hiawatha*, p. 19.
73. Schoolcraft, *Hiawatha*, p. 20.
74. Magnaghi, *Native*, p. 102.
75. Verwyst p. 4.
76. Tilton p. 11, 28-29.
77. Tilton p. 25.
78. Parker, "Introduction," p. 45.

79. Magnaghi, *Upper*, p. 59.
80. Parker, "Introduction," p. 2.
81. Hambleton and Stoutamire p. 44; Bremer p. 308.
82. Cleland, *The Place of the Pike*, p. 19.
83. Cleland, *The Place of the Pike*, p. 19.
84. Cleland, *The Place of the Pike*, p. 19.
85. Cleland, *The Place of the Pike*, p. 20.
86. Cleland, *The Place of the Pike*, p. 21.
87. Hambleton and Stoutamire p. 19; Cleland, *The Place of the Pike*, p. 21.
88. Cleland, *The Place of the Pike*, p. 22.
89. Cleland, *The Place of the Pike*, p. 84.
90. Magnaghi, *Upper*, p. 60.
91. Cleland, *The Place of the Pike*, p. 22-24; Cleland, *Rites of Conquest*, p. 228.
92. Blackbird, Chapter 6.
93. Chute p. 67-68.
94. Kidder, *Ojibwa*, p. 112.
95. Chute p. 191, 205-6, 358.
96. Magnaghi, *Upper*, p. 75; https://en.wikipedia.org/wiki/Samuel_Morse#Telegraph.
97. Williams p. 92.

Chapter 3: Marriage and Mining

1. Bourgeois p. 16-17.
2. Chippewa County Marriage Records. Charles Makatak-wat to Charlotte Madjikijiki.
3. Chute p. 22.
4. Kawbawgam-Nolin Manuscript.
5. Cleland, *Rites of Conquest*, p. 250.
6. Berger, "Mah-je-ge-zhik Was Remarkable Man."
7. State of Michigan Supreme Court. Jeremy Compo vs. The Jackson Iron Company, p. 20.
8. State of Michigan Supreme Court. Jeremy Compo vs. The Jackson Iron Company, p. 21.
9. Lingle; Madosh Folder 497.3 B23d.
10. Terando-Cadotte documents.
11. Boyer, "Charlie Kawbawgam," p. 4-6.
12. Magnaghi, *Native*, p. 92.
13. Rydholm, *Superior Heartland*, p. 100; Kawbawgam-Nolin Manuscript.

14. State of Michigan Supreme Court. Jeremy Compo vs. The Jackson Iron Company, p. 24.
15. 3Rs Team p. 5.
16. Terando-Cadotte documents.
17. Kirtland deposition p. 67-68.
18. 1884 Susan Ge-Shik; Mead p. 19-20.
19. Mead p. 20; State of Michigan Supreme Court. Jeremy Compo vs. The Jackson Iron Company, p. 25, 31.
20. Bourgeois p. 16-17.
21. McCann, "Charlotte Kawbawgam vs. The Jackson Iron Company." Part 2. p. 18.
22. Magnaghi, *Native*, p. 115.
23. Boyer p. 5; Lingle p. 2; *The Mining Journal*, "Kaw-baw-gam: Interesting Facts…"; Rydholm, *Superior Heartland*, p. 137.
24. *The Mining Journal*, "Kaw-baw-gam: Interesting Facts…"
25. Swineford p. 91; Maynard p. 2.
26. Stone p. 16.
27. Swineford p. 93.
28. Swineford p. 93.
29. Swineford p. 94.
30. Swineford p. 94-95.
31. Stone p. 19.
32. Stone p. 20-21.
33. Stone p. 27-31.
34. Stone p. 25; Madosh Folder.
35. Stone p. 27.
36. Maynard p. 2-4.
37. Stone p. 39-41.
38. Stone p. 42.
39. Stone p. 44.
40. Swineford p. 96.
41. Stone p. 44.
42. Stone p. 157, note 38.
43. Stone p. 6-7.
44. Swineford p. 97.
45. Woolson p. 226.
46. Stone p. 46.
47. https://en.wikipedia.org/wiki/Ontonagon_Boulder.
48. Lewis p. 116.

49. Lewis p. 167-68.
50. Kohl p. 60-63.
51. https://en.wikipedia.org/wiki/Ontonagon_Boulder.
52. https://en.wikipedia.org/wiki/Ontonagon_Boulder#Attempt_to_recover_the_boulder.
53. Kohl p. 60.
54. Swineford p. 252-53.
55. Mead p. 9-10; Maynard p. 5; Rydholm, *Superior Heartland*, p. 139; Stone p. 65-68.
56. Kidder, "Charlotte," p. 7; Mead p. 9.
57. Kirtland deposition, p. 67-68.
58. Everett deposition, p. 95.
59. Magnaghi, *Native*, p. 120.
60. Rydholm, *Superior Heartland*, p. 139.
61. *The Mining Journal*, "Marji Gesick's Descendants Lost Case."
62. Pitezel, Chapter 6.
63. Pitezel, Chapter 24.

Chapter 4: Marquette's Founding and Early Years

1. Rydholm, *Superior Heartland*, p. 140-41.
2. Rydholm, *Superior Heartland*, p. 146.
3. "Untitled Manuscripts." Robert J. Graveraet Folder.
4. "Untitled Manuscripts." Robert J. Graveraet Folder.
5. October 13, 1977 article. Title and publication unknown. Graveraet Family Folders.
6. "Peter Dougherty of Grand Traverse"; Rankin, Ernest H., "Untitled Manuscript"; LaLone, "Graveraet Family."
7. Rydholm, *Superior Heartland*, p. 148.
8. Robert J. Graveraet Folder.
9. 1824 George Boyd letter to Lewis Cass. Robert J. Graveraet Folder.
10. "Untitled Manuscripts." Robert J. Graveraet Folder.
11. "Untitled Manuscripts." Robert J. Graveraet Folder.
12. "Untitled Manuscripts." Robert J. Graveraet Folder.
13. Pendill, Olive letter. November 6, 1925.
14. "Peter Dougherty of Grand Traverse" p. 191.
15. Stone p. 73.
16. Stone p. 76.
17. Stone p. 78-81.
18. Stone p. 81.

19. Stone p. 83.
20. Magnaghi, *Native*, p. 116.
21. Magnaghi, *Native*, p. 119.
22. Kawbawgam, Typed Manuscript. 977.495 J63M in Kawbawgam Folder BF 920 Marquette Regional History Center. Probably from 1881.
23. Rankin, Ernest H. "Untitled Manuscript."
24. State of Michigan Supreme Court. Jeremy Compo vs. The Jackson Iron Company, p. 32.
25. State of Michigan Supreme Court. Jeremy Compo vs. The Jackson Iron Company, p. 37.
26. State of Michigan Supreme Court. Jeremy Compo vs. The Jackson Iron Company, p. 37.
27. Bourgeois p. 16-17.
28. "Peter White's Tales…"
29. "Peter White's Tales…"
30. *The Mining Journal*, "Kaw-baw-gam Dead."
31. Swineford p. 105.
32. *The Mining Journal*, "Kaw-baw-gam Dead."
33. Swineford p. 105.
34. Swineford p. 105-6.
35. Boyer, "Charlie Kawbawgam," p. 4-6.
36. Boyer, "Charlie Kawbawgam," p. 5; *The Mining Journal*. "Kaw-Baw-Gam: Interesting Facts…"
37. Boyer p. 5; Longtine p. 220.
38. *The Mining Journal*, "Indian Motif."
39. Bourgeois p. 12.
40. Maynard p. 12.
41. Barney p. 8.
42. "Peter White of Marquette." *The Detroit Free Press*.
43. http://www.mifamilyhistory.org/mimack/military/EarlyMilitary/officerindex.asp
44. "Inspirer of Poems."
45. Williams p. 30-35.
46. Barney p. 6.
47. Rankin, Ernest H. *The Indians of Gitchee Gumee*, p. 21-22.
48. Kidder, *Ojibwa*, p. 145.
49. Stone p. 71; Rydholm, *Superior Heartland*, p. 146. Stone says 1846 but Rydholm says 1847.
50. Maynard p. 11.

51. *The Mining Journal*. "Ellen J. Clark..."
52. Lill p. v.
53. Lill p. v.
54. Niemi p. 6A
55. Maynard p. 9-10.
56. Williams p. 41.
57. White, "Address at the Opening of the Escanaba High School," p. 3.
58. Williams p. 42-43; Rydholm, *Superior Heartland*, p. 158-61.
59. *The Mining Journal*. "The Guardian of Presque Isle."
60. Swineford p. 111; Williams p. 43.
61. Williams p. 47-48.
62. White, "Address at the Opening of the Escanaba High School," p. 4.
63. Magnaghi, *Native*, p. 126.
64. Cleland, *The Place of the Pike*, p. 45.
65. Maynard p. 12.
66. https://en.wikipedia.org/wiki/Escanaba,_Michigan.
67. Stone p. 105-107.
68. 1871 date handwritten on back of photograph, Judge H. Steere Room, Bayliss Public Library; interpretive panel, Water Street, Sault Sainte Marie. The panel says the photograph is from the Bayliss Public Library, so an 1871 date seems more likely.
69. Magnaghi, "Observations."
70. Letter Mrs. Ball to Olive Pendill 1920.
71. Stone p. 93-94.
72. Stone p. 94.
73. Magnaghi, *Native*, p. 123-24.
74. Magnaghi, *Native*, p. 92, 112-13.
75. Verwyst p. 8-9.
76. Blackbird, Chapter 6.
77. Stone p. 94.
78. Letter Mrs. Ball to Olive Pendill 1921.
79. *History of the Precious Blood Cathedral, Part III*, p. 7.
80. *History of the Precious Blood Cathedral, Part III*, p. 7.
81. *St. Mary's Catholic Church Baptisms*. p. 79.
82. *History of the Precious Blood Cathedral, Part III*, p. 15.
83. *The Mining Journal*, "A Day in France"; *The Mining Journal*, "Songs of La Belle France."
84. Williams p. 127-30.
85. Williams p. 131.

86. Maynard p. 10.
87. Kelley, *Marine*, p. 26.
88. Kelley, *Marine*, p. 27.
89. Kelley, *Marine*, p. 28.
90. Kelley, *Marine*, p. 28.
91. James Kelley letter to Peter White 1906.
92. *The Mining Journal*, "Dr. James H. Dawson."
93. Rankin, Carroll W.
94. Rydholm, *Superior Heartland*, p. 132.
95. Dobson.
96. Chute p. 224.
97. Arbric, *Sugar Island Sampler*, p. 79.
98. Arbric, *Sugar Island Sampler*, p. 99.
99. Bayliss et al. p. 91.
100. "Untitled Manuscripts." Robert J. Graveraet Folder.
101. Rankin, Ernest H. "Mystery."
102. Rankin, Ernest H. "Mystery."
103. Graveraet obituary, available at http://www.mainlymichigan.com/Native%20Americans.GRAVERAET-Family-Page.ashx.
104. Barney p. 12.
105. Brinks, *Peter White: A Career....* p. 31.
106. "Untitled Manuscripts." Robert J. Graveraet Folder.
107. Rankin, Ernest H. "Mystery."
108. Rankin, Ernest H. "Mystery."
109. Rankin, Ernest H. "Mystery."
110. Williams p. 23.
111. Rydholm, *Superior Heartland*, p. 315-18.
112. Magnaghi, *Upper*, p. 33.

Chapter 5: Back at the Sault, 1846-1856

1. Cleland, *The Place of the Pike*, p. 32.
2. https://en.wikipedia.org/wiki/Peter_Marksman. See also Pitezel, *Lights and Shades of Missionary Life*, where Marksman is mentioned numerous times.
3. Cleland, *The Place of the Pike*, p. 32.
4. Quoted in Arbric, *City of the Rapids*, p. 110.
5. https://wc.rootsweb.ancestry.com/cgi-bin/igm.cgi?op=GET&db=mychipmans&id=I2363.
6. https://en.wikipedia.org/wiki/Nathaniel_Chipman#Family, https://

en.wikipedia.org/wiki/Henry_C._Chipman.
7. Chipman p. 11.
8. Kappler p. 729-30.
9. Chipman p. 11.
10. Chipman p. 53-54.
11. https://www.ancestry.com/boards/topics.ethnic.natam.intertribal.mi/666/mb.ashx.
12. LaLone p. 6; https://wc.rootsweb.ancestry.com/cgi-bin/igm.cgi?op=GET&db=mychipmans&id=I2363; https://www.ancestry.com/genealogy/records/john-logan-chipman_34772955.
13. Maynard p. 7; Chipman p. 190.
14. https://wc.rootsweb.ancestry.com/cgi-bin/igm.cgi?op=GET&db=mychipmans&id=I2363.
15. https://en.wikipedia.org/wiki/John_Logan_Chipman.
16. LaLone, "Black Cloud—Oshawano Family," p. 5.
17. Dana p. 46.
18. Gilbert. "Memories of the 'Soo.'"
19. Magnaghi, *Native*, p. 104; Lewis p. 187.
20. Dana p. 38, note 4.
21. Chute p. 115.
22. Arbric and Steinhaus. https://www.lakesuperior.com/the-lake/maritime/how-the-soo-locks-were-made/.
23. Magnaghi, *Natives*, p. 126.
24. Lewis p. 223.
25. Gilbert. "Memories of the 'Soo'."
26. Arbric, *City of the Rapids*, p. 128.
27. Arbric, *City of the Rapids*, p. 125.
28. Magnaghi, *Native*, p. 123, 125.
29. Magnaghi, *Upper*, p. 74; Magnaghi, *Native*, p. 125.
30. Magnaghi, *Native*, p. 127-28.
31. Magnaghi, *Native*, p. 124.
32. Kohl p. 425-26.
33. Magnaghi, *Native*, p. 127.
34. Hambleton and Stoutamire p. 72.
35. Magnaghi, *Native*, p. 128.
36. https://www.cmich.edu/library/clarke/ResearchResources/Native_American_Material/Treaty_Rights/Text_of_Michigan_Related_Treaties/Detroit_1855/Pages/Ottawa-and-Chippewa.aspx.
37. https://www.cmich.edu/library/clarke/ResearchResources/Native_

American_Material/Treaty_Rights/Text_of_Michigan_Related_Treaties/Detroit_1855/Pages/Chippewa-of-Sault-Ste.-Marie.aspx.

38. Bourgeois p. 15.
39. *The Mining Journal*. "Anent Charley Kaw Baw Gam." p. 2-3.
40. Gilbert. "Memories of the 'Soo'."
41. Gilbert. "Memories of the 'Soo'."
42. Lewis p. 224.
43. Cleland, *The Place of the Pike*, p. 28.
44. Cleland, *The Place of the Pike*, p. 28-30.
45. Kappler p. 729-30.
46. Magnaghi, *Native*, p. 130.
47. Cleland, *The Place of the Pike*, p. 45-46.
48. Kohl p. 54-57.
49. Kohl p. 367.
50. Kohl p. 372.
51. Kohl p. 428.

Chapter 6: Jacques LePique

1. Kidder, *Ojibwa*, p. 129.
2. Kidder, *Ojibwa*, p. 129, note 96.
3. Kidder, *Ojibwa*, p. 139.
4. Kawbawgam-Nolin Manuscript.
5. Kidder, *Ojibwa*, p. 139.
6. Kidder, *Ojibwa*, p. 144, note 111.
7. Kawbawgam-Nolin Manuscript.
8. Kawbawgam-Nolin Manuscript; Shiras, *Hunting Wild Life*, Vol. 1. p. 417.
9. Kidder, *Ojibwa*, p. 141.
10. Kidder, *Ojibwa*, p. 139-40.
11. Kidder, *Ojibwa*, p. 143.
12. Jack LaPete Folder, Manuscript 977.496 J6SM; Kidder p. 144.
13. Kidder, *Ojibwa*, p. 144.
14. Kidder, *Ojibwa*, p. 81.
15. Kidder, *Ojibwa*, p. 81-82.
16. Kidder, *Ojibwa*, p. 82.
17. Kidder, *Ojibwa*, p. 144.
18. Jack LaPete Folder, Manuscript 977.496 J6SM.
19. Kidder, *Ojibwa*, p. 145; Boyer, "Jack La Pete," p. 23.
20. Kidder, *Ojibwa*, p. 145.

21. Kidder, *Ojibwa*, p. 145.
22. Kidder, *Ojibwa*, p. 145.
23. Kidder, *Ojibwa*, p. 146-47.
24. Kidder, *Ojibwa*, p. 147-48.
25. Kidder, *Ojibwa*, p. 148.
26. Kidder, *Ojibwa*, p. 148.
27. Kidder, *Ojibwa*, p. 148.
28. Kidder, *Ojibwa*, p. 148-49.
29. Shiras, *Justice George Shiras Jr.*, p. 68.
30. Shiras, *Hunting Wild Life*, Vol. 1. p. 13.

Chapter 7: The Kawbawgams in the 1860s

1. *The Mining Journal*. "Glorious Fourth."
2. Bourgeois p. 15.
3. Brotherton, "Old Pictures…," p. 10.
4. Bruner p. 9.
5. Kidder, *Ojibwa*, p. 112.
6. Kidder, *Ojibwa*, p. 112-13.
7. Magnaghi, "Native Americans at Marquette," p. 9.
8. Kidder, *Ojibwa*, p. 72.
9. *Lake Superior Journal*, 22 Oct 1851, vol. 2, no. 23, p. 2. Retrieved from http://www.migenweb.org/chippewa/obits.htm.
10. Anonymous. *History of the Upper Peninsula of Michigan.*
11. Dana p. 42.
12. Dana p. 42-43, including notes 4 and 6.
13. DuLong, vol. 37.1. p. 54-55.
14. DuLong, vol. 37.1. p. 54.
15. Mukkala.
16. Bruner p. 9.
17. Boyer, "Charlie Kawbawgam," p. 7.
18. Longtine p. 222-23; *Chocolay Township History* p. 24, 30.
19. *Chocolay Township History* p. 78.
20. *The Mining Journal*. "Kaw-baw-gam Dead."
21. Bruner p. 9.
22. Nertoli p. 4; Steele p. 166.
23. *New York World*. "Fight Blasted His Career."
24. Magnaghi, *Native*, p. 133.
25. Magnaghi, *Native*, p. 135.
26. Magnaghi, *Native*, p. 137.

27. Magnaghi, *Native*, p. 136.
28. Magnaghi, *Native*, p. 134.
29. Magnaghi, *Native*, p. 134.
30. Chute p. 167.
31. Magnaghi, *Native*, p. 137.
32. Arbric, *City of the Rapids*, p. 130.
33. Magnaghi, *Native*, p. 137.
34. Majher p. 26.
35. Magnaghi, *Native*, p. 133.
36. Magnaghi, *Native*, p. 152; https://en.wikipedia.org/wiki/1st_Regiment_Michigan_Volunteer_Sharpshooters.
37. Magnaghi, *Native*, p. 138.
38. Rupley n.p.
39. Howe. "Visitors Do Research…."
40. *The Mining Journal*. "The Guardian of Presque Isle."
41. *The Mining Journal*. Kaw-Baw-Gam: Interesting Facts…"
42. Rydholm, *Superior Heartland*, p. 427.
43. Madosh Folder.
44. "Background Material…," Madosh Folder.
45. Madosh Folder.
46. "Background Material…," Madosh Folder.
47. "Background Material…," Madosh Folder.
48. Terando letter. Madosh Folder.
49. Magnaghi, *Native*, p. 138-39.
50. Magnaghi, *Native*, p. 143.
51. Magnaghi, *Native*, p. 139.
52. Magnaghi, *Native*, p. 139.
53. Gruber and Fisher. "Marquette Memories and Yours."
54. Gruber and Fisher. "Marquette Memories and Yours."
55. Rankin, Carroll W.
56. Magnaghi, *Native*, p. 139-40.
57. Magnaghi, *Native*, p. 145.
58. Magnaghi, *Native*, p. 143-44.
59. Magnaghi, "Native Americans at Marquette," p. 7.
60. Verwyst p. 348.
61. Verwyst p. 348.
62. Magnaghi, *Native*, p. 141.
63. Cleland, *The Place of the Pike*, p. 34.

Chapter 8: Charlotte Kobogum et al. vs. The Jackson Iron Company

1. State of Michigan Supreme Court. Jeremy Compo vs. The Jackson Iron Company, p. 29.
2. *The Mining Journal*, "Marji Gesick's Descendants Lost Case"; Rydholm, *Superior Heartland*, p. 139.
3. Stone p. 111.
4. Rydholm, *Superior Heartland*, p. 139.
5. Kidder, "Charlotte," p. 7.
6. Mead p. 11; Stone p. 111.
7. State of Michigan Supreme Court. Jeremy Compo vs. The Jackson Iron Company, p. 32.
8. Mead p. 11.
9. Stone p. 111; Mead p. 11.
10. Stone p. 113-16; Mead p. 11-12.
11. Mead p. 10-11.
12. Mead p. 11.
13. Hinsdale p. 155-56, which cites Comp vs. Jackson Iron Col., 50 Mich. 588 (June Term, 1883). Reports.
14. Swineford p. 102.
15. Hinsdale p. 156.
16. *The Mining Journal.* "Jerry Campeau, 80 Years Old, Is Dead."
17. *The Mining Journal.* "Death of Mrs. Compeau."
18. Mead p. 12-13.
19. http://genealogytrails.com/mich/marquette/biographicalrecord3.html.
20. Mead p. 12.
21. *The Mining Journal*. "Again in the Courts."
22. Hinsdale p. 159.
23. Kidder, "Charlotte," p. 1.
24. "Twice Marquette Mayor."
25. Mead p. 12-13.
26. Mead p. 11.
27. Mead p. 14.
28. Mead p. 14.
29. Mead p. 14-15.
30. Mead p. 15.
31. Mead p. 18-19.
32. Mead p. 22.
33. Mead p. 23.

34. Mead p. 18-19.
35. Mead p. 20-21.
36. State of Michigan Supreme Court. Jeremy Compo vs. The Jackson Iron Company, p. 35.
37. Mead p. 20-21.
38. Mead p. 21-22.
39. Kidder, "Charlotte," p. 7; Hinsdale p. 160.
40. Kidder, "Charlotte," p. 13.
41. Kidder, "Charlotte," p. 14.
42. Hinsdale p. 155-56, which cites Comp vs. Jackson Iron Col., 50 Mich. 588 (June Term, 1883). Reports.
43. Mead p. 23.
44. Mead p. 24.
45. *The Mining Journal*. "The Guardian of Presque Isle."
46. Mead p. 26; Hinsdale p. 160.
47. Mead p. 27; Census 1900. Marquette County, Michigan.
48. Mead p. 24.
49. Mead p. 28; James V. Campbell, majority decision in Kobogum v. Jackson Iron Co., October 25, 1889, 76 Mich 498, 43 N.W. 602.
50. Stanley.
51. Mead p. 3.
52. Mead p. 29.
53. *The Mining Journal*. "Indian Marriages."
54. Bond. 1888.
55. Mead p. 30.
56. Mead p. 31; "In the Matter of the Estate of Mary Tebeau Minor."

Chapter 9: Moving to Presque Isle

1. Maynard p. 14.
2. Magnaghi, "Native Americans at Marquette," p. 6.
3. Magnaghi, *Native*, p. 148.
4. Magnaghi, *Native*, p. 148.
5. Magnaghi, *Native*, p. 149.
6. Magnaghi, *Native*, p. 151.
7. Magnaghi, *Native*, p. 136.
8. Magnaghi, *Native*, p. 151.
9. Magnaghi, *Native*, p. 151.
10. Peter White letter to Mayor Alfred Swineford, February 1, 1875.
11. *The Mining Journal*. "The Guardian of Presque Isle."

12. Bruner p. 9; *The Mining Journal*. "An Outrage."
13. Anderton p. 25.
14. *Iron Ore*, January 2, 1903.
15. Boyer, "Charlie Kawbawgam," p. 8.
16. "Death of a Famous Chippewa." *Marine Review*, p. 3.
17. Magnaghi, *Native*, p. 152.
18. *The Mining Journal*. Brief Article about Kawbawgam Killing a Catamount.
19. Magnaghi, *Native*, p. 153.
20. Mead p. 31; *The Mining Journal*, "The Guardian of Presque Isle"; *The Mining Journal*, "Again in the Courts."
21. Brinks, *Peter White*, p. 57.
22. Tichelaar, *My Marquette*, p. 249.
23. *The Mining Journal*, "Kaw-baw-gam Dead."
24. *The Mining Journal*. "Is 102 Years Old."
25. *The Mining Journal*. "On Presque Isle…." p. 8.
26. Magnaghi, *Upper*, p. 33.

Chapter 10: Family and Troubles

1. *The Mining Journal*. "On Presque Isle…." p. 8.
2. Williams p. 26.
3. Williams p. 26.
4. *The Mining Journal*. "Obituary: Mrs. Madosh."
5. *The Mining Journal*. "Obituary: George Madosh."
6. Marquette County Death Record #45-17; Madosh Family File 920 BF.
7. Madosh Family File 920 BF.
8. Madosh family. Find a Grave website.
9. Kidder, *Ojibwa*, p. 148.
10. Kidder, *Ojibwa*, p. 148; Bourgeois-Kidder p. 152.
11. Kidder, *Ojibwa*, p. 149.
12. Kidder, *Ojibwa*, p. 149.
13. Kidder, *Ojibwa*, p. 149.
14. Kidder, *Ojibwa*, p. 149-50.
15. Kidder, *Ojibwa*, p. 83, 150.
16. Kidder, *Ojibwa*, p. 83.
17. Kawbawgam-Nolin Manuscript. Kawbawgam Family Folder.
18. *The Mining Journal*. "Mrs. Jack LaPique Drowned."
19. *The Mining Journal*. "Dr. Howard H. Kidder's Letter." Also excerpted in Kidder, *Ojibwa*, p. 151.

20. Kidder, *Ojibwa*, p. 150.
21. Shiras, *Hunting Wild Life*, Vol. 1. p. 418.
22. Shiras, *Hunting Wild Life*, Vol. 1. p. 418.
23. Shiras, *Hunting Wild Life*, Vol. 1. p. 417-18.
24. Shiras, *Hunting Wild Life*, Vol. 1. p. 418.
25. Shiras, *Hunting Wild Life*, Vol. 1. p. 418, 420.
26. Shiras, *Hunting Wild Life*, Vol. 1. p. 401.
27. *Marquette Magazine*. "Stories of Interest."
28. Shiras, *Hunting Wild Life*, Vol. 1. p. 421-23.
29. Shiras, *Hunting Wild Life*, Vol. 1. p. 424; *The Mining Journal*. "Obituary: Frederick Cadotte."
30. Shiras, *Hunting Wild Life*, Vol. 1. p. 229-30.
31. Tichelaar, *My Marquette*, p. 200; https://en.wikipedia.org/wiki/Robert_Dollar.
32. Shiras, *Hunting Wild Life*, Vol. 1. p. 400.
33. Census 1900, Marquette County, Michigan.
34. https://www.myheritage.com/names/david_mandosking.
35. Mead p. 27; https://www.myheritage.com/names/mary_tebeau; Mary Mandoski Death Certificate.
36. "Cadotte (Ancestry and Genealogy)." Madosh Folder BF 920.

Chapter 11: Preserving Ojibwa Culture

1. Kohl p. 384.
2. Warren p. ix-x.
3. Kidder, "Camping on Lake Superior."
4. Bourgeois p. 18.
5. Bourgeois p. 19.
6. Kidder, *Ojibwa*, p. 75.
7. Kidder, *Ojibwa*, p. 150.
8. Bourgeois p. 19.
9. Kidder, *Ojibwa*, p. 23.
10. Kidder, *Ojibwa*, p. 23.
11. Bourgeois p. 19.
12. Bourgeois p. 13-14.
13. Kidder, *Ojibwa*, p. 21-23.
14. Chute p. 209.
15. Bourgeois p. 19.
16. Kidder, *Ojibwa*, p. 101.
17. Kidder, *Ojibwa*, p. 101.

18. Kohl p. 436-38.
19. Kidder, *Ojibwa*, p. 74.
20. Kidder, *Ojibwa*, p. 75.
21. Kidder, *Ojibwa*, p. 76.
22. Kidder, *Ojibwa*, p. 116-21.
23. Kidder, *Ojibwa*, p. 129, note 98.
24. Kidder, *Ojibwa*, p. 129, note 96.
25. Kidder, *Ojibwa*, p. 130.
26. Kidder, *Ojibwa*, p. 130.
27. Kidder, *Ojibwa*, p. 35.
28. Kidder, *Ojibwa*, p. 36.
29. Bourgeois p. 4.
30. *The Mining Journal*, "Voices of the Ojibwa," p. 4.
31. Howe. "Visitors Do Research…."
32. Howe. "Visitors Do Research…."
33. Bourgeois p. 18; Homer Kidder, Find a Grave website.
34. https://en.wikipedia.org/wiki/Alfred_V._Kidder.
35. https://en.wikipedia.org/wiki/Tristram_Randolph_Kidder.
36. https://web.archive.org/web/20060803221038/http://www.mnsu.edu/emuseum/information/biography/klmno/kidder_alfred.html.
37. Berger, "Great American Archaelogist from Marquette."
38. Alfred Vincent Kidder letter to Dr. Leslie A. White, May 29, 1941.
39. *The Mining Journal*. "Alfred Kidder to Leave."
40. Alfred Vincent Kidder letter to Ernest Rankin, February 13, 1962; Stafford, p. 423.
41. Shiras, *Hunting Wild Life*, Vol. 1. p. 420-21.

Chapter 12: A Local Celebrity

1. Barbour, p. 22-23.
2. White, "My Recollections of Early Marquette," p. 3-5.
3. Peter White letter to Mr. Dickinson, August 18, 1888.
4. Brinks, "Peter White," p. 1; Peter White letter to President Grover Cleveland, March 1, 1893.
5. Williams p. 187.
6. *The Mining Journal*. "Kawbawgam's Snowshoes."
7. https://en.wikipedia.org/wiki/Gaetano_Trentanove.
8. Rydholm, *Superior Heartland*, p. 330.
9. Rydholm, *Superior Heartland*, p. 332.
10. *The Mining Journal*. "Father Marquette."

11. https://en.wikipedia.org/wiki/Jacques_Marquette_(Trentanove).
12. Rydholm, *Superior Heartland*, p. 332.
13. Rydholm, *Superior Heartland*, p. 332-4; Marquette, Jacques Statues Folder; "Pere Marquette Edition." *The Mining Journal*. July 15, 1897.
14. Rydholm, *Superior Heartland*, p. 334.
15. "Unveiling Day Jubilee."
16. EHR/JPW, "Father Jacques Marquette Statue."
17. Rydholm, *Superior Heartland*, p. 334.
18. Rydholm, *Superior Heartland*, p. 334.
19. Loomis p. 74; Rydholm, *Superior Heartland*, p. 334.
20. Husar, p. 9D.
21. *Mackinac History*, p. 6; https://en.wikipedia.org/wiki/Gaetano_Trentanove; *The Mining Journal*, "His Features in Enduring Marble," May 25, 1898.
22. Census 1880, Chippewa County, Michigan.
23. *The Mining Journal*. "Anent Charley Kaw Baw Gam."
24. "Angel of Death Summons Augustine Gager and Several Others."
25. Gilbert. "Memories of the 'Soo'."
26. *Enquirer and News*. "Albion's 'copper-colored sons of the forest.'"
27. Gilbert. "Memories of the 'Soo'."
28. Stanley p. 16; Bourgeois-Kidder p. 16; *The Mining Journal*, "Voices of the Ojibwa," p. 4.
29. *The Mining Journal*. "Glorious Fourth."
30. *The Mining Journal*. "A Day in France"; *The Mining Journal*. "Songs of La Belle France."
31. Stanley p. 16.
32. *The Banker's Magazine*. Vol. 46. p. 236.
33. Stone. "The Kawbawgam Pictures."
34. R. L. Polk & Co.'s Directory, p. 58.
35. Magnaghi, "Native Americans at Marquette," p. 8.
36. Kirk letter 1939.
37. Robb.
38. *The Mining Journal*. "60 Years Ago."
39. *The Mining Journal*. "Bust of Koboggam."
40. *The Mining Journal*. "60 Years Ago."
41. Howe. "Visitors Do Research…."
42. *The Mining Journal*. "Archeologist Kidder."
43. Boyer, "Kawbawgam," p. 8; *Mining Journal*, "Kawbawgam's Snowshoes"; Wittler, Personal Email, January 13, 2020.

44. Williams p. 26.
45. *The Mining Journal*. "Kaw-baw-gam Dead"; Stanley p. 16.
46. *The Mining Journal*. "Indian Motif."
47. Williams p. 28; *The Mining Journal*, "Thirty Years Ago."
48. Charlie Kawbawgam Death Certificate. #816. Marquette County, Michigan. Michigan Department of State Lansing.
49. White, Peter. "Kaw-baw-gam 1902."
50. *The Mining Journal*. "City Brevities." December 31, 1902; *The Mining Journal*. "On Presque Isle…"
51. *The Mining Journal*, "Kaw-baw-gam Dead"; Mead p. 31.
52. *The Mining Journal*. "On Presque Isle…"
53. Bruner p. 9.
54. Magnaghi, "Native Americans at Marquette," p. 10.
55. *The Mining Journal*. "On Presque Isle…"
56. *The Mining Journal*. "On Presque Isle…"
57. Maynard p. 18. Maynard quotes this but doesn't provide his source.
58. Magnaghi, "Native Americans at Marquette," p. 9.
59. *The Mining Journal*. "On Presque Isle…"
60. *The Mining Journal*. "On Presque Isle…"

Chapter 13: Legacy

1. Kawbawgam Statue Subscription Form.
2. *Evening Wisconsin*. "Goes Back to Italy."
3. Kosciuszko Monument. Wikipedia. https://en.wikipedia.org/wiki/Kosciuszko_Monument.
4. *Evening Wisconsin*. "Goes Back to Italy."
5. "Statue of Kaw-Baw-Gam."
6. Trentanove letter to Koepcke, June 11, 1903.
7. Trentanove letter to Koepcke, August 12, 1903.
8. *Mackinac History*, p. 6; Gaetano Trentanove. https://en.wikipedia.org/wiki/Gaetano_Trentanove.
9. Anderton p. 25.
10. Bruner p. 10; Boyer, "Charlie Kawbawgam," p. 9.
11. *The Mining Journal*. "Natural Monument to Chippewa Chief."
12. Stanley p. 14.
13. https://en.wikipedia.org/wiki/John_Smith_(Chippewa_Indian).
14. Mead p. 31.
15. Stanley p. 16.
16. *Lake Superior Journal*, January 1903.

17. Boyer, "Charlie Kawbawgam," p. 9.
18. Magnaghi, *Upper*, p. 33; Magnaghi, "Native Americans at Marquette," p. 12.
19. Mary Mandoski Death Certificate.
20. *The Mining Journal.* "City Brevities." May 28, 1904. p. 8.
21. *The Mining Journal.* "Obituary: Frederick Cadotte."
22. *The Mining Journal.* "Obituary: Raymond G. Trevillion."
23. https://www.myheritage.com/names/david_mandosking.
24. Madosh Family Folder BF 920.
25. Cleland, *Rites of Conquest*, p. 246; https://en.wikipedia.org/wiki/Mount_Pleasant_Indian_Industrial_Boarding_School#The_children.
26. Cleland, *Rites of Conquest*, p. 246-48.
27. *Mount Pleasant, Michigan Boarding School.*
28. "Augustus Madosh." https://www.ancestry.com/genealogy/records/augustus-madosh_130619592.
29. *The Mining Journal.* "Obituary: Henry Melvin Madosh"; *The Mining Journal.* "Obituary: Michelle Richarda "Madosh" Kohn."
30. Leander August Madosh. https://www.ancestry.com/genealogy/records/leander-august-madosh_130619524.
31. Leander August "Lee" Madosh. Find a Grave website.
32. Madosh, Personal Interview. Madosh, Peter Headstone; *The Mining Journal.* "Obituary: Helen Marie Madosh."
33. Cleland, *Rites of Conquest*, p. 270-71.
34. *Sault Evening News.* "Johnston to Push Claims of Indians."
35. *Sault Evening News.* "Indians Urged to Enroll Now."
36. Sundstrom.
37. Kawbawgam Folder 977 496 J 63m.
38. *The Mining Journal.* "Charley Kawbawgam Reminiscitur."
39. Boyer, "Charlie Kawbawgam," p. 9; *The Kawbawgam: 1928.*
40. Cleland, *Rites of Conquest*, p. 230, note 4.
41. Prusi and Sargent, "Redmen Indian Logo Gets National Attention."
42. *The Mining Journal.* "School Logo Too Macho?"
43. *The Mining Journal.* "MSHS Students Vote Again on Logo Decision."
44. Rydholm, "U.P., Indians always got along."
45. Dupras and Rydholm. "Letter to the Editor." *The Mining Journal.*
46. Bleck.
47. *The Mining Journal.* "Redmen Logo Lawsuit Dismissed."
48. *The Mining Journal.* "Logo Debate Boils Over."
49. Paulsen.

50. Berger, Adam. "Historically Speaking."
51. *Chocolay Township History* p. 115-16.
52. Graham p. 131.
53. *The Mining Journal*, "Scout Pageant."
54. Fletcher p. vii.
55. McCann, "Charlotte Kawbawgam vs. The Jackson Iron Company." Part 2. p. 18.
56. Traver p. 25-27.
57. Traver p. 311-12.
58. Traver p. 30.
59. Traver p. 14.
60. Mead p. 3.
61. Traver p. 70.
62. McCann, "Charlotte Kawbawgam vs. The Jackson Iron Company." Part 2. p. 18.
63. McCann, "Charlotte Kawbawgam vs. The Jackson Iron Company." Part 2. p. 18.
64. http://aisp.msu.edu/people1/people/matthew-fletcher/.
65. Fletcher p. xv.
66. Kawbawgam Family Folder.
67. Carter. "Kawbawgam Village Project."
68. *Chocolay Township History* p. 102.
69. *Chocolay Township History* p. 101.
70. Hoyum.
71. McCann, "Charlotte Kawbawgam vs. The Jackson Iron Company." Part 2. p. 17.
72. http://www.shawano.michdar.net/dar2.htm.
73. https://www.nmu.edu/nativeamericanstudies/home-page.
74. Henry p. 30-31.
75. Henry p. 44.
76. Henry p. 46.
77. Henry p. 53.
78. Pepin.
79. Cabell. "Eastside Zoning."
80. www.MarjiGesick.com.
81. Poquette.
82. Arbric, *City of the Rapids*, p. 253.

Appendix: Alleged Photographs of the Kawbawgams and Their Relatives

1. Wentworth p. 66-69.
2. Rankin, Ernest H. "Accounts of Early Indian Missionary…"
3. Rydholm, *Superior Heartland*, p. 133.
4. Deo, Personal Email, July 16, 2009; Deo, Personal Interview, July 3, 2019; Tinder p. 53, 90.
5. Rankin, Ernest H. "Accounts of Early Indian Missionary…"
6. Reuter, p. 49.
7. Gruber, Michelin, and Wittler.
8. Gruber, Personal Email, January 22, 2019.
9. Deo, Personal Interview, February 4, 2020.
10. Chute p. 220.
11. Deo, Personal Email, July 16, 2019.
12. Tinder p. 90.
13. Mead p. 5; Tinder p. 49, 67, 74; Cutler, quoted at http://www.pa-roots.org/data/read.php?5487,732664.
14. Deo, Personal Interview, July 3, 2019.
15. "Charles Brotherton" p. 1-2.
16. "Charles Brotherton House" pamphlet.
17. Brotherton diaries.
18. Strom.
19. Deo, Personal Interview, February 4, 2020.

Index

D

L

Photo Credits

Chippewa County Historical Society, Sault Sainte Marie, Michigan—16, 29, 33, 34, 36, 120

Jack Deo, Superior View, Marquette, Michigan—176, 188, 217, 221, 222, 224, 253, 274, 278, 328, 329 (left), 330 (bottom), 331, 333

Judge Joseph H. Steere Room, Bayliss Public Library, Sault Sainte Marie, Michigan—88

Marquette Regional History Center, Marquette, Michigan—x, 15, 27, 46, 52, 55, 57, 63, 69, 70, 78, 79, 81, 90, 98, 99, 100, 101, 105, 106, 108, 113, 121, 133, 139, 142, 143, 151, 154, 168, 169, 180, 182, 184, 185 (bottom), 187, 189, 193, 197, 199, 203, 204, 207, 208, 210, 213, 227, 228, 232, 240, 246, 251, 254, 257, 259, 261, 262, 263 (top), 264, 267, 268, 272, 285, 299 (bottom), 300, 306 (bottom), 307, 321, 325, 327, 329 (right), 330 (top), 334

Peter White Public Library, Marquette, Michigan—256 (right), 265 (left)

Tyler Tichelaar, Marquette Fiction, Marquette, Michigan—14, 30, 32, 37, 138, 185 (top), 250, 255, 256 (left), 263 (bottom), 265 (right), 289, 290, 299 (top 2 photos), 306 (top 2 photos), 308, 309, 312, 314, 315, 317, 318, 319

Wikipedia—12, 26, 38, 60, 116, 128, 140

A Special Request

If you enjoyed this book, please write a book review for it at Amazon, Barnes & Noble, Goodreads, or another bookseller or booklover website. Authors rely on book reviews and word-of-mouth to sell their books. Readers also rely on reviews to help them make their decisions on which books to purchase and read. Just a couple of sentences from you can have a huge impact. The author thanks you for your time.

Be Sure to Read All of Tyler R. Tichelaar's Upper Michigan Books

IRON PIONEERS
THE MARQUETTE TRILOGY: BOOK ONE

When iron ore is discovered in Michigan's Upper Peninsula in the 1840s, newlyweds Gerald Henning and his beautiful socialite wife Clara travel from Boston to the little village of Marquette on the shores of Lake Superior. They and their companions, Irish and German immigrants, French Canadians, and fellow New Englanders face blizzards and near starvation, devastating fires, and financial hardships. Yet these iron pioneers persevere until their wilderness village becomes integral to the Union cause in the Civil War and then a prosperous modern city. Meticulously researched, warmly written, and spanning half a century, *Iron Pioneers* is a testament to the spirit that forged America.

THE QUEEN CITY
THE MARQUETTE TRILOGY: BOOK TWO

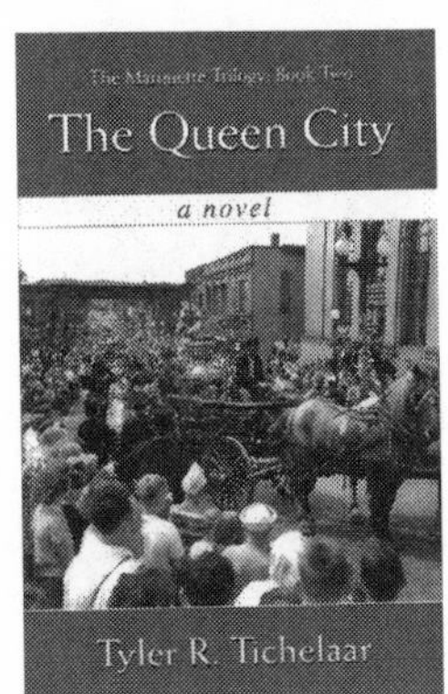

During the first half of the twentieth century, Marquette grows into the Queen City of the North. Here is the tale of a small town undergoing change as its horses are replaced by streetcars and automobiles, and its pioneers are replaced by new generations who prosper despite two World Wars and the Great Depression. Margaret Dalrymple finds her Scottish prince, though he is neither Scottish nor a prince. Molly Bergmann becomes an inspiration to her grandchildren. Jacob Whitman's children engage in a family feud. The Queen City's residents marry, divorce, have children, die, break their hearts, go to war, gossip, blackmail, raise families, move away, and then return to Marquette. And always, always they are in love with the haunting land that is their home.

SUPERIOR HERITAGE
THE MARQUETTE TRILOGY: BOOK THREE

The Marquette Trilogy comes to a satisfying conclusion as it brings together characters and plots from the earlier novels and culminates with Marquette's sesquicentennial celebrations in 1999. What happened to Madeleine Henning is finally revealed as secrets from the past shed light upon the present. Marquette's residents struggle with a difficult local economy, yet remain optimistic for the future. The novel's main character, John Vandelaare, is descended from all the early Marquette families in *Iron Pioneers* and *The Queen City*. While he cherishes his family's past, he questions whether he should remain in his hometown. Then an event happens that will change his life forever.

NARROW LIVES

Narrow Lives is the story of those whose lives were affected by Lysander Blackmore, the sinister banker first introduced to readers in *The Queen City*. It is a novel that stands alone, yet readers of *The Marquette Trilogy* will be reacquainted with some familiar characters. Written as a collection of connected short stories, each told in first person by a different character, *Narrow Lives* depicts the influence one person has, even in death, upon others, and it explores the prisons of grief, loneliness, and fear self-created when people doubt their own worthiness.

THE ONLY THING THAT LASTS

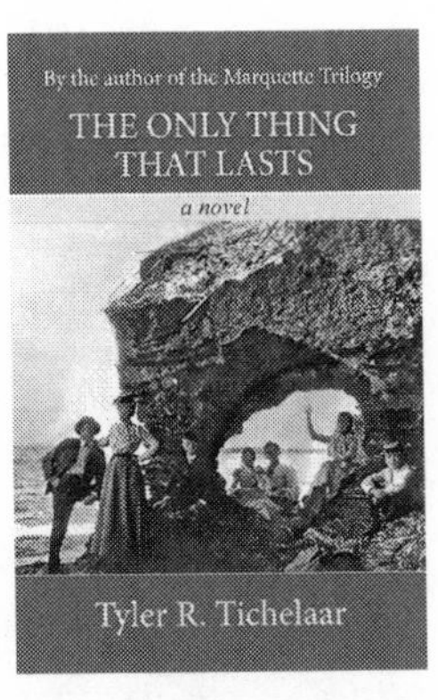

The story of Robert O'Neill, the famous novelist introduced in *The Marquette Trilogy*. As a young boy during World War I, Robert is forced to leave his South Carolina home to live in Marquette with his grandmother and aunt. He finds there a cold climate, but many warmhearted friends. An old-fashioned story that follows Robert's growth from childhood to successful writer and husband, the novel is written as Robert O'Neill's autobiography, his final gift to Marquette by memorializing the town of his youth.

SPIRIT OF THE NORTH: A PARANORMAL ROMANCE

In 1873, orphaned sisters Barbara and Adele Traugott travel to Upper Michigan to live with their uncle, only to find he is deceased. Penniless, they are forced to spend the long, fierce winter alone in their uncle's remote wilderness cabin. Frightened, yet determined, the sisters face blizzards and near starvation to survive. Amid their difficulties, they find love and heartache—and then, a ghostly encounter and the coming of spring lead them to discovering the true miracle of their being.

THE BEST PLACE

An irritating best friend gained during a childhood spent in a Catholic orphanage, a father who became a Communist and went to Russia in the 1930s, and 3:00 a.m. visits to The Pancake House. Such is the life of Lyla Hopewell. But in the summer of 2005, when her old boyfriend Bill has a heart attack, her best friend Bel really gets on her nerves, and Finn Fest comes to Marquette, things will change for Lyla.

WHEN TEDDY CAME TO TOWN

Former U.S. President Theodore Roosevelt was on campaign on the Progressive "Bull Moose" ticket, but his break from the Republican Party had caused him to have many detractors. When a small town Michigan newspaper editor accused him of being drunk while campaigning, Roosevelt decided to make an example of him.

Matthew Newman, reporter for the New York *Empire Sentinel*, should have seen his assignment to cover the trial as the opportunity of a lifetime. But Matthew is also a native of Marquette, Michigan, where the trial will be held. Matthew left Marquette long ago and does not relish returning to deal with a distant sister and her drunkard husband, or to attend his niece's wedding, set for the weekend after the trial begins.

WILLPOWER: AN ORIGINAL PLAY ABOUT MARQUETTE'S OSSIFIED MAN

There are some stories that deserve to be told. As a young boy, Will Adams' soft tissues were becoming harder, turning him into a living statue. Others faced with such a dark future might have felt sorry for themselves, turning inward. Not so for Will; his disease brought about an amazing creative burst of energy. His true story is as inspiring today as it was more than 100 years ago.

MY MARQUETTE: EXPLORE THE QUEEN CITY OF THE NORTH—ITS HISTORY, PEOPLE, AND PLACES

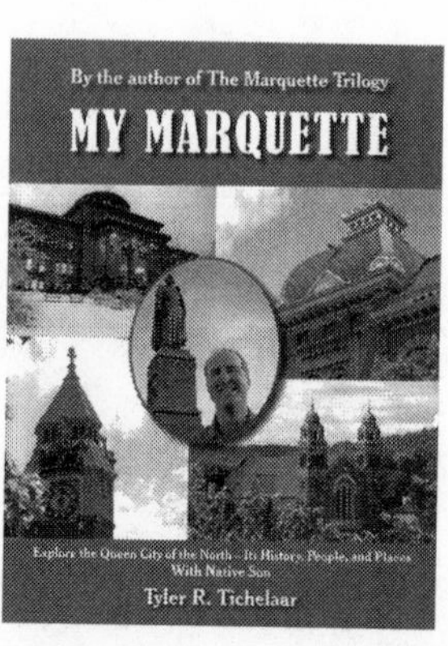

My Marquette is the result of its author's lifelong love affair with his hometown. Join Tyler R. Tichelaar, seventh generation Marquette resident and author of *The Marquette Trilogy*, as he takes you on a tour of the history, people, and places of Marquette. Stories of the past and present, both true and fictional, will leave you understanding why Marquette really is "The Queen City of the North." Along the way, Tyler will describe his own experiences growing up in Marquette, recall family and friends he knew, and give away secrets about the people behind the characters in his novels. *My Marquette* offers a rare insight into an author's creation of fiction and a refreshing view of a city's history and relevance to today. Reading *My Marquette* is equal to being given a personal tour by someone who knows Marquette intimately.

HAUNTED MARQUETTE: GHOST STORIES FROM THE QUEEN CITY

Founded as a harbor town to ship iron ore from the nearby mines, Marquette became known as the Queen City of the North for its thriving industries, beautiful buildings, and being the largest city in Upper Michigan.

But is Marquette also the Queen of Lake Superior's Haunted Cities? Seventh-generation Marquette resident Tyler Tichelaar has spent years collecting tales of the many ghosts who haunt the cemeteries, churches, businesses, hotels, and homes of Marquette.

Now, separating fact from fiction, Tichelaar delves into the historical record to determine whom the ghosts might be, which stories have a historical basis, and which tales are simply the fancies of imaginative or frightened minds.

Hear the chilling tales of:

- The wicked nun who killed an orphan boy, and how the boy continues to escape from his grave
- The librarian who haunts a local hotel while mourning for her sailor lover
- The drowned sailors who climb out of Lake Superior at night
- The glowing lantern of the decapitated train conductor
- The mailman who gave his life so neither rain, nor sleet, nor snow would stop the U.S. mail
- More ghostly ladies in floor-length white gowns than any haunted city should have

Haunted Marquette opens up a fourth dimension view of the Queen City's past and reveals that much of it is still present.

For more information on Tyler R. Tichelaar's Marquette Books, visit:

www.MarquetteFiction.com

And be sure also to check out Tyler's other titles

THE GOTHIC WANDERER:
FROM TRANSGRESSION TO REDEMPTION

CREATING A LOCAL HISTORICAL BOOK:
FICTION AND NONFICTION GENRES

THE NOMAD EDITOR:
LIVING THE LIFESTYLE YOU WANT, DOING WORK YOU LOVE

KING ARTHUR'S CHILDREN:
A STUDY IN FICTION AND TRADITION

THE CHILDREN OF ARTHUR HISTORICAL FANTASY SERIES
Arthur's Legacy: The Children of Arthur, Book One
Melusine's Gift: The Children of Arthur, Book Two
Ogier's Prayer: The Children of Arthur, Book Three
Lilith's Love: The Children of Arthur, Book Four
Arthur's Bosom: The Children of Arthur, Book Five

About the Author

TYLER R. TICHELAAR HAS A PhD in Literature from Western Michigan University and Bachelor and Master's Degrees in English from Northern Michigan University. He is the owner of Marquette Fiction, his own publishing company, and of Superior Book Productions, a professional editing, proofreading, and book layout company. He is also the former vice president (2007-2008) and president (2008-2019) of the Upper Peninsula Publishers and Authors Association. Tyler is especially proud to be a seventh generation Marquette resident.

Tyler began writing his first novel at age sixteen in 1987. In 2006, he published his first novel, *Iron Pioneers: The Marquette Trilogy, Book One*. More than twenty books have followed. In 2009, Tyler won first place in the historical fiction category in the Reader Views Literary Awards for his novel *Narrow Lives*. He has since sponsored that contest, offering the Tyler R. Tichelaar Award for Historical Fiction. In 2011, Tyler was awarded the Marquette County Outstanding Writer Award, and the same year, he received the Barb Kelly Award for Historical Preservation for his efforts to promote Marquette history. In 2014, his play *Willpower* was produced by the Marquette Regional History Center, with assistance of a grant from the Michigan Humanities Council. He has twice been nominated for the Pushcart Prize for his short stories.

While Tyler also writes on such diverse topics as nineteenth century Gothic fiction and Arthurian historical fantasy, he remains engrossed in writing about Marquette and Upper Michigan as microcosms for the greater American story. He has many more books in the works.

Visit Tyler at www.MarquetteFiction.com.

Made in the USA
Columbia, SC
03 July 2022

62657915R00269